CONFLICTING WORLDS

New Dimensions of the American Civil War

T. Michael Parrish, Editor

TWELVE

TALES

OF

CIVIL

WAR

SOLDIERS

War's Relentless Hand

Mark H. Dunkelman

Louisiana State University Press
Baton Rouge

Published by Louisiana State University Press
Copyright © 2006 by Mark H. Dunkelman
All rights reserved
Manufactured in the United States of America
FIRST PRINTING

DESIGNER: Melanie O'Quinn Samaha
TYPEFACE: ITC Galliard
TYPESETTER: G&S Typesetters, Inc.
PRINTER AND BINDER: Edwards Brothers, Inc.

LIBRARY OF CONGRESS CATALOGING-IN-PUBLICATION DATA

Dunkelman, Mark H.
War's relentless hand : twelve tales of Civil War soldiers / Mark H. Dunkelman.
　　p. cm. — (Conflicting worlds)
Includes bibliographical references and index.
ISBN-13: 978-0-8071-3190-9 (cloth : alk. paper)
ISBN-10: 0-8071-3190-3 (cloth : alk. paper)
　　1. United States. Army. New York Infantry Regiment, 154th (1862–1865)　2. New York
(State)—History—Civil War, 1861–1865—Personal narratives.　3. United
States—History—Civil War, 1861–1865—Personal narratives.　4. New York
(State)—History—Civil War, 1861–1865—Regimental histories.　5. United
States—History—Civil War, 1861–1865—Regimental histories.　6. Soldiers—New York
(State)—Cattaraugus County—Biography.　7. Soldiers—New York (State)—Cattaraugus
County—Social conditions—19th century.　8. Cattaraugus County (N.Y.)—Biography.　I. Title.
II. Series.
E523.5154th .D87 2006
973.7'4470922—dc22

2006003090

A book whose characters pass through Buffalo,
Utica, New York City, and Hedgesville, West Virginia,
has to be dedicated to
Amy and Dan
and
the rest of the Rowland family:
Jake and Allison;
Justin, Sarah, Lucy, and Jude;
and Jennifer.

Contents

Introduction

Each of these twelve tales begins in a cemetery, at the grave of a Civil War soldier, and proceeds to resurrect some chapters of his story.

Cemeteries are tranquil places. Quiet ruled during my pilgrimage to the soldiers' graves. Often the only sounds were those of nature: trees rustling in the wind, the chatter of birds and squirrels, the lowing of a cow. Rarely did I encounter another person. The edgy hustle and bustle of everyday life seemed far removed from these calm oases. The long-dead soldiers were truly resting in peace.

Cemeteries are concealing places. Death buried the soldiers' tales—of love and passion, pain and loss, triumphs and gaiety, troubles and grief—under the stark cover of chiseled headstones. All the emotions, sensations, expectations, and realizations of human lives were smothered beneath the sod. For a while, certain tales of the departed had been kept in remembrance by loved ones. Sparked by some reminiscent incident or an old photograph, generations passed the stories along. But over time, the tales often vanished into oblivion.

Graves conceal the tales of roughly 3 million men who served as soldiers and sailors for the Union and the Confederacy. As individuals, how are they remembered today?

Family plays an important role. Descendants recollect many soldiers through a dim web of photographs, relics, and legends. Most families have a history lover who is adept at rekindling memories. Budding genealogists come across Civil War ancestors, document them, and outline their service for new generations. Most soldiers are recalled by direct descendants, while collateral relatives keep the memory of young men who died unwed and childless. If an individual Civil War soldier is remembered today, chances are it is by his family.

Some soldiers are commemorated in the written record. There is a seeming plentitude of published letters, diaries, and memoirs of men who served in the Civil War. But in fact only an infinitesimal percentage of the millions of soldiers are recorded in the vast literature of the war, much of which sticks to grander themes: famous campaigns and battles, the lives of prominent generals. Walt Whitman (who will appear in one of these tales) famously said that the real war would never get into the books. As for the war, so for most of the soldiers.

If a Civil War soldier is not remembered by his family or recorded in a publication, he essentially remains lost to history. His soldier's legacy—the letters and tintype he sent home, the relics he preserved—has been lost or discarded or sold (often to scatter in the collectibles market). No one visits the archives to request his minimal military and pension records. In sweeping published sagas of Northern and Southern armies, he is invisible as an abstract pawn or a mere statistic. His tale, untold, has vanished.

This book tells the stories of a dozen soldiers of the 154th New York Volunteer Infantry, a regiment raised in the western part of the state. Why have I chosen to chronicle these twelve soldiers, all members of the same unit?

For some forty years, since I was a teenager, I have studied the Civil War through the prism of the 154th New York. During that time I have collected everything I could find that would shed light on the service of the regiment and the experiences of its 1,065 soldiers. The collective history of the 154th can be simply summarized. The regiment was raised in the summer of 1862 in Cattaraugus and Chautauqua counties in response to President Abraham Lincoln's call for three hundred thousand three-year volunteers. It organized at Jamestown, New York, and was transported by rail to Washington. It spent its first seven months in northern Virginia in camps at Arlington Heights, Fairfax Court House, and Falmouth, interrupted by a brief march to Thoroughfare Gap in the Bull Run Mountains. In May 1863 the 154th was badly bloodied in its first battle, Chancellorsville. Two months later it was decimated at Gettysburg. Transferred by rail to the western theater in the fall of 1863, the regiment took part in the Chattanooga and Knoxville campaigns. After a restful stay in winter camp at Lookout Valley, Tennessee, the 154th fought a string of battles and skirmishes during the 1864 Atlanta campaign. It then followed William Tecumseh Sherman on his famous March to the Sea and through the Carolinas. Immediately after the war the regiment participated in the Grand Review of the victorious Union armies in Washington, and was mustered out of the service in June 1865 at Bladensburg, Maryland.

While the exploits of the 154th New York as a whole are well documented, the stories of most of the regiment's individual soldiers remain obscure. The bare bones of their service records (revealed in the regimental muster rolls), thinly fleshed out with sparse notes of their later lives (culled from pension files), provide only the sketchiest outlines of their tales. Their official record exists; their personal record is missing.

With a few soldiers, I have had better luck. Thanks to the kindness of descendants of scores of the 154th's soldiers, of friends who know of my interest, and of dedicated people who work in libraries and historical societies, I have had the good fortune to locate, copy, and transcribe more than fourteen hundred wartime letters, dozens of diaries, and a roomful of other material relating to the regiment, all of which provides a wealth of information about the 154th New York and many of its men. This extensive documentation has enabled me to reconstruct the stories of certain soldiers in considerable detail.

The enduring fame of the regiment's best-known soldier came posthumously. When his corpse was found on the Gettysburg battlefield in July 1863, the only clue to his identity was clutched in his stiffened hand—an ambrotype photograph of three little children. A massive media campaign was launched to identify the devoted father and locate his family. As newspaper and magazine articles spread the story across the North, photographic copies of the children's portrait were mailed to anxious inquirers. A month after the first article appeared, the widow and orphans were located in Portville, Cattaraugus County, New York, and the deceased was identified as Sergeant Amos Humiston of the 154th New York.

As another great wave of publicity broadcast the gratifying news across the land, the Humistons became celebrities. A flood of sentimental prose, poetry, imagery, and song celebrated the loving father and his "Children of the Battle Field." The widely circulated *Frank Leslie's Illustrated Newspaper* imagined Amos's touching death tableaux in a woodcut. The now famous photograph of the three tykes and one of their martyred Pa—retouched to add a uniform and beard—sold in great quantities. The children's cherubic faces also appeared on sheet music and in engravings. Ultimately, the story inspired a Sunday school fund-raising drive, leading to the founding of a soldiers' orphans' home in Gettysburg, which became the postwar home of Humiston's bereaved widow and children. But the orphanage, the great good born of the little family's tragedy, was also fated for a melodramatic and sad ending. After years of nurturing hundreds of children, the institution closed under a cloud of scandal and corruption.

Sergeant Humiston's story is certainly the most famous to emerge from the history of the 154th New York. It is in fact one of the best-known human interest stories of the entire Civil War. A fixture in Gettysburg books and a favorite of journalists, it has been related in print countless times in the century-plus since Amos fell, and more than a dozen times in the years since my Humiston book, *Gettysburg's Unknown Soldier,* came out in 1999. There is a monument to Amos near to where he died and a display on the incident at the Gettysburg National Military Park's visitor center. Plentiful copies of the Humiston children's photograph survive and change hands routinely in Internet auctions.

Amos Humiston was not the only soldier of the 154th New York whose story combined drama, tragedy, pathos, and plot twists. But he was the only member of the regiment who became a widely chronicled celebrity. This volume's dozen soldiers never made a national media splash or were documented in widely read books (with two notable exceptions). To the public at large, from the Civil War era to today, these twelve men have remained obscure, their tales unknown.

Although they are largely silent in recorded history, their voices echo in faded letters, worn diaries, and postwar reminiscences. Turning to those and other materials, I have sought to breathe some life back into these twelve soldiers, to reconstruct a bit of their world during the Civil War. Their tales illuminate some dark corners of the war's history. With them we veer off the wide road trod by mighty armies into the narrow byways of human hopes and fears, horrors and heartbreak, love and loss. Each of them shares with us his unique, personal tale, revealing experiences that strike us with empathy and emotion.

As with Sergeant Humiston, family is woven into these soldiers' stories. In one tale, a wife writes to her soldier husband, "Oh, if war's relentless hand should make you its victim and you should return no more to your little ones and Mary, she would not be long behind."[1] In countless terrible ways, soldiers and their families were touched by war's relentless hand. Imagine the extent of sorrow in those long-ago days, when death took more than six hundred thousand soldiers, including five chronicled in these tales; when an unknown number of veterans died of war-induced causes after their discharges, as in two of these tales; when countless others were disabled for life, as in three of the tales; and when surviving soldiers and their families—as in two tales—fell prey to other traumas. The full human cost and grief of the Civil War can never be calculated. These twelve stories can only hint at it.

These tales can, however, teach us much about Civil War soldiers: how their resilience, perseverance, and devotion to cause and comrades sustained them in meeting hardships and horrors; how they were further nourished by the love of their families and the support of their home communities; how their spirits were buoyed by religious faith or sunny optimism or carefree cockiness; how they bore up when they were wounded or injured or ill; how they cared for each other in life and death. These common soldiers often displayed uncommon virtues.

I heeded four primary criteria in selecting the dozen subjects. First, the soldier's story had to be memorable, vivid, and gripping in personality or plot line. Second, it needed to be supported by ample documentation—there is no fictionalization in this book. Third, it had to depict one of many fates that lurked in waiting for Civil War soldiers. As the tales reveal, the soldiers—and their families—faced no shortage of troubles and traumas. Finally, each tale had to differ substantially from the other eleven. Because all twelve men served in the same regiment, they could expect a certain common experience. But the vagaries of war dispersed the members of the 154th New York; each of the twelve fell to his singular fate.

The soldiers (and occasionally their loved ones) are often quoted in the tales. In composing their letters and diaries, they occasionally misspelled words and generally ignored punctuation. To smooth the narrative flow, I have taken the liberty of correcting those flaws. Otherwise their words are quoted exactly as written.

Portraits of nine of the soldiers illustrate their respective chapters, allowing us to put faces to their tales. Two of them are pictured with their wives, who figure prominently in their stories. Unfortunately, no portraits have been located of three of the soldiers. When the time came to place the tales in order, alphabetically by surname proved to be an ideal sequence.

In telling their stories, I felt close to these twelve soldiers. I hope that as you read the tales, you will feel close to them, too. Still, I remain humbled and haunted by how little I know about these men and their loved ones—and by how many tales remain untold.

War's Relentless Hand

CHAPTER ONE

Corporal Joel M. Bouton

Company C

Gettysburg National Cemetery contains the graves of 3,555 Union Civil War soldiers. Rows of markers, set in great concentric semicircles around a towering monument, are divided into sections representing eighteen states, the U.S. Regular Army, and unknowns. The sweeping arcs of granite are set flat against the grass. Every few inches, like printing on a tickertape, the name, company, and regiment of a fallen soldier are cut into the stone. Most of the inscriptions are easy to read; some of them retain blacking applied years ago. The New York State lot is the cemetery's largest, with 867 graves in seven rows, designated Sections A to G. As I walked the largely unshaded plot on a sultry May afternoon, the stones baked in the heat.

I sought one soldier's grave in particular. He and eleven other members of the 154th New York Volunteer Infantry were killed or mortally wounded at Gettysburg. Initially the twelve were buried on the battlefield near where they fell, or close to the hospital where they expired. The remains of two were recovered and returned home for burial. Eventually, the ten other corpses were reinterred in the national cemetery, three of them as unknowns. Their graves were scattered in the three outermost rows, Sections A, B, and C. I was looking for Section C, Grave Number 94.

I wandered for a while before I found the stone. The inscription read, "J. M. BOUREN. CO. C. REGT. 154."

It reminded me of an often-quoted remark made by William Tecumseh Sherman. Years after the Civil War, in an address to a veterans' reunion, Sherman provided a caustic definition of heroism. Surveying the old soldiers in his audience, the general declared, "I think we understand what military fame is—to be killed on the field of battle and have our names spelled wrong in the newspapers." After his death at Gettysburg, Joel Morse Bouton's name was never misspelled in newspapers. But through a clerical error or a stonecutter's mistake, his surname was misspelled on his headstone, making him, according to Sherman's acid characterization, forever a hero.[1]

If not for a friend, little would be known about Joel Bouton. His family and early years are shrouded in obscurity. He was born in Greene County, New York, about 1839. Some twenty years later, the Bouton family appeared to consist of Joel, his mother, and his sister. The three lived apart. Joel resided in the Westchester County village of South Salem, a short distance from the Connecticut border. His sister and her husband were about 150 miles west, in Binghamton, the Broome County seat. More than a hundred miles farther west, in the Cattaraugus County village of Portville, lived Joel's mother. She was, presumably, a widow. Nothing is known of Joel's father.

Joel's doings in South Salem are uncertain. He might have been staying with relatives; the village was home to several Boutons. It seems possible he was attending the local academy. Whatever the circumstances, in South Salem Joel met Stephen E. Hoyt, and the two young men became fast friends. When Joel left South Salem in the late summer of 1860, he charted his ensuing adventures in correspondence to Steve Hoyt.[2]

Two years later, when he became a soldier, Joel continued to write to Hoyt. Joel was a prolific correspondent, also writing to Mother Bouton, of course, to other family and friends, and to newspapers back home. Then, abruptly, his letters ceased. When word came that Joel was gone, loved ones tucked the missives away for safekeeping. But in the many years since, all of the correspondence—including the newspaper columns—has been lost, except for Steve Hoyt's batch of letters from Joel.

Joel Bouton was an atypical member of his regiment. Three-quarters of the members of the 154th New York were farmers, and most of the others were lumbermen, mechanics, laborers, and tradesmen of various sorts. Many of the men spent virtually their entire prewar lives in Cattaraugus or Chautauqua County, toiling on family farms and receiving rudimentary educations at nearby common schools. Only a few attended local academies or distant colleges in preparation for professional lives, or broke away from the farms to ramble for a period. Joel did both. Most of his comrades remained tethered to farms and local communities for their entire lives, with the notable exception of their Civil War service. Many of their biographical sketches and obituaries jump directly from their births to their military service, having nothing to say about their unremarkable prewar lives on the farm.

Joel, on the other hand, lived a largely independent and carefree life for two years before he enlisted, meandering from place to place and from job to job. And he left a record of his rambles in his series of letters to Steve Hoyt. Prewar letters from the homebound farmers are rare, leaving our knowledge of their personalities and daily lives blank. Only when they went off to war did the farmers begin writing a great flood of letters home, many of which survive today to inform us of their adventures. Joel's antebellum wanderings, in contrast, gave him plenty to write about, and he was a steady correspondent.

Most extant Civil War soldiers' letters were written to family. In the absence of Joel's letters to Mother Bouton, we are fortunate that Steve Hoyt kept his set and that it has been preserved through the years. Only in the Hoyt letters does Joel Bouton speak of his interests and occupations, his cares and concerns, as war clouds gathered and the storm broke over the land.

Joel's letters to Hoyt are generally brash, robust with youthful optimism and brimming with confidence. He spoke to his friend as a confident, forthright young man confiding to a boon companion, his sometimes blustery bravado seasoned with a willingness to poke fun at himself. No doubt Joel's letters to Mother Bouton took a different tone, especially after he enlisted. Surely he used pleading language when he wrote to her from the army. After all, he had volunteered against her wishes.

"Hey! ho! there," Joel began his first letter to Hoyt, extending a whimsical invitation to participate in a favorite pastime: "Say Steve, won't you go fishing? . . . Come! It's a capital day, the bull-heads will bite like everything, and if you will go we will hook some of Ed Hull's apples, and have a first rate time." Since leaving South Salem, Bouton had rambled around New York State far to the north and west. Most of his stops were in villages in Broome County, not far from his sister's home in Binghamton. At Chenango Forks he spent three days at a great camp meeting, a religious revival attended by an estimated ten to twenty thousand of the consecrated and the curious. "I had a good time there you'd better believe," Joel declared, but his pleasure did not derive from spiritual nourishment—his interest was in "some pretty young ladies" among the crowd. The hunt for attractive young women was to be a frequent topic in his letters.

Joel's wandering came to a halt on September 6, 1860, when he arrived at his sister's home in Binghamton. The next day he began working as a painter with his brother-in-law. "I expect to work at painting," Joel wrote, "until it is time to commence a school." He had applied to teach at four or five schools, but he had high hopes of being appointed principal of the school in his sister's ward, where he could earn forty to fifty dollars per month and have "a steady place as long as I suit."

In the meantime, with the momentous 1860 presidential election looming, politics beckoned. Joel was shy of his twenty-first birthday and ineligible to vote, but he still took an active interest in the campaign. During his first week in Binghamton he attended three political rallies. The first featured a speech by Daniel S. Dickinson, a local Democratic party kingpin and former New York State senator, lieutenant governor, and U.S. senator. The Democrats had split along sectional lines and were fielding two candidates for president: Stephen Douglas of Illinois, largely backed by Northerners, and John C. Breckinridge of Kentucky, the choice of Southerners. Two other candidates were vying for the presidency: Tennessean John Bell of the Constitutional Union party and the Republican, Abraham Lincoln of Illinois. Dickinson, oddly, was backing Breckinridge. Joel made no comments about his speech.

On the night of September 11, Joel showed his true political colors when he attended a meeting of the Republican Wide Awake Club. Most of the members, like Joel, were young men. While the Lincoln supporters were busily engaged in passing resolutions, they were interrupted by the clangor of an alarm. The men rushed from their meeting hall and found Court Street swarming with people. Cries of "Fire! fire!" came from every direction, bells tolled, and five or six fire companies rumbled to their work. Joel had not witnessed a fire in many years. He and his excited companions ran several blocks to the scene of the blaze, only to discover a chimney fire at the American Hotel. Unimpressed, the Republicans returned to their hall and finished their business.[3]

Joel continued his activities with the Binghamton Republicans as the presidential campaign heated up in the following weeks. "I tell you, Steve, we have a flourishing Wide Awake Club here," he wrote on October 8. "We came out on parade a week ago last Saturday for the first [time]. We expect to have a torch light procession this week." The Wide Awakes met and demonstrated frequently to drum up support for their party. They typically marched at night, wearing matching black oilcloth capes and caps and carrying torches made of oil lamps attached to rails, symbolic of their candidate, the Rail-Splitter Lincoln.

Joel found time for amusements aside from politics. He attended a presentation by a Boston spiritualist and a show of Van Amburg's menagerie. He spent a week on a painting job in the town of Windsor. "It wasn't a splendid place," he complained, being "40 miles from the world into the bushes" and "18 miles from nowhere." But his stay was brightened by meeting a beautiful young lady, "about 25 years old [and] the color of a mulatto." She was engaged, but Joel was still able to inform Hoyt, "U C I had a splendid time." (Joel was fond of using abbreviations like "U C" and "B 4" in his writing.) Females were much on his mind. In a bit of doggerel at the close of his letter, he prescribed a remedy for winter's approaching snowstorms and moaning winds: "If when in bed they do wish to keep warm, / They must surely get married and that very soon."[4]

That night Joel began taking a two-week course at a teachers' institute. On November 17 he wrote to Hoyt from his new place of employment, a schoolhouse about three miles outside of Binghamton. His first students, he noted, included "some nice little scholars." Among them were about a dozen who were "a great deal larger than I am," including a couple of "pretty nice young ladies." Joel's big news concerned the recent election of Abraham Lincoln as president and the celebration it inspired. "Last week it was all excitement about election," he reported. "I tell you, Steve, we had a grand jubilee after election in Binghamton. . . . Such a powwow I never was to as there was there on election day." He also noted the typically rowdy behavior of the voters: "They got to fighting and everything else that was bad." Throughout mid-nineteenth century America, election day was marked by drunkenness and brawling.[5]

Aside from the presidential election, Joel's interest in politics and current events was erratic. In his letters to Hoyt he paid little heed to the sectional crisis convulsing the country. He wrote next on Christmas Day of 1860. South Carolina had seceded from the Union five days before, but Joel did not mention that portentous act. Instead, relaxing after a holiday dinner of "roast turkey and various other good things," he wrote about his teaching. His students now included six young ladies, among them three boarders, one a beauty from Pennsylvania. "I have a spelling school every two weeks," he added, "and we have a reading circle in full blast, of which I have the honor to be president." He and another dozen teachers were about to attend a teachers' association meeting in Windsor. "There are some young ladies going," he noted, "and I am in hopes it will be sleighing." Sleigh rides were traditional rites of winter courtship, a way for young men and women to spend time together unchaperoned. Joel also was attending weekly Saturday night meetings of Binghamton's Young Men's Debating Society, where he heard a lecture on Russia delivered by Charles Sumner, the famous abolitionist senator from Massachusetts. Senator Sumner himself bore the scars of sectional animosity. Only a year before, he had resumed his senatorial seat following three years of recuperation after a vicious beating in the Capitol at the hands of a South Carolina congressman infuriated by a Sumner anti-slavery speech.[6]

By the time of Joel's next letter, February 1, 1861, Mississippi, Florida, Alabama, Georgia, and Louisiana had also left the Union, and that day Texas seceded. Within the next week, delegates from the departed states met at Montgomery, Alabama, adopted a constitution as the Confederate States of America, and elected Jefferson Davis as their president. But Joel dismissed the disintegration of the United States with a joke: "Secession does not effect my business much," he wrote, "as I do not have to buy much cotton." Instead of addressing the grave national crisis, he related personal minutia: recovering from a cold, hoping to go on sleigh rides, and attending two weekly singing schools. "We have one in my school house, and one down on the creek about a mile and a half from here," he wrote. "There are lots of pretty girls down there but they are so noisy that we can't sing much." As usual, thoughts of girls preoccupied him. "I have got to have one [even] if I take a married one," he declared, "but I guess I can get one."[7]

As school approached the end of its term in March, Joel announced a move. "I expect to start for the west just as soon as I can get my pay," he informed Hoyt. "I am going home to live this summer, as mother is very anxious that I should come." He would please Mother Bouton by joining her in western New York. And a new occupation beckoned in Portville. Oil had been discovered in the region and drilling operations were to commence when warm weather arrived. Joel spent his last days in Binghamton in a social whirl: "I have engagements for every night this week but one." He went to maple sugar parties and dreamed of fishing for suckers. Spring was coming.[8]

Joel arrived in Portville about noon on April 3, 1861. "Since then I have been pretty busy," he informed Hoyt five days later, "as we are preparing to move." Within a week, he and Mother Bouton moved to Olean, a larger town immediately to the west of Portville and the center of the area's oil boom. "The oil excitement is very great about here at present," Joel observed. Drilling had commenced in Olean; one well had been bored to a hundred feet. "The demand for coopers is very great," Joel noted; he was thinking about making barrels for a while to earn some good money. "There are but few of that profession in these parts, and they cannot get near enough barrels to put their oil in and some have had to let it run to waste on the ground for want of something to put it in." But for the time being he had not decided for certain what to do during the upcoming summer. He was passing the time fishing for trout and pike and shooting pigeons.[9]

By the time of Joel's next letter, the Civil War had erupted with the firing on Fort Sumter by Confederates in South Carolina. The news electrified the North. The booming of Sumter's guns, a Cattaraugus County historian later wrote, "reverberated across the hills and streams from ocean to lake" as a signal to arms. President Lincoln's immediate call for volunteers to suppress the rebellion met with a wildly enthusiastic response. Olean was gripped by war fever and erupted with a burst of patriotism. "We have lots of war excitement around here," Joel wrote on April 29. A local militia company was "all prepared to start and they have got their tents pitched, and are encamped in regular military style, up in the park right in the center of the village, so that we have plenty of martial music and parading about these times." The great Northern mobilization had begun.

For all of his seeming indifference to the secession crisis, Joel was jolted by Sumter's shock. He longed to enlist. But he met with resistance that proved to be insurmountable. "I tried to coax Mother to let me volunteer but she would not [permit it]," he wrote. "She said that she should not live till fall if I went, so I had to give it up." Mother Bouton used another ploy to bolster her refusal. She stood her son up against the doorpost to see if he was tall enough to be a soldier. At age twenty-two, Joel had reached his full height of five feet, six inches. He was too short to enlist, Mother Bouton insisted. "So," Joel lamented, "I expect I shall have to give up the idea of being a soldier just at present." His determined mother would require some strong convincing to change her mind and allow him to volunteer.[10]

Brimming with patriotic ardor, yet thwarted by maternal command, Joel watched enviously as the local volunteers departed for the front. "I wish that I was with them," he wrote wistfully. Responding to Hoyt's news of a patriotic ceremony in South Salem, Joel declared, "I should really like to have been out to your flag raising," citing his love for the Star Spangled Banner and quoting lines from Francis Scott Key's anthem. He contemplated disobeying his mother's injunction and returning to South Salem to enlist. "When you get a company formed in Salem that is likely to be accepted," Joel informed his friend, "I wish to have you send me word and I will try to come out and go with you."[11]

But as the war escalated in the summer of 1861, Joel remained a civilian. He spent two weeks aboard a raft with a load of oil barrels. (Perhaps he had followed his inclination to work as a cooper.) The course was down the Allegheny River, through the Seneca Indian Reservation, which flanked both sides of the stream for miles. "We camped out in regular Indian style," Joel noted, "and for about half of the time we were on the Indian reservation right amongst the Indians themselves." He planned to travel to a nearby county to work during the haying season. During his free time he went fishing and picked blueberries. At Olean's Independence Day celebration, he watched three illuminated balloons ascend into a night sky blossoming with fireworks. He attended a camp meeting and the Spaulding and Rogers Circus. But the war constantly intruded on his easygoing life. Even at the circus the conflict surfaced, Joel reported: "The old clown made a rousing union speech."[12]

"I am sorry to hear that the martial spirit of old Salem is so lukewarm," he wrote to Hoyt in August, responding to a report of lackluster recruiting efforts in that town. "If I was out there," Joel added, "I should be almost tempted to harangue the people to fly to the defense of their firesides." Another group of volunteers had left Olean for the front, he reported. But by this time, Joel appeared to be having second thoughts about enlisting himself, couching his reluctance in humorous terms. "I have about made up my mind that I shall not go," he wrote, "as they say that [the enemy would] just as soon shoot a fellow down there as not; at any rate they shoot very careless and I don't believe it is a very good place for a fellow unless he is married and [has] got a scolding wife." Instead of volunteering, Joel tended the peas, beans, squashes, and cucumbers in his mother's garden.[13]

Following a month's visit to Binghamton during the fall of 1861, Joel returned to Olean to attend the local academy, probably taking teachers' classes established by the state university regents. His late start put him behind in his lessons. "I have had to study by steam power," he admitted, "to get along with them again." Joel plunged enthusiastically into school life. He was senior editor of the Olean Academy newspaper, writing articles and editorials and editing student contributions. And he anticipated a forthcoming school dramatic production, especially the nightly rehearsals, which would offer opportunities to "enjoy the society of so many of those dear charms that steal the heart away." About twenty teenaged girls were students at the academy, "some of the finest feminines," he assured Hoyt, "that you ever had the pleasure of meeting."

November brought Joel's first opportunity to vote. More than a dozen state and county offices were decided in the 1861 election. With one exception (for state canal commissioner), Joel voted the straight Republican (or "Union State") ticket. "The Democrats would not unite on a union ticket," he reported with satisfaction when the results were announced, "and the Republicans have whipped them higher than a kite."[14]

As the new year of 1862 dawned, politics and the war faded from Joel's letters. Instead he chronicled his busy social life. School work left plenty of time for leisure pursuits. Among his favorites were ice skating parties and sleigh rides, both of which offered chances for closeness to girls. "I tell you I think there is a

great deal more sport to skating now than it was before the ladies participated,"
he told Hoyt. "It is quite a pleasure to get one of the dear creatures in your arms
to show her the great secret of the art—(skating I mean)." Sleigh rides brought
a half dozen or more couples together. Sometimes the excursions lasted all night;
two rides ended with breakfast.

As much as he enjoyed their company, Joel was conflicted when it came to
relationships with women. "As for myself," he declared, "I have about concluded
to live a life of single blessedness, as I find that the great passion I have for the fair
sex is fast dying out of my composition; and as they are pretty expensive property
at the present day, I have concluded that it will be best for me to devote my funds
to some other purpose." He belied that statement, however, when he announced
that since his arrival in Olean he had wooed four different sweethearts. He admitted that he was a bit of a cad. "I go with one for a while, then discard her for
another," he confessed. "They all seem to feel pretty bad to have me leave them
and try to keep me, but it won't do. In a place like this where there are so many
young ladies, a fellow can just as well change every now and occasionally as not—
unless he wants to go with some particular one through the walk of life, which
you know is not my sentiment." Apologizing to Hoyt for a belated answer to a
letter, Joel blamed it on the social whirl. "You will pardon me, I am sure, when
I tell you it is the fault of the girls that you have not heard from me before," he
wrote. "I never went [out] so much in my life as I have been this winter; almost
every night I go somewhere." [15]

With the approach of spring and the end of the school year, Joel wondered
how to occupy himself. "Our school closes two weeks from tomorrow," he informed Hoyt on March 11, "and then I expect to have other fish to fry. I do not
know what I shall do this summer yet." He had applied for teaching positions
at two large Olean village schools, "yet the trustees think that a female teacher
will do in the summer and they will teach cheaper, so you see the women are a
bother to me in more ways than one." With employment prospects uncertain in
Olean—the oil boom had gone bust—his ambitions turned elsewhere, down the
Allegheny and Ohio rivers. "I think some of going down the river this spring if I
cannot get into any business that suits me," he wrote. "If I do I shall go to *Cincinnati* and take a tramp through Ohio—and see if I cannot find a place where a
fellow can make a fortune." [16]

Thoughts of Ohio vanished when Joel found a satisfying job in his hometown.
By May of 1862, he was working as a typesetter for the *Olean Times*. The weekly
newspaper dated from 1860, when a subscription of twelve hundred dollars was
raised to start a Republican organ in the village under the editorship of L. M.
Gano. "I like the business the best of anything that I ever have worked at," Joel

wrote on a sheet of Gano's copy paper, "[and] the more I do at it the better I like it. I can set as many type as some compositors that have worked at it [for] years." In his spare time, he played baseball with a local club and fished to his heart's content. "I once in a great while allow myself the indulgence of going to call on some nice young lady," he added, "though I am weaning myself from them as much as possible—and I find that my love for them is fast dying away." With his new job, it appeared that Joel was set for the summer and beyond—as long as he did not change his mind again and head in some new direction.[17]

Joel Bouton's rather carefree life came to an abrupt end on July 26, 1862, when he enlisted at Olean to serve for three years in defense of the Union. He never explained to Steve Hoyt what made him finally decide to volunteer, or how he convinced Mother Bouton to allow him to go, or if he ignored her demands that he stay. "Probably you have heard that I am a soldier of the U.S.," he simply wrote, "which is the case, and I like it very much." After his recent stints as house painter, student, teacher, raftsman, and typesetter, Joel had found his final occupation. From now on, his adventures would be determined by the activities of his regiment, the 154th New York, and the vagaries of fate.

Joel found his initiation to army life fairly easy to take. "Where we are camped it is nothing but play to do our duties," he reported from Camp James M. Brown, the regimental rendezvous at Jamestown, in neighboring Chautauqua County. "We have lots of fun here of all kinds, I tell you—more than you can find in any civil life." But this easygoing existence was tempered by other realities. "It is well for soldiers that they can enjoy themselves," Joel observed, "as they are deprived [of] many of the luxuries and conveniences of home." Lodged in rough barracks, subsisting on mediocre food, the green soldiers already had fond memories of civilian life.

Joel was appointed a corporal of Company C—composed of recruits from Olean and surrounding towns—by the company commander, Captain Lewis D. Warner. Had the men been allowed to elect their noncommissioned officers, Joel expected to be voted orderly sergeant. But Warner, a widely respected Portville carpenter, joiner, and lumberman, had appointed the sergeants and corporals. Joel claimed (inaccurately) that the captain had shown partiality to men from his hometown. "But I am satisfied," Joel conceded, "as my position [as corporal] clears me from doing picket duty and is two dollars per month more pay, besides a good chance of promotion." Joel was mistaken about his corporal's rank exempting him from picket duty. And at fourteen dollars per month, a corporal's pay was actually only one dollar more than a private's.[18]

On September 24, 1862, Corporal Bouton and the rest of Company C were formally mustered into the service of the United States at Camp Brown. Joel was listed in the company's descriptive book as having a dark complexion, black eyes, and black hair. Five days after the muster-in, the 154th New York departed western New York for the front. Joel's next letter was written on October 26 from the regiment's camp near Fairfax Court House, Virginia. Now he could offer Hoyt an authentic glimpse of army life at the front.

Seated on a stout stick of firewood propped up on two bricks, a folded newspaper on his lap for a desk, Joel wrote in the dim light of a candle wedged in the socket of a bayonet stuck in the ground. He and his tent mates, "three as hale and hearty boys as ever shouldered a musket in defense of their country," had combined their shelter tent halves—sheets of cotton drilling—to create an enclosure about twelve feet long, six feet wide, and four feet high in the center, with one end thatched shut with pine boughs and hay, the other covered with a rubber blanket. Their beds were made of hay spread over the ground, topped by their woolen blankets and overcoats. At one end of the tent a cheerful fire blazed in a small pit. "Without the rain is coming in torrents," Joel reported, "which ever and anon beats through our cotton roof giving us a shower bath free gratis, while a fine little stream flows under the edge of the tent."

"I have been sick about two weeks since we landed on the sacred soil of Virginia," he wrote, without specifying his ailment. But he added that he survived the rigors of the regiment's first march from Arlington Heights to Fairfax, covering about twenty miles over two days, in good shape: "We had very heavy knapsacks but I got along with mine first rate." And he expressed approval of army fare. "We live first rate for soldiers," he wrote; "have fresh beef, soft bread and coffee, which with the little extras that we get from the sutlers makes everything on the squeegee." (Sutlers were civilian vendors who sold foodstuffs and sundries to the soldiers.)

Still, life had taken an ominous turn. "I am not as patriotic as I used to be when I was at home reading the newspapers," Joel admitted, "but I expect to meet with many hardships and can stand it now that I have got fully initiated. But still [I will] hail with joy the day when this war is through with." When that hoped-for day would arrive was uncertain; no doubt grim work must be done before it arrived. "I hope that it may be my lot to escape unhurt from this," Joel wrote, "but I am ready for the battle at any time, as that is what I came for."

Joel was displeased with what he saw as the government's strategy of conquering the rebellion by sapping the Confederacy's resources rather than attacking its armies. "I don't believe in this inactivity," he declared. "This exhaustive policy is a poor one in my opinion. It is exhausting our resources as fast as that of the enemy. I don't believe we can ever starve the Rebels into submission; the only way is to whip them to it, and the sooner we commence this job in earnest the sooner we shall be through with this unpleasant business." [19]

The job seemed under way in November, when the Eleventh Corps, including the 154th New York, was ordered on a reconnaissance to seek the enemy in the vicinity of Thoroughfare Gap, in the Bull Run Mountains. The corps marched west to the gap, but no Confederates were found. The expedition ended inconsequentially with a return to Fairfax. "When we came into our present camp about two weeks ago," Joel reported from Fairfax on December 7, "it was a thick woods, so thick that a company could not dress up in a line. But now it has all disappeared, for more than 50 acres we have cleared entirely ready for the plough." After denuding their campsite of timber, the men had to haul firewood on their backs for more than a quarter-mile, a chore Joel described as "no fun by any means." There was talk around camp that the regiment would soon go into winter quarters. "I hope so," Joel wrote, "for we are poorly provided for now, having nothing but the shelter tents," which were inadequate to keep the soldiers warm. "We have the blues some today," he admitted, "on account of the cold weather." Recent days had brought snow and "cold enough to freeze the bark off a dry pine tree," he reported, "and I tell you we have had gay old times since in trying to keep warm, which has been a vain attempt. Last night was the most seedy old time I have seen since I was a soldier. We had *ducks* rest all night." Generally Joel composed his letters in pen and ink, "but it is as much as I can do to hold a pencil this morning."

Low spirits induced by hardships were compounded by other factors. "As the thing looks now, it does not appear as if we were a-going to have much fighting to do," Joel supposed, "but there is no telling what will turn up." Beyond the uncertain military situation, Bouton sensed a vast corruption in the war effort. "There is more humbug in the thing than I thought of before I enlisted," he wrote. "It is nothing more than a gigantic speculation." Officers had been heard to say that they hoped the war would last their full three years' term of service—and even longer—so they could collect their ample pay. "I tell you that the war on our side has been conducted on the money-making principle entirely," Joel declared, "and if officers had received no larger pay than privates, I honestly believe that this would have closed long ago." This feeling was shared by many of the soldiers.

But Joel's spirits had not been entirely dampened, as a personal description revealed. "Soldiering agrees with me first rate," he informed Hoyt, "as you may judge when I tell you that I weigh 21 pounds avoirdupois more than I did when I enlisted and twelve pounds heavier than I ever did before in my life. And oh! such whiskers. I have nine fine silky hairs on one side of my chin and six on the other. Can you beat that? I think it is for a man's health to wear whiskers, or else I should cut mine off."[20]

By the time of Joel's next letter, January 7, 1863, the regiment had marched to Falmouth, Virginia, across the Rappahannock River from Fredericksburg. Fortunately it arrived too late to take part in the recent battle of Fredericksburg, which had been a dismal and bloody disaster for the Union cause. "We were not in the fight, although we expected when we left Fairfax to have a hand in," Joel reported. "During our last two days' march we could hear the cannonading very distinctly, but it played out the night we drew up on this side of the river and we heard nothing more except a few scattering reports the next morning." Northern soldiers and the public at large castigated the Army of the Potomac's commander, Major General Ambrose E. Burnside, for the ignominious defeat. But Joel exonerated the hapless general, citing the Confederate army's strong defensive position, the force of public opinion that compelled Burnside to give battle at a disadvantage, and the relatively low ratio of Union losses to men engaged.

Although the Fredericksburg fiasco cast a pall of depression over the army, Joel retained a chipper outlook. "I am as healthy as a buck," he bragged. "Weigh 150 pounds, and I think if I was out there I could go down on the river and holler louder than you can." The regiment's living conditions had improved. A winter camp had been platted "on a grand scale with very broad streets," and cozy huts kept the men warm and comfortable. "They are constructed of mud and logs," Joel reported, "principally logs, with our tents for roofs. In one end we have splendid fireplaces made of stone, sticks, mud, and bricks, which not only furnish us with plenty of heat and light but cook our provisions to perfection."

From their riverside camp, the men had a good view of the Confederates on the opposite shore. "When it is clear we can see them very distinctly, lounging around their campfires," Joel noted. The New Yorkers' first contact with the enemy was benign. Standing picket along the riverbanks, Union and Confederate soldiers commiserated across the cold, rushing water. War weariness told on both sides. "It's d——d cold," Joel reported a Confederate picket yelling one night to his counterpart of the 154th. "I wish Jeff [Davis] was on this side of the river, and Old Abe [Lincoln] on that standing picket tonight. I think they would come to terms devilish quick." Another rebel told one of the New Yorkers "that if it could be left to them two to settle the thing that they would throw down their guns, shake hands, and go home." The Confederates declared that "they do not know what they wanted this war for," Joel reported. "They were living well enough before it broke out and had no cause for complaint."[21]

"Well, Steve, I have not yet seen any fighting yet," Joel wrote in his next letter, "but came pretty near it in the last proposed crossing of the Rappahannock; and no doubt we should have seen bloody work if it had not been for the rain." He referred to the notorious Mud March of January 1863, which saw a promising army movement bog down in sucking mire under torrential rains, leading to the dismissal of Burnside as commander of the Army of the Potomac and his replacement by Joseph Hooker. Following that debacle, the 154th New York moved to another winter camp, "on a hill somewhere in Virginia," as Joel put it, "I guess not far from Stafford Court House." It was their best camp yet, he declared, but "we have built winter quarters four times and I hope we shall be permitted to stay where we are until spring, for I am getting tired of lugging logs and mixing mud to build huts with."

For four months the regiment had moved from camp to camp, but it had yet to meet the enemy in combat. "It is pretty dangerous work to fight," Joel conceded. "Still I shall awfully hate to go home and say that I have never been in any battle." The impatient North should not fault her common soldiers for failing to meet the enemy, Bouton believed, if the generals would not actively campaign. "We are willing to do our duty in any way and if the officers in command of us do not see fit to lead us against our common enemy, I don't know as we are to blame and think that we ought to be entitled to a little credit for having a willingness to fight."[22]

But when Joel wrote again on March 3, he was still languishing in the same camp near Stafford Court House. "We are having very pleasant weather," he reported, ". . . and the roads are getting better faster; and then I suppose we shall have to get up and skedaddle again for some place—the Lord only knows where—and I don't know as it makes much difference, as lying still so long in camp is getting to be *somewhat* monotonous." He optimistically added, "I think from the situations of affairs now that we shall not have to stay down here another winter."

The Stafford camp was beautiful, Joel reported, situated in a pleasant location, with its company streets lined with rows of pine, cedar, and holly. "And what an additional ornament do you suppose was added to them yesterday?" he asked Hoyt. "Hoops! Yes, sir! And not barrel hoops either, or such as little boys and girls chase through the streets, but crinoline, such as encircle the human form divine." Much to his delight, a party of female visitors had invaded the male preserve of the camp. "There were four of the *'dear critters'* made their appearance amongst us and gladdened our eyes once more with the sight o' them, which I assure you was a great treat; and you ought to have seen the heads stuck out of the tents as they passed. One fellow was so eager that he run out without a shirt on."

"We have a peculiar drill to go through when we meet a female down here," Joel wrote slyly to Hoyt. "It is this. Present arms—close (clothes) up—lie down—draw rammer—ram cartridge. There is one time and two motions to each command but the last, when the recruit makes as many motions as he has a mind to. You can guess how each command is executed. Such is military." Did Joel actually perform his double entendre "drill" with a woman in camp? He left it to his friend to guess.[23]

A few weeks after the women roused the camp, the regiment still had not moved. Joel explained why the opening of the spring campaign was delayed. "We still stay in these quarters," he wrote, "for the reason that the roads are such that it is impossible to get away, and as it rains about every other day, [we] don't know when they will be any better." In the meantime, he had plenty to keep him occupied:

> I have one letter for publication and three private ones that I want to write tomorrow, besides drill, dress parade, a lesson to get in the tactics, write in my diary, besides many other camp duties that all take time, and that is about a fair standard of daily routine in camp, with about two days every week for camp guard or picket. So you see we have enough to keep us busy through the day, and in the evening lights have to be put out at half past eight.

Joel was paying more attention now to the last-mentioned rule; just twelve days before, he had been arrested for having a light lit after taps. What punishment—if any—he received was apparently too inconsequential to warrant mention.

"I have so much writing to do that you will have to put up with short letters most of the time," Joel apologized to Steve. In addition to his personal correspondence, he wrote letters to the press. Having written extensively for school publications and worked for a newspaper, it is not surprising that Joel became an army correspondent for his old employer. One of his messmates, Sergeant Amos Humiston (who thought Bouton was "a first rate fellow"), noted that Joel wrote on a regular basis to the *Olean Times* and a newspaper in Cuba, New York, keeping the home folk informed of news from the regiment.[24]

Joel had big news for Steve Hoyt the next time he wrote, on May 18, 1863. At last the 154th New York had seen combat. Joel described the maneuvers leading up to the terrible ordeal in a lighthearted fashion. Using mock biblical language, he related how "it came to pass" that "our regiment, yea! even the 154th," left its Stafford camp on April 13 and marched up "that renowned river—even the Rappahannock" to Kelly's Ford, where it spent two weeks picketing the river-bank. He described how the 154th crossed the river in pontoon boats on the evening of April 28 and held the opposite shore while a bridge was laid. He dismissed the harmless fire from Confederate pickets that splashed into the water while the crossing was made: "The enemy were few, even as scattered mullein stalks, and we were not molested by them." Having spearheaded the Union advance, the regiment rested while it watched the crossing of three Federal army corps, "the hosts of Abraham [Lincoln], even Abraham the First, a mighty host even as the trees of a small woods."

Dropping the Old Testament tone, Joel mentioned the 154th's looting of the bountiful farm owned by the ford's namesake: "We had fun jayhawking old Kelly, a rich Secesh." He described the regiment's march to the Rapidan River as guard to the baggage train, and the subsequent tramp to a clearing in the Wilderness woods near Chancellorsville.

He did not describe the ensuing battle, but instead sent a soldier's letter (perhaps one of his own) clipped from the *Olean Times*, "which will save me considerable writing." That letter no doubt detailed how the 154th New York and the rest of the Eleventh Corps were surprised and routed by the famous flank attack of Confederate general Thomas J. "Stonewall" Jackson on the evening of May 2, 1863, how the regiment and the rest of its brigade fought a forlorn and brief holding action against the overwhelming rebel onslaught after most of the rest of the corps had fled to the rear, and how the 154th lost 240 casualties out of 590 men present for the fight—a 40 percent loss rate and the fourth highest regimental casualty count suffered in the Union army at Chancellorsville. "We were in a very hard fight for about an hour," Joel merely informed Hoyt, "and taken at a great disadvantage, but our boys fought their maiden battle well and our brigade received all of the praise that the Eleventh Corps got." Indeed, in the aftermath of the battle, the 154th's brigade was singled out for acclaim while the rest of the Eleventh Corps was condemned for its poor performance.

Joel overestimated the duration of the regiment's fight, however. The 154th made a stubborn stand for perhaps twenty minutes to a half hour before being isolated, outflanked, and driven by the exultant enemy into the woods toward the safety of other Union lines. Many fell during the chaotic retreat. "When we retreated you ought to have seen your humble servant run," Joel told his friend. "About 6 or eight rods behind me were a lot of the rebs coming with fixed bayonets, yelling, 'Surrender, you Yankee son of a b——h!' But I could not see the point, and they did not get this child, no not they. I had the satisfaction of administering to one of them one of Uncle Sam's blue pills during the engagement, but it was mighty unpleasant to be chased so by them. I was fortunate enough to escape without a scratch, although I had a very close call; but a miss is as good as a mile." He added flippantly, "Besides, a man that is borned to be hung can't be shot."

Sooner than he could imagine, Mother Bouton's son was shot. It happened only eleven days after he survived Chancellorsville, back in the safety of the Stafford Court House camp. Joel was standing picket on the night of May 13 when he accidentally fired his musket. The muzzle was pointed toward his left foot. Joel's second toe was mangled; a surgeon amputated it.

Self-inflicted wounds were often deliberate—several members of the regiment intentionally shot themselves or hacked their limbs with axes to be discharged from the army. That was not the case with Joel. His wound was the result of an embarrassing mishap; he had no intention of using it as a ticket to return home. Short a toe but irrepressible as ever, he intended to recuperate and to continue to serve. His wound was "getting along finely," he assured Hoyt, "and I guess I shall be able to go with Old Joe [Hooker] when he again crosses the river, which I hope won't be delayed any longer than is necessary for me to get all right." [25]

Luckily for Joel, he had a month to mend before the next march. In the meantime, the regiment again moved its camp and named the new bivouac in memory of its adjutant, Samuel C. Noyes Jr., who had fallen at Chancellorsville. "A splendid camp," Joel called it, "the finest that we have had since we came to Virginia. It is in a large oak woods where we have a beautiful shade and some swings and gymnastical appliances." Perhaps Joel used the makeshift apparatus to strengthen his injured foot; rest certainly helped him to heal. Easy times were had in the idyllic new surroundings. "We are having very fine weather and very pleasant times just at present," he wrote. "In fact we have had scarcely any duties to do since the last fight."

Hoyt had apparently made some critical remarks about the Chancellorsville defeat to his army friend. Joel responded defensively, "You seem to think that we did not accomplish much the last time we crossed the river; but notwithstanding that we did not gain all that was planned to do nor all that the country was hoping for, still we inflicted on the enemy one of the severest blows that they have received since the commencement of the war, and two or three more of the like will use up entirely the reb army of Virginia." Another move was in the offing,

Joel thought, "the nature of which I am unable to form any idea of, as it is one of the most mixed things that I have tried to ferret out." Distant gunfire was heard from camp; rumors flew, and the soldiers were ordered to keep ready to march.

"Something is in the wind," Joel sensed. As always, he was ready to drift wherever the breezes took him.[26]

Steve Hoyt probably never learned the details of what happened next. Six days after Joel wrote to Steve, on June 12, 1863, the 154th New York began a long trudge that carried it in choking dust and sweltering heat through drought-parched Virginia and across the Potomac River into Maryland. It was the hardest march the regiment had yet made. Distances of more than twenty miles were covered on some days. Straggling was common. "The men were very much crippled with sore feet," Captain Lewis Warner reported, "and . . . we would have passed as a detachment of the Invalid Corps." Corporal Bouton's nine-toed feet no doubt ached as much as the rest, but he managed to keep up and stay with the regiment.[27]

The march of July 1 carried the regiment from Emmitsburg, Maryland, across the Mason-Dixon Line into Pennsylvania. Orders were received to proceed at the double-quick. As Joel and his comrades picked up the pace, the distant booming of artillery and crackling of musketry grew more distinct. In mid-afternoon the regiment halted in a cemetery at the crown of a hill overlooking the village of Gettysburg. There the exhausted men filled their canteens, gobbled a quick lunch of salt pork and hardtack, and cleaned and loaded their rifles. Beyond the sprawling village's rooftops and spires, on distant plains and ridges, clouds of gun smoke rose from the battle lines. At about 3:30 P.M., the 154th New York and the other regiments of its brigade were ordered to rush from Cemetery Hill to cover the retreat of the rest of the Eleventh Corps—the same dangerous task they had faced at Chancellorsville.

Joel hurried with his regiment down the hill and into the village. Gettysburg was in chaos. The advancing column parted a steady stream of fugitives as it made its way through the streets. Panicked civilians were fleeing their homes. Wounded soldiers crowded the sidewalks. As the line passed a church, shells began to strike and burst nearby. The men steadily pressed on. They followed Stratton Street to the northeastern outskirts of town and filed through a carriage gateway into a fenced brickyard.

The 154th New York, with a regiment on its right and another to its left, formed its line in front of the beehive-shaped brick kilns and advanced to a post and rail fence at the northern edge of the yard. There the men were ordered to kneel and reserve their fire until the enemy was close enough to make a volley effective. In front of Company C, at the center of the regimental line, a ripe wheatfield covered a gentle slope, the golden tassels waving placidly in a gentle breeze. Joel had no sooner crouched behind the fence when an awesome and intimidating sight met his eyes.

A Confederate line of battle crested the rise, stretching out of sight to the right and left, fluttering red battle flags marking eight regiments of two brigades—a force far outnumbering the meager Union line, and outflanking it at both ends. The enemy line advanced a bit, halted, and unloosed a volley toward the brickyard. A pall of smoke hovered over the wheatfield, then through it the Confederates came charging. The Union regiments opened fire. Darts of flame and billows of smoke erupted from the fence line. The enemy staggered momentarily, then came on again, an unstoppable human avalanche.

As rapidly as they could, Joel Bouton and the rest of Company C loaded and fired their muskets. As the smoke thickened and the roar of gunfire grew, Corporal Richard H. Kerr of Company D made his way to Joel's side, put his hand on Joel's shoulder, and bent to shout something into his ear.

At that moment, a Confederate bullet penetrated Joel Bouton's skull and killed him instantly.[28]

"Corp. J. M. Bouton is reported killed," Captain Lewis Warner wrote on July 10 to the *Olean Times*. Nine days later a Cattaraugus County civilian who had journeyed to Gettysburg to ascertain the 154th New York's casualties reported that Joel had been "seen dead on the field." On August 19, Captain Warner notified the *Times*, "Corporal Bouton was said to have been killed on the 1st day of July, at Gettysburg, and as he has not been heard from among the prisoners, I think there is no doubt of his death."[29]

Word eventually reached Stephen Hoyt, who sorrowfully bundled Joel's letters and put them away as mementos. Little did Hoyt know he was preserving the only known portrait of his friend: a young man brimming with boundless enthusiasm and optimism, embracing life as it came to him, cheerfully skipping from town to town, from job to job, his fishing pole bobbing with a big catch, a date with a pretty girl set for the evening—happily thriving in the prime of his brief life, until the war put him beneath his misspelled headstone in Gettysburg.

CHAPTER TWO

Private Milton H. Bush

Company K

Cattaraugus County basked under drifting clouds in a bright sky on a balmy mid-July day as Phil Palen and I wended our way along back roads past fields and farms and woods. A long-time friend, Phil is an avid local historian with a strong interest in the county's Civil War legacy. His knowledge of area highways freed me from juggling maps and the steering wheel, and our meandering conversation made a pleasant ride even more enjoyable.

Driving through the township of Conewango, we passed numerous Amish homesteads. The road was spotted with clods of manure from buggy-drawing horses. Lines of black and white clothes dried in the breeze next to houses while straw-hatted, bearded men and bonneted women tended to their tasks. At the top of a slope on Seager Hill Road, we pulled into the driveway of Rutledge Cemetery. I followed two shallow dirt ruts worn into the grass to the middle of the two-acre cemetery and parked in the shade of a tree, near a clump of white hydrangea.

The air was redolent of cows and hay. Except for the occasional swish of a passing car and the distant hum of a motor, the cemetery was quiet. A small stream flowed silently at the foot of a steep drop-off at the back of the lot. Maples, yews, cedars, Norway spruce, and a lone catalpa dappled the well-kept grounds with shadow. Small flags dotting the grass marked the graves of veterans and attested to Conewango's devotion to serving her country.

Not far from my car, in the shade of a cedar next to the drive, one flag floated beside a small granite obelisk. The marker commemorated the Bush family—a patriarch, Milton Bush, and his three wives; a teenaged daughter from the first marriage, from the second an infant girl and a young adult son. The flag flew for the son, Milton H. Bush. Milton was a Civil War soldier, but no reference to his service was carved into the stone.

In fact, Milton Bush does not rest beneath the Rutledge Cemetery obelisk that bears his name: his inscription is a cenotaph, made in his memory by his family despite the fact that he is buried elsewhere, far from his western New York home.

Milton Bush is interred in the Nashville National Cemetery in Tennessee. He was one of approximately 16,500 Union soldiers moved to the burial ground after it was established in 1867. The corpses came from battlefield and hospital graveyards in a wide region around Nashville. Union general George H. Thomas established the cemetery in the town of Madison, about six miles north of Nashville, intentionally locating it adjacent to the Louisville and Nashville Railroad. Thomas wanted to make sure that everyone aboard a train along that line would see the graveyard and realize the sacrifices that had been made to preserve the Union.

Milton is buried in Section J, Grave Number 13580. A standard marble stone, simply carved with a shield enclosing the grave number and his name and state, marks his final resting place.[1]

If it were not for a simple clerical error, Bush might well have lived a long life and been laid to rest beside his family in their hometown cemetery. Slapdash bookkeeping by green officers, a strict adherence to regulations, and the glacial grind of military bureaucracy were not listed as the official cause of his death—but they had doomed Milton Bush.

The tragedy of errors began on September 1, 1862, when Milton enlisted in his hometown of Conewango, New York, to serve for three years. He was one of ten Conewangoans signed up over the course of a week by their townsman, Stiles B. Ellsworth, a civil engineer who would be appointed a sergeant of the company he was helping to form. Why Bush volunteered is uncertain. Perhaps he was fired by patriotism; maybe he was pressured by his peers, infected as they were with war fever. Whatever his motivation, Milton's enlistment can only be viewed as a mistake, in light of what soon happened.

He was twenty-one years of age and stood five feet, eight inches tall, with a pale complexion, blue eyes, and light brown hair. He had spent his young life on the family farm in Conewango. His father and namesake was a widower with four children when he had married Aurelia Hitchcock in 1840. Milton Hitchcock Bush was born to the couple in Conewango on May 5, 1841. His sister Alice, born in 1852, lived for only three months. Milton was about seventeen when his mother died in 1858. In 1861 the elder Bush took a third wife, Aurelia's older sister, Diantha Hitchcock. In addition to his father and his stepmother-aunt, Milton probably left some step-siblings behind when he and his fellow recruits left Conewango for Camp James M. Brown in Jamestown.[2]

Camp Brown was located about a mile south of Jamestown's center, at the Chautauqua County Agricultural Society's hilltop fairgrounds. The exhibition buildings, set between a pine grove and a half-mile racetrack, had been appropriated and adapted for military uses. Floral Hall was now a barracks, Dairy Hall and Mechanics' Hall were linked by a new building to form an immense dining hall, and other new structures served as kitchens, store houses, and more barracks. By the time Milton arrived, approximately seventeen hundred recruits were housed at Camp Brown, increasing the population of Jamestown by more than half. Crowds of visitors flocked to the old fairgrounds and added to the hubbub. Compared to the quiet Bush farm, Camp Brown was like a busy city.

Life in camp was devoid of the comforts of home. The men slept on straw-filled bed-ticks in hemlock-plank bunks. Complaints about scanty and unpalatable food were near universal. Duties were light and haphazardly performed. Still, the men chafed at their lack of freedom. Passes to leave camp and visit the village were seldom issued. But the tall fence and novice guard details surrounding Camp Brown proved to be porous. Running the guard became epidemic. It culminated when the guardhouse was burned to the ground during a riotous mass escape.

Privacy was virtually impossible. Knots of men gathered to sing, play baseball, attend prayer meetings, drink whiskey, read their Bibles, or gamble on card games, depending on their wont. Some blustered about going to Dixie to give the rebels hell; others quietly contemplated what was to come. Many thought of the families and friends they were leaving behind. They vented their homesickness in a flow of letters home.[3]

Milton had not spent much time at Camp Brown when he understood he had made a mistake: he did not want to be a soldier. Struck by this grave realization, he considered his options. As the muster-in approached, he took the only step available to escape his dilemma. He hired a substitute. Milton was the only member Company K—and the rest of the newly formed regiment—to buy his way out of his commitment, to renege on his patriotic promise with a payment.

How much Bush paid Gustavus J. Ackley to take his place in the ranks of Company K of the 154th New York is unknown. The deal was reportedly made on September 23, 1862, two days before the company was mustered into the service of the United States for a term of three years, unless sooner discharged. Ackley was perhaps visiting friends at Camp Brown when he agreed to substitute for Bush. He was a Conewango farm boy of about seventeen years of age; he fibbed and swore he was twenty-three to conform with regulations. Ackley was given a physical examination and approved for duty by the regimental surgeon, Henry Van Aernam. Captain Henry Hugaboom of Company K then agreed that Ackley should be accepted and mustered in place of Bush, and the regiment's colonel, Addison G. Rice, consented to the substitution.

Rice was a lawyer and politician who had served in the prewar militia and probably had a rudimentary knowledge of military regulations. In approving the Bush-Ackley substitution, he obviously saw no legal impediment to the switch. In the bustle of preparing the regiment for its muster-in, Rice did what he had to do to effect the Bush-Ackley agreement and left the details to Company K's captain. Unlike Rice, Henry Hugaboom was a middle-aged farmer with no knowledge of the intricacies of military procedure. This created a problem.[4]

Rice ordered papers drawn up releasing Bush from the regiment and formalizing the substitution agreement. With the document in hand, Milton packed his belongings, left camp, and returned to Conewango a free man.

Ackley remained at Camp Brown and two days later Company K was mustered in. Gus must have been surprised when his name was not called in its proper alphabetical order during the muster. Apparently he instead answered to Bush's name when it was called. Hugaboom either did not notice or overlooked that error. In addition, Ackley was not listed on the company muster-in roll; Milton Bush was. Hugaboom also missed that slip. Nevertheless, the farmer-turned-captain signed his name to the roll beneath a certification, on his honor, that the list exhibited the true state of his company and that each man had answered to his own proper name in person. Only in subsequent musters was Ackley carried as a private of Company K and Milton Bush dropped from the rolls.[5]

So off to the war went Gustavus Ackley in Milton Bush's place. While Bush went about his life at home through the fall and winter, the principals in his exchange arrangement left the army, one by one. First to go was Colonel Addison Rice, who had raised the 154th New York with the understanding that he would deliver it to the front and be relieved of command by a veteran officer from Cattaraugus County (and Rice's former law partner), Patrick Henry Jones. Within two months after the regiment reached Virginia, as per agreement, Rice returned home and Colonel Jones assumed command.

Next to leave was Gus Ackley, whose career as a soldier was short. "Gustave Ackley is not very well," a member of Company K reported only nine days after the 154th New York reached Virginia. "Day fore yesterday he was very sick." Less than two months later, on December 9, 1862, Ackley was discharged on account of disability at Fairfax Court House. He seemed to convalesce quickly on his return home. He graduated from the University of Buffalo, studied medicine with a prominent Conewango physician, and hung his shingle in the nearby village of Cattaraugus, where he was practicing at the end of the war. (Ackley's career as a doctor was brief; he died in Cattaraugus during the winter of 1865–1866.)[6]

Last to go was Captain Henry Hugaboom. The day before Ackley was discharged, Hugaboom was sent to a hospital at Georgetown, D.C. His health continued to plague him on his return to the regiment a month later. Worse, he was unsatisfactory as a leader. "I have been disappointed in our captain," wrote Private George W. Newcomb of Hugaboom. "He is a perfect dead head. There is no fire in him. He sits around like a stout bottle."[7]

Hugaboom tendered his resignation on March 4, 1863, and left for his Cattaraugus County home the next day. "He resigned on the account of his health," wrote Private Newcomb. "He thought he would not be able to stand the privations of camp life." Some members of the company, however, wondered if Hugaboom's failing health was the real reason for his resignation. Newcomb recalled that the men had purchased a sword for their captain and presented it to him at Camp Brown before leaving for the front. Hugaboom had accepted the gift with a short speech, declaring he would stand by the men until the sword was worn up to its hilt. Now that Hugaboom was gone, Newcomb wrote, "Some think that he was afraid there would be a chance to use it before long and he resigned on that account." Six months after he accepted the sword with a brave vow and led his company to the front, Henry Hugaboom was back on his farm.[8]

So the matter might have ended, with Bush (and Ackley, Rice, and Hugaboom) happy at home, had Colonel Patrick Jones not made an interesting discovery in January 1864, at the 154th's winter camp at Lookout Valley, Tennessee. While attending to the plentiful regimental paperwork, Jones noted that Bush's name had been carried on the rolls of Company K. But there were no accompanying remarks to indicate that he had been discharged or otherwise lost to the company. To Jones, Bush was still a soldier—a soldier absent without leave.

The colonel ordered the company's new commander, Captain Arthur Hotchkiss, to notify Bush "to report to his company in default of which he would be charged with and arrested for desertion." Hotchkiss did not know Bush, or the circumstances of the case. He had been promoted from another company to replace Hugaboom. Despite his status as an outsider, Hotchkiss had become a favorite with his men; unlike Hugaboom he had a military bearing, and he was personable with the boys. Captain Hotchkiss obeyed Colonel Jones's order and wrote the letter to Bush, which made its way from Lookout Valley to Conewango.[9]

For a year and a half, Milton Bush had enjoyed his freedom as a civilian. The months had passed in the familiar cycle of work on the family farm—shearing sheep, cutting hay, delivering milk to cheese factories, harvesting oats, corn, apples, and potatoes. Conewango farmers were tapping maple trees on snow-blanketed hills and readying their kettles for making sugar when Hotchkiss's letter arrived.

We can only imagine Milton's surprise and dismay when he read Hotchkiss's letter. He had made a deal which had freed him from military service, and now, inexplicably, he was ordered into the army, under threat of a capital offense. He contacted his former captain, Henry Hugaboom, who no doubt was dumbfounded and embarrassed at the fix Bush found himself in—a predicament that Hugaboom was largely responsible for. Hugaboom agreed to accompany Milton to the front and do what he could to resolve the matter. Together, the two left Cattaraugus County and made the long trip to Tennessee.

Bush and Hugaboom arrived at the 154th New York's Lookout Valley camp on March 23, 1864. Hugaboom met with Colonel Jones, who told the former captain that nothing could be done to rectify the case and free Bush. Within days, Hugaboom left for home, leaving hapless Milton to fend for himself. Shortly thereafter, Corporal Marcellus W. Darling of Company K summarized the situation, placing much of the blame for Bush's predicament on Hugaboom and expressing pessimism about Bush's chances of escaping the army's clutches:

> Our old captain, Hugaboom, has been here. He came with Milton Bush but has gone back and left Bush, and I guess we shall have to make a soldier of Bush, for I think there is no way he can get out now. After any one is mustered into the United States [service], it is harder to get out than out of state prison. In the first place, Hugaboom was to blame in telling Bush that anyone could take his place, for it is an impossible thing to have it done after he is mustered into the United States service.[10]

Private Milton Bush was in the army, but he was there against his will. He insisted to Colonel Jones that the presence of his name on Company K's muster-in roll was a clerical error and that he was "morally if not legally discharged" from the service by the agreement made with Captain Hugaboom and Colonel Rice. Most likely he presented the original papers as evidence. Milton then requested an honorable discharge. Jones agreed. But there would be much more to it than that.

On April 2, the colonel addressed a letter advocating Bush's discharge to the assistant adjutant general of the Department of the Cumberland. Jones outlined the details of Milton's case and closed by stating, "Believing the foregoing facts as stated to be true and that Bush acted in the matter in good faith, I respectfully submit the case to the decision of the commanding general." [11]

Bush's fate was now out of his hands, entwined in the abundant red tape of the army's bureaucracy. Awaiting a decision in the case, veterans of the 154th had their opportunity to "make a soldier of Bush," as Marcellus Darling had predicted. This indoctrination presumably transformed Milton from civilian to soldier, albeit an involuntary one. "Milton is well," Private David S. Jones reported soon after Bush's arrival in camp. His health continued to hold up when the regiment broke camp in Lookout Valley and embarked on the Atlanta campaign in May 1864.

Milton was present for duty when the 154th New York fought in the woods and mountains of northern Georgia during May and June at the battles of Dug Gap on Rocky Face Ridge, Resaca, New Hope Church, and Gilgal Church, with plenty of skirmishing and marching in between. According to Company K's muster rolls, he served in the ranks during that time. By then he was a veteran soldier—and a survivor, having escaped harm as the regiment's casualty lists lengthened. But on June 22, 1864, Milton's luck turned. That day he was sent by railroad from the vicinity of Kennesaw Mountain, Georgia, to Ward 1 of the Army of the Cumberland's General Field Hospital near Chattanooga, Tennessee. Surgeons there described him as convalescing from remittent fever. [12]

Two days later, on June 24, Milton was put aboard one of the special hospital trains that ran regularly three times a week from Chattanooga to Nashville. He and the other patients were carried aboard on stretchers, which were suspended from straps lining the walls of the cars. The locomotive was painted red to identify the train as a hospital conveyance to the roving bands of Confederate guerillas who periodically harassed the railroad. Milton's train made the trip safely, and he was admitted to Division 1 of the Cumberland General Hospital at Nashville on June 25. His complaint was now listed as chronic diarrhea. [13]

In Nashville, Milton Bush's luck ran out entirely. He died on July 7, 1864. The final diagnosis was inflammation of the bowels. [14]

Milton was interred in the Cumberland Hospital's burial grounds and his name, regiment, and date of death were painted on a wooden headboard marking his grave. There he rested until he was reburied in the Nashville National Cemetery.

Colonel Jones and the 154th New York were in the vicinity of Atlanta on August 26, 1864, when the adjutant general's office of the War Department in Washington issued Special Order Number 282. A decision had finally been rendered in Milton's case. Extract 63 of the order read, "Private Milton H. Bush, Company K, 154th New York Volunteers, now with that Regiment will be discharged [from] the service of the United States, upon receipt of this order at the place where he may be serving." By the time Colonel Jones read it, the order that might have saved Milton's life had arrived some two months too late.[15]

CHAPTER THREE

Corporal Martin D. Bushnell

Company H

Back in the mid-1970s, Frank M. Bushnell and I spent a half-hour in a cemetery in his hometown of Napoli, Cattaraugus County, lying on our bellies in the grass. We were peering at the marble headstone of Frank's granduncle, trying to make out the epitaph. Over the grave flew two American flags. One fluttered in a bronze holder, the star-shaped badge of the Grand Army of the Republic. The other was incised at the top of the stone, its rigid stripes forming perfect waves. Beneath the carved flag was a rusted frame that once held a photograph of the deceased. Under the frame were inscribed Frank's ancestor's name, regiment, and date of death. Below the inscription, at the bottom of the stone, was a four-line verse, worn shallow by the passing years. Try as we might, Frank and I could not make out the last two lines.

Almost thirty years later, I returned to South Napoli Cemetery with Phil Palen. As we crested a hill on the quiet Hardscrabble Road, near the intersection of the Manley Hill Road, Phil pointed out a small white sign with the red letters, "IN." No other sign identified the place. We pulled into the dirt drive; as in most of the small country cemeteries in Cattaraugus County, the drive made a U through the grounds to an exit, with a central spur. Giant twin maples towered near the center of the cemetery, but most of the plat was bathed in sunlight and the lawn was striped with long, late-afternoon shadows of headstones. Like the other Cattaraugus County cemeteries I visited, the grounds were well tended, the grass neatly mowed, the stones upright. These resting places were not marred by the vandalism I had seen in some historic cemeteries in New England.

But damage had nevertheless been done. Not far from where Frank Bushnell now rested, near the hill's crown, his ancestor's marble stone had been badly eroded by acid rain. All of its inscriptions were difficult if not impossible to read, and only a newer granite stone at the foot of the grave enabled one to identify its occupant. The four lines of poetry at the bottom of the marble had been eaten away. But now I knew what they said, having discovered them in the writings of their author:

> Sleep on, our loving brother, sleep,
> This marble shall thy memory keep,
> But deeper on our hearts are graven
> The thought that we shall meet in heaven.

In the lines of that quatrain lies the intersection of two lives.

"The Yankees are in the pocket!" The shrill scream of a little neighbor girl startled Mrs. Fannie Jackson awake. She had dozed off over a newspaper she was reading on the warm Sunday of May 8, 1864. The cry came again: "The Yankees are in the pocket!" Fannie was wide awake now, and rose from her couch. For several days cannonading had thudded to the north, in the direction of Dalton, Georgia. Fannie had assumed that a Union army advance—if it came—would carry the Yankees seven miles east of where she lived, through Resaca, where the railroad ran. But now they were here, in the pocket—a cove near the pass in the mountains called Snake Creek Gap, where Fannie had her home.

Her first thought was to hide some valuables, but she dismissed it. The Yankees would find anything she tried to conceal. Walking to her gate, she watched Confederate troops rushing by. They told her Sherman's whole army was moving through the gap. The infantrymen hurried on, and the road was again deserted and quiet. But soon Fannie heard the rhythmic thumping of hoof beats as a distant rider approached. As he neared her yard, she perceived that he was a Yankee cavalryman.

The horseman galloped up to Fannie's gate, drew and cocked his pistol, and fired a barrage of questions at her. How long ago had she seen any Rebs? How large was the Confederate force? How far to Resaca? Where was her husband? Before he was through, a regiment of Yankee horsemen milled beyond the fence, many of them repeating the same questions to her. They threatened to take her mule, hitched to the fence, which set her three young children to crying. At length a kindly trooper stopped the interrogation, and suggested that Fannie remain indoors. He added that he would keep an eye on her mule. But soon the commanding officer ordered the mule to be confiscated. As the beast was led away, Fannie joined her children in tears.

That night, Union pickets camped near the house. They turned their horses out into the farm's fields to graze on the wheat, corn, rye, and oats. Darkness brought silence, but the Jacksons spent an anxious and sleepless night, expecting a battle to erupt at any moment. At sunrise shots were heard nearby. As the hours passed, the din of musketry swelled to fill Fannie's ears. Along the road in front of the Jackson home, Yankees double-quicked toward the uproar and ambulances clattered toward their gruesome work as officers shouted orders above the tumult. Fannie's children, pale with fright, screaming, crying, trembling, clutched desperately at her skirts. War had come in terrible earnest to Snake Creek Gap, and to Fannie Jackson.[1]

Fannie A. Oslin Jackson had spent all of her twenty-eight years in northern Georgia when the Yankees penetrated the pocket. She fondly remembered her childhood in the sparsely settled timbered hills of Cobb County. The Oslins ran a farm, a mill, a sawmill, a cotton gin, and a blacksmith shop. Fannie helped with housework, with spinning and weaving, with sowing corn and tending the garden. A tomboy, she played town ball, cat, and marbles, and beat all but one of the neighborhood boys in footraces. She regularly attended church and Sunday school and an annual Methodist camp meeting. She took lessons in a small one-room log cabin schoolhouse. At age thirteen she was sent to school for two years in the village of Atlanta, boarding with a relative.

At the Oslin home on Christmas Eve of 1850, Fannie married Zachariah N. Jackson. She was sixteen years old; Zack was nineteen. He was a childhood friend and neighbor, a schoolmate and church fellow. The couple lived with Zack's stepfather for two years before buying their own farm. Seven years later they sold it and bought another fifty miles north, in Gordon County. Along the way, they raised two boys and two girls. In 1863 their youngest child—a four-year-old named Joe Brown Jackson after Georgia's governor—died after a brief illness.

In the antebellum years, Fannie gave little thought to national affairs. She had her hands full tending to her home and family. As a native Georgian, she loved "the sunny vales of the South," in whose sacred soil her ancestors were buried. But she deplored secession when it came. And the root cause of the war, she felt, was slavery. "My early life was spent among slaves," she wrote in later years. "I loved my colored mama as my own, but from my earliest recollection, I felt as if slavery was wrong." Her grandparents owned many slaves. Her father owned eight slaves until a financial reverse forced him to sell all but two. Fannie loved to watch the blacks sing and dance during corn shucking bees. And yet she harbored a fear of them, dreading they would rise in insurrection and slaughter the whites. She seldom saw them abused and consequently felt she saw slavery "in its mildest form." Nevertheless, Fannie believed slavery "a dark spot on American civilization . . . so foul an evil." Etched in her memory was one horrific scene: the corpse of a slave, savagely whipped by his master and left in a field to die. "His back was a perfect jelly."

Fannie and Zack were strong Unionists, and many of their northern Georgia neighbors shared their sentiments. Fannie believed the area, if allowed the chance, would have voted against secession, but a convention of popularly elected delegates from throughout the state had voted Georgia out of the Union. By the time the Yankees came to Snake Creek Gap, Fannie knew of local Union men who had lived for months in mountain caves or burrows dug near their homes to escape conscription into the Confederate army. Sympathetic friends fed the fugitives. And there were so many Confederate deserters in the mountains that state troops had been ordered to hunt them out, without much success.

Zack Jackson was serving as a lieutenant in the Confederate army, but he was not a willing volunteer. Hearing widespread rumors of impending conscription, he had enlisted in a regiment of Georgia state troops for a year, thinking that after his tour of duty was completed he would be exempt from further service. Fannie had reluctantly acquiesced to his decision. A few months later, the Confederate Conscription Act of April 1862 forced Zack's regiment to serve a term of three years, unless the war ended sooner. It seemed that Zack would be absent from home for a long time—if indeed he was fortunate enough to return.

Fannie visited Zack several times at his regiment's encampments in Savannah, Charleston, and Chattanooga, and he got home occasionally on leave. He expressed to her his hatred of the rebellion and the Confederacy, and his devotion to the old flag. He vowed that if the army retreated past their home, he would desert and go north with her and the children. As the two parted after his last visit home, Zack told Fannie, "Trust in God. Do right and God will care for us as He has done in the past." Then Zack turned to go. Fannie recalled, "As he passed out of sight over the hills he waved a farewell; then tears gave me relief." [2]

Fannie managed to take care of the family in her husband's absence, but it was hard. When she was prostrated by illness, she rented the farm at Zack's urging and took the children to her parents' home in Cobb County. On her recovery she returned to Gordon County, but after consulting with Zack she sold the farm and bought another one ten miles away—the place at Snake Creek Gap. The great battle at Chickamauga had raged some twenty miles to the north in September 1863, just before she moved. "My friends thought it was madness for me to go nearer the contending armies," Fannie noted, but Zack told her he would rather have her within Union lines than in Confederate territory. Her father urged her to return to Cobb County, but she refused. "I will not go," she wrote, "but will stay at our home and take the fortunes or misfortunes of war that are in store for me."

"The house was small and much dilapidated" and the farm's fields were stony, Fannie wrote of her new home. She admired the wild, mountainous landscape surrounding the gap, but she longed for the improvements of civilization. And life in wartime north Georgia was harsh. Many of the men were away in the army. Slaveholders had fled south to protect their valuable human property. Left behind were women and children, living in increasing privation. Northern manufactured goods, on which Southerners had so long relied, had been cut off by the blockade of Confederate seaports by Union warships. Inflation soon put commonly purchased goods out of reach, and the home folk had to make do with what they could produce on their own. So, Fannie observed, "What women and children could not do had to be left undone."

Fannie spun and wove all the fabric for her family's clothing, a coarse flannel she called "Dixie silk." The lack of cards—wire brushes to comb cotton before spinning—complicated and lengthened the process. Barks, roots, leaves, berries, and rocks were used instead of manufactured dyes to color the homespun cloth. When the price of salt—a necessity to preserve meat—reached ninety dollars a barrel, she dug up the brine-saturated earth beneath the smokehouse, doused the soil with water in an ash hopper to rinse out the dirt, and boiled the resulting brine until the water evaporated and left dark but useable crystals. When the cost of leather soared, she tanned the hides of beeves she slaughtered. She made shoes by pairing cowhide soles with cloth uppers.

Spinning occupied nights; daytime was given to working the farm. Fannie successfully chopped wood, hoed with a team, and built fences, but she had trouble sowing grain and plowing. She protected herself from the sun with a Shaker bonnet she made of rushes from the swamps, trimmed with a strip of her grandmother's old dress. Her mule's frequent balkiness plagued her: it would not cross a mud puddle unless she led the way, and it seemed to do the opposite of what she wanted when plowing fields. "I presume I did not understand muleology," she wrote. Hard work and slim prospects were interrupted by bad luck.

One night, Fannie stood guard with an old gun to protect her only hog—for which she had paid sixty-nine dollars—from theft. After she slaughtered it the next day, the meat was pilfered. Confederate troops stationed nearby showed no compunctions about stealing from the home folk. Then the Yankees came, and she lost what little she had left.[3]

Five days after the Yankee penetration of the pocket, late in the evening of May 13, 1864, the chief quartermaster of the Union army's Twentieth Corps lay down for a much needed rest in his newly pitched tent near the yard of a little house. Lieutenant Colonel William G. Le Duc settled into his blankets but could not get to sleep. He was disturbed by a sound—he thought it might be the muffled cry of a baby. Unwrapping himself, he carefully picked his way around debris and along a broken-down garden fence to the house. Later that night, he described the place in a letter to his wife. "The house was a log cabin, weather boarded, a building with one room and with a window—that is a square hole in one end, with a shutter hung on hinges on the outside—no sash or frame for glazing." Peering through the opening, he saw the single bed and the entire floor covered with wounded or sick soldiers. Caring for them was a woman; she was preparing food or medicine by an open fire. There were three children in the house, but not a baby in sight.

Fannie Jackson noticed the colonel peeking through the window and asked if there was anything she could do for him. He inquired about the crying baby. There was no baby in the house, Fannie replied. The cry came again. "There," Le Duc said, "don't you hear it?" The children giggled. Fannie explained that the youngsters' pet lamb was hidden under a box in a shed. The colonel had mistaken its lonesome bleating for a baby's cry. The lamb was all the family had left, she told the officer. Sheep, cows, hogs, chickens, bacon, meal, garden crops—all had been swept away by the army. She maintained her composure as she told Le Duc of her losses, but "every tone of her voice was a tear."

Fannie explained how she had offered her home to a Union army surgeon as a hospital and volunteered to serve as a nurse. Le Duc, touched by her courage and compassion amid the wreckage of her home, had his orderly give some food and water to the lamb. Then he presented Fannie with two sacks of corn and some pork. As he left, she tearfully told him, "I am—very much obliged to you, sir." That night, the colonel's eyes misted as he described the scene to his wife. "If I don't write as well as usual," he commented, "it is because I do not see quite clearly."

The next morning Le Duc returned to the ramshackle house. "He expressed great sympathy for us in our situation," Fannie later wrote; "that he had been watching me take care of the sick and wounded at my house; that he had a wife and children at home and would surely feel sad indeed if he thought they were situated as we were." He brought medicine for Fannie's sick son, and gave the children a pile of newspapers and magazines. On May 15 he visited again and presented the family with more corn and pork, and some sugar, coffee, and hardtack. He asked Fannie what she planned to do when the army left. She told him she did not know.

On the morning of May 16, as he prepared to leave Snake Creek Gap, Le Duc provided Fannie with a letter of recommendation stating she had been "unwearied in her humane attentions to all the sick and maimed who have thronged her house," and requesting "all the kindness and attention that can be shown and should be shown to a polite and kind hearted lady whom with her three young children the misfortunes of war have rendered bitterly destitute." She received similar letters from a Union surgeon and a chaplain, who were likewise impressed with her faithful nursing of their wounded.

Fannie was deeply grateful. Her farm was in ruins and she was impoverished, but these letters offered her a chance to make a livelihood. Years later she wrote of Le Duc, "He had been so kind and sympathetic that we felt that we were parting from a dear friend, though he had been camped by us but a few days. I could only thank him and ask God to bless him for his kindness to us. I could not express my thanks as I would like. There are times when the heart is too full for expression—this was one."[4]

"For two weeks I ate and slept but little," Fannie recalled, "giving all my time and strength to alleviate some of the suffering with which I was surrounded." She bathed the men's wounds, changed their bandages, served them water, brushed swarms of flies away from their prostrate forms, brought them flowers, talked, read, and prayed with them. She also cared for refugees, women and children made homeless by the fighting. She ate barely "enough to feed a kitten," and catnapped on her pantry and kitchen floors. She scrubbed and washed the house in a futile effort to keep it clean, and she tried to ignore the terrible stench of fifty dead horses rotting nearby. The hospital spilled from her house into the smokehouse, a layer of men filling the suspended floor, another layer sheltered beneath. Then the hospital overlapped her yard, and tents full of sick and wounded stretched two hundred yards to her spring. All the while, the distant battle thundered.

Finally the fighting moved south, and the hospital at the Jackson home was disbanded. Two days after the last maimed soldier was removed from the cabin, Fannie and the children went down the valley and stayed with friends for two weeks. She returned to Snake Creek Gap once, to find that her corn crib, stables, and part of the house had vanished, chopped to flinders as fuel for soldiers' camp-fires. She spent one last terrifying night in her shattered home. The grounds were now a graveyard and she feared wolves would come down from the mountains to feast on the dead. All night long owls hooted and two dogs ran around the house in an endless circle, howling dolefully. "I never thought I was superstitious," Fannie later wrote, "but somehow I never think of that night without shuddering." Heartbroken by the desolation, she left her home, never to return.[5]

On the spring day when Fannie Jackson's nap was interrupted and her life turned topsy-turvy, a battle raged about ten miles to the north of her home, at Dug Gap on Rocky Face Ridge. As part of an assault by two Union brigades, the 154th New York charged up the mountain in the face of stinging gunfire and tumbling boulders loosened at the crest by its Confederate defenders. The day was warm, the slope was steep, the climb was slow. On reaching the protection of the palisades that gave the ridge its name, the panting soldiers halted to catch their breath. Then the regiment was ordered to fix bayonets and mount the summit. Through crevasses and over the immense rocks the men struggled, only to be cut down when they emerged on the mountaintop. The color sergeant planted the national flag on the crest and was instantly killed. Others fell in a scramble to rescue the color. It was finally secured, and the regiment fell back down the mountainside, carrying their wounded to safety, leaving their dead and some captured behind. One out of four men was a casualty—fifty-five of them in all—but Martin Bushnell survived the ordeal unharmed.

Dug Gap was Bushnell's first significant battle with the regiment. Illness had kept him away from the 154th when it fought at Chancellorsville and Gettysburg. Skirmishing in Tennessee the previous fall had given him but a slight taste of combat. Now, in the mountains and valleys of northern Georgia, he would experience battle after battle as Sherman's army drove toward Atlanta.

Martin was a long way from home, and a long time from returning.

In 1840, Chauncy Bushnell bought seventy-five acres of land on the present-day West Branch of the Bucktooth Run Road in Napoli. He and his wife, Emeline (Woodworth) Bushnell, had settled on the property several years earlier and carved a farm out of the wilderness. Following custom, they first built a log cabin, and after clearing fields, erecting fences, and making other improvements, they constructed a frame house for their growing family. Martin Dewight Bushnell was born to the couple on February 15, 1842, the third of an eventual five children. He spent his youth on the family farm, attended the local common school, and furthered his education at the nearby Randolph Academy. By 1862 he was back in his hometown, where he enlisted on August 15 at age twenty, to serve three years. Bidding his family farewell, he went off to the war.[6]

At Camp Brown on September 25, Martin was mustered in as a corporal of Company H of the 154th New York. The company descriptive book listed him as five feet, eleven inches tall, with a light complexion, blue eyes, and light brown hair. He was present during the regiment's early movements in Virginia until December 10, 1862, when he entered a hospital at Fairfax Court House, Virginia, stricken with bronchitis. Eleven days later he was admitted to the hospital at Fort Schuyler, in New York City's harbor. A long convalescence ensued. Martin was released in June 1863, and on July 1—the same day his regiment fought at Gettysburg—he addressed a letter to his parents from a distribution camp near Washington. "I could have got into the Invalid Corps had I thought [it] best," he wrote, "but I did not prefer belonging to a crippled brigade. Whenever I was examined by a surgeon, I was sound as a rock. I could not afford to do as I had seen some do, with crutches and 17 canes." Martin was determined to do his duty, not to evade it by faking a malady.[7]

After he rejoined the 154th New York, it was transferred to the west in September 1863. In October the regiment spearheaded the movement from Bridgeport, Alabama, to Lookout Valley, Tennessee, which opened the celebrated "Cracker Line" and relieved the besieged Union army in Chattanooga. During the march the regiment fought a skirmish at Wauhatchie, Tennessee, on October 28, and Martin faced fire for the first time. In a letter to a friend back home in Napoli, he proudly described how the 154th, "cheering and hurrahing eagerly," dashed across a field and up a steep, brushy hill and sent a regiment of rebels "to hunt their holes in the mountain."[8]

More triumphs followed. The regiment played a insignificant role in the great victory that routed the Confederates at Chattanooga in November, but Martin nevertheless bragged, "You of course know that we did a big thing, not only for ourselves, but [for] our country's glorious cause." Over the winter, he and his comrades basked in the recollection at their Lookout Valley camp, where snug huts and ample rations provided them with "high and aristocratic living." Martin assured his hometown friend, "We are very refined in style and manners, as it is of course necessary for soldiers to be." He added, "I hope that my brief description of our living will not make you envy me my comfort. I must say that I almost do yours teaching school. I am thinking that I shall be very rusty if I live to get home in regard to literary matters, but I guess I will know how to *shoulder arms* and *right-face*. Well all right, my duty is here and let it be performed here."[9]

As the 1864 spring campaign season approached, Martin's spirits remained high. He boasted that he was "as tough as a pickled owl" and as fat as a Dutch woman. "The weather is beautiful and everything [is] going well," he wrote in March. "The boys all appear happy and many enjoy life *tip-top*." At a review of their brigade, the men paraded jauntily to "sweet and lively national airs" played by a brass band. "We displayed *our best military skill*," Martin wrote, "which you know *must be great*." With cocky confidence, he awaited the coming ordeal.[10]

In April 1864, Martin was detailed to daily duty as a corporal of the 154th New York's color guard, a post of great honor and great danger. In coming battles, he would be the target of concentrated fire by the enemy as they sought to bring down the flags—those precious emblems were symbolic of the regiment's very essence. He would do all he could to safeguard the colors and prevent them from capture by the Confederates.

May brought Sherman's advance into Georgia. After the fight at Dug Gap, the regiment went on to battles at Resaca and New Hope Church, where the soldiers charged over pine-clad red clay hills scarred with log entrenchments. The month closed with a week of almost constant skirmishing. The 154th lost fifteen men in the various actions following Dug Gap, but Martin survived unhurt. On June 3 he summarized the recent fighting in a letter to his parents, and offered some reassurance.

> We are now experiencing what may very well be called real field service and I stand up [to it] very well. . . . We had a terrible rain yesterday. We were standing in line of battle, all the time saying with a grin, "Who would not be a soldier?" It is hard, but all live in hopes of better times. You will please be as little concerned about me as possible. I trust that all will be well with me, my fate be what it may. My chance and situation is no worse than thousands of others. I have always felt I should survive this war, the end of which cannot be very far distant.[11]

His chances would diminish, but Martin would indeed survive the war. A week and a half after he wrote his letter, two days of battle near Gilgal Church cost the 154th New York severely in casualties. On June 15 the regiment was deployed as skirmishers in front of its brigade, the men darting from tree to tree while exchanging fire with the entrenched enemy. When the Confederates retreated the 154th went after them exuberantly, following them impetuously to the rim of another line of breastworks, which brought them at last to a halt. More than a score of men fell in the charge. The regiment remained in an exposed position the next day, pinned down by Confederate musketry and taking more casualties. Martin again escaped harm.

Days later, his fighting ended. On June 24, 1864, the 154th New York passed a pleasantly warm day behind breastworks near Kolb's Farm, Georgia, with only the usual skirmishes interrupting the quiet. The Union line stretched along the edge of a woods. Across a large clearing, almost a mile away, the Confederates were similarly dug in at a forest's edge. That afternoon, at about 4 P.M., Martin Bushnell fell prey to fate.

He and a comrade were sitting behind the breastworks, idly watching a card game. Martin had his hands folded around his knees and his feet propped up on a rock or a log when a stray minié bullet zipped from the Confederate line and smashed into his right ankle, fracturing the bones into shards. An hour later, in the division field hospital behind the line of battle, Surgeon James Reiley of the 33rd New Jersey covered Martin's nose with a chloroform-soaked cloth. The young soldier's body went limp. Wielding a knife, Reiley made a continuous cut around Martin's leg about four inches above the shattered ankle, and scraped tissue away from the bones. The surgeon then grasped his saw and rasped through the bones. After tossing Martin's severed leg aside, Reiley sutured a long flap of flesh and skin from front to back over the stump.[12]

"Am suffering much from wound," Martin recorded in his diary the next day. Private Abner L. Perry of Company A, a fellow Napolian, brought his comrade a bed and pillow, and Martin began to rest more comfortably. "He is doing well," reported Private Emory Sweetland of Company B, a steward in the hospital, adding, "He was a first rate soldier." On June 26 Martin noted, "I am feeling better. The day passes with but little suffering."[13]

But on June 27 he wrote, "Today I have to endure more pain." That day the hospital came under enemy artillery fire. In a confused scramble, surgeons and attendants moved their patients about a mile to the rear. Martin was initially left behind. As shells exploded around him, he screamed for help. Some attendants returned and carried him away. They had no sooner done so when the tent that had sheltered him was ripped apart by a shell.

During the jostling, Martin's stump began bleeding profusely. Surgeons cut through his stitches to staunch the hemorrhage, and sewed the flap together again. Now they feared the flap would slough off. The case had taken a dangerous turn.

"My limb is sore and painful," Martin reported on June 28. At eleven o'clock that morning, he and other patients were loaded aboard ambulances. For five hours they lurched and swayed over roughly rutted roads before arriving at Big Shanty, site of the Army of the Cumberland's General Field Hospital.

"Good luck breaks upon me," Martin wrote the next day. "I find myself in the hands of a cousin, Dr. Milton Woodworth. I pass the day with some pain. It is very warm." On hearing some of the hospital attendants refer to the surgeon in charge of the hospital by name, Martin had wondered if the doctor might be a relative—Martin's mother was a Woodworth. The doctor was sent for, and he and Martin discovered they were first cousins. They had never met before.

On the last day of June Martin wrote, "Nothing new occurs. I am feeling about the same. Am receiving good care from the hands of a lady, Mrs. Jackson." [14]

Eight days earlier, on June 22, 1864, Fannie Jackson had resumed her career as a Union nurse when she joined the General Field Hospital of the Army of the Cumberland, then stationed near Resaca. After reading the recommendations of Colonel Le Duc and the other Union officers, and mulling the story of her straitened circumstances, Dr. Milton C. Woodworth had approved Fannie's application. He promised her a position as a nurse in his hospital and accreditation from the Western Sanitary Commission. The two hit it off during an interview over dinner. Woodworth judged Fannie as "a true honest intelligent lady." Fannie found the doctor to be "very jovial, affable, friendly, and kindly disposed." [15]

Within days after she commenced her duties, the hospital moved to Big Shanty and its headquarters were established in a large house. There, on June 29, Fannie was approached by Dr. Woodworth. He told her he had discovered a cousin of his among the wounded. Woodworth had never met the young man before—but, the doctor joked, "If he is kin to me, he obviously must be a good and clever fellow." Woodworth wanted Fannie to give special care to his cousin. Rather than be sent to the rear with the other wounded, this patient would stay in the hospital until he recovered enough to be sent home. Without good care, the doctor emphasized, he was sure to die.

Woodworth took Fannie to his office and introduced her to Martin Bushnell. "I was drawn to him at first sight," Fannie wrote. He was lying on a cot, wasted from loss of blood, and exhausted by the extreme heat. "He looked so pale and pitiful," she thought. "His large, broad forehead and classic brow showed an intellect of high order. His face showed signs of great suffering, while his clear blue eyes expressed a spirit of resignation. I felt drawn to him at once and had pity and sympathy for his sufferings."

Woodworth told Martin that Mrs. Jackson was to be a mother and sister to him.

"His classic face, resigned submissive look, and helpless condition made me feel I had a patient who would be patient and a pleasure to take care of," Fannie noted. Martin was moved into a room adjoining hers, and his care at her hands began. "He was weak, the heat was oppressive, and I had to be with him all the time," she wrote. At Martin's bedside, Fannie came to admire her patient even more.

"A more noble, patriotic, unselfish soldier I never met," she declared. "I watched over him by day and night during the long hot days of July and August, and never [heard him utter] a complaint. His life was suspended as by a thread during those weeks of weariness and pain. . . . The long days watching with such a patient sufferer endeared him, and he became to us as a brother." To help Martin tolerate the heat, she replaced his woolen uniform with a silken paisley robe. During her first days of nursing him, Fannie described her routine:

> He is good-natured and it is a pleasure to care for him. I sit beside him at night and fan him till he goes to sleep. He is very nervous and the nights are very warm. I fan and bathe his hands, arms, and neck with cold water; talk, sing, and read to him; and keep his mind entertained and make him as comfortable as possible.[16]

Fannie and Martin traced their summer together in their diaries. Early in July the hospital moved south by rail to Marietta, where it was set up next to the tracks in a grove, with a commodious house as headquarters. Fannie and Martin were assigned a room, but he spent the first night in a tent in one of the wards — his first separation from his nurse. She hurried to him early the next morning. "When I went in he looked at me sadly with big tears in his eyes and said, 'Are you going to leave me in this ward?' I told him that I had now come for him. His countenance changed in a moment and his tears were dried, and with a smile on his face he was moved into our room." That day Martin wrote, "I am enduring considerable pain." Fannie noted, "When I examined his stump, green flies had gotten to it and the larvae would soon have hatched."[17]

The only time Martin complained, Fannie noted, was when she was away. Soon after arriving in Marietta, she spent a couple of days on a visit to her father, who was living nearby. "I lie in my room all alone a greater part of the time and am lonesome and uneasy," Martin noted in his diary during her absence. When Fannie returned, she worried about her patient's condition:

> Martin complained of being very lonely while I was away. His symptoms are of the most alarming kind. He has spells of perspiring so freely that it exhausts him very much, and he is so restless. I sit and fan him till he is asleep or under the influence of morphine, which is given him every night. When he is well under its influence, I steal away as quietly as possible but am near, and if anything is wanted I can attend to him.[18]

Martin seemed to improve a bit over the next several days. "I am on the gain a little," he noted on July 14. "Have steady but not very severe pain." Three days later, a Sunday, he was carried to the porch to hear the hospital's chaplain preach. On the afternoon of July 23 he was lugged aboard a railroad car; the hospital was moving again. But the train sat motionless overnight and did not pull away until the following morning, when it swayed south to Vining's Station. There the hospital's tent city was set up in another grove alongside the railroad, and headquarters were established in a plantation house just vacated by General Sherman. Once again, Martin and Fannie were assigned a room. "I feel very well until near night, when I endure much pain," he wrote. "He is feeling pretty well," she wrote, "but the flaps have sloughed off his stump and its looks as if the foot had been chopped off, though it is beginning to heal some." She added an ominous note: "Fears are entertained that the stump will never be healthy." Gangrene had infected the wound.[19]

An additional cot was set up in their room for the mother of a wounded officer, who had come from Ohio to care for her son. The hospital chaplain often joined the trio for evening prayer meetings. Long lines of ambulances arrived from the front, where Sherman's men were battling for Atlanta. As new patients filled the hospital, trains loaded with convalescents steamed for the rear. A garden between the house and the main hospital grounds was converted into a cemetery. Soldiers' corpses, wrapped in blankets with their names and regiments written on scraps of paper pinned to their chests, were brought on bloodstained stretchers and laid in rows awaiting burial. Black swarms of buzzing flies crawled over the inert forms. Every day, Fannie walked each row, and read each name. One night, as the booming of a thunderstorm mingled with the distant thudding of artillery, she was overcome by emotion and broke down, weeping bitterly.[20]

By August Martin was feeling better and he began writing letters to family and friends. He sat in a chair for the first time on August 2; on August 10 he stood for the first time and hobbled around the room, clutching Fannie's shoulder for support. "He is lively and eats heartily," she noted. "He tells me to 'heft' his grub and bring in all I can carry." As her patient improved, she got to know him better. "He is intelligent, of an amiable disposition, and an entertaining talker. He is really much company for me and a real comfort. I knew but little of his temperament and disposition till lately. He had suffered so much he was not himself."[21]

In mid-August Fannie paid another visit to her father, and Martin once again lamented, "I live alone." Soon after her return, their room took in another lodger—Dr. Woodworth's wife, Jennie, who impressed Fannie as "a plain, sensible woman and a devoted wife." Fannie noted, however, that the doctor did not spend much time with his spouse. "He seems to be taking to his 'tea' a little too much," she wrote disapprovingly. Dr. Woodworth had a taste for liquor. The hospital stores provided him with an unlimited supply and there were plenty of drinking companions.

Fannie's opinion of the surgeon was changing. "Dr. Woodworth was a good surgeon and of more than ordinary ability," she later wrote; "he was a profound thinker and had good common sense; he was very jolly and witty." But sometimes she found his joking to be tiresome, especially his jibes at the black hospital helpers, and she was annoyed when he had fun at her expense. He was fond of introducing her to strangers as "Mrs. Jackson, our matron from the Rebel army," or, "Mrs. Jackson, one of the Southern animals we are domesticating," or, "Mrs. Jackson of the Southern Conthieveracy." To Fannie, such silliness was inappropriate when they were surrounded by constant sorrow.[22]

Martin continued to recuperate. "Very warm today. I walk about 10 rods from the house for the first time going out," he wrote on August 24. "Martin walked to his dinner today," Fannie recorded. "I held him to keep him from falling. It is almost like a child learning to walk, only he is more careful. As he is so much better now, I have much time to do work in the wards." In the next few days, Martin continued to take occasional short walks using crutches.[23]

Returning to the hospital on September 4 after a short visit to Resaca, Fannie was greeted by Jennie Woodworth and Martin with important news: "Atlanta has fallen." Sherman's army had entered the city two days before. On September 6, the hospital was ordered to move into Atlanta. The latest crowd of sick and wounded were sent by rail to the rear, the hospital tents were struck, baggage was packed in boxes, and everything was loaded aboard boxcars for the eleven-mile trip to the city. Martin and Fannie made the journey on September 8 and were assigned quarters in a small brick house in the center of the new hospital grounds.

As Martin continued to convalesce, he made his first excursions outside the General Field Hospital. On September 11 he visited friends at the hospital of his Second Division, and three days later an ambulance from the 154th New York arrived to take him for a visit to his regiment. About a week later he welcomed a reciprocal visit from a comrade of Company H, Corporal Edmund J. Finley, who had been wounded in the nose at Dug Gap. "Martin is still with us and can walk pretty well with his crutches," Fannie wrote during this time, "though I still dress and care for his wound."[24]

While Martin improved in body and spirit, Fannie became increasingly despondent and anxious, tormented with suspense about the fate of her husband in the long, bloody campaign just ended. Her tension was broken by a sudden surprise. After supper on September 24, Jennie Woodworth asked Fannie to accompany her to the hospital office. The two were talking when a clerk came to the door and announced, "Mrs. Jackson, Zack is at the barracks." Zack Jackson was held there as a prisoner of war, but through the efforts of Dr. Woodworth, Colonel Le Duc, and others, he was released to Woodworth's custody.

Dr. Woodworth and Zack arrived at the hospital the next evening. "Mrs. Woodworth, Martin, and all the officers of our mess were assembled in my room awaiting their arrival," Fannie wrote. "A more lively, jovial crowd had never been seen in the hospital. I really think that they enjoyed my husband's return about as much as I did myself." A lavish supper was served in the gaily decorated kitchen tent, after which Dr. Woodworth presided over a mock wedding of the reunited couple. For Martin, the joyous occasion was not without some pain. "In the confusion and excitement of the hour," Fannie wrote, "Martin got up and, forgetting his limb was gone, started to walk and fell to the floor." Martin had previously complained of the phantom limb phenomenon—he sometimes felt that his lost foot was still attached and in great pain. A spiritualist member of the hospital staff had explained that he was feeling his "spiritual foot." After falling at the party, good natured Martin joked that he had tried his spiritual foot, "but it would not go." [25]

A week later, the close-knit Bushnell-Jackson-Woodworth family was broken up. On the morning of October 1, 1864, Martin boarded a northbound train to return home on a furlough. Fannie bid her young friend a tender farewell, and picked up a pen to record her thoughts.

> Martin started for home today. I felt very sad at parting with him. I had cared for him so long that he seemed a part of the family. When he bade me good-bye, he said that the days I had cared for him and the sleepless nights I had spent beside his cot had created in him a brotherly feeling toward me that would last as long as his life.
>
> I have sad fears of his stump ever being healthy, but it improves slowly and he walks well on his crutches. He is a noble young man and a patriotic soldier. When one has taken care of a person for four months as I have of him, one learns much of that person's general character, and a real attachment is formed.[26]

Martin made his way home by railroad and steamboat, arriving in Napoli on October 11. He spent most of the next month on the Bushnell farm, generally feeling well and enjoying quiet times that bordered on dullness, breaking the routine with occasional visits to relatives. To while away the time he entertained visitors, read, and wrote to Fannie Jackson and Dr. Woodworth. "We received letters from Martin Bushnell regularly," Fannie noted. "They were compositions of the highest order, lively and vivacious, showing a well-balanced mind. He said that his stump called for me every day to come and dress it." She of course sent loving replies to her "Dear Brother Martin." Martin also wrote to regimental comrades. In response to one such letter, First Lieutenant George C. "Guy" Waterman, a fellow Napolian, offered some cryptic advice: "You must take care of yourself and not get *'Shot'* (in the neck I mean) and keep that 'stump' away from the girls and look out for Martin D. Bushnell and you are all right."[27]

Having yet to be discharged, Martin was still under the control of the military. At the expiration of his furlough, on November 14, 1864, he was admitted to Sisters of Charity General Hospital in Buffalo. For the next seven months he languished in the hospital, fighting boredom as best he could. His wound appeared to be better, and he was fitted for an artificial leg. In the spring of 1865, a string of unforgettable events interrupted the tedium. The joy engendered by Richmond's fall and Lee's surrender was soon dampened by horror at the death of Abraham Lincoln. "Yes, the assassination of our beloved President was a most atrocious deed," Martin wrote to his parents. "It was a great shock and loss to our nation, yet I think it will prove a more severe blow to the rebellion . . . as our people are more than ever indignant and traitors have not merciful 'Father Abraham' to deal with now."

On April 27, the train carrying the remains of President Lincoln stopped in Buffalo on its way from Washington to Illinois. Martin took part in a funeral procession that wound through city streets packed with people, below buildings draped in black crepe and half-staff flags hung in black streamers, to St. James Hall, where the casket was displayed for a public viewing. He described the scene in a letter to his family.

> There was a large and magnificent hearse constructed for the occasion which was drawn by six white horses shrouded with crepe. There was a procession more than two miles long composed of soldiers, citizens, and all kinds of societies and orders too numerous to mention. . . . Invalid soldiers like myself had the honor of riding in carriages a little ways behind the hearse. There was a continual tolling of bells kept up and at regular intervals the firing of cannon. As we halted, a prayer and speech was made. The whole scene was marked with solemnity and the day one long to be remembered by me and all who love the name and memory of Abraham Lincoln.[28]

On June 29, 1865, Martin was transferred from Buffalo to Central Park Hospital in New York City. This facility, formerly a Roman Catholic convent school, specialized in prosthetics and was popularly known as "Stump Hospital." There, on August 12, Martin was finally discharged from the service on account of total disability. He also received a brevet promotion to first lieutenant, New York State Volunteers, for gallant and meritorious service. Twelve days later he was back in Buffalo, where he applied for a pension. Guy Waterman supplied an affidavit in support of Martin's case, stating he was with Bushnell at Kolb's Farm and witnessed his wounding. In January 1866, Martin was granted a pension of eight dollars per month, retroactive to the date of his application.

He returned to the Bushnell farm in Napoli and settled back as best he could into the routine. But as Fannie Jackson had feared, his stump never healed properly. In May of 1866 Martin traveled from Napoli to seek treatment from his cousin, Dr. Woodworth, in Warren, Ohio. It was a fatal mistake.

Milton Woodworth was trapped in a downward spiral of alcoholism. As Fannie later noted, "The little cloud of drunkenness, at first not larger than a man's hand, grew to be a dark pall, overshadowing [his] whole life." Dr. Woodworth was headed for a divorce from his loving wife, Jennie, on the grounds of drunkenness, and commitment in an asylum for inebriates. Martin was apparently unaware of the seriousness of his cousin's condition. He placed himself willingly in the surgeon's hands.

On June 5, 1866, Woodworth amputated the stump. A few hours after he put down his scalpels and saw and sutures, Martin Bushnell died. He was one of the many uncounted casualties of the war—one of an untold number who died from the effects of service-related wounds or illnesses days, weeks, months, or years after they were discharged. His remains were returned home to be laid to rest.[29]

Fannie Jackson continued her hospital work after Martin's departure. Before Sherman abandoned Atlanta for his March to the Sea, the Army of the Cumberland's General Field Hospital was moved to Chattanooga, where Fannie was reassigned to Hospital Number 3. Zack Jackson, who had taken the oath of allegiance and entered government employ, joined the U.S. Military Construction Corps. "It seems so quiet now," Fannie wrote in Chattanooga, "after the stirring events of the summer." In February 1865, while she was at dinner, her tent caught fire and she lost bedding, some clothing, and "some poems that Martin Bushnell had composed while I was nursing him."[30]

Fannie was relieved of duty on September 6, 1865, and accepted a commendation for faithful service. Before the Jacksons left Chattanooga, Fannie wrote, "Each one of us received some substantial token of Martin Bushnell's remembrance and friendship for us; not one was left out." The family moved to Iowa for three years; while there, Fannie got news of Martin's death. The Jacksons then relocated to Kansas. In 1874 Fannie applied for a Federal pension, which was denied. But she obtained William Le Duc's address from his brother, a member of the Kansas state legislature, and wrote to her old friend for help. Le Duc added his testimony to a sheaf of affidavits from former army surgeons, and her 1892 application for a nurse's pension was approved. Fannie was receiving a pension of thirty dollars per month when she died at Olathe, Kansas, on February 19, 1925.[31]

Fannie never forgot her wartime encounter with Martin. As the years passed, she retained vivid and sentimental memories of several of her former patients. But none of them reached the cherished place she reserved in her heart for Martin Bushnell. Remembering him a half-century after they parted, she wrote, "Martin was an intensely patriotic, kindhearted gentleman, a devoted Christian, and a kind friend. I am sure that I was made better by nursing him so long; he was so patient and kind."

In 1867 she gave birth to a son she named Oslin Martin Jackson in Bushnell's honor. For more than fifty years she kept up a correspondence with the Bushnell family—with Martin's parents, Chauncy and Emeline, until they died in the 1880s; then with Martin's younger brother Frank until his death in 1909; and finally with Martin's niece, Myrtle Bushnell Waite. Chauncy and Emeline died without ever learning the details of their son's wounding, Fannie revealed. "Whenever he began to talk about it, his mother would cry so bitterly that he would not tell her all."

Beginning in 1894, Fannie made three visits to Martin's family in Napoli. "At no place did I receive a heartier welcome," she wrote, "than at the Bushnell home." Before Emeline Bushnell died, she asked Fannie to suggest an epitaph for Martin's headstone. Fannie, touched by the honor, responded with the verse that was carved in the stone.

Around 1910 Fannie made her last visit to Napoli. From the Bushnell home she went to South Napoli Cemetery and placed a wreath of wax flowers on Martin's grave. Her memento remained there for years, a symbol of the deep bond of affection linking a Southern nurse and her Northern patient.[32]

CHAPTER FOUR

Private William F. Chittenden

Company D

Lot 80, Section F, of Mount Hope Cemetery, in Lansing, Michigan, is a large, grassy, open spot, ringed by tall trees. The grave of William and Mary Chittenden is marked by an upright granite marker, rough-hewn but for a smoothed rectangle incised with their surname. Their given names and dates are absent. No individual stones mark their graves, and it does not appear that such stones have been covered by the sod in this well-kept cemetery. Nor is there a marker or flag to distinguish William as a Civil War veteran. In virtual anonymity, identified only by their last name, the couple are buried together.

Six decades before they were laid to rest in Mount Hope, during the Civil War, death had reached to embrace the Chittenden family. Mortality hovered over all Civil War soldiers and their families, of course. Many acknowledged that they could be taken at any time. But for most, the thought was fleeting—a quick icy brush across their consciousness, a shuddering sense of their own demise. During the war, frequently and intensely, the Chittenden family felt the cold touch. William and Mary alternately feared and invited death's grasp, prayed to keep it away and prayed to have it arrive, sought it and spurned it. Time and again, they felt it wrap around them or their children, constrict and tighten, and then loosen and let go.

On the morning of Sunday, August 31, 1862, at Camp James M. Brown in Jamestown, New York, William Chittenden opened his pocket testament and read the last two chapters of the Revelation of St. John the Divine. He was struck by the beauty of the description of the new Jerusalem, the holy city lit by God's glory, with its walls of gold and gates of pearls and foundations of jewels, a place where there would be no more tears, nor sorrow, nor pain, nor death. There was the home wherein he would reunite with his beloved Mary and little Hiram and Clyde, were they not to meet again on earth. To William, the prospect seemed all too possible.

He put aside his Bible, took a pencil and paper, and began to write his first letter home. "My eyes are wet with tears," he informed Mary, as he contemplated "that lovely and familiar home picture which I may never behold face to face again on earth." He was weary of life's pilgrimage, he declared; his desire was strengthened to meet her in that spangled heaven, where the wicked ceased from troubling and the weary were at rest. But he owed her an apology for "some trifles" that occurred between them when he left home. "I said trifles," he wrote, "but if you could look into my heart this morning you would see the mistake"—the misunderstanding had not been a mere trifle. He knew her heart was deeply wounded. He pleaded with her not to think him selfish, to forgive him for wronging her so deeply. He was penitent; it was his sincere desire to become a better man. He appreciated her kindness. He knew her motives were prompted by pure love for him.

Putting his letter aside to attend a religious service, William listened as a preacher warned against the vices of camp life—profane language in particular—and urged his listeners to seek the blood that cleansed away sin; for of all men, soldiers were most liable to be immediately called by God. After the sermon, William resumed writing. He foresaw a somber future, darkened by his wicked heart and inconsistent life, and the unpleasant circumstances of his leaving home.

He explained to Mary his motivation to serve, his willingness to face death. "I did not expect a life of pleasure in the army, but I feel more than ever that it is my duty to serve my country with my life if necessary." Was liberty worth bleeding and dying for in 1776? he asked rhetorically. Did not the present generation have a duty to transmit unimpaired to their descendants the priceless heritage they had inherited from their fathers? So he would serve, no matter where. Rumors in camp speculated about the newly organized regiment's destination. "It matters little to me where we are sent if it is where we are most needed," he wrote. "What I can do I feel willing and anxious to do, and the quicker the better."

After pausing for a prayer meeting and supper, William finished his letter as darkness fell. Gazing at a photograph of his wife and sons, he wrote, "I have just taken a look at the ones I love best on earth, and what feelings do you think are swelling the bosom of a companion and father?" He wished he could embrace them all. He asked Mary to kiss Hiram and Clyde for him, to keep up good courage and hope for the best.[1]

Only the basic facts survive regarding the prewar lives of William Fletcher Chittenden and Mary Jane Wheeler. Both were natives of the Cattaraugus County town of Yorkshire. William, born on September 5, 1835, the first of seven children of Hiram and Emaline (Payne) Chittenden, grew up on the family farm and planned a life in agriculture. Mary Jane, the second of nine children of Martin W. and Sarah N. (Hamilton) Wheeler, was born on January 16, 1836. She and William were wed on November 18, 1857, by the Reverend Thurston T. Horton of Yorkshire's First Baptist Church. Their son Hiram Martin Chittenden was born on October 25, 1858; Clyde C. Chittenden arrived on August 19, 1860. William owned a modest farm on present-day County Highway 55 in Yorkshire, between the Pleasant Valley and Keller Road intersections. According to the 1860 U.S. census enumerator, his real estate was valued at one thousand dollars and his personal property at two hundred dollars.[2]

When the war came, Harrison Cheney, a school teacher and farmer from the neighboring town of Freedom, made a yeoman's response to President Lincoln's call in July 1862 for three hundred thousand three year volunteers. Cheney recruited all ninety-four men of Company D of the 154th New York from six townships in the northeastern corner of Cattaraugus County. William Chittenden was one of eight men Cheney signed up in Yorkshire on August 5, 1862. Among the others was William's brother-in-law, Nathaniel S. Brown, who was married to Mary Jane's younger sister Nancy.[3]

Separated by the service, William and Mary commenced a correspondence of extraordinary frankness, intimacy, and—ultimately—desperation.

After apologizing to Mary for his unpleasant leave-taking, William was heartened a week later to receive a letter from her "full of tender affection." Whatever had marred their parting was now forgotten. He immediately responded, using stationery illustrated with a woman's portrait and a verse from the popular song "The Girl I Left Behind Me." The food at Camp Brown was almost intolerable, he reported; he had felt quite sick in recent days. And the men were struggling to adjust to military discipline. The previous evening, Captain Cheney had marched the company in a body to obtain drinking water. "To be deprived of that which flows so freely for all of God's creatures," William observed, "is something we are unused to."

Much of his letter concerned matters at home. He advised Mary on the disposition of their sow and pigs, but told her that in regard to other concerns she should rely on her own judgment and the advice of family (referred to colloquially as "friends"). He hoped that she could make things as easy as possible for herself. "My heart aches when I think of the hardships you will be subject to," he declared, "and at times I think I have wandered from the path of duty by leaving my family to serve my country. . . . Do not let your pathway be darkened by anticipating coming trouble," he urged her. "Dark and stormy hours may be ahead of us, and it will be wisdom in us to be prepared for the worst by putting our trust in an arm stronger than that of flesh."[4]

When he wrote again three days later, he was feeling better and had stood a tour of guard duty. Crowds of citizens, he informed Mary, were daily visiting camp to take leave of their loved ones. He was touched by their partings:

> I wish you could be here and see them. Here is a young soldier with his sweetheart, perhaps the one chosen to share life's joys and sorrows. Here another with his young wife by his side, and in his arms he carries a little one. Another picture shows a family group, the father and mother leading the little ones entrusted to their care and brothers and sisters and in fact all with some present for the loved ones shortly to leave them perhaps forever.[5]

From their surviving letters, it is unclear whether Mary and the children visited Camp Brown, or if William returned home on furlough for their final parting. But a flurry of activity soon separated the family by hundreds of miles.

William stood in the ranks as a private when Company D was mustered into the U.S. service on September 24, 1862. In the next week the regiment made the long railroad journey from Jamestown to the nation's capital. After a comfortable trip to Elmira in well-appointed passenger cars, the men experienced "hard riding" in rough boxcars from Elmira to Baltimore, and an even worse passage from Baltimore to Washington in "the poorest class [of] old cattle and hog cars." William noted that "one of the two assigned to Co. D was so old and rotten as to be unsafe." He thought he had stood up to the ordeal as well as any of his comrades, but he admitted he might be the first "to fall out by the way." His health was precarious; it would be a constant concern. He was getting over a cold but was bothered by a lingering cough.

From Washington the regiment crossed the Potomac River on the Long Bridge to Camp Seward on Arlington Heights, Virginia. From the hilltop, William had a splendid view of sailboats and steamships plying the river. Along the shoreline, as far as the eye could see, camps full of soldiers crowned every hill. He reported scanty rations, and water poorer than a Cattaraugus County mud puddle. Although "very tired and worn out" from his first march, he was feeling better.[6]

In the following days he visited one of the strong forts that guarded the heights, took part in his first drill and review, and had his photograph taken to send home. He wrote to Mary every day or two, filling up sheets of paper before sending them off. He philosophized about the war, describing it as "an expensive and destructive business" that would make thousands of well-to-do citizens penniless and ruin the morals of many promising young men, "for it is a school where vicious seeds are sown with a lavish hand." If he should never return home, and she should be spared to see Hiram and Clyde grow to manhood, he wanted Mary to warn them of war's evils.

He ached with longing for his family. "If a man has a comfortable home with loved and tender ones by his side, he little knows how great a sacrifice he is making by leaving them for a soldier's life," he declared. "Nor are the hardships and dangers to which he is exposed the greatest sacrifice he has to make. All this I could endure for my country without much complaint, but the greatest trial is to be deprived of your society and the children's." He was never meant to be a wanderer, he admitted, and the farther he went from home the more he treasured the kindnesses Mary had showed him. He asked her forgiveness for past unkind words and acts, and promised better behavior if he ever came home. Every time he lay down to sleep he thought of lying by her side; he often thought such togetherness would never happen again. "But I will go no farther and confess I have been looking too much on the dark side of the future, which is my way when discouraged or unwell," he wrote. He feared the change in climate and diet would debilitate him—"But hope for the best and be prepared for the worst should be our motto."[7]

By candlelight on the night of October 10, William described feeling "quite used up" after a day of drilling and attending to a sick comrade who had enlisted with him at Yorkshire. "I have been troubled with the dysentery and it makes me feel quite weak," he reported, "but [I] do not apprehend much trouble." As he wrote, news arrived that had the men shouting with excitement. The regiment was ordered to Fairfax Court House, to join the corps of Major General Franz Sigel. William approved. "I think push along [and] keep moving would be a good motto," he wrote. "It would be better to wear out [on campaign] than die in camp from inaction."

He wrote the next day lying on the damp ground in his tent, cold and shivering under his blanket after cooking breakfast and washing dishes for his mess in the rain. Troops were passing the regiment's camp, and preparations for their own march were under way. There were a good many who would not be able to carry their knapsacks, William observed, and some who would not be able to march at all. He vowed, "I shall not give up until obliged to."

Orders to move out came at breakfast on October 12, and the men bustled to strike their tents and pack their knapsacks. After a ten-mile tramp under his heavy load, William pitched his tent in the rain and wrote a few lines to Mary, reporting that he was tired but stood the ordeal better than he expected. The regiment reached Fairfax the following day. William found the village to be of "little importance" and "small pretensions." He described the region between Arlington and Fairfax as "the most desolate country I ever saw," with old, ruined buildings and few inhabitants.[8]

On October 20, William addressed a letter to Mary under "painful circumstances"—the first death in camp had taken a member of Company D. In great detail, William described how the ailing Private John L. Myers spent his last days, how his brother and tent mate Edmond Myers awoke the previous night to find John in a fit, and how the surgeons had been helpless to prevent his death, attributed to congestion of the brain. Myers's death, William wrote, "shows most conclusively that whether in camp or [on] the battlefield, death is the most certain and yet the most uncertain of events. That it will come none can question; but when, none can determine." Myers left a wife and small children, William informed Mary—"which will enable you to know how to sympathize with the mourners."[9]

At home in Yorkshire, Mary Jane Chittenden struggled to adjust to her husband's absence. Writing a hasty letter, distracted by the noisy teasing of little Hiram and Clyde, she confessed uncertainty about her ability to manage the farm. "Oh, William, this is business which I do not like," she lamented. "I never was cut out for a man or to do a man's business and I do not know how to get along with it." She begged him, "Write freely about your business and tell me how you want things done. You do not know how it cheers me to have your advice about the farm work." She wished she could get a letter from him every day. And she worried about him. "I want you to let me know if there is any prospect of your fighting soon," she wrote, "and if you have to march or prepare for battle at any time, write—if not but a few words—and let me know. Oh, how I hope and pray that this rebellion will soon end and our loved ones will come to our arms again."

Mary also struggled with a crisis of faith. "Oh, how I wish I could say that I was a child of God," she wrote. Her heart was evil, she confessed; she feared she could never be a true Christian. "Oh, my loved one, pray for me, that I may be one of those who shall have a home in glory," she begged. Only then could she and William be promised togetherness for eternity—"that if we meet no more below, we may be [a] family unbroken in the kingdom of God."[10]

On the evening of October 6, weary after a day of digging carrots and potatoes, picking corn and beans, and building a fence, Mary wrote to William until sleep overcame her. Three days later, she continued her letter with some bad news: the children were sick. "I am afraid the whooping cough is going to use them rather hard," she wrote. "Oh, William, how I wish you were at home," she added. "The future looks dark to me. The war will continue until all our friends are killed I fear. . . . Oh, William, be careful for my sake. Be careful of your health and life lest your Mary lays low with a broken heart. May God speed the happy day when you with others shall return to the arms of the loved ones left behind."[11]

In her next letter Mary reported, "I think the children may be a trifle better," but she admitted that their improvement was barely perceptible. "I can tell you it is a task to take care of them," she wrote, "and I think I shall be very thankful when they get over the whooping cough." Her longing for her husband had intensified. "Oh," she exclaimed, "how much I think of you of late." Instead of becoming more reconciled to his absence, it seemed progressively harder for her to bear. Every night thoughts of him kept her from sleeping. Sad scenes of her past unkindness to him filled her soul with bitter grief. Emotions overwhelmed and upset her when a hired crew of men came to thresh the farm's grain. As she served them dinner, she could hardly control her feelings because her William was absent from the table.

Fearing the worst, she imagined herself joining William in death: "Oh, if war's relentless hand should make you its victim and you should return no more to your little ones and Mary, she would not be long behind. She would soon lie low, and the loved ones separated here below would (if prepared) clap glad hands 'on the other side of Jordan.'"

Then she put the somber thought aside. Keep up good courage, she urged, do not worry about matters at home (for it would do no good), and be careful of your health and life. "Rush into no danger that can be avoided," she admonished. "Think of Mary and how she would stand even between you and the deathly missiles if possible, and be careful, *oh so careful*."[12]

Writing one night after completing her evening chores, bothered by a severe headache, Mary complained about an unspecified slight she had received during a trip to the village of Yorkshire Center. "I had my feelings hurt very much this morning," she reported, "and oh, William, how my heart went forth to the absent one. It seemed as though my heart would burst with grief." She had made up her mind to ignore her neighbors as much as she could, "and live by myself till William comes home." Her hurt feelings had caused her headache, she thought—"and I have no William here to lighten my cares or soothe my aching brow and *heart*."

Mary felt better two days later, when she wrote at intervals while preparing breakfast. It was barely daylight, but the boys—who had recovered from the whooping cough—were up and singing, "as happy as birds." "I am singing to Pa," said Clyde; Hiram wished his father would come home for a hug and kiss. But the boys' happy chatter did not entirely brighten her mood. "I do not think there is 10 minutes at a time when I am awake that you are not present in my thoughts," Mary wrote. "Oh, how I wish you were here to eat with us. It seems so lonesome at the table without you." [13]

As October closed, Mary spent an evening writing of her longing for William.

Oh my dear, could I but fly, think you I would sit here and converse with you in this way? No, I would soar swiftly away till I found the cherished friend, and with my head resting on his bosom pour forth all my joys and sorrows in his ear who has so often listened and seemed so ready to share all my troubles. But this cannot be. We are far apart now and know not how long we shall be thus severed, "perhaps forever." But oh! let us pray [to] "Our Father" that he lay not his chastening rod too heavily upon us. [14]

But even as Mary wrote, the rod was descending on the Chittendens.

November brought the 154th New York's march to Thoroughfare Gap in the Bull Run Mountains. For more than a week before the move, William's health troubled him. He was excused from duty and spent three days confined to his tent. On the eve of the march, Captain Cheney asked him if he would be able to keep up. "I told him I should try it," William wrote, "and go as far as I could."

On the morning of November 2, the regiment waited while an endless stream of troops and wagons flowed down the road. William took advantage of the delay to respond to a letter from Mary. He was thankful to hear that the children were better; he wished that he could clasp them both to his heart. "This may be a pleasure not in store for me," he wrote, "but [I] will hope for the best and try to be prepared for what awaits me." He assured Mary that his breast swelled with emotions of love and tenderness for her. He voiced regret at the hard work she had to do, and offered thanks and approval for the way she was managing the farm. Then he quit writing as the march began.

One day the soldiers suffered from the heat ("I never sweat more in my life," William wrote); the next day they donned their overcoats to keep warm. That night they did not pitch their tents, and they awoke in a rainstorm. They passed through the decrepit village of Centerville and over the battlefield of Bull Run, where there were "abundant signs of the fight": cannonballs and shells strewn in every direction, tree limbs cut down by the firing, and numerous graves of those "who fell in the fray, never to behold their homes again." Unlike many of his comrades, William spared Mary a detailed description of the battleground's most gruesome sights.

After marching for three days, William reported he felt somewhat better, but was "far from being well." He was determined to "keep up with the company as long as I can and share the dangers with the rest of the boys." He promised Mary he would "take as good care of my health as possible and keep all I can from harm's way." [15]

The march continued in biting cold and swirling snow. William was warmed by tea and a pair of mittens provided by Mary. Passing through a rich and hitherto unravished countryside, he was disgusted to observe "the reckless disposition for plunder showed forth by our officers and men" as they foraged for turkeys, hens, sheep, pigs, and apples. He was particularly appalled by a member of the regiment who robbed a young lady of her jewelry and offered her father fifty cents "for liberties with her person." To William, this miscreant was "as deserving as death as the meanest rebel." [16]

By the time the regiment reached Thoroughfare Gap, William was bothered by chronic coughing. He hoped to soothe it with licorice or horehound candy, but none was available. Molasses, he found to his displeasure, had an emetic effect. He again assured Mary that he would do all he could to preserve his health. "I desire as much as any one can to return to my family and home," he wrote. "It is my greatest earthly wish, stronger than life itself; for were it not for you and the children, it would not make but little difference whether in southern soil or at home my bones are laid." He was not discouraged or ready to give up, he was quick to add. He looked with bright hopes to the future, when the wicked, ruinous war would close "and those who prize the comforts of home above the scenes of strife and carnage may return in safety to their friends." [17]

But his health continued to deteriorate. As the regiment prepared to return to Fairfax from the gap, William sought medical care. The surgeon prescribed some medicine and ordered Chittenden to be sent to one of the general hospitals in the rear. "I have long dreaded it," William wrote, "but it may be for the best, as I may be better taken care of." His comrades had been very kind to him, he hastened to add, brother-in-law Nat Brown in particular. "Mary, do not let this worry you," he admonished, "for I think it may be for the best." He claimed he had been frank in describing his predicament, as bad as it was, and hoped to write more favorably soon, "but we are in a world of afflictions and know not how soon it may come to us." He would keep up good courage; he asked her to do the same. "Mary," he pledged, "my whole heart and affections are yours until death." Three days later, he was sent to a Washington hospital.[18]

After days of gloomy downpours in Yorkshire, a foot of water filled the cellar of the Chittenden home. Upstairs, little Clyde stood by a table watching his mother write a letter. He had graduated from dresses to short pants, "almost a man," Mary proudly wrote, although "he hurt his finger pretty bad the other day and he cried for Pa as hard as he could." Hiram asked his mother to tell Pa to come home, "he don't want him to stay there and let the men shoot him." Mary, too, bemoaned her husband's absence. She saw him in her dreams. "Oh, if this cruel war would ever close," she wrote, "but I fear it never will until our loved ones are all slain. Oh, William, why did I ever let you go? . . . Why did I not hinder you when I could?" But she dismissed her "vain talk" of what might have been. She pled to him to be careful for her, whose heart "mourns in silence at morning, noon, and night for the loved one far away." She apologized for her low spirits. "Oh, William, you will not thank me for such a letter as this," she admitted, "but to tell you my troubles makes them far easier for me to bear." Writing of her sorrows, her heart felt lighter. She would willingly bear all her afflictions if she knew he would live to return to his family again. She tried to end her letter on an upbeat note: "Goodbye, and do not let anything I have written serve to cast you down, for I want you to enjoy yourself the best you can and I will do the same."[19]

But try as she might, Mary could not stop worrying. Time and again she clasped "the silent pen" to share her thoughts and feelings with her husband. "Oh, William, how often I wish my heart were open as a book before your eyes," she exclaimed, "that you might read my every thought of you. You would then fully know how full of love and tenderness your Mary's heart was for you." In recurring dreams he returned to her, but when she awoke the illusion was dashed. "Oh, how long before the dream will be a reality," she wondered, "or can it never be?" She peppered him with questions about his health. "If I could know you were alive and well, I should feel much better than I now do." She begged him to send a letter with every mail, "for I feel so anxious to hear from you, for you are in so much danger, so near the enemy, it almost chills my blood when I think of it."[20]

Her despair reached dangerous depths:

My heart is so full this morning that it seems as though it would burst unless I let some one share its sorrows; and who have I but you to disclose my heart's secrets to? Oh, William, I would almost willingly lay my little ones in the grave that I might have nothing to detain me on this earth, for indeed my life is a burden to me. I have no desire to live now [that] you are gone. You will think me hard to write thus to you, but if I write at all I must write my feelings. The blinding teardrops fill my eyes and I can hardly see to write. I do not wish to complain, and yet I would rather die than live in the way I have to. I never was calculated to endure the hardships of the life I now lead; and not only this, but I live in constant fear of the awful news that he who is so dear to me is slain upon the battlefield. Oh, my God, grant to save me from this last bitter cup and I will try by thy grace to bear all other trials more submissively. . . . My heart is filled with wild despair. I almost go frantic at times. I cannot compose my mind. It seems one bitter dream of sorrow, from which I fear I shall never awake.[21]

But Mary's nightmare had scarcely begun.

"I was very sorry to hear you say that you could easier part with our little ones than with your unworthy husband," a dismayed William wrote in response to Mary's lament. "Oh, my dear companion, never let such a thought enter your mind again—though I know you love them as tenderly as I can." He prayed that God would spare the lives and health of each member of their small family, so they could enjoy a happy reunion. "Do not feel discouraged any more, but cheer up," he urged. "Hope for the best and try and view things on a brighter side." He blamed himself for her low spirits. "I must assume a more cheerful tenor in my correspondence with you or be unable to read your letters" because of their sadness. "It pains me much to read of your anguish and suffering on account of my absence," he wrote.

Oh, try and be courageous, ever trusting in the Almighty for sustaining grace. I know your times are hard, and my feelings are often pained when I think of your trials. My own sufferings are nothing when I think of my dear family, so far from me, and the hardships you endure. Truly we did not fully realize all things before I enlisted. Could we but have looked even a little way into the future, I should no doubt [have] been at home now with my dear family. . . . I know you cannot help thinking of the dangers to which I may be exposed. . . . But it is much the best way, I think, to ever be hopeful and not dwell so much on coming trouble.[22]

But William's letters from the hospital gave Mary more reason to worry. For the first time, he disclosed the true state of his health. For more than a month he had suffered from chronic diarrhea; then he was overcome by typhoid fever and lung disease. He needed help to walk when he arrived at Harewood Hospital in Washington; his mouth was parched, his head burned with fever. "You may think it strange that I did not write more particularly about my cough and what ailed me now," he admitted, "but I did not feel able then." When she blamed him for concealing his condition, he meekly replied, "I done as I thought best, hoping to be better soon." But he had not improved.[23]

At Harewood he was housed in a tent, open to the wind, without a floor or stove. Clad in a thin cotton shirt and drawers, confined to his bed, he was so weak he had to rest between writing short passages to Mary. When he finally dressed and ventured outside, he could barely walk. "Our fare is hardly sufficient to make us gain strength," he noted. Meals consisted of tea or coffee, beef or mutton soup, toast, and water. "I feel that it will be a long time before I shall be well again," he confided as November waned. "My constitution is not strong enough for a soldier. I feared it would be so, but had hopes that I might be more rugged."[24]

He felt better a few days later, although still troubled by a sore throat. "If I had my strength I should feel quite like myself," he declared, but he remained weak. He was pleased to receive letters from Mary, forwarded from the regiment by Nat Brown, but he gently rebuffed her request to come to Washington to nurse him. Not only would it be imprudent and inconvenient for her to leave home and travel alone, he pointed out, but there were no accommodations for female nurses at the hospital. Knowing how her active imagination tended to make things worse than they really were, he confessed he had not given her a detailed account of hospital life, sparing her tales of patients neglected by nurses and unnamed "scenes of a touching character." Again he pledged his devotion to her, and encouraged her to maintain good spirits. "I hope when the days of war and carnage are over that we may spend many happy days together, and then we can recount to each other bygone trials in the quiet retreat of our own happy home with those little darlings whom I should like to clasp with their mother to my heart."[25]

That dream was soon in dire jeopardy.

Hog-slaughtering on the Chittenden farm was followed by a spell of bitterly cold weather. On December 8, 1862, Mary wrote to William to inform him that Clyde was sick. "I did not intend to say anything to you about it," she wrote, "but I thought if I were in your place I should rather know." The two-year-old had a sore throat. Mary guessed it was only a canker, but she had sent for a doctor nevertheless. As she wrote, Clyde was sleeping peacefully; Mary urged William not to worry about him. But then she added a postscript to her letter. "William, the doctor is here. He says Clyde has got the diphtheria, but he thinks he will get along if nothing happens." Mary knew, however, that diphtheria was sweeping Yorkshire—and the epidemic was killing some of its victims.[26]

After midnight Mary woke from a brief nap to watch over "little Clydie" and give him medicine. She passed some of the lonely hours writing to William. It seemed to her that Clyde was no worse, but the doctor had told her "it would be nothing strange if he should be taken worse suddenly and not live but a few hours." Mary would rely on faith to withstand the trial. "I want to feel to leave my little one in the arms of the Good Father," she wrote, "knowing He will do all things well. . . . Let us William try and give all our hearts to God, knowing that all earthly joys are but for a moment, and let us lay up all our treasures in heaven that we may one day find them in that paradise where sorrow never enters."

Later that morning, with Clyde cradled in her lap, she continued her letter, knowing how her husband's "anxious heart" would fill with hope and fear for news of his son. "William, this is the strangest disease I ever saw," she wrote. "One hour Clyde will be around to play and the next he will seem very sick. I just stopped writing long enough to swab his throat, which is a very hard job." Mary had sought help from both the Chittenden and Wheeler families, but little was forthcoming. Her brother Edgar Wheeler, recently discharged from the 105th New York after losing a thumb at Second Bull Run, lived with her at the farm, but spent the daylight hours working outside. So, Mary regretfully noted, "I am alone with the children in the house most of the time." She wished she could embrace William, "whose heart would echo back every anxious throb of mine," but in his absence she placed her trust in God's strength and wisdom.

Still later that morning the doctor returned. During his visit Mary finished her letter so he could post it in the village. "He thinks Clyde is better to day," she reported, "and I sincerely hope this may be the case." She would do her best for the boy, she promised, and would keep William well informed.[27]

In the next five days Mary wore herself out caring for the children—for Hiram, too, had caught the diphtheria. Every hour or two, day and night, she gave the boys doses of medicine. As the days passed she only found time to change her clothes once. She regretted missing the funeral of a niece, dead of diphtheria. Just when it seemed she could stand the strain no longer, relatives and friends relieved her and she was able to get some much needed sleep.

The doctor visited often. Hiram's throat was badly swollen and hurt him a great deal, but he seemed to improve steadily. Clyde, on the other hand, remained dangerously ill. His appetite was sporadic and he was cranky. Most of the time he wanted to lay in his cradle; he slept often. Writing one evening after the doctor called, Mary suggested to her husband, "William, you must try and be prepared for whatever awaits you. Our little Clyde may leave us for a brighter home, and God helping me, I mean to try and be prepared for each coming trial."

The next morning, after another night of little sleep, Mary continued her letter. She wished she could say the children were better, but she could not. "My dear," she informed William, "I fear we shall not all be again permitted to meet on this side [of] the grave. If you could, I think it would be advisable to try and get a furlough and come home." But then she realized the futility of that suggestion: "Clyde will either be better or else done with earth and its sorrows long before this could reach you and you get home."

Before Mary sealed her letter, Hiram made a request. She gave the four-year-old a pencil, wrapped her hand around his, and guided him to write:

> Dear Pa, come home and see little Hiram and Clyde. I take all the medicine the doctor gives me so I can get well and see Pa when he comes home. I will kiss you if you will come home and see me. I want to see my pa pretty bad. Goodbye from your little Hiram.[28]

When William received Mary's letter he first read Hiram's note, "not without dropping a few tears as I remembered the dear little ones as last I saw them, and how Hiram called Pa to come back." He wanted to respond to Mary immediately, but feared he could not control his emotions. So he left his hospital tent for a secluded spot, "where none but God can witness my grief." He urged Mary to put her trust in God and assured her that he felt deeply for her. While he wished to be optimistic, he realized that little Clyde might already have left the "vale of tears, sorrow, and suffering" for heaven. "I can write nothing to encourage you," he confessed, "but wish you to carry all your cares to the lamb of God and so live that we may meet our little ones where sickness, pain, and sin will never disturb us more." He wrote of his sick sons, "Oh, my dear, how gladly would I lay down my life for them if the sacrifice would be called for—though their father's heart is not as free from sin as theirs is, nor am I prepared to meet my God."[29]

The next morning William added a few lines, wishing Mary a good morning and "a greeting to my little ones if alive." In his imagination, he had followed Mary through each trying ordeal. He wished he could be with her, so their tears could mingle and they could sooth each other's aching hearts. "Oh, it is sad to hear such news so far from home, and no way to hasten to them," he wrote. "After I went to bed last night I was thinking of you and how hard it would be for you all alone under such sorrows, and it seemed as though my heart would break. I could feel no worse if by your side, even if to follow our little boy to his last resting place." He had hopes both boys were alive and feeling better, but, "if not I know they are better off and freed from a world of sin and pain."[30]

"That dreadful scourge diphtheria is more dreaded by me than most any other that flesh is heir to," William wrote. "Before this reaches you," he told Mary, "our darling boy, around whom so many of our fond hopes have clustered, may lay in the cold embrace of death, never more to respond to our call in his playful way." He admitted, "I almost dread the next news I shall hear, but will hope it may be well."[31]

With Clyde crying for her, Mary hastily closed another letter to William. Relatives and neighbors came by during the evenings to help her, she reported, but she spent daytimes alone with the two sick children. "But God gave me strength to bear it," she declared. Finally a friend had come to stay full time and help. The diphtheria epidemic continued to claim victims. Another Yorkshire child of their acquaintance had died of the disease, Mary reported, desolating a family. "Let us thank God that this is not the case with our home."[32]

Clyde's neck remained swollen, but it seemed to Mary that he was improving. The doctor planned to lance the swelling. For the time being, however, he was letting it be, thinking it was beneficial and would hurry the disease out of the boy's system. As Mary reflected on her situation, she strangely conflated the children's sickness with her husband's service in the army, and made some startling confessions.

> Oh, my dear, how thankful we should be that our little ones are alive. But William, strange as it may seem to you, never once since they have been sick have I breathed a prayer to God for their recovery. But oh, how ardently I plead for strength to bear all my grief without a murmur! How could I ask for those little ones to live in this cruel, sinful world? How much rather would I see them laid in the silent tomb than torn from my arms in early manhood to go to the battlefield, and how often I have thought I would sooner part with them than with my William so far away—and if this sacrifice was called for, I should have tried not to murmur. But God has spared them thus far, and I pray my Father it may be for some noble purpose.[33]

Mary spent a quiet New Year's Day 1863 with her brother Edgar and their father. The holiday was enlivened by the receipt of a letter from William, which "seemed much like a visit." She responded immediately, beginning a letter before she served supper and continuing it in the evening. "Little Clydie is gaining [as] fast as can be expected," she reported, "but he cannot walk a step yet." The boy had not walked for three weeks. The doctor had not lanced his swollen neck, with beneficial results.

> The swelling on his neck runs wonderfully yet, and everyone thinks it is all that saved his life. If it had not have come out on the outside, it seems as though he could not have lived. But God saw fit to spare his life, for what [reason] He alone knoweth. May He grant in his infinite mercy that it may be for good and not evil. Oh, William, how I have tried to be resigned about my children. I have tried to say, "Father thy will be done," and if God had taken my little ones to dwell with him I should have tried not to murmur, for I should have felt that they were freed from a world of sin. But still I think I feel truly thankful that I have them yet with me.

While her worries about the children lessened, Mary's concern for William continued unabated. She repeatedly asked him to obtain a discharge if possible and a furlough if not. Reviewing his case, she could not see how the authorities could refuse him a discharge. He had tried so hard to keep up with the regiment and had stayed with it until his comrades had to carry him to the hospital, where his health had worsened and he was nothing but an expense to the government. He could never stand a soldier's life, she maintained. If he was sent back to the regiment he would be disabled again within two weeks, to be returned to a hospital if not laid in a grave. The Northern people were enraged, she wrote, to see their sick soldiers kept to die and be buried in Southern graves far from home. "It almost chills my blood when I think how our soldiers are treated," she declared. She meant to put her trust in God and be prepared for whatever awaited, "but my daily prayer is that my William may return to me ere his health is ruined forever, or a grave far away is closed over his form."[34]

Eight days after Mary wrote, William was granted a sixty-day furlough, and he returned to Yorkshire for a joyous reunion with his family.

Despite the pleasure of William's return home, the Chittenden family still faced dangers. Young Hiram remained seriously ill when his father returned to the army at the expiration of his furlough, and William had doubts the child would recover. "You know not how I felt when I left home that morning (I hope not for the last time)," William wrote Mary from Virginia, "but it seems like tearing ones heart strings asunder to bid adieu to friends so dear." His own health remained precarious and did not improve as he was shuttled from place to place on his return to the South.

He reported back at Harewood Hospital on March 10, 1863. On April 3 he was sent to a convalescent camp near Alexandria, Virginia. There a surgeon took his pulse, checked his tongue, and admitted him to a barracks, where he was informed he would be sent to his regiment. The following day another surgeon, without even examining him, prescribed a dose of medicine and a quinine pill. Then he was sent to a nearby distribution camp. Feeling despondent, he informed Mary of his uncertain status. His health was poorer than when he left home. He felt he would never regain it. There was a chance he could be transferred to a hospital in a northern city, but he expected to be sent to the regiment. The first leg of that journey would be a four-mile walk to Alexandria, "and I do not feel that I can walk a mile." Lonely, ill, homesick, and unsure of his future, he told Mary, "I dare not write to you as I feel."[35]

On April 12 William returned to the regiment at its camp near Stafford Court House, Virginia. When the 154th broke camp the following day and embarked on the march that led to Chancellorsville, Private Chittenden was left behind with other convalescents. Eleven days later he was admitted to the Second Division, Eleventh Corps hospital at nearby Brooks Station. Confined to his tent during a rainstorm, he told Mary, "I have little to encourage me here." Regimental comrades informed him he would receive a discharge, but some patients had been waiting more than a month for their discharge paperwork to be completed. Then the hospital filled with the wounded from Chancellorsville, and the surgeons were preoccupied with amputations and other operations. "There are suffering soldiers on every side of us," William noted. One of them was his brother-in-law, Nat Brown, who was wounded in the forehead. (Brown would survive, only to be tormented by pain from his wound for the rest of his life.)[36]

Captain Harrison Cheney and a company comrade from Yorkshire visited the hospital with some reassuring news from regimental surgeon Henry Van Aernam. "They both said the doctor told them that he should have me discharged as soon as possible," William informed Mary, "but I can not give you any more encouragement than this at present." Van Aernam himself came by the next day. "He said he had no doubt as to the final result of it, but it would take time as the doctors here were so busy with the wounded that for a while at least other things would have to be neglected"—and William's discharge would have to come from one of the harried hospital surgeons. Van Aernam promised to do what he could to hurry the process and advised William to be as patient as possible.[37]

Adding to his misery, his body broke out in boils. Writing to Mary offered solace. "It is about the best way I have of spending the lonely hours, for a great many times when I have commenced to write I have felt so lonely and discouraged that it seemed as though I could hardly write. . . . I have felt relieved in my mind after writing awhile, for it is like conversing with my dearest friend." Were it not for that great privilege, he felt, his condition would be doubly hard to bear. Soon he wrote to Mary every day, encouraging her as best he could, offering her advice regarding farm business, pouring out his love to her and the children, hoping for future blessings. But solemn notes slipped through his optimism—"I am far from being well," he wrote, and "at times the way seems rather dark."[38]

Finally, on the last day of May, came the long-awaited good news. Surgeon Van Aernam accompanied him to an interview with a hospital surgeon and explained his case. "My papers of disability are made out," William told Mary, "and if nothing happens, I hope to soon be ready for a homeward journey."[39]

"Little Clyde is asleep and Hiram is standing by my side," Mary wrote after her husband's return to Virginia. "He wants me to tell Pa that we have made some [maple] sugar and he wants you to come home and get some." With her letter, she enclosed two items—a diarrhea cure clipped from the *New York Tribune* ("which may be of use to you and others"), and a poem of her own composition. "Please accept this poor effort at poetry," she wrote, "for it came from the heart if not very good." In her verses, Mary once again voiced the pain of separation, and pondered the possibility of joining William in death.

> 'Tis evening's hour and o'er the earth
> Night her dark mantle gently spreads,
> And thousands [of] stars bedeck the sky,
> And o'er the earth their glory shed.
>
> But all alone I sit tonight,
> With heart so sad I can but mourn;
> For he whose love was my delight
> Far! to the cruel wars has gone.
>
> Ah! ah! that sad that bitter hour
> When from my arms he went away;
> Ne'er while my reason holds her powers
> Can I forget that parting day.
>
> The parting kiss, the fond embrace,
> The last warm presence of the hand;
> The sad "goodbye" and faint "God bless
> You," while I fight for freedom's land.
>
> Oh, should he ne'er return again
> To cheer my lonely home and heart,

Not far behind would I remain
But meet him soon, where friends ne'er part.

But all my cares I'll cast on Him
"Who watchest with a fathers care,"
And "Bring him to my arms again,"
To God shall be my daily prayer.[40]

Spring brought more work on the farm. Mary's father trimmed the orchard, potatoes were planted, and a hundred pounds of maple sugar were put up. There was another cow to milk, and newborn lambs and a calf to tend to. Mary's brother Edgar was so rough with the animals that she took over caring for them. As busy as she was, despite nature's warm green renewal, Mary still could not shake her despondency:

> You will excuse me, my dear, if I unburden my full heart to the ear of my only true earthly friend, for I feel that I am alone in this world, sad and lonely—tired of the burdens of life. Gladly would I lay me down to rest where the "wicked cease from troubling" if I had no little ones to need a "mother's care." You said in your letter that it seemed to you at times that we should never all meet again below. I have often thought since you left "Our Home" that if you ever returned, ere then death might leave his footprints in our little circle. . . . I can truly say that if it were not for the hope of your return, life would have but few charms for me. The coming summer will have naught of happiness for me if you do not return. Since you left I have taken but little comfort, except when I would lay aside the cares of life and go before my maker and pray him to comfort me with his spirit. . . . Oh, William, I will hope and pray that you may speedily return, and while life lasts this shall be my daily petition to God until answered, which I feel quite confident will be some day.[41]

But the lonesome days continued to pass and Mary struggled with her burden. "The memory of those sad days when my little ones were so sick and I almost sick and friendless watched over their suffering forms wasting with disease (both day and night) brings the blinding teardrops to my eyes," she wrote. As for the present, "If it were not for the hope of your return," she told William, "my heart would sink beneath the load it carries. . . . I do not wish to burden your mind with my cares, but I feel sad to have you sick so far away from home."

Thinking of others whose soldier loved ones were casualties of battle, Mary tempered her anguish. Close to home, her sister Nancy longed for word from her wounded husband, Nat Brown. "I fear he is worse or dead," Mary wrote, "but oh, I hope not for her sake." And so many families were in mourning. "I will try and be patient in regard to your absence," Mary told William, "for when I think how many hearts are almost broken for their loved ones, who they can never behold again, I try to feel thankful that God has spared your life thus far, and at his throne of grace [I] plead for your return."[42]

And finally, blessedly, her prayers were answered, and the long-hoped-for day arrived.

On June 3, 1863, Second Lieutenant John Mitchell, commander of Company D of the 154th New York, signed a certificate of disability for the discharge of Private William F. Chittenden. Before his sickness, Mitchell noted, William "was a good soldier, prompt and ready for duty always." The examining surgeon listed the cause of Chittenden's disability as phthisis pulmonalis—tuberculosis. "He has been under treatment since last November and unfit for duty," the doctor noted. "Both lungs are far advanced in disease, rendering the patient completely prostrate; he is in fact in the last stages of consumption."[43]

The prognosis proved wrong. William survived. Claiming that his condition prevented him from doing half of the manual labor he performed before the war, he was admitted to the pension rolls in 1864, to receive eight dollars per month for a total disability. The Chittendens' crisis was over. Despite his frail health, William and Mary enjoyed many years together after his return home.

With their wartime correspondence ended, no intimate record of their postwar lives survives. Only the sketchiest outline can be drawn. A daughter, Ida Lunette Chittenden, was born to the couple on June 16, 1864, about a year after William's homecoming. In 1888, William, Mary, and Ida moved from Yorkshire to Cadillac, Michigan, where Clyde had preceded them; in 1895 the three moved to Lansing, where William worked as a florist. William died at his Lansing home on June 2, 1923, aged eighty-seven. Mary died there on September 13, 1924. She was eighty-eight.[44]

Having escaped their wartime brush with death, the Chittenden boys matured into men of prominence. After his early years "under the active and wholesome discipline of the farm," Clyde Chittenden attended an academy, took college courses, and studied with a Cattaraugus County law firm until he moved to Michigan in 1883. In Cadillac he built a successful law practice and lumber business and was elected circuit court commissioner and judge, prosecuting attorney, and state senator. Clyde was praised as "a man of decided strength of character whom no obstacles can deter nor difficulties discourage."[45]

Hiram Chittenden eclipsed his brother's prominence, achieving national distinction as a military engineer and historian. He was a student at Cornell University when he received an appointment to West Point by Congressman Henry

Van Aernam—the former surgeon of the 154th New York who had facilitated his father's discharge from the army. Hiram graduated from the U.S. Military Academy with high honors in 1884 and attended the Engineer School of Application. He then served as an engineer officer in the Department of the Platte, developer of the road system in Yellowstone National Park (and the park's chronicler), Federal commissioner of Yosemite National Park, and chief engineer of an army corps during the Spanish-American War. He also authored several works of engineering and history, including a classic study of the American fur trade. Hiram held the rank of brigadier general on his retirement from the army.

Van Aernam was proud of his part in Hiram's rise. Chittenden was "the best *soldier material* at my command when I named him for West Point," the doctor wrote. "It has made a great change in *his life* certainly—from milking cows on his father's poor farm on 'Blue Hill,' to his present position." Van Aernam's appointment certainly helped boost Hiram Chittenden to a rewarding and renowned career. But Hiram, like his brother Clyde, had a solid foundation upon which to build. According to the *Dictionary of American Biography*, "[Hiram] Chittenden was a man of the highest character."[46]

That both brothers were praised for their strength of character is no coincidence. Their worthiness was nurtured by the compassion of their parents. Against great odds, William and Mary had struggled to regain health and hope for themselves and their boys. They had found strength in religious faith. They had clung to life and reaffirmed living. They had reunited the family and kept it together. Van Aernam disparaged the Chittenden's poor farm, but the place was rich in love.

CHAPTER FIVE

Captain Alanson Crosby

Company D

From the center of the Cattaraugus County village of Franklinville, I drove east on Cemetery Hill Road and soon came to the iron gates of Mount Prospect Cemetery. As the blacktopped drive wound uphill to the middle of the neatly tended grounds, I encountered a mound, fifty feet in diameter, consecrated to the town's Civil War veterans as "The Soldiers' Rest." At its center towered a graceful granite monument, simply decorated with carvings of crossed rifles and a star, surmounted by a statue of a stalwart color-bearer—a "Tribute of Franklinville to the Patriots of 1861–1865," dedicated by the town in August 1906.

The crowd's attention on that long past summer day focused on Franklinville's surviving veterans, then in their senior years, stooped and gray. Many of them wore the blue uniform of the Grand Army of the Republic, with badges identifying them as members of Franklinville's Post Number 508. When the GAR men had formed their post fifteen years before, they had named it in memory of one of their town's martyred soldiers, Captain Alanson Crosby of the 154th New York. Crosby was buried in Mount Prospect, and in the coming years, the aged veterans at the ceremony would join him, one by one.

Now the monument stood watch over the graves of a dozen members of the 154th New York. I wanted to visit them all on this lovely summer day, Captain Crosby's in particular, but a problem loomed. Mount Prospect was the largest cemetery I visited in Cattaraugus County, with thousands of stones scattered over thirty-five acres. This picturesque place—with its rolling landscape, leafy canopy of mature trees, and plentiful stones—called for a lengthy and leisurely prowl. But the afternoon shadows were long, and I had an appointment in another town in an hour. There was no way I could hunt the twelve graves in that short amount of time.

Luckily for me, Mount Prospect's caretaker, Donald B. Forrester, and his assistant, Jeff Bushnell, were still on duty. At the cemetery office, I went through the alphabetized listings in the big ledger book of burials and jotted down the section letters and plot numbers of the graves I wanted to visit. With Donald in the lead, Jeff behind him lugging several smaller plot books, and me following, we began to work our way through the various sections. A fifteen-year veteran at the cemetery, Donald strode sure-footed from one veteran's grave to the next. A couple of times I noticed that he walked backward, an ever-present cigarette dangling from his mouth, and sidestepped gravestones as if he had eyes in the back of his head.

With the two men's help, it was easy to find the tall obelisk marking the grave of Captain Crosby. It stood near the edge of a circular roadway, not far behind the looming monument atop Soldier's Rest. From its face, I took in a serene view of a valley and surrounding hills, green, dark, and cool under the brilliant sky. Turning, I examined Crosby's obelisk. The deep-cut inscriptions in the white marble were rounded at the edges after years of exposure, but still legible. About halfway up the obelisk a carved flag—whose stars and stripes had long since worn away—waved inside a circular cut. Below it, I had no trouble making out the epitaph's salient facts: Crosby was wounded in battle on June 16, 1864, and died in Officers Hospital at Nashville, Tennessee, on July 9, 1864, aged twenty-eight years, three months, and two days.

After his death in Nashville, Alanson Crosby did not immediately rest in peace. Most Civil War soldiers were buried as promptly as possible, near the places they died. Those who fell on the battlefield in close proximity were dragged together and laid in a common trench; isolated dead were put in single graves. Those who succumbed in hospitals were interred in nearby burial grounds. Only later—most often in the postwar years—were their remains exhumed and reburied in the nearest national cemetery.

Rare were the soldiers who left enough money, or whose families were wealthy enough, to have their remains shipped north for burial in hometown cemeteries. Alanson Crosby was one such soldier. When he died, an inventory of his effects included his clothing, a valise, a rubber blanket, a buffalo robe, and $356.79 in U.S. notes. After contacting Alanson's kin, an officer in Nashville used the money to arrange for the disposition of the body.[1]

Crosby's corpse was embalmed, placed in a metallic coffin, and shipped by railroad to Ellicottville, the Cattaraugus County seat. It arrived on July 15 and was taken to the home of Alanson's brother-in-law. On Sunday, July 17, the remains were conveyed to the home of Crosby's parents in Franklinville. Then the coffin was carried to the Methodist Episcopal Church in Cadiz, a hamlet in the township, for the funeral service. About two hundred mourners packed the church and hundreds more, unable to enter, waited outside. After the service the pall bearers, followed by the grieving family, carried the casket across the road for burial in the Cadiz Cemetery. "We can only add, in brief, our sympathy and condolences with the aged parents and the younger members of the family," concluded a report of the funeral by the *Cattaraugus Union*. "The young soldier fills an honored grave."

But the honored grave proved to be impermanent. At an unknown date, Alanson's remains were disinterred and moved to Mount Prospect Cemetery. This quite likely occurred soon after Mount Prospect was established in 1877. Franklinville residents had long pushed for a new cemetery. Led by their townsman Henry Van Aernam, the former surgeon of the 154th New York, they had formed an association, organized a corporation, purchased the land, and dedicated the grounds with solemn ceremony. Their lovely new cemetery was a source of great civic pride. Crosby's family wanted him to rest in this fine place, with its specially designated Soldiers' Rest, and so they moved him there. Since the move to Mount Prospect, Alanson Crosby's remains have laid undisturbed.[2]

Crosby's corpse was afforded special treatment when it was shipped home to be laid to rest. His funeral also was special. The large outpouring of grief revealed the public's esteem for the young man. The mourners believed that great promise had been cut short by his untimely death. Most small towns, North and South, sent men like Alanson Crosby to the war: up-and-coming young men of prominent families, well-educated professional men, men destined to rise in rank as officers in the military, men who would return home to heroes' welcomes and assume their rightful places as pillars of their communities. They were men, in short, who were the country's future leaders. They were men who were cut down wholesale in four years of carnage.

Their contemporaries pictured them—and we continue to picture them—brandishing swords at the head of their charging men, urging their prancing steeds through gun smoke toward the enemy, waving shot-torn flags in defiance when the fatal bullet hit. But death did not call on Civil War soldiers with a gallant air to offer a picture-perfect, bloodless swoon into eternity. It appeared suddenly—a terrible, swift bolt from nowhere that struck men down brutally into mud and dirt.

That was how Alanson Crosby fell: abruptly and harshly, without a hint of the glamour that Civil War romance attached to its martyrs. And yet, before he breathed his last, Alanson displayed stoic dignity and murmured noble sentiments. Thus he was afforded a hero's death—a death worth celebrating with the most high-flown sentiments of Victorian rhetoric. Alanson rose above the mundane circumstances of his wounding to expire in a manner befitting the brave and promising officer his contemporaries held him to be. On his deathbed, he achieved romantic martyrdom.

As he lay dying, Alanson might have recalled the time when death almost snatched him under the most absurd of circumstances, quite unfitting for a Civil War hero: stark naked, in the middle of a raging river.

Fugitives in enemy territory, two escaped prisoners of war stood on a mountaintop at sunset, gazing at the last great obstacle between them and safety. Hundreds of feet below, the Potomac River cut through a gulf, its waters about a half-mile wide, dark, turbid, and swollen by heavy rains. First Lieutenant Alanson Crosby and Second Lieutenant John Mitchell of Company D, 154th New York, stared at the river. "At a time when our minds were less wrought up with anxiety for escape," Crosby later wrote, "the thought of plunging into its boiling and whirling current would have been madness." But the two men had overcome numerous hardships and dangers in their flight and were filled with reckless confidence. The Maryland shore beckoned irresistibly.

Crosby and Mitchell climbed down the cliff to the water's edge, stripped off their clothes, rolled them in bundles, and strapped them to their backs. They paused for a brief look across the surging river before plunging into the water. "About six rods above us the current was broken up by a ledge of rocks, and thrown into a foaming and seething torrent," Crosby noted. "Where we were struggling below, it was full of whirlpools and eddies through which it was next to impossible to swim." As the two men floundered through the roiling water the heavy bundles on their backs became saturated, dragging them beneath the waves with every stroke they took. Exhausted, their arms turned leaden. Slapped away by the river, their hats danced off downstream. "It was evident we could not reach the opposite shore without the interposition of a miracle," Crosby recalled.

> I looked back to see if it would be possible to return to our starting point. We were far out in the stream near the center. It would be useless to turn back. A wide sea of whirling waters encompassed us. I tried to touch the bottom, but in vain. We were fast failing. Our strokes were growing feebler and slower. Our position was nearly vertical in the current, with nothing but the face above the water.

Then, to Crosby's horror, Mitchell sank beneath the froth. "I supposed he was gone; and that I should follow him in a few minutes I had not the least doubt." But Mitchell bobbed to the surface and the two struggled on.

> Death stared us in the face with all its ghastly horrors, and we were rapidly sinking into his insatiable jaws. Hope died within us, and a sullen despair, a sort of stolid indifference, came over us. The terror of our situation vanished, and a thread of recollections flashed through our minds. It seemed as if the memories of a lifetime were crowded into one moment.

At that climactic instant, Crosby's foot came to rest on a submerged rock, and he clung to it "with the desperation of a new born hope." The current threatened to sweep him off his toehold back into the deep water, but he caught his balance, braced himself, and stood safely. Mitchell was nearby and Crosby yelled to him over the river's roar. Sinking, surfacing, gasping, spitting, Mitchell thrashed his way to Crosby's rock.

> There we stood, in the rushing torrent up to our shoulders, rocking back and forth in a fierce struggle to maintain our position. The bundles on our backs must go, or we would soon go with them to a watery grave; that was certain. Hitherto we could not get them off, but now was an opportunity. They went tumbling along on the rough current—boots, coat, unmentionables, waistcoats, underclothing and all.

Freed of their burdens and reinvigorated by their short rest, Crosby and Mitchell pushed off the rock. They were pleased to find that the current near the Maryland shore was less rapid and rough, and without the weight of their wet clothes they managed to cross the last channel safely and reach the bank, exhausted, faint, and sick. "The only wardrobe we had left consisted of a 'finger ring,'" Crosby wrote. "In that unique and scanty costume we crawled, for we could not walk, out of the water and up the bank." [3]

Only faint outlines remain of Alanson Crosby's prewar life. He traced his line to a soldier grandfather, Colonel Jedediah Crosby, who commanded a regiment in the War of 1812. The colonel's four sons, including Alanson Crosby Sr., came to Franklinville in 1830 and settled on a hill that was dubbed with the family name. The third and last child of Alanson and Cornelia (Wright) Crosby, a boy named after his father, was born at Crosby Hill on April 2, 1836. Young Alanson attended the common schools in Franklinville. Unlike most of his classmates, he continued his education, matriculating at a university in Kentucky and studying at the Poughkeepsie (New York) Law School.

Returning to Cattaraugus County, Alanson polished his legal skills by reading law in the Ellicottville firm of Rice and Jones—which brought him into the circle of Addison G. Rice, the future organizer of the 154th New York, and Patrick Henry Jones, the regiment's future commander. Those contacts would stand him in good stead in the coming war. Crosby was admitted to the bar in May 1859 and practiced for a while in Ellicottville before joining the law office of Alexander Sheldon in the nearby village of Randolph.[4]

When Addison Rice organized the 154th New York in the summer of 1862, his former pupil entered the war. During the regimental enrollment drive, Crosby (no doubt with Rice's endorsement) was appointed an authorized recruiting agent by New York State governor Edwin D. Morgan. The young lawyer quickly got to work with a harangue at a rally in Ellicottville. "His handsome face glowed with enthusiasm," a witness reported, "and his voice rang out clear, bold and spirit-stirring, as the notes of martial music." Crosby closed his oration with a bold reference to the Star-Spangled Banner: "Living, that FLAG shall gladden my eyes, and, dying, its folds shall enshroud me." There was a brief silence as he took his seat; then the audience erupted in "a tumult of applause."[5]

Crosby and Benjamin Giles Casler, a storekeeper from the town of Cold Spring, opened a recruiting office in Randolph. In July and August of 1862, Alanson signed up twenty-five of the ninety-seven enlisted men who formed Company A of the 154th. Casler and Baker Leonard Saxton, an Ellicottville blacksmith, enrolled the others. Alanson himself enrolled on August 8. The company was the first from Cattaraugus County to be organized in response to the call for volunteers and to report to Camp James M. Brown in Jamestown. One of its members boasted, "A more intelligent mass of men were never seen in a Company."[6]

In recognition of their work in recruiting the company, Saxton, Casler, and Crosby were awarded commissions by Governor Morgan as captain, first lieutenant, and second lieutenant, respectively. In August, Alanson made a special trip to Albany to ensure that the company's papers were in order so as to secure its place as first in the still-evolving regiment. On August 30 he forwarded a roster of the company for publication in the *Cattaraugus Freeman,* the Republican newspaper published in Ellicottville. "It is sufficient to say that we have the *best* company in camp," he wrote. "This is conceded by all. We have been compelled to transfer ten men to other companies on account of having more than enough. Hurry up enlistments in Cattaraugus," he added, "so we can be off for Dixie. The boys are *spoiling* for a fight." But the impatient men had to bide their time for a month before they left Camp Brown. Crosby and the rest of the officer corps were mustered in on September 26, 1862. Three days later Colonel Rice's regiment was off to Dixie.[7]

Unfortunately, Alanson's letters to his family are not known to survive. He did, however, leave a written record in a series of letters to the *Cattaraugus Freeman*. Intentionally composed for publication, they were primarily chronicles of the regiment's service, devoid of their author's intimate revelations and innermost thoughts about his own experiences. Alanson initially wrote journalism, not expressionism. But as time passed, his personal opinions emerged from the orotund camouflage of his public prose.

He announced his goal in his first letter, sent from camp at Fairfax Court House, Virginia, on October 23, 1862. "It is now nearly a month since the 154th Regiment left Jamestown for the seat of war, and no account of its progress has yet been publicly given to the friends of the brave boys who compose it," he observed. "As almost every family in your vicinity has a representative here, it may be of interest to some of your readers to know how we reached our destination, and some of the incidents connected with our journey, and our soldier-life in the sunny land of Dixie."

The men left Jamestown in the best of spirits, he reported. At Elmira, New York, they were supplied with English-made Enfield rifled muskets, reportedly captured from a blockade-runner. "They are excellent guns," Alanson declared, "and when the Cattaraugus and Chautauqua boys draw a line on a 'secesh' miscreant, he will not hesitate long to come down." Their ride through Pennsylvania was "a complete ovation": "Men, women, and children vied with each other in wafting us tokens of approval as we passed along." He was especially appreciative of the reception they received in Williamsport, where the townsfolk distributed "all sorts of good things" to the soldiers, and the young ladies of a seminary ("kind, fair, hospitable, and patriotic creatures") filled their canteens with coffee and "came pretty near winning the hearts of some."

Baltimore, with its large population of Southern sympathizers, presented a study in contrasts. When the regiment marched through the city from one depot to another, Alanson wrote, "I saw many ruby lips curl and fair faces distort themselves with attempts to express scorn for the brave volunteers who were hastening to the defense of their native land." On the other hand, "There were many good Union greetings, and the Stars and Stripes waved proudly by fair hands from hundreds of windows as we passed along."

Washington afforded the men a look at the "silent grandeur" and "majestic proportions" of the Capitol.

> To those who never saw it before (and there were but few who had) it was an object of no little interest. Associated, as it is, with everything grand and glorious in our

past, and portentous and gloomy in our present history, how could it be otherwise than an object of pleasing, yet painful interest?

"I dare say many patriotic resolves went up from the hearts of our noble volunteers when their feet first trod the traitor soil of Virginia," Alanson wrote. What the men found was desolation. Crosby compared the ruin of the Old Dominion to Herculaneum. On the march from Arlington Heights to Fairfax Court House, he saw only a few inhabited homes. "The people have nearly all united their destinies with *Jeff. Davis,* and the Union soldiers occupy their houses for barracks." Entire villages were deserted. "The withering hand of war has wiped them out forever, and nothing remains to indicate their former existence but decaying ruins." Fairfax he described as "a rickety, one-horse affair . . . in the worst stages of dilapidation." He and a few companions made a brief excursion to Falls Church, where they enjoyed a dinner of hoe-cakes made by a Virginia crone. She was old enough to be Methuselah's grandmother, Alanson guessed; he wondered how she survived in her deserted and denuded neighborhood.

Colonel Rice was about to return home to Ellicottville, although his prearranged successor (and former law partner), Colonel Patrick Jones, had yet to report for duty. Rice "has done well in getting the regiment organized and into the field," Alanson observed, "and the men regret that he could not remain with them permanently." But Crosby could not have been too concerned about the change: the switch in colonels would pass him from one supportive patron to another.

So far, soldiering seemed to agree with Alanson. He composed his letter during his first tour of picket duty, "in the depths of a Virginia forest, with nothing but a portfolio to write upon." Thirty men were under his command, "and we all feel the importance of our mission. I like the business so far, and would like to be stationed on the out posts all the time during this pleasant weather." The green soldiers were ready for action. "We expect to move in a few days," Alanson wrote. "I think we shall have fighting to do soon. When it comes the 154th will do its share."[8]

"The 154th has seen much of the 'pomp and circumstance of glorious war' since I wrote you last, although its most terrible features have not yet been presented to us," Alanson began his next letter to the *Freeman* on December 8, 1862. Indeed, the routine duties of drill and picket had become "irksome and monotonous" to the soldiers before an order came to advance from the Fairfax camp. Despite their ignorance of their destination or role in the mission, their "hearts beat high," thinking they were bound for Richmond with the grand Army of the Potomac. But the resulting movement to Thoroughfare Gap fizzled out inconsequentially.

Alanson described the strong but abandoned Confederate fortifications guarding the approaches to Centerville, a village that he judged to be a one-horse town before the war, now home solely to bats and owls. He detailed the wreckage of the Bull Run battlefield, where "the woods and roadside were filled with graves," many of them washed away to reveal the rotting corpses. He wrote of the village of Haymarket, "the most pleasant and thrifty looking place I have seen in Virginia," which was burned in the night by the Union troops. Alanson did not say so, but members of the 154th participated in the arson. "Of course nobody approved such an unprovoked act of vandalism," he wrote. "The inhabitants were all rank *secesh,* however, and the perpetrators of the shameful deed probably console themselves with the reflection that it helped to accelerate the blow that is expected to 'break the backbone' of rebellion."

Near Thoroughfare Gap the soldiers finally found countryside unscarred by war. Local farms provided a plentiful bounty. "The way fresh beef, pork, fowls, honey, apples and vegetables came into camp was a caution to all traitors," Crosby wrote. The inhabitants were all staunch secessionists, but voiced a wish that the war would end. "The impression is prevalent," Alanson wrote after conversations with several local folk, ". . . that both sides have had enough of war."

Refuting an insinuation by the *Cattaraugus Union* that the Union troops had fallen back from Thoroughfare Gap to their Fairfax camps in disorder, Alanson stated, "Such is not the fact. We were not on the retreat by any means, and certainly had no motive to hurry. We marched back in first rate order." He added, "This regiment has not felt a *panic* yet, and until greater danger approaches than anything yet seen you may safely depend it will not."

In contrast to the 154th's steadfastness, Alanson cited the response of civilians back home to the threat of conscription into the army. He mocked "the three or four thousand lame-backed, sore-livered, squint-eyed, bad-kidneyed, broken legged patriots, whose dreadful maladies were produced by sudden exposure to the draft" in Cattaraugus County. "The boys in the army laugh at the poor fellows' trepidation." While civilians cowered at the prospect of serving their country, seventeen members of the 154th had perished since arriving in Virginia. At the front, Alanson declared, "These cold winter evenings make us frequently think of home but we indulge in no vain desires to be there." And yet, he admitted, "Occasionally a wish is expressed by some homesick boy, that he might have one more nice sleigh ride with the 'girl he left behind him.'"

His former law teacher, Colonel Patrick Jones, was in command of the regiment, Alanson reported, "and universally liked by officers and men." Not surprisingly, Crosby was among several officers recommended by Jones to the adjutant general of New York State for promotion. Commissioned a first lieutenant on March 17, 1863, he was mustered in at that rank in Company D on April 4.

"I have got me a young 'contraband' to do cooking and general housework," Alanson wrote in closing his letter, using the term applied by the Yankees to escaped slaves. "He is a bright boy, 10 years old. I captured him when on picket one day, and find him to be a valuable prize." That said, Alanson forfeited the opportunity to address the controversial topics of African American slavery and emancipation. How long the youngster remained in Crosby's employ is unknown—Alanson never referred to him again.[9]

"Since I last wrote you, another year has passed away, leaving a sad record of private griefs and national disasters," Lieutenant Crosby began his next letter to the *Freeman* on March 9, 1863, from the regiment's camp near Stafford Court House. Pondering the progress of the war to date, he noted that the spirit of the Northern people had wavered between extremes of joy and despair in response to events. As the conflict entered its third year, "it is difficult to determine what progress has been made, or whether in fact any permanent success has crowned the Union arms."

The failure of the Federal cause, he felt, could not be blamed on the soldiers. "Their dauntless courage, heroic valor, patient suffering, and cheerful obedience to the harshest precepts of military law," he declared, "have covered them with immortal glory on every battlefield from Maryland to Texas. *Their* fame, at least, is secure."

But the Northern people questioned the lack of success, and wondered who was responsible. The North was superior in population, wealth, and power—why could she not speedily crush the weak and impoverished South? Alanson cited three reasons. First, the government had failed to demonstrate a "wise, consistent, and *determined purpose*" in its conduct of the war. Second, the Lincoln administration's repeated changes of commanders of the Army of the Potomac "has, in my humble judgment, done more to demoralize the army than all the rebels in Secessia ever could do." Ironically, Alanson recommended another change to resolve the situation—reinstate Major General George B. McClellan to command. No matter that McClellan had twice commanded the army, and twice disappointed Lincoln. "There is no disguising the fact," Alanson wrote. McClellan "is the idol of the Army of the Potomac," and his return to command would generate such enthusiastic joy among the soldiers "as would make traitors quake and turn pale with consternation."

Despite McClellan's absence, Alanson hastened to add, "the army is far from the state of demoralization, which some of the persistent penny-a-liners would have the people believe." The new commander, Major General Joseph Hooker, was rapidly gaining the confidence of the men. Crosby believed the army's morale was as good as it had been when fresh in the field.

The third problem Alanson pointed out was politicking by Northern newspapers. "They dishearten and disgust the soldiers with their ill-natured bickerings and low partizan abuse," he declared. "Let all political journalists and demagogues remember that there are thousands of brave men in the field, whose different opinions embrace all the various shades of political doctrine, and that when a column of billingsgate is launched from the press at any distinctive political organization, it reaches the army and causes strife and bitterness." Could the brave soldiers not be spared the painful thought, he asked, that "they have left such a despicable constituency at home?"

His discourse completed, Alanson summarized the regiment's movement from Fairfax to Falmouth and its participation in the Mud March. He reported that an inspector from headquarters had complimented the 154th on the best kept camp in the corps. Alanson noted:

> The regiment is rapidly becoming proficient in drill and discipline, and if any fighting is to be done, the boys would be happy to participate. There has not existed so cheerful a spirit among them since we came here as now exists. You may depend on it, they will reflect credit and honor to the counties that sent them here if they have an opportunity. . . . I think the horizon begins to light up a little. The clouds are lifting, and the light beams faintly, feebly, through the thick darkness of our national distress. In the approaching campaign, let wise counsels prevail and skillful generals lead us, and a few short months will behold Treason prone in the dust.[10]

A few short months passed and treason still stood rampant, having once again defeated Union counsels less wise and generals less skilled than those at the command of Robert E. Lee. Eleven days after the 154th New York was shattered at Chancellorsville in early May 1863, Alanson wrote to the *Freeman*. But his letter was brief, merely an introduction to a long list of the regiment's casualties. "By publishing the same," he wrote, "you will, perhaps, relieve the friends of our brave boys from much anxious and painful suspense concerning them. Our casualties are very heavy,"—there were 223 names on his incomplete list—"which cannot be wondered at considering the determined resistance our regiment made to the overwhelming numbers of the enemy that were precipitated upon us. *Every man proved himself a hero!* When old soldiers, that have faced the storm of war on a hundred battlefields, broke and fled from the terrible conflict, our noble fellows stood until surrounded on three sides, and then withdrew under a murderous storm of bullets and shell." Closing his note, he promised, "When I get a little leisure, I will give you a more detailed account."[11]

He never got around to it. Instead, his next letters had an amazing story to tell.

Alanson related his grand adventure in two private letters. Both recipients deemed them worthy of publication in the newspapers. Manley Crosby shared a hurried and concise note from his younger brother with the *Cattaraugus Freeman;* Samuel G. Love, a former major of the 154th New York, turned over a floridly verbose missive to the *Jamestown Journal.* In both, Alanson briefly described the 154th's role at Gettysburg, "the fiercest, bloodiest, most glorious and decisive battle of the war"—how the regiment was sent under fire to confront an overwhelming Confederate force, how it stood "firm as the Pyramids, fighting with the desperation of a forlorn hope, a murderous fire all the time raking them in front and flank," and how only a handful of the men were able to cut their way through the enemy and escape when the regiment was surrounded and forced to surrender after a fierce hand-to-hand melee.

But Alanson's story really began with his capture. He and the other captives were rushed to the rear, over the carnage-strewn battlefield, and spent the next two suspenseful days trying to interpret whether the thunderous sounds of battle signified victory or defeat for their Union comrades. "The intense interest and anxiety experienced by the prisoners during the remainder of that great engagement," he wrote, "can perhaps be imagined, but not described." The Northerners' emotions swung from weeping despair to tearful joy as the fortunes of battle shifted and rumors were contradicted or confirmed. Waking on the morning of July 3, Alanson thought himself in the throes of "a vague and feverish dream" as he contrasted the bucolic countryside, with its white cottages and farmhouses, dewy fields and gardens, and floral-scented air, to "the thousands of wounded soldiers, crippled horses, broken caissons, and dismounted cannon around us."

That morning the captured Union officers and enlisted men were separated, and any communication between the two groups was prohibited. In the afternoon of July 3, the captives heard the distant climax of the battle—the massive Confederate artillery barrage and subsequent doomed infantry attack on the Union center. "It was the most awful, grand, and terrible sublime spectacle I ever witnessed," Alanson asserted. The Union victory secured, that night the prisoners savored a sound, contented sleep.

As Independence Day dawned, the Yankees expressed their joy with rousing renditions of patriotic songs until silenced by a Confederate officer, who restricted their musical performances to hymns. Around noon a thunderstorm drenched the men just as they began their march toward Richmond prisons. Steady rain was still falling when they were herded into a cornfield for the night. Exhausted and hungry—they had received nothing to eat since their capture but what little food they could barter from their guards for pocket knives and other trinkets—they fell asleep on muddy stalks and stubble in the pelting rain.

The march of July 5 carried the prisoners to the summit of the Blue Ridge Mountains at Monterey Springs, Pennsylvania. The following morning they received a ration of flour, which they mixed with water, rolled flat, and baked on stones set in fires. "My experience in the culinary art being quite limited," Alanson wrote, ". . .the result of my effort convinced me that my talent for *brick making* is better than for *bread making*." Flour was all the food the prisoners would receive during their march, except for "a few choice pieces" of beef, "cut from the flanks or behind the horns."

For the next two days the captives marched about thirty-five miles, all the way from Monterey Springs across the Maryland panhandle to Williamsport on the Potomac River, without stopping to eat or rest. They arrived at the river on the afternoon of July 7, baked some flatbread, and fell asleep in a torrential rain. July 8 was consumed in the laborious process of ferrying about 180 captive Union officers across the Potomac in a boat that could hold but 40 at a time. "That night," Alanson noted, "we slept on the 'Sacred Soil' of the Old Dominion, near the river." Unbeknownst to Crosby, that soil was now part of newly minted West Virginia, which had entered the Union as the thirty-fifth state just weeks before.

Until crossing the river, the prisoners had hoped to be rescued by pursuing Union cavalry. "After crossing the Potomac," Alanson wrote, "all hopes of escape were abandoned." On July 9 the men marched until midnight and encamped in an orchard near the banks of a large pond, Big Spring, somewhere between Martinsburg, West Virginia, and Winchester, Virginia.

The morning of July 10 was bright and beautiful, Crosby recalled; the countryside glowed green and fresh after the recent rains. Above his head, birds chirped in the fruit trees, then darted away to skim over Big Spring. Viewing the scene, Alanson was swept by a sudden resolve:

> The happy, exhilarating influence of that morning, and the joyous freedom of the
> birds, as I gazed upon the lovely prospect everywhere around, roused a sudden and

irrepressible desire for liberty, and I determined to attempt an escape from "durance vile," at whatever hazard. The thought of a weary march over the burning roads at that sultry time of year, and imprisonment in a filthy tobacco warehouse, perhaps for months, with nothing but adamantine biscuits for food, strengthened my resolution and stamped it with the seal of fate.

Putting away his half-eaten flatbread, Alanson approached his fellow regimental officers, seeking a partner to join his plan. Only one of them agreed to make the attempt—Alanson's fellow lieutenant in Company D, John Mitchell, "a bold and brave soul," Crosby judged, "as reckless of danger as he is fond of excitement and adventure."

"No time was to be lost," Alanson wrote. The prisoners had finished their breakfast and would soon be on the road. After a quick and quiet discussion, Crosby and Mitchell launched their scheme. Holding their handkerchiefs—which had doubled as flour sacks—at arm's length, the two strolled between two lines of guards toward the pond, clearly indicating they intended to do some laundry. To their right when they reached the water's edge was a steep bank, eight or ten feet high and covered with short, thick bushes and vines.

"The plan was to watch [for] an opportunity when the guard did not see us," Alanson wrote, "and plunge into the thicket and lie concealed until the column moved off." But the nearest guard was too attentive. Precious seconds were slipping away, so Crosby improvised. Sitting on the bank, he engaged the guard in conversation. While the two were talking, Mitchell crawled into the bushes out of sight. But Alanson seemed trapped by his new-found Southern acquaintance.

> I was in a great dilemma how I could get into the thicket also. The order to "fall in" was given, and the guard stepped upon the bank and commenced rolling his blanket. I pulled out my handkerchief and commenced washing it again, and when his eye was withdrawn stealthily crept into the bushes with the Lieutenant. The foliage was very dense, and it was impossible to discover a person unless the leaves were parted. We lay close to the ground in breathless silence, when the sentinel came past our hiding place, at the foot of the bank, looking for us. Fortunately he did not see us and went back. He probably thought we had joined the others while he was rolling his blanket and preparing to march.

The two lay concealed until the dull thumping of the marching column receded in the distance. "You can perhaps imagine our emotions," Alanson wrote, as "the birds came around, twittering and singing so gaily, that we thought perhaps they were congratulating us on our happy deliverance." But more dangers lurked. They could not stand to stay in the thicket until dark, but to reach a distant woods meant exposing themselves to the sight of the nearby turnpike for a distance of almost three hundred yards—and the roadway was filled with enemy ammunition wagons, stragglers, wounded men, and cavalry detachments. They decided to do the unexpected.

> So we crawled out of the bushes and deliberately walked off across the field, expecting every step to hear a challenge to halt or a rebel bullet whistling past us. But no challenge or bullet came, and we succeeded in reaching a fence, over which we climbed, and getting down on the ground, went about fifty rods "snake fashion," until a small hill concealed us from the pike.

They had scarcely stood up and started for the adjacent woods when they saw two Confederate soldiers approaching them on the other side of the fence. They threw themselves on the ground, and the Confederates passed without noticing. After hurrying into the edge of the woods, they sat at the foot of a tree and discussed plans, agreeing to wait until nightfall before moving again. Then they were startled by a sound—two Confederate soldiers had just jumped the fence and were coming in their direction. Even though they were in plain sight, all Crosby and Mitchell could do was sit perfectly still and hope to avoid observation. It worked; the Confederates passed on. Deciding that hiding in bushes was not so bad after all, the escapees crawled under some shrubbery in a fence corner and awaited darkness.

At nightfall, Crosby and Mitchell crept up to the fence and waited for a break in the line of Confederate wagons rumbling down the turnpike. After darting across the road, they set off in a northwesterly direction, using the North Star as their guide. They groped their way through corn and wheat fields, struggled through tangles of brambles and forest undergrowth, and climbed hills and descended into valleys where they crossed streams and swamps. In the middle of the night the tired and hungry men stopped for an hour's nap by a straw stack in a field, sinking into the damp pile and shivering in the cold fog. Refreshed by their rest, they continued on, soon becoming soaked to the skin as they traversed dew-drenched wheatfields.

As dawn lit the eastern sky, the two decided to approach an isolated house along their route to seek some food. After carefully ascertaining that there were no Confederate troops about, they entered the cottage and found an elderly woman and her teenaged daughter. "The daughter was quite handsome and appeared intelligent," Crosby wrote, "so of course our conversation was chiefly with her." The apprehensive women feared that Crosby and Mitchell were Confederate spies on the hunt for conscripts and Unionists. "I have seen rebel officers before [wearing] the Union uniform," the girl declared, "going through the country for the same purpose you are, but you will not find any one here to force into your army." Only when the men displayed letters they had received from the North directed to them as members of the 154th New York did the women relax their guard and admit to being "unconditionally for the Union." The whole family was loyal, the girl professed. "But we have to be very careful with our sentiments here," she added, "for we are the only Union family in the neighborhood, and it would not do for us to talk too much." The women were delighted to serve the Yankees a hearty breakfast and adamantly refused an offer of pay. They showed Crosby a map, and he sketched an escape route in his pocket diary. The women then stuffed the officers' pockets with provisions, filled a canteen with milk, and sent them on their way with fervent best wishes for success.

Fog still clung to the valley as the fugitives clambered up a rocky mountainside. From the flat atop the ridge, they took in the panorama spread below and exulted. They felt free from danger and reckoned that they were only hours away from free soil. Shouting gleefully, the two offered boisterous farewells to Jefferson Davis and the Confederacy and resumed their journey along the summit. But their freewheeling attitude almost doomed them. With their guard down, they suddenly were shocked to see two Confederate soldiers heading their way. They dove behind some large rocks and hid. The Confederates passed by, almost over their heads, but continued on.

Descending the slope toward the little village of Hedgesville, West Virginia, Crosby and Mitchell heard the voices of children at play. Creeping cautiously, they discovered four small boys, two white and two black. The Yankees approached the youngsters and asked if there were any soldiers in the village. "Oh, yes sir, right smart of them," a boy replied. "Are they Rebel or Union soldiers?" "Rebels, sir." Further questioning revealed that enemy cavalry pickets surrounded the village—and one was just below them, at the foot of the mountain. Once again, Crosby and Mitchell had escaped a close call. "We begun to think that perhaps Providence was not entirely neutral in the matter," Crosby reflected. "Had it not been for those children our northward journey would have terminated at Hedgesville."

There was nothing to do but reclimb the mountain. On reaching the summit they held a brief conference and decided to make a wide detour around the village and strike the Potomac farther upstream. For the rest of the day they traveled over ridges and across ravines. They were following the crest of a lofty mountain at about sunset when they came to a sudden halt. Below them tumbled the Potomac.

Dripping wet and naked but for their rings after their perilous crossing of the river, Alanson Crosby and John Mitchell spied a black man cutting wheat in a nearby field. They shouted to him to get them some clothes. He looked at the two for a moment and ambled off toward a house on a hilltop. Supposing he would soon return with some garb, Crosby and Mitchell lay down on a patch of grass to wait.

A long time passed. Finally, the black laborer and several white men rode up to the two officers. In response to their request for clothing, an elderly man, who seemed to be the leader of the group, responded forcefully. They would not be furnished with any clothes, he declared; they did not deserve any. They were "infernal rebels" who had crossed the river to rob, steal, and plunder, and it was a wonder and a pity that they had not drowned in the Potomac. He ended his diatribe by ordering the two to get up and go with him to the headquarters of Union colonel James A. Mulligan, some three miles away at Clear Spring, where he hoped justice would be swiftly meted out to them.

As anxious as Crosby and Mitchell were to reach Union lines, they expressed one reservation: "We had some doubts about our toilet being exactly *a la mode* for a visit." Angered by their disobedience, the old man tried to trample them with his horse. The officers defended themselves with stones and the confrontation quickly sputtered out. As tempers cooled, Crosby and Mitchell, realizing they were dealing with a Union man, revealed their identities. The change in the old man's attitude was immediate and dramatic. "If his rage had been terrible a few minutes before," Crosby wrote, "his surprise and chagrin was now unbounded." With tears in his eyes he apologized profusely for his behavior and ordered his associates to fetch some clothes. Soon Crosby and Mitchell were clad in old shirts and patched blue overalls and mounted behind a couple of the horsemen for the ride to the old man's house.

Their host informed them they must spend the night, that the Confederate army was still on the Maryland side of the river about ten miles below, and that enemy scouting and foraging parties were prowling in the vicinity. If any came, he would pass the two off as his sons. Crosby and Mitchell gladly accepted the invitation. "We were perfectly at ease," Crosby noted, "for looking as we did nobody would have dreamed that we had seen an army in our lives."

The next morning their haberdasher provided them with chip hats "that looked as if they had descended to that family from an antique ancestry." Mitchell received "a pair of old shoes that seemed to be laughing at their own ludicrous appearance," Crosby wrote, "and my feet were graced, *one* with an old canvas gaiter, and *the other* an old boot with the leg cut off." Shortly thereafter, the two were presented to Colonel Mulligan as alleged Union officers. The suspicious colonel questioned them closely until convinced of their true identities. After a hearty laugh at their unsoldierly appearance, Mulligan hospitably invited them to share dinner around a large, flat rock by the roadside.

With a pass from the colonel in hand, the next morning Crosby and Mitchell set out for their regiment. They had to circumnavigate the Confederate army, and the journey consequently took them two and a half days and carried them as far north as the Pennsylvania line. They rejoined the 154th New York on July 15 at Hagerstown, Maryland. "Our appearance among our old comrades occasioned the greatest surprise and merriment," Crosby wrote. "The hardships and fatigues we had endured, and the clothes we wore rendered our appearance more like ragged and half starved rebels than Union officers." [12]

After his escape adventure, Alanson's public pen went silent. No longer did he describe his experiences at the front in letters to the newspapers. One contributing factor may have been a lack of time brought about by expanded duties. A second and more immediate reason was that he soon had a lengthy hiatus away from the regiment.

The day after his return to the 154th New York, Crosby was mustered in as first lieutenant and adjutant, to date from July 1; he had been commissioned as such on June 12. As adjutant, Alanson was the chief assistant to the regimental commander and in charge of much of the regiment's business, particularly correspondence—which might have left him little time or inclination for writing on the side. His promotion to the 154th's field and staff officer corps took him away from the men of his company, who regretted the separation. A note in the *Cattaraugus Freeman* observed that Crosby "was a great favorite with the company to which he belonged, and the boys disliked to have him leave them under any consideration. After his promotion, therefore, his old comrades arrested him for desertion, tried him by a court-martial, convicted and sentenced him to be shot! He was subsequently pardoned, after being very gravely lectured upon the enormity of his offence!" [13]

A week after his promotion and mock trial, a special order detailed Adjutant Crosby, together with two other officers and six enlisted men of the 154th, to proceed to New York State to take charge of drafted men in rendezvous at Elmira. The detail left camp on July 24, 1863. Alanson spent the next nine months in the war's backwater, overseeing recruiting, guarding draftees in Elmira, and accompanying new troops to the front. It was soft service, perhaps given in reward for his recent hardships. During the posting he made several visits to friends in Ellicottville; the local newspapers described him as "a good officer and a capital fellow" who was "looking well and hearty." His detached service over at last,

Crosby left Ellicottville for the front on April 18, 1864. The *Freeman* opined, "The lieutenant is a brave and dashing officer, and will give a good account of himself."[14]

He arrived at the 154th's camp in Lookout Valley, Tennessee, on April 28, and six days later the regiment embarked on the Atlanta campaign. As the almost incessant marching, skirmishing, and entrenching—and the occasional pitched battle—unfolded in north Georgia, Alanson again trod in the vicinity of death. But he survived the fights at Rocky Face Ridge, Resaca, and New Hope Church. Along the way, he was involved in an incident remembered by some of the men as a macabre joke. When darkness ended one of the fights, the weary soldiers dropped to the ground and fell asleep. That night orders were received to build breastworks in front of their position at once. Adjutant Crosby went along the line waking the officers and men, often being cursed for his efforts. One soldier, ignoring several calls, refused to budge. Suspecting he was feigning slumber to avoid the coming labor, Alanson grabbed him and gave him a vigorous shake. The fellow remained inert. Alanson then seized him by the shoulder, flipped him over, and was stunned to find him a corpse, a victim of the battle.[15]

As the campaign continued, Alanson received another promotion. His commission as captain was dated May 18, 1864; he was mustered in as such with Company D on June 9. Six days later, the 154th New York was deployed as skirmishers to cover the brigade front and drove the enemy from Gilgal Church, midway between Pine Mountain and Lost Mountain, through rugged woods for about a mile, to the vicinity of Mud Creek. Despite the loss of twenty-one men killed or wounded, it was a heady victory for the regiment. Savoring the moment, the exultant men cheered and growled like tigers as they chased the rebels. Once again, Captain Crosby survived the battle.

That night the men piled logs, gathered brush, and dug dirt to build entrenchments. On the morning of June 16 the regiment was ordered from the protection of its breastworks into the second line, where it was exposed to enemy infantry and artillery fire from the crest of a ridge. Until they could dig in, all the men could do was hug the ground and hope they would not be hit.

Laying low, Corporal Samuel Hogg of Company H huddled with his back resting against Alanson's side. When the captain asked him for tobacco, Hogg cut a slice from his navy plug. As Alanson filled and lit his pipe, Hogg began to crawl away downhill. Suddenly the corporal heard the sickening sound of a bullet hitting flesh and bone and a groan from Alanson. For the rest of his life, Hogg wondered whether his movement had triggered the enemy shot.[16]

Private Emory Sweetland of Company B, an attendant in the regimental hospital, was cautiously approaching the 154th's line when he saw Alanson raise himself up on an arm and convulse, crying, "Oh my God, I'm hit!" Sweetland rushed to the captain, tore open his vest, and found a bullet hole, clotted with blood, on the left side of his chest. The shot had broken his fourth and fifth ribs. Sweetland and Assistant Surgeon Corydon C. Rugg rolled Alanson onto a gum blanket and carried him to the rear—a movement that attracted more Confederate fire. Many of the shots whizzed overhead; others pierced the blanket and Sweetland's and Rugg's uniforms. But the medical men delivered Alanson to an ambulance without further harm.[17]

As suddenly as that, Alanson Crosby was gone from the regiment—no longer a physical presence, now a memory and a statistic. His comrades knew his wound was severe, but thought he would survive. Colonel Patrick Jones, in reporting the regiment's casualties in a letter to the *Cattaraugus Freeman,* wrote, "Capt. Crosby, it is said, will recover. He needs care and some courage and all will come out right." After treatment at the division hospital, Crosby and other wounded members of the regiment were sent by rail to Chattanooga. On June 18, as the train stopped at Resaca, Georgia, Private Stephen R. Green of Company E, on duty there, went through the cars to see his comrades. "His ribs was broken; rather a bad wound," Green reported of Crosby, "but not dangerous I think."[18]

Captain Commodore Perry Vedder of Company H visited Alanson in the hospital at Chattanooga. "Never can I cease to remember the sad scenes of that day of parting," Vedder later wrote to Crosby's brother, Manley. In flowery, sentimental, and spiritual terms, Vedder portrayed Alanson as a soon-to-be martyred hero.

When I went into the room where he lay, he was in a calm and gentle slumber. I sat down upon the foot of his bed and silently looked upon his features, so pale, yet so serenely beautiful. Oh, I wish you could have seen him then. He seemed to be dreaming of happy days departed, or of some that dwelt in future hope. Smiles of sweetest radiance played upon his countenance, as if the spirit of innocence was moving upon the surface of his untroubled soul. This, I thought, is a dream of immortality, and I wept like a child. When he awoke he took my hand in his, and said: "Com, I cannot live, I am going to die." I endeavored to make him forget the sad thought, but it clung to him with the power of revelation. He talked to me of the joys of his childhood hours—the happy days he had passed with his sister and you—of father and mother, and of friends and companions. He was very weak, and every few moments would close his eyes and breathe more softly, and act as if communing with himself. He would awake again from this peculiar slumber, with his spirit invigorated and lightened, seemingly by its contact with holy things in its contemplative flight to the great Unknown.

I remained with him a long time, and the last words I ever heard him speak were words of loftiest cheer. "I believe my country is right, and I deem it glorious to die in her cause." This he said in a low tone, his eyes earnestly resting upon the blue, unclouded sky, beyond which his mind already beheld the glorious Infinitude.[19]

"I hear that Crosby has been sent to Nashville," Sergeant Horace Smith of Company D recorded in his diary at a distribution camp in Chattanooga on June 30. In Nashville, Alanson lingered for little more than a week. On July 9 he succumbed at Officers Hospital to "traumatic pneumonia" resulting from his gunshot wound. None of his regimental comrades were present to comfort him or record his last moments.[20]

News of Crosby's death reached the 154th New York on July 15. "Another officer gone," Major Lewis D. Warner lamented in his diary, "who a short month since was in full health and expecting long life." In a letter written for newspaper publication later that month, Warner presented a formal eulogy for the fallen captain:

He was a young man of very prepossessing manners and appearance, of good moral character and of fine mental qualities, an ornament to society as well as to his profession (that of a lawyer). The announcement of his death, coming unexpectedly as it did, has cast a gloom over the regiment with which he has so long been connected, to the members of which he had become endeared by his many excellent qualities, as a soldier, companion, and friend. I feel that I can say for his late companions in arms that they sympathize with his family and friends at home in their bereavement, and would add this testimony as to the worth of the departed, while they drop a tear over his grave.[21]

As the word spread, other tributes were offered. "Poor Crosby is dead, another victim to this rebellion," Horace Smith commented privately in his diary. "His name and memory will long be cherished with reverence and respect by all his comrades in the army, both officers and privates, for he was a friend to all." Colonel Patrick Jones eulogized Crosby as a "brave and gallant soldier, a bright lawyer, and a young man of great promise." Commodore Vedder penned an homage in his letter to Manley Crosby:

Alanson's death fills me with more than common sorrow. In the peaceful walks of life we were friends and associates, and I ever found him generous and high-minded. Since we were soldiers, mutual hardships and dangers bound us firmly together by that eternal chord of friendship and attachment known only to the brotherhood of arms. Mine, outside of his circle of relatives, is not an individual grief. From the heart of Georgia a voice of sadness comes, and wherever a member of the 154th New York is found, there is unmingled woe.

In the smoke and flame of battle he never paled, but was always in the front, where his fiery and heroic spirit inspired the souls and nerved the arms of all to strike for God and Freedom. I might give you examples of his calmness and daring in battle, but no words of mine can add luster to his honored, glorious and imperishable name.

Bury him where the sunshine at eventide may play upon his grave, for his life was pure; plant flowers upon his grave, for his death was gentle.[22]

Public encomiums appeared in newspapers in the weeks after Alanson's death. "Capt. Crosby was a lawyer by profession, a young man of much promise, of fine culture, excellent abilities and pleasing address," an anonymous eulogist declared in the *Cattaraugus Freeman*. "Thus at the early age of 27 years another of our most gifted and beloved young men has laid down his life upon the altar of his country. To his aged parents, and to his other relatives and numerous friends, we tender the assurance of our heartfelt sympathy in their sad and painful bereavement." Members of Ellicottville's bar met to pass solemn resolutions of sympathy to the Crosby family and of tribute to their departed colleague, requesting the village newspapers to publish the same:

Resolved, That as a friend, kind, noble, generous, of high hopes, and, as a member of the bar, of unblemished integrity and ambitious of distinction, we mourn and lament his sudden death; and while we mourn, we will ever bear in remembrance his purity and dignity of character, his social and intellectual accomplishments, his noble patriotism, and his unflinching bravery. That, although a man of peace, educated to our profession, and loving its pursuits wherein distinction awaited him, he left all behind, and at the call of his imperiled and bleeding country he bounded to the front with sword in hand to do battle against her traitorous foes. Great and noble in actions as well as thoughts, his death grand and glorious—he sleeps in a patriot soldier's grave—his deeds and virtues a proud monument for all time.[23]

By proclamation of President Abraham Lincoln, Thursday, August 4, 1864, was appointed as a day of national humiliation and prayer. The president requested the people of the United States to assemble at their preferred places of public worship to confess and repent their sins and to beseech the Almighty to suppress the rebellion, to preserve them as a united people, to grant them and their armed defenders courage and endurance, and to soften the hearts and enlighten the minds of the rebels that the war might end before their own utter destruction.[24]

On the appointed day, an anonymous writer penned a woeful letter to the *Cattaraugus Freeman* from New Haven, Connecticut. The previous day a newspaper had informed this old friend of Alanson Crosby's death. "And ever since," he wrote,

> a great silence has fallen on my soul, wherein I walk as in a dream. Yet, through it all, a sound, nay, no sound, but rather silence audible, has haunted me unceasingly, like a faint, far-off echo of the words: "I have seen the end of all perfection!" Last night it would not let me sleep; faint and far off it seemed indeed, yet it was more distinct than the fitful wind or the fast-falling rain: today it has come back with me into the busy world, and makes itself heard above all the din of city life. Shall I break the spell? Shall I banish this ghostly echo by writing of it here?

For this mourner, warm memories of Alanson spawned bitterness toward the agents of his death.

> How plainly I see him as I saw him last, in all the glow and pride of youth, of brilliant talents, of superb, surpassing beauty! His splendid eyes, blue and quiet in repose, but black, deep, blazing, in the excitement of conversation, shine now with all their wonted cordial brightness. I hear his musical voice, his merry laugh—how can I think of him and death together! Can it be true? I listen, and again that dreary monotone fills the strange silence in my soul. Yes! I have seen an end to all perfection. Dead—dead,—Another of our best and bravest gone to heap the hetacomb to the foul demon Slavery! Another victim to this accursed rebellion! How long, oh Lord, how long, shall thine enemies triumph over the desolation they have wrought!

The eulogist noted Alanson's popularity in the 154th New York:

> I was not surprised . . . to learn how swiftly and surely he had endeared himself to his entire regiment—how he was the chosen friend and ally of every private; how, if a favor was wanted by any of the men, Lieutenant Crosby's influence was sought, and never sought in vain; how he adjusted their difficulties, wrote their letters, was, in a hundred nameless ways, always at their service, and how every soldier of them would have laid down his life for "the Lieutenant."

Contemplating the loss, the mourner was again consumed by anger. "It seems to me that the entire North, when it sees its bravest and most beautiful thus consumed, must awake to the same fierce hatred of the rebellion and its guilty cause." His bitterness vented, Alanson's friend closed by proposing a toast:

> Come, pledge me in a glass of pure cold water—fit beverage for a Fast Day, and for all days—let us drink, standing and in solemn silence: "Immortal honor to our

Fallen Brave—success to the cause of Truth and Freedom—death and eternal infamy to the rebellion and to rebels—and confusion, shame, and equal infamy to all
their sympathizers at the North."[25]

Beneath the mourner's letter, the *Freeman* ran the latest list of casualties from
the 154th New York. The war was grinding on. After he expired, thirty-five of his
regimental comrades—and tens of thousands of more men, Union and Confederate alike—would join Alanson Crosby in death before it would end.

CHAPTER SIX

Captain John C. Griswold

Company F

A couple of miles outside of the Chautauqua County village of Cassadaga, in a triangle formed by County Route 72 and the Tarbox and Shumla roads in the township of Arkwright, I found the graveyard sitting on flat land, ringed by mature maples and surrounded by cornfields. A hoop-topped iron fence rose from bunches of daylilies to enclose the small plot. A wooden sign above the gate identified the place as Christian Cemetery. Atop the sign two American flags stirred in a slight breeze.

On this bright day, lilacs and other shrubs cast islands of shade on the newly mown lawn. In the shadow of one of the bushes, I found the two stones I sought. According to the inscriptions cut into their polished faces, the matching granite wedges marked the resting places of a husband and wife. A flag marked him as a soldier; the script identified him as a Civil War officer.

The inscriptions, simple lines on silent stones, gave no hint of the agonies the couple suffered during the war.

Spring took a winter-like turn in Chautauqua County during the first week of May 1863. For two weeks local farmers had sowed wheat during fine weather, but then the temperature plunged and a steady cold rain fell for three days, with a bit of snow mixed in. The sky was beginning to clear on May 7 when Mrs. Susan Griswold wrote to her husband, John, serving as first lieutenant of Company F,

154th New York, in distant Virginia. Fighting a pounding headache—she had been sewing steadily during the rainy week—she let her emotions spill:

> [I] feel quite down for a few days, not hearing anything from you for so long and expecting you are in battle, that I have cried my eyes almost out of my head. . . . It has become almost second nature for me to cry; but being around amongst folks so much, I have to put a double command over my feelings. If I should give way to my feelings, I do not know what would become of me. . . . Oh, how we do want you to come home; but what will we do if anything should happen that you should not come? Oh, my heart sinks within me to think of it. . . . May God bless you and spare you to return to your wife and child once more. . . . Do write as soon as you can. I have not said half [of what] I would like to say to you, for I cannot tell you my feelings with the pen. . . . I send you my love once more and a kiss.[1]

The very next evening, Susan Griswold received shocking, horrible news. Her dread had become reality. In a list of the 154th's casualties in the recent battle of Chancellorsville, published the previous day by the *New York Herald,* John was reported killed. A few days later a local newspaper, the *Fredonia Censor,* published an obituary:

> Death of Lieut. John C. Griswold.
> In the list of killed in the late bloody battle at [Chancellorsville], we are pained to notice the name of 1st Lieut. John C. Griswold, of Co. F, 154th N.Y.V. Lieut. Griswold was an old resident of the town of Arkwright, in which he had held important positions as a town officer, having been for many years a Justice of the Peace, and three times elected Supervisor, which position he held at the time of entering the service of his country. He was an upright and worthy citizen, and his death will be deeply felt in the community where he lived. His age was about 42. He leaves a family to mourn his loss.[2]

Crushed and heartbroken, Susan dropped into the abyss of grief. She repeatedly called on God to take her, too. It seemed that she could not go on living. It would be sweet to find rest in the grave, she thought, until another consideration struck her: "The Lord put it into my heart," she wrote, "that I must live for the sake of my child." But she could not describe the agony of mind she suffered at the loss of her beloved husband. No words could tell it.[3]

John Cowles Griswold, age twenty-four, and Susan Briggs, age seventeen, had been married in Chautauqua County on January 11, 1844. Both of them had come to the county from elsewhere. Susan was born in Wayne County, Ohio, on October 6, 1826; the Briggs family moved to Chautauqua when she was a young girl. A youthful religious epiphany made her a devout and active member of the Arkwright Christian Church. By Susan's adult years, a large circle of friends and acquaintances held her in high regard for her integrity, her kindness, even for her friendly admonitions and gentle rebukes.[4]

John was born in Sangerfield, Oneida County, New York, on August 1, 1819, the eleventh of twelve children of Seth and Zerviah (Cowles) Griswold. He lost his father at age three. Ten years later, Zerviah brought John and nine of his brothers and sisters to Chautauqua County. The family settled on a lot in Arkwright and cleared a farmstead from the forest. Mother Griswold spent the remaining twenty-six years of her life there; John was the only son who always remained near the pioneer home.

He attended district schools in Arkwright, serving as a trustee during one of his terms. At age eighteen he was captain of a company in the New York State Militia's 169th Regiment, a precursor of his later role in the Civil War. He and Susan had two sons; Cassius M. was born in 1845, and DeWitt C. in 1850. By the outbreak of the war, only Cassius survived; DeWitt had died at age ten. Neighbors regarded John as "a remarkably quiet and peaceable man," whose "whole influence in town was that of a peacemaker." His townsmen elected him as their justice of the peace and their representative on the Chautauqua County Board of Supervisors.[5]

Neighbors also knew John Griswold as "intensely patriotic." When the 154th New York was organized in the summer of 1862, he took an active role in the recruitment drive. At a war meeting in Arkwright on August 29 he enrolled a dozen volunteers; he eventually added another four, for a total of sixteen of Company F's eighty-four enlisted men.[6]

By the time the regiment left for the front, John Griswold realized he now had two families to care for. Susan and sixteen-year-old Cassius would depend on his soldier's pay and advice from afar, but would otherwise be left on their own to get along with their lives. Company F, on the other hand, would require constant, in-person supervision, support, discipline, and counsel—and there were more than eighty of "the boys" to look after. And it quickly became obvious that Lieutenant Griswold, rather than the company's two other commissioned officers, would be the father to those boys.

Thomas Donnelly had enrolled thirty-six of Company F's recruits and was rewarded with the commission as captain. He proved to be a misfit as a leader, and soon lost the men's respect when he revealed himself to be ignorant of military matters and a drunkard to boot. Second Lieutenant Henry W. Myers also proved to be a dud—he would be the first officer of the regiment to submit his resignation, within a month after the 154th reached Virginia.

It was to Lieutenant Griswold that Company F looked for leadership. He inspired trust, confidence, and affection in the boys, who turned to him for guidance through the thickets of army life. Acting in loco parentis to four score men far from home, John Griswold devoted himself to the company.

That devotion soon became obvious to Susan Griswold. John's letters to her were full of news about the Company F boys, which he expected her to pass along to their family members. News of company doings also reached Susan and Cassius from relatives and friends among the soldiers. Acting as a conduit of information between the front and home, and finding much in John's letters about the men of Company F but little to help her with her own difficulties, Susan came to begrudge the hold John's surrogate family had on him. She came to realize that the bonds of esprit de corps tied John to his boys in a special fashion, in some ways eclipsing his ties to home.

While the men of Company F were drawn together by the vortex of war, the home folk remained distant observers—unable, many of the soldiers felt, to ever truly understand what they were going through at the front. In his letters to Susan and Cassius, John tried his best to bridge that gap by conveying to his old family a sense of his new family.

Adjusting to army life presented Company F with challenges. "Myself and the rest of the boys are all well and in good spirits," John informed Susan during the railroad journey from western New York to the Virginia front, but homesickness already undermined their confidence and excitement. "A shade of sadness could be seen overshadowing the countenances" of the boys, John observed, "a sure indication that the thoughts of home and loved ones were crowding on the mind." After an unpleasant ride of two days in crowded freight and cattle cars and a wearying march from the Washington depot, they spent their first night on Arlington Heights without shelter. In the darkness some of the men drank tainted water and soon fell sick. "The boys begin to think that soldiering is not all fun," John noted, "and if they were home they might [chance the] draft and be d——d." He relayed a special message to Cassius from the boy's friend, Private Homer Adelbert "Dell" Ames: "If you have any idea of enlisting you had better get rid of it as soon as possible."[7]

Griswold himself briefly became ill at Camp Seward, suffering "a violent attack of the camp sickness which is prevailing to a considerable extent among the soldiers." The company rallied to its stricken lieutenant. "The night I was sick, the boys took some hay from the teams belonging to our regiment and put [it] into our beds which made it very comfortable," John reported, adding, "I think the boys will take good care of me when necessary." During the regiment's first lengthy march, from Arlington to Fairfax Court House, John "bunked in with some of the boys" during a rain-swept night that left some of the men drenched. He worried about two sick men who had been left behind, wondering whether they had communicated with their families. One of them had lost a pair of drawers and needed a change; John "let him have a pair of mine trusting luck to get another pair." The other men were generally well except for occasional attacks of diarrhea. "They are in tolerable good spirits, but most of them think that if they were out of this they could not be caught again," John wrote. They particularly disliked cooking for themselves and sleeping in open tents on frosty autumn nights. "But they will probably get used to it and like it better by and by."[8]

Days later a torrential rainstorm struck. "The boys are complaining, grumbling, swearing, etc. about their tents," John wrote, "and not without just cause, for they are miserable things in cold or storm." But the discomfort, Griswold judged, "is only a foretaste of what we may expect [during] the coming winter." Thoughts continued to turn homeward. "We would all of us like to be in old Chautauqua a day or two to go to a few neighborhood pairing bees and eat apples [and] pumpkin pies and drink cider and grow fat." Homesickness was sometimes tinged with fatalism. "We think of the friends we have left behind," wrote Private Henry A. Munger to Cassius Griswold, "and I do not know but we have left them forever, but I hope not." He added that Cassius's father "is well and seems to enjoy camp life middling well."[9]

At the Fairfax camp, John engaged in a familiar ritual: he had his photograph taken to send home to his family. In front of a painted backdrop of tents, a cannon, and a flag, he struck a grim-faced pose for an ambrotypist. As he stood stiffly for the long exposure he proudly wore a new sword, a gift from the boys of Company F.[10]

In response to Susan's letters, John reported himself very glad to hear that her health was good and she was "so smart and riding about the country." He urged her to "be careful of yourself and not run too much risk" and to "keep up good courage and enjoy yourself as well as you can." But his references to her and home were fleeting. Instead, his letters were dense with details about the company and its activities. Particular emphasis was given to the sick.[11]

Company F left thirteen sick men at Fairfax Court House when the regiment marched to Thoroughfare Gap in November 1862, among them Henry Munger and his brother Austin. During the stay at the gap, Lieutenant Griswold received permission to return to Fairfax to look after the patients. He found Henry Munger and four other men huddled by the fireplace in an upstairs room of an old house. "I got them into a more comfortable room in a building used for a hospital," he reported, "where they could have better medical attention."

Then he traveled to the Alexandria hospital where the rest of the men were being treated. There he received a shock—Austin Munger was dead, a victim of typhoid fever and erysipelas. "My feelings at this announcement I cannot describe," John informed Susan. "[It was] so unlooked for and unexpected, as the last time I saw him he thought himself and I supposed him to be gaining." Susan shared John's letter with two Fredonia newspapers, both of which published an excerpt as a "Tribute to a Deceased Soldier":

> Austin is no more. His moral worth and integrity at home were known by all his acquaintances there. In camp, his virtues lost none of their purity or steadfastness. His quiet and gentlemanly deportment, his unobtrusive and peaceful manners, his cheerful performance of the duties of a soldier, secured to him the good will and friendship of both officers and men. He is the first victim in our Company in the cause of our Country. Why should it be one of its best members?[12]

"To carry the news to Henry is a burden I would gladly avoid but cannot," John confessed to Susan. He described the scene on his return to Fairfax. "The news of Austin's death fell with crushing weight upon Henry. The first burst of grief and afterwards his silent sorrow is sad to behold." Henry himself suffered from camp fever and rheumatism, but his prognosis was good. Others were less fortunate. Griswold was soon swamped with sick men when he was ordered to look after a number of them sent by the division from Thoroughfare Gap, including fifteen from the 154th New York. He found them in a church at Fairfax Station, with nothing to eat but hardtack. He obtained some soft bread, coffee, and sugar from the post commissary, spent the night with the men, and conveyed them the next day to a military hospital. "So you see they are getting sick pretty fast," John informed Susan after listing Company F's patients. "I have had a tour of it and hope I shall not have another." He commented to Cassius, "I have seen so much of sickness the last week that I am tired of hearing the word 'sick.'"[13]

But his hospital visits and reports of the sick continued. On November 27, Thanksgiving Day, he looked in on the Company F boys and made arrangements to have Henry Munger, whose condition had not improved, transferred into better quarters where he could receive better care. There was another death to report: Private Oscar W. Brown, "a noble boy, respected by all," had succumbed to typhoid fever at a Washington hospital. While much of John's holiday letter concerned the hospitalized men, some of his thoughts turned homeward. "How I should like to have been with you today and enjoyed a good Thanksgiving dinner," he told Susan; he had dined on bread and sugar. He was pleased to learn that a woman friend was staying with his wife. "I wish my stockings were at home a day or so," he wrote, "as there is some awful holes in the heels." He also wished he could be home to help Cassius put up firewood for the winter.[14]

A busy month passed before John had the opportunity to write again. The 154th marched for a week through snow and mud from Fairfax to Falmouth. The regimental wagons, carrying his trunk and writing materials, lagged behind. When they finally arrived at the new Falmouth camp, extreme cold prevented him from writing. At last, with a fireplace in his tent to warm his fingers, he wrote a long letter to Cassius. In describing the march, he mentioned he had carried the musket and knapsack of Private William D. Harper, who was unwell, in addition to his own traps. After his writing was interrupted by a flurry of duties—drills, an inspection, a picket tour, filling out a muster roll—he reported that he was still wearing his tattered socks: "I am going to make a bee some evening and mend them up if I don't get sick of it." He asked his wife to send him a cravat lengthy enough to wrap a couple of times around his neck for warmth.[15]

At the Falmouth camp, Lieutenant Griswold's perspective broadened beyond the company and regiment. For the first time, the 154th New York was in the presence of the enemy. The Confederate army's camps and fortifications were in plain view across the Rappahannock River, and pickets from the two sides fraternized along the riverbanks. The recent Union defeat in the Battle of Fredericksburg, "which resulted so disastrously to our cause," Griswold noted, ". . . has dampened the spirits in the army." Morale was so bad, he wrote, that "we found the soldiers in a condition bordering on insubordination. Some regiments went so far as to declare that they would never go into another fight with the rebels, that there was no use in trying any more for we could never subdue them by force, that it was nothing but a damned nigger war [referring to the new policy of emancipation], and that the sooner it was settled on some terms the better."

Political issues compounded the malaise. "While the two armies are gunning at each other across the river," John observed, "our generals and cabinet, with the help of congress and political demagogues, are having a hand to hand fight at Washington in the shape of court martials, cabinet making, and quarreling over this and that policy of conducting the war, and thus losing advantage of the best weather I ever saw for military operations." These factors, combined with "the extremely divided sentiment of the people at the North, created a feeling of despondency in the minds of the soldiers that was truly gloomy and discouraging."[16]

Political commentary, however, remained a rarity in Griswold's letters. His focus continued to center on Company F. Several moves of their winter camp caused "much swearing" among the men. "The indications are that we shall stay here a few days," John wrote after the 154th arrived near Stafford Court House in February 1863, "probably just long enough to get fixed up to be comfortable, and then leave for parts unknown. . . . We have built cabins three times this winter and are going to work at it again." He was sick, having caught a cold while marching through the rain, sleeping on the ground, and over-exerting himself in building his hut. But the surgeon prescribed some powders and a dose of hot pepper tea at bedtime, which broke his fever and cured him. "The boys are generally well and in good spirits," he reported, but sickness still sent some to the hospital. "If they had got up a little gumption and stayed with the company and not got so awful homesick," John thought, they would have stayed well.[17]

Snug in their newly built cabins, the men ignored the rain and snow and mud outside (except when they had to stand picket in it), and enjoyed the bounty sent in boxes from home—"all the delicacies and luxuries of the season": dried beef, sausage, pies, cakes, preserves, butter, and cheese. "If a person were to look in at our meals," John thought, "they would suppose we were living at a first class hotel." Savoring these gifts from home "puts one in mind of long evenings passed in the society of the donors of this treat," he declared. "Give my thanks to those who so kindly remembered me in filling this box." He added, "It troubles us some to think of coming down from such fare to hardtack, salt pork, and coffee, but soldiers must learn to accept the good as it comes and make the best of that which is not so agreeable."[18]

John pled guilty when Susan accused him of not writing often enough, but he offered an excuse. "There [are] a hundred things continually arising to hinder one from writing at any time he would wish," he declared, "but I will try to keep even with you if I can." She was considering a springtime trip to Michigan, but health problems gave her pause. "You ask me what you shall do," John wrote. "This is a hard question. But I can tell you what you must not do—that is, doing work that is beyond your strength and endangering your health until it is more thoroughly established. . . . Take your choice as circumstances seem to direct, but do not by any means go to work beyond your strength." This note of solicitude was followed by a request for a new hat, a pair of suspenders, buckskin gloves, and some leather shoe taps, with detailed instructions for packing the items in an iron-hooped box, surrounded by dried apples and doughnuts.[19]

Two weeks later, John indulged in a rare bit of sentimental longing. "Your last letter was truly refreshing," he told Susan. "It seems so natural to take a regular feeling occasionally. If I could only see your eyes, snap! the scene would be life like and exhilarating." When Thomas Donnelly returned to camp a few days later after a ten-day furlough home, he brought the next best thing: Susan's photograph. "Captain Donnelly has just come in," John wrote. "He brings the likeness of a gal that I would like to see. I think she has improved in appearance considerably since I left."[20]

After a separation of six months, the Griswolds sought to reunite, either by John returning home on a furlough or Susan visiting the front. Neither plan proved practical, however. "As to getting a furlough," John wrote, "it will not come our [company's] time for another in some time; and before that we shall probably be on the march and no more can be got. But if I could [come home], I fear you could not make up your mind to let me come back, and then I should be in a fix." Nor was a visit by her to camp to his liking. "As to your coming down here to help me, I don't know what in Tophet I could do with you here," he wrote. "You could not march and keep up, and I have no idea they would let you ride one of the mules, for they are so poor they can hardly carry themselves; so on the whole, I guess you had better stay where you are."

Instead of a reunion, he offered some lighthearted advice:

> As to what you shall do yourself, I don't see as you need to worry yourself about it. If you have a good place to stay, just make yourself at home, eat your rations when dealt out to you, spin street yarn as much as you are able, go a-visiting when you can and wish to, be as lazy as possible, keep as contented and cheerful as you can and not trouble yourself about that which cannot be avoided. Pursue the course thoroughly through the summer and if it does not agree with your system and improve your health, I shall have to prescribe some other course for next winter. . . . So just make up your mind to submit to the rules and regulations of the War Department.[21]

John's next letter was written on the eve of a march. Spring had brought a new campaign season. Their destination was unknown, but the Company F boys correctly speculated that they would move up the Rappahannock River in preparation for a general advance by the army. Four of the men would be left behind sick, John reported, and one—"reduced to a skeleton almost by chronic diarrhea"—was to be discharged. "The rest of the boys are well and in good spirits," John wrote. "It will come rather tough at first to leave our comfortable bunks and camp [and go] out again," he added, "but we hope we shall not have any more very cold weather."[22]

Two days of marching brought the 154th New York and the other regiments of its brigade to Kelly's Ford, "a miserable godforsaken place" in John's opinion.

During the second day's tramp "we were hurried through pretty sharp," he reported, covering eighteen miles and wearing the men out. He set the scene at the ford for Susan:

> Here we are again, on the banks of the Rappahannock, watching the rebs on the opposite side of the river with our battery of three-inch rifled cannon looking defiance at them from a rise of ground on the bank, while in turn they are grinning at us with an equal number of artillery pieces from the opposite side, thus presenting the appearance of two Kilkenny cats with their backs up, ready to pounce upon each other and tear one another's eyes out.

Captain Thomas Donnelly left the company at Kelly's Ford, having submitted his resignation. "The boys of Co. F are glad of it," wrote Private William Charles. Command devolved on Lieutenant Griswold. He and his men chafed at their brigade's isolation at the ford. In a note to Susan on April 26, 1863, John complained, "We cannot communicate with our friends nor hear from them or what is going on in the world outside of our lines, which are very limited in extent, but if the rebs do not nab us soon we shall probably be in a situation to send and receive our mail occasionally. . . . We are all well as usual," he wrote in closing. "We know nothing of what is going on around us therefore have no news to write." Two days later the 154th crossed the Rappahannock and headed to Chancellorsville.[23]

While John's letter was in transit, early and sketchy news of the fighting in Virginia reached Chautauqua County. On May 5, Susan wrote a distraught letter to her husband:

> It is with trembling hand and aching heart that I attempt to write a few lines to you, not knowing whether you ever will receive it or not, expecting you are in a very dangerous place. We hear you are not held as reserve, no, you are in advance, which, it seems to me, [means] you are in more danger than before. But all I can do is to weep and pray for your safety. It seems that the Lord must spare you. Keep up good courage and trust in providence. Put your whole trust in him who is able to save, and be very careful and not run any great risk. If I could share the danger with you, it seems I could stand it better; but I know not. I dare not indulge the thought one moment that you will never come home. I cannot tell you my feelings with the pen. You can better imagine what they are than I can tell you. . . . If you knew how anxious I am to hear from you, you would drop a few lines to me if it was possible; but I do not know as it is when you are on the move. Then is the time I feel the most anxiety about you; to think you are in battle and then not to hear from you. It seems some of the time I cannot endure it.[24]

Three days later came the news of John's death, and Susan's world fell apart.

An agonizing week passed. Then letters began to arrive from Company F. Second Lieutenant Dana P. Horton wrote to Susan on May 11, offering "all of the information I can" regarding John. It was not much, but it offered a glimmer of hope. "He was wounded in the arm and started to leave the field. I see in the papers he is reported killed, but I think he is taken prisoner and not killed, but I do not know for certain." Dell Ames wrote the following day. "Lieut. Griswold is missing," he informed Susan.

> He was wounded in the arm and bled pretty hard. The rebs was so close on to us that we had to run for our sweet lives and I don't know if he got off from the field or not. . . . If he was taken prisoner we may not hear from him in a good while, and if he is in any hospital we will hear of it in a short time, and I will let you know if we hear from him in any way. . . . Lieut. Griswold was thought everything of by the company and he was a good commander as I want over me. He done justice to them all and they all liked him well, and they feel bad not to see him in command of the company. But I am in hopes that he will come out all right yet.[25]

John was alive—perhaps—but the uncertainty of the reports filled Susan anew with anxiety. "It seemed I could not stand it," she wrote. "I thought it would make me sick. Some of the time I was so weak I could hardly walk across the house." But as letters continued to arrive, the situation clarified. "We have just heard from your husband by way of flag of truce," Lieutenant Colonel Henry C. Loomis wrote on May 14. "He is not dead, but severely wounded and a prisoner. We did not learn particulars. He will probably recover." Lieutenant Horton, with "great gratification," wrote again on May 15. "One of my wounded men has been paroled and sent back to our hospital and he says that Lieut. Griswold was wounded in the arm and taken prisoner. He said he stayed with Lieut. Griswold one night and they sent him to Richmond." Former captain Thomas Donnelly wrote from his Chautauqua County home on May 21, "I have just received a letter from Lieut. Col. [Loomis], and Mrs. Young has received a letter from her husband, and both letters speak of Mr. Griswold being wounded and a prisoner in Richmond." Donnelly added, "All looks bright."[26]

John himself dictated a letter to Susan—his wounded arm prevented him from writing—but the missive disappeared into postal limbo between the Confederacy and the United States. Weeks would pass before the letter would leave Richmond for Chautauqua County. It read:

Libby Prison, Richmond, May 22, 1863

Dear Wife,

I am here in the hospital department. I was wounded in the right arm near the shoulder; no bones broken. I am doing well and things are as comfortable as I could expect in this place. I expected to start for home tomorrow, but am disappointed. I shall have to wait till next time. We are not allowed to write only ten lines, so I shall have to bid you goodbye for this time. I am as ever yours, etc.

John C. Griswold[27]

While John's letter was in transit, more welcome news arrived from Company F. Dana Horton received a letter from Susan on May 23, which he read with "intense interest" and responded to immediately. The previous night, letters had reached camp from members of the company who had been captured at Chancellorsville, paroled by the enemy, and sent to the parole camp in Annapolis, Maryland. As a condition of their release, the parolees had sworn an oath not to take up arms again until they were exchanged for similarly paroled Confederate captives. They confirmed that John was in a hospital in Richmond with a flesh wound in his arm. "Mrs. Griswold," Horton wrote, "I think that our much loved Lieut. 'G' will soon be exchanged and will soon be at home with you and his many friends, which will be very happy to see him." The company also awaited his return. "We should be very much joyed to see him with us again, entirely recovered from his wound," Horton stated. He added a personal note. "Please give my respects to your son. I have often [heard] Lieut. Griswold speak of him and yourself, so it seems almost as if I were acquainted with you. You must keep up good spirits, for I think the Lieut. will soon be exchanged."[28]

Lieutenant Griswold "has not been paroled yet," Dell Ames reported on May 24, "but he may be in a few days. I hope so anyway. . . . I hope he will be exchanged in a short time." Nine days later, Lieutenant Horton relayed good news. "I have just heard from your husband," he informed Susan. "He is at Annapolis, Md., and is getting along very well indeed. As he did not say anything about writing to you, I thought I would send you a short note. . . . He has to get someone to write for him, as he cannot use his right arm yet."[29]

Finally, a month after the battle, Susan received a letter from John. Written on May 30 in the unfamiliar hand of one Alex R., it was sent from St. Johns College Hospital in Annapolis.

My dear Wife,

I arrived at this place on Tuesday night last [May 26] and went into the hospital on Wednesday morning, where I have pleasant quarters and am very glad to get out of Rebeldom. I was taken sick a few days before leaving Libby Prison, but my health is now much improved and my arm is doing as well as can be expected under the circumstances. I was shot through the right arm above the elbow. . . and became so weak from the loss of blood that I was unable to leave the field, and was therefore taken prisoner. . . . As soon as my health is a little recruited I intend to get a leave of absence if possible and come home for a while. My time is passed very pleasantly here, there being a library attached to the hospital which furnishes reading matter, and in strolling around the college yard which is large and well shaded. As soon as you receive this write to me.[30]

"I have just received your letter," Susan rushed to respond on June 3, "and I feel to say thank God for his goodness in sparing you to write to me once more. I feel today the dead's alive. We have mourned you as dead." She described to John her agony on hearing the report of his death, her desire to rush to his side (thwarted by lack of means), and the kindness of Company F men in keeping her informed. But the shock of the past weeks still numbed her.

Dana and Dell wrote to me, but I did not feel satisfied of what your condition was. Some of the boys would write home [that] you was not wounded very bad, nothing but a flesh wound, and some thought you soon would be able to come back there . . . but Dana thought you would not be able to do duty for some time, therefore he thought you would come home, so his letters got up some hope in my mind that I should see you once more.

By now, Susan was desperate for a reunion with John, either in Annapolis or at home. Her pleading was tinged with despair.

If it is possible for you to come home you must do so, for I cannot have it so that you must stay down there and suffer, as I cannot do anything for you nor see you. If you cannot come home, do let me come down there and see you once more. Oh, have I not suffered enough on account of this war? I feel there is not much happiness on earth. Must I suffer on still more and more on account of this war? Oh, what have I done that I must suffer so much? But if you can come home, that will pay me for all the suffering. This anxiety of mind is so hard to bear. . . . It is cruel, but I suppose I must stand it. What cannot be cured must be endured.

But Susan's sadness was not only for herself. "It makes my heart ache to think of the miseries all over this country on account of this war," she wrote. "The tears that were shed after that battle! It was a very solemn time here, there was so many missing." Six members of Company F had been killed or mortally wounded, the home folk had learned; five others were wounded and seventeen were missing. "When I think where you was," she concluded, "I think it was nothing but the hand of providence that saved you; but thank kind providence for his goodness."

She pleaded to John to weigh his loyalties to his family and to the cause, and closed with a tender expression of her love.

> My continual prayer is Lord spare my dear husband to return to his family. If you should be any worse or anything should happen, let me know right off. Telegraph to us, or have it done. If I could see you, it seems it would be the happiest moments of my life, but I sometimes am fearful that I never shall have that privilege. But I live in hopes. Hope keeps the heart whole. Hain't you stayed there long enough? It is more than you ought to do for your country. I think your family ought to come in your affections first. . . . I send a kiss to you. You know there never was a woman [who] loved her man better than I do you.[31]

John received Susan's letter on June 8 and responded immediately through the medium of another scribe. He was "sorry to hear that you had heard such bad news of me" but pleased to report that "my wound is healing fast [and] everything is very favorable at present." He gently declined Susan's suggestion that she come to Annapolis. "Indeed I should be pleased to see you, but under the present circumstances I think it would seem unsafe, for I don't know how long I may stay here, nor where I may be ordered; so I think it advisable to defer it for awhile." He assured her that he intended to obtain a leave of absence and return home at the first opportunity. But another loyalty tugged at him. "I feel very anxious to visit the Company and shall do so as soon as I can get permission."[32]

Every day for a week Susan sent someone to the post office to look for John's response. When it arrived on June 12, she replied within an hour. "It seemed as if I could not wait so long" for a letter, she declared, ". . . but thank God, one has come at last." While she wrote, John's long-delayed letter from Libby Prison arrived. Now she poured her heart out to her husband. His letter was welcome,

> but oh, how much rather would I see the writer (or the one that caused it [to be] wrote). Can I wait much longer? I am afraid you will keep putting me off till you can't come home, or you get well enough to go back to your company. Can you be so cruel as not to come home or let me come and see you? Perhaps I am a little too fast. I will say if you can [not] possibly come, why can't you resign? You must. How can you stay there and suffer so much and keep your wife and child in such continual anxiety about the dearest of husbands and fathers? Oh, do come home! It is more than I think I can stand. Oh dear! oh dear! it is so hard this war. Oh my God, when will this war end, this awful misery cease?

She felt a great interest in the soldiers, Susan asserted, and she was very grateful to the members of Company F who had kept her informed of John's situation. "If you go to the company," she told John, "tell Dana Horton that I shall never forget his kindness to me, and Dell Ames [too]." But she commented bitterly on John's desire to return to the company—her rival for his devotion:

> You say you are very anxious to go to your company and shall do so. I fear you are more anxious to go there than to come home. You will say I am a little jealous, and I think I have reason to be. If you felt as I do, you would start for home as soon as you could. But if I could only know you would come home, I should feel better than I do. But I hope for the best. How hard to have our loved ones sick and wounded, away so far from us, where we cannot see them nor do anything for them! Oh, how can I endure it? But all we can do is to commend them to a merciful God. How hard my lot seems to be, and yours too—but thanks to a merciful God that you are still living. . . . I hope the next we hear from you, you will be on the way home or ready to start. I guess I have said enough about that. If you do not come before long, I shall start down there and hunt you up, whether you want me or not.[33]

John responded calmly to this impassioned letter. His wound was healing slowly, but he still had no use of his arm and continued to rely on someone to write for him. As he dictated, he made no mention of Susan's wish to visit him in Annapolis. He informed her he had applied for a leave of absence, "but as there is so much red tape wound around all military transactions, it will take a number of days to ascertain the result." Nevertheless, he declared, "I am bound to get home in as short [a] time as possible," even if he had to go to Washington to obtain his leave.

But his loyalties were still conflicted. "I have heard nothing from the company since I last wrote," he noted. "Still I should like to hear from them, as I think so much about them. I feel it my duty to be with them as they are on the move, but circumstances won't permit it."[34]

In the end, John Griswold had it both ways—he returned home on a furlough from the hospital, after which he rejoined Company F. Nothing is known of his visit to Susan and Cassius; no written record survives. By early August 1863 John was back with the company, stationed on the banks of the Potomac River at Alexandria, Virginia. After weeks of rest at home in a comfortable bed, he resumed sleeping in a wall tent on a bed of hay, covered with an old army blanket and a quilt. The men were on duty guarding conscripts as they were shipped by rail to the front. Griswold was a captain now, having been commissioned as such on May 27, to rank from April 13 (the date of Thomas Donnelly's resignation). On the sick list because of his lame arm, his only duty was to supervise the company business, overseeing paperwork that had fallen into disarray during his absence. Once again he resumed his correspondence with Susan, his writing limited by his aching hand. As before, his letters were filled with news of the Company F boys.

In September he received unsettling news from Susan: she was not feeling well. "Be as careful of your health as possible," John admonished his wife, "and not get down again." For the first time, he considered leaving the service. "I hope the time will come ere long that I can get out of this creditably," he informed Susan, "but [I] see no way at present, only through the Invalid Corps, and as long as the regiment is here I had rather be with it than in that corps." The Invalid Corps—later called the Veteran Reserve Corps—was composed of disabled veteran soldiers unfit for active duty at the front but capable of performing limited duties in the rear as guards, hospital attendants, garrison troops, and the like.[35]

The easy duty at Alexandria ended suddenly when the Eleventh Corps was ordered to the western theater of the war. He would have tried to avoid making the trip, John assured Susan, but the order was so sudden it was all he could do to ready the company for the movement. "I begin to think the tender mercies of war are cruel," John wrote, "but [I] shall have to make the best of it for the time being." The men had hoped to remain in Alexandria, he noted, "but it does not seem to be our fortune to get an easy berth [for] any length of time." The regiment boarded railroad cars in Washington on September 26, 1863, and rode for six days and nights—"a long and tiresome journey," according to John—before arriving at Bridgeport, Alabama. The weary, dusty men refreshed themselves with a bath in the Tennessee River and appraised their new surroundings. Bridgeport consisted of a burned depot and a destroyed railroad bridge, situated in a rough, mountainous wilderness—an "out of the way, god-forsaken place," John judged. "We think we are nearly out of the world."[36]

While the Company F boys built fortifications, cut logs for corduroy roads, and stood picket, John remained restricted to supervisory duties. "My hand and arm gains but little," he reported. "I have not much use of it yet. The cold affects it very much." When the regiment marched upriver in late October in the movement that opened the famous Cracker Line and relieved the siege of Chattanooga, John—"not being well at the time and also a cripple"—was left behind in charge of other disabled soldiers at the Bridgeport camp.[37]

When he rejoined the regiment it was camped in the shadow of Lookout Mountain, in rugged countryside dotted sparsely with "miserable log houses." Confederate artillery atop the mountain attempted to shell the 154th's valley camp daily, but the trajectory invariably caused them to overshoot. When the regiment left Lookout Valley to take part in the battle that drove the Confederates from the mountains and ridges surrounding Chattanooga, John was excused from duty and left behind in camp, "wait[ing] with anxiety to hear the particulars." By the time he notified Susan of the "grand cleaning out" of the enemy, the regiment had continued on a march to the relief of besieged Knoxville, Tennessee. John remained at Lookout Valley, awaiting his comrades' return and worrying about new reports from Susan that she was "running down again." [38]

She had moved from Arkwright to a rented house in the larger village of Fredonia, reportedly to enable Cassius to attend a better school. John fretted about the move and the extra burden of housekeeping it entailed. "You can now better understand why I did not seem more willing for you to keep house," he chided his wife. "As long as you were gaining I was contented, but now it is otherwise. The best thing you can do now is hire somebody to do your work before you get so that you will have to hire 2 or 3 to take care of you." By the time Susan received that bit of advice it was irrelevant. Soon after she settled into her new home, John learned, "she was prostrated upon a bed of sickness." [39]

Early in December 1863, dire news arrived from Susan. John immediately addressed a request to the commander of the Lookout Valley camp: "I have the honor to apply for a leave of absence for thirty (30) days to visit my wife in Chautauqua Co., New York, who is *very sick* and not expected to live but a short time." The chain of command endorsed the request and the leave was granted. [40]

A friend later described John's visit home:

He was privileged with a furlough from December until towards the middle of February, during which time he accompanied his beloved companion, and gave her what comfort and consolation he could. . . . It became necessary for his return to his company, and he took the last look and gave the last farewell, and again turned his back upon all that was near and dear to answer the call of his Government, to enter again upon the vicissitudes and deprivations incidental to a soldier's life, while his heart was bleeding from the lacerations of a fearful foreboding that he never again would see the companion of his bosom this side of heaven. [41]

This sentimental account was inaccurate in one particular: John had been granted a twenty-day leave rather than the thirty days he had requested, and when it expired his request for an extension was rejected. He nevertheless stayed with Susan for several more weeks. As a consequence, when he finally arrived back in camp at Lookout Valley in mid-February he was arrested for absence without leave and ordered to await a hearing by a military commission. At the end of the month he was exonerated by the examining board and released for duty. "The boys in the company feel nice to think they have got the captain back again," wrote John's nephew, Private Milon J. Griswold. "I felt sorry for Aunt Susan to have him come back and have her so sick," Milon added, "but I hope that we may all live to get back to our homes and friends once more."[42]

John resumed writing to Susan. He suppressed any mention of his worries about her and gave no signs of his forebodings. He avoided any reference to her condition whatsoever, concentrating instead on newsy chatter. In a quick note sent from Nashville on his way to Lookout Valley, he told her he was well, mentioned it was warm and rainy, gave tidings of one of the Company F boys, and reported he was about to leave for Chattanooga. But he hungered for news from her. "Have Cassius or someone write immediately and often," he requested. "I will write again when I get to the company."[43]

His next letter provided details of his trip, more news of Company F boys, another weather report, and the latest military rumors. But this dispassionate recital gave way to his greatest concern: indecision about his future. Should he stay at the front as duty demanded? Or should he resign and return home to his ailing wife? "I have not yet fairly concluded what I had better do," he admitted, "or what they will do with me." Colonel Patrick H. Jones had asked John to remain in the service if he thought his health could stand it. "I think I will stay awhile and try it," John concluded, "but your situation at home worries me and I hardly know what to do." Having made up his mind to stay for the time being, he urged Susan to write often. "I am getting very anxious to hear from home," he wrote. "Hope to hear soon."[44]

When the next letter from Susan arrived, it was encouraging. Her health was "gaining." It left John "indulging in the hope that at a not distant day our little family might be united and enjoy some of the comforts of life in each other's society."[45]

"The news came like a thunderclap in a cloudless day," John wrote to Cassius on March 14, 1864. Susan was dead; the end had come on March 4. Her remains had been laid to rest in the graveyard. The funeral service had been held at the Arkwright Christian Church, the minister expounding on Micah 2:10: "Arise ye, and depart; for this is not your rest." A letter from a relative, followed quickly by one from Cassius, had brought the sad tidings. Stunned, John voiced his grief to his son. "The polar star around which all our hopes and affections and all those sweet influences that make home desirably centered is stricken from its orbit," he wrote, "leaving a blank that can never be filled." John counseled resignation to the teenager—"It is hard as you say, but she cannot be recalled and we must submit"—and urged him to honor his mother's memory. "Do not forget the admonitions and counsels of your dear mother," he wrote. "She reposed great confidence in your integrity and the uprightness of your intentions. Do not let that confidence be misplaced, but remember her many virtues and pattern [your conduct] after them."

John rued his absence from Susan's deathbed and funeral. "To think that I could not be with her during her last illness, or even to see her consigned to her last resting place" filled him with woe. And he was staggered by his own uncertain future. "I feel very lonely and discontented," he confessed to Cassius, "more so than I have ever been before; and sometimes think I will quit the service and go—*where*—with no place to call home." His surrogate family of Company F offered some consolation. "Perhaps I am as contented here as I should be anywhere," he acknowledged, but in the end he felt hopeless: "I feel at present that it was of small amount what became of me." [46]

While John agonized about what to do, an overnight storm blanketed Lookout Valley with more than a foot of snow. The next day he shook with cold chills and felt a fever coming on; then diarrhea laid him low. His declining health complicated his deliberations about his future. "Unless I get considerable better I shall have to quit the service," he wrote to a niece. "If Susan was alive and I had a home to go to, I should not stay any longer than to get discharged; but under present circumstances I presume I am more at home here than I should be anywhere else." He added, "It is hard to think of one's home being broken up by the death of a loved wife and mother, but the worst is past and it is of little moment what becomes of me now." [47]

Disease and despair drove John to death's door. "We are pained to learn," the *Fredonia Censor* reported, "that information has been received that Capt. John C. Griswold, of the 154th, is very low with inflammation of the bowels, and no hope is entertained of his recovery." But the boys of Company F rallied around their captain, tendering him with "as good care as could be given a man here in this country," as Dell Ames put it. Private Marvin M. Skinner nursed him every day; at night other men took turns watching over him. At this low point, John finally submitted his resignation. "I had rather he would have stayed with us," Dell Ames wrote, "but his health would not admit of it." Ames was writing a letter to Cassius for John on May 1, 1864, when the papers arrived. Captain Griswold's resignation had been accepted and he was discharged to date April 28, 1864, for disability from his Chancellorsville wound. Meanwhile, John's health had improved. "He has had a hard sickness," Dell informed Cassius, but "he is on the gain now and I think that he is out of danger. . . . He says that he is coming home just as soon as he is able."[48]

John returned to Arkwright and picked up the pieces of his life. In the following months and years he resumed his duties as justice of the peace, served several terms as justice of sessions, and again represented the town on the county board of supervisors. "In every position," a chronicler wrote, "he was the same kindly conscientious and true man and was highly esteemed in the town and county." A post office was named Griswold in his honor. He was pleased to watch his son Cassius mature into a respected man and prominent citizen of Arkwright. John even remarried, in 1868. He was wed to Alice Hill longer than to Susan—but, tellingly, when he died at his Arkwright home on July 24, 1892, he was laid to rest beside his first wife.[49]

Mourners paid tribute to his character. An obituary writer for the *Fredonia Censor* noted:

> His kindness to all who needed his assistance, his strict integrity and his devoted patriotism which led him to risk his life for his country, all these noble attributes are known as household words in all this region where he was so well known and highly respected. Surely such a record is to be esteemed rather than the accumulation of vast wealth. His best monument is the love and respect with which his memory will be cherished in the hearts of all his friends and neighbors.[50]

The Chautauqua County Board of Supervisors eulogized him in a special memorial. "His memory is revered and cherished with sincere affection," the supervisors decreed, "and it was not only the just but the universal verdict in all the region where he was so long and thoroughly known, that a noble pioneer, a brave patriot, and above all a good man, had died, when John C. Griswold passed from mortal vision."[51]

Both tributes concentrated on John's Civil War service, providing details of his wounding and capture, his return to duty, and his subsequent illness—for "it was as a brave, patriotic soldier that he made the record which most entitles him to our admiration, and which makes his memory a priceless legacy to his descendants." But the accolade John Griswold perhaps would have appreciated most was a simple line from one of the old Company F boys, William Harper, whose knapsack and musket John had carried on a march thirty years before. In a memoir of his service Harper wrote of Captain Griswold, "He was as good a man as ever commanded a company."[52]

CHAPTER SEVEN

Private William Hawkins

Company B

Geese honked and cows lowed in the distance as I explored East Otto Cemetery. On the outskirts of its eponymous Cattaraugus County village, the long, rectangular burying ground, lined by maples at a quiet crossroads, climbed and spilled over the edges of a hillside. A bit away from the dirt road near the cemetery's center, just below the hill's crest, I found the stones marking the grave of William Hawkins. A granite monument was identified only with his surname. Beside it, a flag in a GAR holder decorated an older, gray-veined marble headstone. I could make out a waving American flag cut into the top of the stone, and below it the inscription, "William Hawkins, Co. B, 154th Regt. N.Y. Vols. . . . Born—1834; Died—1906."

The ellipsis indicates three lines of indistinguishable script, washed away by acid rain. There is no way of knowing for certain, but those lines quite possibly referred to Hawkins as a survivor of one of the deadliest places of the entire war.

A crowd filled the new Methodist Episcopal Church at the crossroads in East Otto on the evening of Saturday, September 2, 1882, for a special ceremony. The meeting place had been chosen by the honoree for a specific reason. The church had replaced one that had stood on the same spot from 1853 to 1880, when it was destroyed by fire. In that old church, on a Saturday twenty years before, William Hawkins had enlisted to do his part in putting down the rebellion. Now, while a band played and the audience settled in the pews, Hawkins greeted friends and fellow veterans of the 154th New York, who had come to honor the old soldier on the site where his great ordeal had begun.

The crowd gathered to commemorate Bill Hawkins as a survivor of the most infamous prison camp of the Civil War—Andersonville, Georgia, where some forty-one thousand Union captives had been held under horrifically squalid conditions during the last fifteen months of the war. Almost thirteen thousand of those prisoners had died and were buried in tidy rows of graves at the Andersonville National Cemetery.

Conducting the ceremony were two residents of nearby Ellicottville—Edwin D. Northrup, a lawyer who was working on a history of the 154th New York, and Byron A. Johnston, a former captain of the regiment. The previous year, the two men had visited the old stockade at Andersonville and come away with a special memento for their friend Bill Hawkins. Now, as the hushed crowd listened intently, Northrup made a speech, called Hawkins to his side, and presented him on behalf of his regimental comrades with a gold-headed cane. Its shaft was a pine pole cut from the notorious stockade. Gripping this souvenir of sorrow, Bill took the stand and offered a brief account of his capture and imprisonment and the miseries he had endured. Some other men made a few remarks before the meeting ended at a late hour. "Taking it all in," a reporter noted, "the scene was a memorable one."[1]

Hawkins was no doubt appreciative of the gift and the public remembrance of his service and sufferings, but he needed no reminder of the horrors he had survived for seventeen months as a prisoner of war. They were engraved in his memory.

Bill Hawkins gave his age as twenty-six when he enlisted at the East Otto church on August 30, 1862, but it seems he was a few years older. The year of birth carved into his headstone (1834) indicates he was twenty-eight at enlistment, while a list of East Otto's soldiers compiled by the town clerk at the end of the war gave his birth date as March 31, 1832, making him thirty years old when he enrolled. Little is known of his early life. He was born in Canada and came with his parents, John and Lucy Jane (Salmon) Hawkins, to Cattaraugus County at an unknown date. By 1860 Bill was working as a laborer on an East Otto farm. At an unknown date he took a wife, Elizabeth Murcer, but the marriage was short-lived. Mrs. Hawkins died of unknown causes on February 5, 1862. Six months later, Bill enlisted. He was five feet, nine inches tall, with a sandy complexion, gray eyes, and brown hair.[2]

Dan B. Allen, a newly minted lawyer turned soldier who was to be captain of Company B, enrolled Hawkins at the church. Bill was mustered in as one of the company's eighty-two privates on September 24, 1862. By July 1863, Dan Allen was lieutenant colonel and the 154th New York's commander. Bill Hawkins was still a private. He was known as Company B's barber. He sat his customers on stumps; as he worked, hair piled up around him a foot deep.

Over nine months of service, Bill had witnessed death in the hospital and on the battlefield. When an East Otto neighbor, Private Warren Bradley of Company G, expired in a Virginia hospital after a short illness, maddened by fever, Bill was at his side. At Chancellorsville, men had fallen all around Bill, shot to pieces and ripped apart by shells. As terrible as those experiences had been, Bill was fated to encounter death on a scale unimaginably vast.[3]

His ordeal began at Gettysburg. After rushing down Cemetery Hill and through the streets of the town on the afternoon of July 1, 1863, three regiments of Colonel Charles R. Coster's Union brigade formed a line of battle along a fence in Kuhn's brickyard. Their mission was to make a stand there in Gettysburg's northeastern outskirts and allow their fellow Eleventh Corps regiments, which had been overwhelmed by the Confederates on the plains to the north, to retreat unmolested to Cemetery Hill. The 154th New York held the center of Coster's line. As Bill and his comrades commenced firing, they could see the enemy advancing in overwhelming numbers and sweeping around the brigade's right flank. Bill had a sinking feeling—Coster's men were "to be sacrificed" in this attempt to cover the retreat. The situation was indeed hopeless. When the regiments to the right and left of the 154th broke for the rear, Colonel Allen ordered his men to retreat. In the confusion of the moment, Bill and others missed hearing the order and lost precious seconds before they attempted to escape.[4]

Bill dashed through a garden near the brick kilns, intent on reaching the relative safety of the town. But the brickyard was surrounded by Confederates and bullets whistled through the air. Bill dropped to the ground. He saw his captain, Simeon V. Pool, try to escape through the brickyard gate, where a Confederate officer ordered him to halt. Pool ignored the demand until the officer leveled a revolver at him, whereupon Pool and much of his company surrendered. Sweeping through the brickyard, Confederates found Bill and added him to the herd of prisoners from the 154th. They numbered 173 of the unit's 265 soldiers who had fought in the battle—65 percent of the regiment's force.

After separating the officers from the enlisted men, Confederate guards marched the prisoners back over the battlefield to the shelter of a knoll. They wove their way through the detritus of combat—sprawled dead and writhing wounded, and hasty surgeons busy at their grisly work at a field hospital. That evening, the Yankee enlisted men were issued rations of stringy old beef. The officers, segregated on the other side of a fence, received nothing. Bill and the others built fires and broiled the beef until it was black. Then, yelling their officers' names, they tossed pieces of meat over the fence. It was "a ludicrous sight," Bill thought, to watch Captain Pool and the other half-famished officers "running like a flock of turkeys" after the scraps of charred beef.

While the men ate, Confederate officers addressed them. The Yankees were given two choices: accept a battlefield parole or remain prisoners of war. In accepting a parole, a prisoner swore under oath that he would not take up arms against his captors until he was formally exchanged for an enemy prisoner of equal rank. Violators, the Confederates warned the Yankees, would be shot or hung. After the Confederates made their proposal, the 154th New York men gathered to discuss it. Union general-in-chief Henry W. Halleck had recently complicated the parole process with an order halting prisoner exchanges. Some of the captives believed that Halleck's order forbade battlefield paroles. Others thought that they would be held for no more than two weeks and then be paroled. After some back-and-forth on the issue, the men voted to reject the rebel battlefield parole offer and remain prisoners of war. It was a fateful—and for many a fatal—decision.[5]

On the Fourth of July, with the battle over, the defeated Confederates began marching their captives south through Maryland. Several days later the prisoners were ferried aboard flatboats across the flooded Potomac River, and began to plod south up Virginia's Shenandoah Valley. During the march, Bill Hawkins demonstrated an entrepreneurial bent that would stand him in good stead in the coming months. He was a wheeler-dealer, one quite willing to work in commerce's shady corners. As a result he was able to make money, buy food, and keep himself well-nourished compared to many of his fellow prisoners.

After crossing the Potomac, Bill managed to sneak into the gaggle of officers and find Simeon Pool. The captain asked Bill to march with him and serve as his "waiter" by providing food. Bill agreed on one condition: that his company comrade, Private Alansing Wyant, be allowed to join them. Pool acceded to Bill's request, and Wyant joined Hawkins with the officers.

Word of their coming had preceded the Yankees, and Virginians along the route were quite willing to sell provisions to the hungry prisoners at inflated prices. Having had "hardly a mouthful to eat on the way," as Bill put it, crowds of famished Yankees—those who still had money in their pockets—swarmed to the civilians' makeshift markets. But after paying five dollars for a single loaf of bread and similar inflated prices for other edibles, Bill quickly exhausted his own and Simeon Pool's savings. The waiter now had to rely on his wits to procure food for his captain and himself.

Bill turned his blankets and other traps over to Wyant so he could work unimpeded. His first strike was at a roadside house, where a swarm of prisoners surrounded the proprietress and her wares: a two-foot-high stack of blackberry pies. Bill chitchatted with the woman a bit and asked the price for a pie. She named an exorbitant figure. So Waiter Bill bided his time, inconspicuous in the milling crowd of prisoners. When the woman turned away to wait on other customers, he grabbed a half-dozen pies and disappeared. Somehow he also came up with some bread and butter. Bill and Captain Pool invited Captain Edward Porter of Company I to join them in ducking behind some bushes, where they devoured "a glorious meal." Impressed, Porter offered Bill ten dollars to wait on him as well. Bill cockily replied that he would take the money later; he "could get stuff without [it]."

Down the road, at a neatly fenced house, Bill asked the resident if he had any victuals for sale. The man handed Bill a loaf of bread; Bill gave him two dollars. Then Bill asked for butter. He would sell it if he had any, the man replied, but there was none to be found. So Bill asked for his change. "How much?" asked the forgetful Virginian. "Two dollars," Bill responded, and the dupe returned Bill's payment in full. At another house farther along, Hawkins asked a fearful woman if she had anything to eat. She seemed oddly immobile. She soon revealed that she was straddling a basketful of eggs beneath her dress. Bill asked her to put two dozen into his hat, and as a crowd of prisoners clamored for more eggs, he made his escape without paying.

Bill even managed to bilk the Confederate guards out of extra food. On one occasion when they issued hardtack to the prisoners, Hawkins managed to grab so much that Captain Pool sent the surplus to his Company B men.

The prisoners' march ended at Staunton. As Hawkins and Wyant parted from the officers, Bill filled Captain Pool's haversack with provisions. "Bill," Pool remarked, "your money must be most all gone." Hawkins pulled out a roll and counted fourteen dollars in Confederate bills—more cash than he had started with. "You must look out," Pool warned his waiter, "or you'll be caught at it." Then the men parted.

During the stay at Staunton, the Confederates stripped the prisoners of their tents, blankets, and canteens. Many of the men had worn out their shoes and were barefoot; their uniforms were reduced to ragged shirts and pants. And many of them had traded little knickknacks—jackknives, combs, scissors, razors, pencils, paper, pens, and the like—for food. The value of those small items was now lost, and would be sorely missed.[6]

On the night of July 23, the prisoners of the 154th New York were loaded aboard flatcars and boxcars for the railroad journey from Staunton to Richmond. They arrived in the Confederate capital the following evening and marched from the depot across a nearby bridge onto Belle Island. This eighty-acre patch of land sat just downstream of a fall line in the James River; the swift current rushing by its shore discouraged escape attempts by water. The prison camp consisted of about six windswept, treeless acres on the river front. The landward sides were enclosed by five-foot-high earthworks. Confederate guards were posted atop the parapet at intervals of forty feet. At the river, a ten-foot upstream segment was reserved for drinking water. Below it, a thirty-foot stretch was used for bathing, and below that 150 feet of shoreline served as the camp's latrine. Inside the compound, some sixty tent-lined streets branched off a main avenue. The prisoners were divided into squads of fifty and assigned to specific streets. The camp's intended capacity was three thousand. Over the summer, the population would swell to about twice that many.[7]

Bill and his friend Alansing Wyant stuck together. Their first night on the island they received rations of bean soup and a quarter of a loaf of fine white bread, "so light," Bill noted, "there was little substance of it." While Wyant used his pocketknife to carve a wooden spoon, Bill plucked a few black bugs from their small cup of soup. When he quit, Alansing asked, "Are you going to skim any more?" No, Bill replied, and they downed their soup, bugs and all—a practice that became standard. The following morning they received another piece of bread and some beef. Twice a day, the same monotonous and unnourishing rations were issued. Bill, accustomed to the riches he had enjoyed on the march through the Valley, did not adapt well to the prison's spartan menu. He soon went nine days without a bowel movement. When he glimpsed the camp cookhouse beyond the earthen enclosure, where Confederates emptied sacks of beans, "dirt and all," into the soup, his appetite soured further. When autumn came, cornbread was substituted for the white bread. The prisoners' digestive tracts were ravaged by the rougher fare. The wheat bread constipated the men; the corn meal gave them diarrhea.

Hawkins and Wyant shared a conical Sibley tent with more than a dozen other men. They were lucky to have that ragged shelter—many of the prisoners lived in the open air. Bill had a small woolen blanket and a rubber blanket to cover him, but in his threadbare uniform he suffered much in fall's colder weather and winter's ice and snow. The tent's dirt floor was packed as hard as rock. Bill's sides were rubbed raw from lying on the adamantine surface. The soldiers had to sleep spoon fashion—snuggled together like a stack of spoons—to fit in the tent and to gain the benefit of body warmth. After lying in one position for a length of time on cold nights, a stiff man would call out, "Ain't you about ready to turn over?" and all would rotate in tandem.

Worried that the prisoners might run the guard, the Confederates prohibited nighttime visits to the riverside latrines. As a result, the camp streets soon became "a horrid place," Bill observed, filled with excrement and other filth. The sinks themselves resembled "a slaughter house," Bill noted, "from the blood that passed the men." In the winter—one of the coldest in recent memory—prisoners froze to death in the filthy streets or on hard-packed tent floors. And hunger led the men to do what no one but a prisoner could imagine. Bill saw men scoop up beans from other men's vomit and eat them.

Some relief arrived in the dead of winter with a shipment of clothing from the U.S. government. Captive Union officers, held at Libby Prison in Richmond, were permitted onto Belle Island to distribute the garments to their men. Captain Pool made the trip and reunited with the Company B boys, and they spent an enjoyable hour visiting with Pool. Bill was sick; he "looked as much like a skeleton as a man well could and [still] be alive," the captain observed. As the two parted, Pool gave the last of his money—a five dollar Confederate bill—to Hawkins and told him to use it to buy medicine. Bill protested, saying Pool would need the money as much as he would, but Pool insisted and Hawkins kept the bill.[8]

Money—and the food it could buy in the prison's black market—was literally a matter of life and death to the captives. Consequently fear gripped them when the Confederates began a systematic search of the prison population. The Yankees were taken outside the pen on a regular basis to be counted. When guards began herding groups of seven or eight prisoners into a tent to be searched, word swiftly spread that the captives were robbed. Rumor had it that some were strip-searched. When Bill's squad's turn came up, the men hid their money as best they could. Some uncapped their rounded brass buttons and stuffed them with bills; others concealed cash in their mouths. Bill had a quarter, given to him by a company mate who had divided his silver among his comrades. He left the coin and some worthless "shin plasters" (privately issued banknotes) in his wallet, and secreted his valuable cash by opening his pants and stuffing the wadded bills under his foreskin.

Bill entered the search tent and spotted two buckets, one almost full of U.S. greenbacks, the other awash with Confederate currency. A table was stacked with silver coins. Beside it stood a red-headed sergeant armed with a Bowie knife and a revolver. An assistant to prison commandant Lieutenant Virginius Bossieux, the sergeant was known throughout Belle Island as a sadistic bully who pounded the prisoners with a club. When Bill gave the sergeant his wallet, the Confederate scorned the shin plasters but grabbed the quarter. With a "terrible threat," he asked Bill if that was all he had. Yes, Bill lied, and the sergeant released him with his hidden treasure intact.

Bill prospered when he went into business with a regimental comrade, Private Allen L. Robbins of Company K, an artful forger of U.S. greenbacks. Robbins produced the counterfeit cash by painstakingly drawing in ink on common plain stationery. He managed to obtain enough supplies of ink and paper to churn out more than five hundreds dollars' worth of phony bills. Robbins was the supplier; Bill was the passer. His modus operandi was to approach Confederate guards—the more ignorant the better—during the day, show them a legitimate greenback, and arrange to buy pies or other goods under cover of darkness. After night fell, Bill would meet the guard at a prearranged spot and quickly and surreptitiously make the exchange—paying for the goods, of course, with one of Robbins's counterfeit bills. Some of the guards, Bill was pleased to note, were too stupid to tell a two-dollar bill from a five. Food in hand, Bill would "astonish the boys with a good meal."

Every now and then Bill enjoyed a special triumph over a dim-witted guard. One day, without telling his comrades, he took a poorly counterfeited two-dollar bill from his squad's kitty and bought a plug of tobacco from an older Reb guard, receiving an authentic dollar greenback in change to boot. On returning to his tent, Bill asked the boys to find the phony deuce. Alansing Wyant, Private Buel Bishop of Company B, and the other men searched in vain for the missing bill. Hawkins then revealed the tobacco and the greenback and told his story. The men were overjoyed, Bill noted with pleasure, and they divided the tobacco evenly.

Other Union prisoners were counterfeiting money in addition to Robbins; Bill estimated that thousands of dollars in fake bills were produced. After a while the guards were on the lookout for this "Belle Island money," as it came to be called, but Bill still found it easy to trick them. A guard would naively ask whether a greenback was good; with apparent sincerity, Bill would assure him it was, and the guard would pocket the fake and hand over the pies. Bill was at the riverside latrine one day when a Reb sergeant told him that nineteen members of his company had accepted more than four hundred dollars of worthless Belle Island money.

But life as a black market trafficker was not without its dangers. Confederate authorities ordered the guards to arrest all so-called "traders," take them to a guardhouse, and relieve them of their booty. As Bill was loitering near a corner of the pen one day, he approached a young guard to set up a deal. Mindful of his orders, the guard leveled his musket at Bill and ordered him to come closer. Pretending he was afraid, Bill feigned an annoying itch on his bare foot. With some quick slight of hand, he put his wad of bills between his toes, wiggled them into the sand, and buried the cash. Meanwhile, by threatening to report the guard for some offense, another prisoner talked the youth out of arresting Bill.

As the clampdown on trading tightened, the practice became more perilous. Guards occasionally took potshots at traders, sending them scurrying to their tents. Several were killed. Sometimes a guard would pretend to accept a trader's bribe and allow him to escape. But it was a trap—other guards, armed with revolvers, would apprehend the prisoner, take all of his money, and turn him back into the pen. Bill's tensest moment came when some fellow prisoners seized him. They were informers. They dragged Bill to a guard and reported he was a trader. A Confederate lieutenant—possibly Commandant Virginius Bossieux—interrogated Bill "savagely"; Bill emphatically denied the charge. As the two debated, another Reb officer rushed up and reported five or six traders working at the other end of the pen. Seeking bigger game, the lieutenant ordered Bill to stand still and hurried off. Bill's legs "would not stand still," and he scurried away and hid.

Other Union prisoners preyed on the traders. A group of about thirty-five captive sailors, camped in the pen's southwest corner, kept a watch out for speculators. When they spotted one they grabbed and robbed him. Annoyed by these turncoats, Bill and large number of other prisoners formed a posse to "whip them out in force." "But the tars, who were hard-fisted fellows, had got wind of it," Bill reported, "and when the attack came, they came out of their tents like bees armed with clubs and routed the army of invasion in a short time, and it was not repeated."

Malnourished, poorly clad, haphazardly sheltered, overcrowded, filthy, vermin-ridden, wallowing in their own waste, the prisoners were ravaged by chronic diarrhea, dysentery, typhoid fever, smallpox, and pneumonia. Bill became "very sick," although he did not specify his malady. For a long time the sickest prisoners were taken out of the pen, loaded aboard an old scow, and ferried across the James to hospitals in Richmond, where most of them died. Bill helped carry several of his comrades to the scow, among them Alansing Wyant and Buel Bishop. Both of them died in the city. Late in the winter, the Confederates built a hospital on the island. Reporting there for medicine, Bill often saw prisoner nurses do their best to succor the living, but the grounds nonetheless were littered with corpses. Many of them were almost if not entirely naked. "The bodies of the dead at Belle Isle," Bill reported, "were nearly stripped of clothes."[9]

Desperate to avoid becoming emaciated, naked corpses themselves, prisoners used bribes to secure their release. Prisoners were to be paroled in the order they entered the pen, but some members of the 154th New York managed to bribe Lieutenant Bossieux with five hundred dollars in cash to get their names moved up the list. When the ruse worked and they left the island, sad disappointment washed over those left behind. Bill was sitting next to one of the plotters, Corporal Clark E. "Salty" Oyer of Company G, when the word came one evening. As a list of parolees was being read, Bill said to Oyer, "Salty, I guess you ain't going to get out tonight—you will have to come down with another five hundred dollars." Just then, Oyer's name was called. He leaped to his feet, said, "Goodnight, Bill!" and departed. Oyer later recalled the "sad and hope-lost faces" of Hawkins and the others, while another of the lucky party remembered Bill being "too full [of emotion] to speak."[10]

One of Bill's tent mates, Private Samuel W. Simmons of Company H, took a more reckless tack to leave the island: he attempted to escape. Simmons and a company comrade, Private Alfred Matteson, concocted a plan to get over the pen's earthworks and cross the river. Simmons told Bill he would just as soon be shot attempting to escape as stay in the prison and starve to death—"they would," he said, "die there anyhow." Bill tried to dissuade him, but Simmons was determined. On the night of October 14–15, 1863, he and Matteson armed themselves with long poles, bid Bill and the others goodbye, and left the tent. Bill was so certain they would fail and be shot that he lay down with his blanket over his ears, hoping to muffle the blast of the muskets that he felt certain would take his comrades' lives.

On receiving a signal from other prisoners that two guards had vacated the northwest corner of the pen, Simmons and Matteson scrambled over the embankment into a ditch and ran along the riverbank until they found a suitable crossing place. Using their poles for balance, they leaped from rock to rock to the middle of the James and then jumped as far as they could into the rushing water. Simmons sank to the bottom, bobbed to the surface, and struggled through the cold water, finally crawling ashore in Richmond on his hands and knees. There he surrendered at a Confederate camp. Matteson was drowned; his corpse was swept downstream until it snagged in a fish net or an eel rack, where it was found on October 20. Matteson's remains were returned to the island and buried by his regimental comrades the following evening.

Simmons was escorted to the island on October 20 and confined in a guardhouse which shared a common wall with the cook house. Through cracks in the wall he spied loaves of bread piled against the partition. Using his case knife to saw through some nails, he freed a board so he could get at the bread. He also managed to finagle extra rations, so that by the time he was sent back into the pen, Bill noted, he was "as fat as a hog." But reduced to the usual scanty rations, Simmons's health began to decline. Bill cautioned his friend to take better care of himself, or he would not live very long. Simmons became deeply discouraged and began to court trouble, hoping to return to the guardhouse and the bread pile. He never made it. He died of fever on New Year's Day, 1864.

Despair, the prisoners knew, could be just as deadly as diarrhea or dysentery.

In February 1864, prisoners began to be sent from Belle Island in detachments of several hundred each. Rumors swept the compound that they were headed to a new prison in the Deep South. Late on the night of February 18, another group of six or seven hundred men joined the exodus. Among them was Bill Hawkins. Ailing and infirm, he could barely walk. He clung to the arms of other prisoners, but each weakened man he grabbed told him, "Don't take a hold on me, or I can't get there myself." A surgeon viewing the skeletal prisoners estimated that nine out of ten of them weighed less than a hundred pounds. Another doctor noted that many of them had lost their sanity.[11]

At the Richmond depot the emaciated Yankees were loaded aboard freight cars outfitted with makeshift seats. As the train began to roll south, a cold wind whistled through the slats of the ramshackle cars. Bill greased his exposed limbs with lard, wrapped himself in his blanket, and monotonously stamped his feet to keep his circulation flowing. Many other men, less vigilant, became frostbitten. The following night, during a brief stop, the prisoners were issued rations. As the swaying train continued its southward journey, two members of the 154th New York succumbed to the cold and privation and died. At the next stop, in Raleigh, North Carolina, their corpses were removed from the car and buried.[12]

The train rolled on for two or three more days without a stop, the prisoners forced to remain in the fetid cars without food. One of the men traded his coat buttons for a guard's rations. Finally the cars slowed to a halt. Peering from the boxcar, all Bill saw was Georgia pine woods; there was not a building in sight. When he jumped from the car his numb legs gave way and he tumbled to the ground. The prisoners were fed some cornmeal bread and coffee made from burnt johnnycake. During the rest, Bill removed his stiff woolen shirt and formed it in a circle over a fire to kill the lice that infested it. Then he clambered back into the car for the final leg of the journey.

About March 1—Bill had lost track of the date—the train pulled into its destination: Andersonville, Georgia, where a new prison camp had accepted its first inmates the previous week. As the Yankees shuffled the quarter-mile from the depot to the prison, they had to make several stops to rest. Some of their once-frostbitten legs were now black with gangrene. Then they entered their new home—a sixteen-acre plot of stump-studded dirt, bisected by a small stream and surrounded by unfinished fifteen-foot-tall pine log walls. There were no barracks or tents to house the prisoners. Bill spent his first night at Andersonville wrapped in his greasy blanket. When he awoke the next morning, it was soaked through with dew.

Rations at Andersonville were as poor and meager as on Belle Island. Cornmeal and bacon were the staples. The cobs were ground together with the kernels, and the resulting cornmeal was so coarse that it gave the prisoners diarrhea. Bill and his mess broke the solder on a canteen and punctured one of its halves to make a sieve to filter out the ground cobs. The mess also had a small tin pail they had brought from Belle Island. They used that precious utensil—four or five of them owned it in partnership—to cook their meals. Water from the creek was good at first but quickly became foul with refuse from the upstream cookhouse and the prisoners' excrement—the men used the stream's swampy borders as a latrine. Soon the prisoners were digging wells throughout the stockade to get fresh water.

The prison's two gates were set in the stockade's west wall, one to the north and the other south of the stream. Bill and a group of 154th New York men set up camp on a slope near the north gate. His companions included Privates Franklin L. Goodrich of Company B and John Hogg and Loren Phillips of Company D, Corporal George W. Bailey of Company G, and Sergeant Peter Messinger of Company A. Bill and Frank Goodrich shared the shelter of a blanket set up like an awning on four poles. Another stout pole was used as a support for the weak and sickly men to grab when they stood up.

Bill's trading days were behind him. To make money at Andersonville, he instead relied on an old skill and revived his barbering trade. Somehow he obtained a razor and shears and opened shop under his blanket awning. The prison's going rate for a shave and haircut was ten cents. As the months passed, Bill made twenty-five dollars as a barber.[13]

Customers were easy to come by. When Swiss-born Captain Henry Wirz arrived to take command of the prison in early March 1864, the stockade held more than seven thousand Yankees. By the beginning of May the population exceeded the pen's capacity of ten thousand. Then came a great influx of prisoners from the spring and summer campaigns. Among them were approximately three thousand men who had surrendered on April 20 at Plymouth, North Carolina. Those "Plymouth Pilgrims," as they came to be called, included many members of the 85th New York, among them a number of men from Cattaraugus County. Having recently reenlisted, they entered the stockade in new uniforms, flush with bounty money; some, Bill noted, carried as much as five hundred dollars in cash. The Pilgrims instantly fell prey to the scams and swindles and worse depredations of the old prisoners. The Cattaraugus County men camped down-slope from Bill's mess and became steady customers at his barbershop. All of the 85th New York men that Bill knew failed to survive Andersonville.

By the end of May more than seventeen thousand men crowded the stockade, another thousand were in a new hospital which had been established outside the pen's southeastern corner, and nearly fifteen hundred others were buried in the prison cemetery. By the end of June the stockade held more than twenty-five thousand miserable prisoners. A ten-acre addition to the north end of the pen opened on July 1 and was quickly filled. On August 12, 1864, the stockade recorded the largest population of prisoners in its existence, almost thirty-three thousand. At that time, Andersonville was the fifth largest city in the Confederate States of America.[14]

On May 12, 1864, a commotion stirred the prison as cries of "fresh fish!" rang near the gates—the usual call made when new prisoners entered the stockade. Among them were several members of the 154th New York who had been captured four days earlier at the Battle of Dug Gap on Rocky Face Ridge, Georgia. Three were members of Bill's Company B: Corporal Thomas R. Aldrich and Privates Charles F. Allen and Orso C. Greeley. Bill found them in line with the other fresh fish. Tom Aldrich never forgot Bill's greeting: "My God, *Tom,* I am glad to see you, but sorry to see you here." Aldrich was dismayed by the pathetic condition of his long-suffering comrades. "The boys all looked like skeletons, with hardly clothing enough to cover their nakedness," he wrote, "and it was a tough sight for us that had been well fed and well clothed."[15]

Aldrich, Allen, and Greeley were assigned to Bill's squad. Bill and his tent mate Frank Goodrich asked the three newcomers to live with them in the barbershop. Aldrich noted that despite the inadequacy of Bill's tent awning, "he was what they called an aristocrat" compared to many of the pen's unsheltered prisoners—and the target of greedy envy by the have-nots. Contributions by the new men made Bill's mess even better off. Tom Aldrich's haversack was full of coffee, hardtack, and sugar, and he had a small piece of pork. He gave all of the food to Bill and Frank, "the most of it for Goodrich, as he was sick and weak and

I knew he was not long for this world." That first day, Aldrich cooked a familiar old army meal for Goodrich: hardtack, pork, and coffee. The dinner "seemed as though it gave him a new lease of life," Tom wrote, "and he acted better and was better as long as it lasted." But when Goodrich finished eating, Aldrich noted, his spirits drooped—"It seemed to make him homesick after it was gone."

Other items Aldrich brought into the pen were of longer lasting benefit. "My piece of tent and rubber [blanket] came handy for shelter and made quite a shanty," Aldrich reported. He judged their quarters to be "a great deal better than nine-tenths of them had." While Aldrich's equipage improved the mess's living conditions, Bill's prison savvy helped the fresh fish cope with the harsh realities of stockade life. "Hawkins had been [a prisoner for] 10 months," Aldrich wrote, "and was fully posted and knew how to work all the cards that could be worked for the benefit of himself or his friends." [16]

But guile could only go so far to sustain life at Andersonville. Monsoon-like rains commenced on June 1 and continued for twenty-two straight days, churning the stockade's grounds into a sea of mud. The little squad's tent was beaten into the muck by the deluge, but they raised it and considered themselves lucky that they were not among the thousands lying unsheltered in the mire. For a month of unrelenting misery, Bill described the dismal life in a terse diary. Fist fights among the prisoners were commonplace, he wrote, even though the combatants were so weak they could hardly stand up. Small gangs of prisoners excavated tunnels in escape attempts, but all of the diggings failed, detected by the Confederates or betrayed by informants. Every morning bloodhounds bayed beyond the stockade walls as they set off into the woods in search of runaways who had fled outside work details. Hopes would sweep the stockade, raised by stories of Union victories and imminent exchange, only to be dashed when the rumors proved to be false. Fresh fish arrived by the hundreds, worsening the already intolerable overcrowding. "When the men lay down," Bill observed, "they lay so thick that one could not walk without stepping on some." Rations diminished to a small pint cup of uncooked cornmeal or unwinnowed boiled rice and a small piece of rotten bacon per man per day.

Every day, scores of sick men were carried outside on ragged blankets to the hospital. Among them was Bill's tent mate, Frank Goodrich, who made the trip on June 21. Frank's comrades never saw him again; he died of chronic diarrhea on July 8. Sometimes sick men were refused admittance to the hospital for lack of room and were returned to the stockade, where they lay dying in the mud and rain. Greeley was sick; Aldrich was passing blood; Bill himself at one point "could not sit up" and "could not eat any." Every early summer day, forty to sixty prisoners died. They were collected in rows next to the stockade's north end, then tossed like cordwood into wagons for the trip to the prison cemetery. Prisoners made a habit of walking along the rows of dead looking for friends. The corpses' ghastly faces, "covered with dirt and sand and marks of agony and suffering," haunted Bill. During June's constant rains, interments halted. When the downpours finally ceased, some three hundred dead awaited burial. Bill could only describe it as "horrid." Why in God's name, he wondered, did the government not work out an exchange agreement to free the prisoners from this hell on earth? (The Federal government had halted prisoner-of-war exchanges in 1863 to protest Confederate policy toward black captives.)[17]

"Very warm, hottest weather I ever saw," Bill wrote on June 25, after the rains had stopped. "One man died across the street from us this morn and . . . he was the largest man I ever saw." But "that is the way they go," Bill noted. "It makes no difference, tough or weak; we don't know how soon we may be stricken down." Rain fell again four days later. "Could not sleep," Bill wrote, "—lice and rain." His hands were bloodstained and his fingers calloused from cracking lice. Except for a five-dollar bill he was keeping as "seed money," he was broke. "No rations yesterday," he noted on the Fourth of July, "and [today the] Rebs promised double rations. It came and was nothing but maggotty mush." Famished new prisoners gobbled it down, but the old hands—"used to starvation"—refused to eat it.

Fifteen feet inside the stockade walls, strips of wood nailed atop stakes paralleled the perimeter, forming a "dead line" beyond which the men were forbidden to venture. Bill twice witnessed prisoners cross the dead line. Both times, the barrier lived up to its name. The first case involved Thomas Herburt, an Illinois veteran widely known as "Chickamauga" after the battle that had cost him his right leg. Herburt's enjoyment of "fun and sport," Bill noted, aggravated his fellow captives. Worse, he communicated frequently with the Confederates, who often granted him passes out of the stockade. But Herburt lost favor with the enemy, Bill reported. They turned him back into the pen, where he was ostracized by his fellow Yankees as a suspected informant. Shunned by friend and enemy alike, Herburt drowned in despair. When a gang of prisoners confronted him on May 15, he responded by intentionally crossing the dead line, yelling for Captain Wirz. The commandant entered the stockade and sent Chickamauga scrabbling back across the line with an armed threat. Wirz looked up to the nearest sentry, perched on a platform attached to the outside of the stockade wall, admonished him to shoot the one-legged Yankee if he crossed the line again, and left the stockade. Herburt stubbornly hobbled past the palings a second time. The chastened sentry took aim and fired his musket; Herburt fell, mortally wounded.[18]

The second case occurred during the summer. Bill saw a cavalryman go to the upstream portion of the creek, hoping to get a drink of water less tainted by grease from the cookhouse. A guard took aim and fired as the man reached under the deadline with his dipper.[19]

In all, guards fatally shot eleven prisoners at Andersonville. A more persistent threat to the captives came from within. Throughout the stockade, gangs of thugs preyed on weakened men, intimidating them, beating them, and robbing them of food, clothing, money, and other possessions. These so-called Raiders were eventually rounded up by squads of organized prisoner vigilantes (dubbed the Regulators), who with Wirz's approval tried them by court-martial and convicted six of the most notorious to death by hanging. Bill witnessed Wirz ride into the stockade on July 11, 1864, and turn the condemned men over to the Regulators, who oversaw the execution. Bill had never had problems with the Raiders, despite the lure of his prosperous barbershop. But he had a poor opinion of the Regulators, who he thought were "little better than the raiders." After conquering the criminals, this "tyrannical little oligarchy" set up its own corrupt police and court system, "entertaining complaints as they pleased," Bill charged, "and trying the same without any form of law or rules of evidence."[20]

By the end of July, Bill was suffering badly from edema, commonly called dropsy. It seemed like his blood was turning into water and pooling in his badly swollen feet and legs. Bill stood as much as he could when the symptoms first appeared, hoping to keep the swelling from spreading up his legs, and spent hours rubbing his bloated limbs. His barbering, of course, depended on his ability to remain erect. But eventually he could not stand without the help of comrades; as he put it, the boys would rally him. "I thought the poor fellow had got to go," Tom Aldrich recorded, "but he was plucky and did not give up." But beneath Bill's outward grit, fear lingered. He later admitted that he "had given up all hope of getting out alive."[21]

By the blazing hot day of August 5, Bill's condition was so bad that his friends carried him out to the prison hospital. None of them expected him to survive for more than twenty-four hours. It was "an awful sight to see the sick ones" that accompanied him, Bill observed. Among them were his comrades Orso Greeley and Charles Allen. Greeley was suffering from scurvy, a common prison malady; Allen, like Bill, was afflicted with dropsy. "Allen was in very bad condition," Tom Aldrich noted; compounding his problem, "He allowed himself to get homesick and discouraged." The trio's hopes were not lifted by their first sight of the hospital: about two hundred moldering tents on a rectangular plot of ground, enclosed by a board fence and surrounded by a pine grove. Hundreds of sick men had been admitted over the past few days and lay unprotected in the scorching sunlight. On each of the first four days of August, an average of 74 men had died at Andersonville, many of them in the hospital. On August 5, when Bill and his friends were admitted, 90 died. The next day 103 sufferers expired, marking the first of many days that saw the death toll exceeded a hundred.[22]

For more than a week, Bill's attempts to sleep were shattered by agonizing cries and pleas for water from his fellow patients. "The sights," he declared, "were terrible." He often witnessed amputations of scurvy-rotted toes and feet. "Come over to the prison yard," he heard one surgeon call to another. "We are going to have some fun—going to take off another Yank's legs." Squatting to defecate, nearly naked prisoners exposed spines covered with sores and maggots. Wherever Bill seemed to look, maggots squirmed. One of the 85th New York's Plymouth Pilgrims, a large man who had been lanced by the surgeons, spent his last several days with his entire torso a wriggling mass of maggots and flies. One day Bill paid one of the prisoner attendants a dollar for a cooked beef's head, stripped of meat down to its nostrils and swarming with maggots. Bill chewed on the nostrils all day. Over the next few days he broke up the skull, blew the insects off the gristle as best he could, and stripped the bones clean. On another occasion he paid fifty cents to enjoy a more appetizing meal—a crane someone had shot in the hospital yard.

Within days after Bill's entry to the hospital, his regimental comrades began to die. On the night of August 9, Bill visited with Private Othnial Green of Company G. Dysentery was killing Green, but he was also suffering from scurvy. His mouth was a horrible sight—his teeth had fallen out of his rotted gums. As Bill shook his hand, Green declared he was going to die. Bill told him he must not give up, but young Green was right; he died the next day. Five days later, scurvy killed George Bailey. For several hours before his demise, he was insensible. Bill had just brought Bailey some corn crust coffee when he died.[23]

Bill was tended daily by a Confederate surgeon, a thick-set man of medium height and dark complexion, with a moustache and goatee and dark eyes. The surgeon treated Bill kindly; Bill felt that his cheerfulness had won the Reb's good will. Nursing Bill was a regimental comrade, Private Russell Lawrence of Company C, one of the Rocky Face Ridge captives. Every day Lawrence measured out Bill's medicine: a thimble-sized beaker of whiskey. Considering the dose inadequate, Bill supplemented it with a natural remedy. Leaning on a staff, he hobbled to a pine tree, collected some resin, and molded it into small balls. Ingesting these pitch pine pills had a salubrious effect on his kidneys. They also seemed to excrete the dropsy fluid from his system, which left him mere skin and bones but more able to get around.

When the surgeon asked Bill to serve as a hospital steward, Russell Lawrence cautioned that he never saw a steward who lived. But Bill's trust in the doctor was sure and he took the post. Besides, the job earned double rations and kept him out of the pestilential stockade. The combination of extra food—however bad—and his pitch pine pills kept Bill alive. He also took advantage of a potential opportunity to communicate with his family back home. On learning that one of the Yankee attendants was planning an escape, he asked the man for a favor. If his escape was successful, Bill wanted him to write to his parents—to let them know he was alive, but not to mention how bad his condition was. The daring Yank donned the clothing of a sick soldier and made his getaway. Bill later learned the fugitive was successful and kept his promise—his letter was the first news the Hawkins family had received of their beloved Bill.

After about two months in the hospital, Bill returned to the stockade. He found a much-changed place. The grounds had been stripped by the prisoners of every reachable stump and root to burn as fuel. Even the dead line had disappeared. And the fall of Atlanta to Sherman's army at the beginning of September had caused a month-long emptying of the prison by the Confederate authorities. Bill estimated a population of between eight thousand and nine thousand when he reentered the pen; by the first week in October it dropped below four thousand. After about two weeks, guards ordered Bill and hundreds of other prisoners to pack up, and they joined the exodus. After the men gathered their pitiful tent scraps and tin cups, they staggered through the gate and left Andersonville and its horrors behind.

Bill and a boxcar full of miserable Yankees rattled along the tracks for three hot days, with scarcely any rations, before reaching Savannah. After a few days in another stockade, they boarded the same old cars and traveled about seventy-five miles to the northeast, to Millen, Georgia, where a new stockade had been built to house the Andersonville refugees. The Millen pen resembled Andersonville in its log construction, but it was almost twice as large and the population—about ten thousand prisoners—was lower than Andersonville at its worst. This plot of root-stubbled dirt was less crowded. Bill found better tents and huts at Millen, but the food was the same sort of slop they had received at Andersonville. He and his companions camped on the upper side of a hill near the gate. All of them were strangers now. He had been separated from old mates like Tom Aldrich. His other old friends were dead.[24]

The prisoners at Millen had "nothing much to traffic with," Bill observed, but it did not matter to him; his trading and barbering days were over. He was dangerously sick. Day after long, slow day, he lay immobile in his tent, helpless. Comrades cooked for him. He was, he believed, "in a dying condition." Much of the time his eyes seemed to be set on some distant, elusive mirage. But Bill's poor health proved to be a godsend. In mid-November 1864 came an announcement: sick prisoners would be exchanged. On November 15, an order came for the weakest and most sickly men to form a line. By the time Bill's friends managed to carry him there, he was the last in a long string of sufferers.

A Confederate surgeon worked his way along the line, examining the men and designating those who should be exchanged. He had just about reached Bill's end of the line when he turned around and began to leave. Bill's heart sank and he slumped to the ground, "hope gone out of his soul." But "God be thanked" for a miraculous interposition: the doctor turned, came to Bill, looked him over, felt the pulse throbbing in his emaciated wrist—and said, "Put down this man's name." As Bill put it simply, "Joy and hope returned."

Bill and some three hundred or four hundred other sick, haggard prisoners were marched out of the stockade to the Millen depot and herded together to await the train. At the edge of the crowd, Bill was pleased to spot his Andersonville doctor friend. He called the man over, shook his hand, and told him his name. The doctor professed to remember Bill. He commented that Bill had not kept himself as clean as he had at Andersonville—many of the prisoners had long since neglected their hygiene. Pointing to some kettles of warm water in a field, he suggested a scrubbing. Bill was going home, the doctor declared, and should look as good as he could. For his part, Bill thought the Rebs just wanted to make the wretched prisoners look as presentable as possible when they were exchanged. But he cleaned up anyway. After his ablution, he and the surgeon exchanged addresses. The doctor wanted Bill to write to him and let him know if he reached home alive.

At the depot, Bill ended his trading career with a spectacular deal. Somehow he hornswaggled one of the Confederate guards to trade uniforms. Bill sweetened the deal by offering an overcoat that he prized highly—throwing in "a big crop" of lice as part of the bargain. The Confederate won that prize in exchange for three dozen eggs and a half-bushel of sweet potatoes. Bill noted proudly, "The overcoat did the biz."

Night fell without the arrival of a train. Prisoners matted the ground near the depot. It was still dark when disappointment arrived in the form of orders to return to the stockade. Stunned, crestfallen, the sufferers shuffled back to the pen in what Bill described as "one of the slowest, saddest processions that ever marched." When the prisoners reentered the stockade, Bill was again toward the end of the line. Inside the gate, the camp commandant, Captain D. W. Vowles, offered some advice. "Boys, I would not go over [to] the other side and mix up with the rest," the Confederate kindly told the huddled men. "You better stay together right here, for I think that in two or three days . . . you will be taken out of here." [25]

The next day Bill had a misadventure with the Regulators, who had reformed to combat crime and continue their high-handed methods of dispensing justice. Regulator police arrested him for stealing a cup—a charge that he vehemently denied—and hauled him before a kangaroo court-martial. Bill resented the judges' "style" as they lectured him from a platform. He was not permitted to call any witnesses, and every time he spoke he was denounced as a liar. Hearing the story years later, E. D. Northrup commented, "Any one who knows Mr. Hawkins personally knows that he could not have been guilty of the charge." But of course, the enterprising Bill had been a thief as well as a trader, a barber, and a hospital steward. In this case, the judges found him guilty and sentenced him to a day's labor cleaning the compound's streets.

He sold some of his produce and made four or five dollars. In his weakness he dared not eat too much himself—although it was hard not to indulge—so he ate sparingly, finding the small portions nourished him "ever so much." True to Captain Vowles' word, in two or three days Bill and a contingent of other sick prisoners were herded from the stockade back to the depot, where they boarded cars for Savannah. Were they headed toward an exchange, or just another prison pen in the city?

The prisoners rested for an hour or two after reaching Savannah. Then the Rebs helped them aboard a scow and they set off down the Savannah River toward the ocean. The bewildered Yankees had no idea where they were headed. Suddenly they noticed "the old stars and stripes" flying above a distant U.S. Navy steamship. All of the prisoners wanted to cheer, but they suppressed their emotions as the scow neared and came alongside the anchored ship. Supervised by two officers, sailors helped the men from the scow to the ship; many had to be carried aboard. They were prisoners no more. Bill saw men, "in their joy and revived hope," get to their feet for the first time in months. Still they kept quiet. Lending the broken men a hand, the officers kept up a constant commentary: "Look at this one," "Oh, see this one here," "Oh, who ever saw such looking men." As usual, Bill was near the end of the line as the scow unloaded. Finally, when the last prisoner stepped from the gangplank to the ship, a hoarse, weak-voiced cheer floated over the water.

The released prisoners immediately began pestering the officers for a meal. Soon they were marched to the middle deck and seated for a hardtack and coffee dinner. "All were so happy," Bill noted. "It would start the tears to hear the poor sufferers talk as they ate." To the famished men, the common ration was a delicacy. Comments like "Oh, how good this tastes" were heard on all sides.

By the time the vessel rendezvoused with a special hospital ship, the officers had identified the sickest parolees. Bill was one of hundreds of ailing men transferred to the hospital boat. It lay at anchor for about two weeks before the patients were judged well enough to sail north. Even with that precaution, fifty men died during the trip from the Georgia coast to Annapolis, Maryland. Bill reported that their corpses were thrown overboard.

At Annapolis the sick ex-prisoners were greeted by the music of a band and, Bill noted, "many mothers, crying." The men were admitted to a hospital and put on a special diet, drawing twenty-five cents worth of rations per day. Bill was still lonesome—he had not encountered any regimental comrades. But he was free of Confederate prisons, and he soon would rejoin his family and friends at home.

Several weeks later, early in 1865, Bill was granted a thirty-day furlough and returned to East Otto. Townsfolk were shocked by his appearance. A doctor described him as "a ghastly skeleton from starvation and exposure." Another resident observed that he barely could walk. Moved by what Bill had endured, the community held a meeting in his honor in the Methodist Episcopal Church, site of his enlistment.

Poor health caused Bill to cut short his visit home and report to a hospital in Buffalo, where he stayed for several weeks. Then, when his furlough expired, he returned to Annapolis. There his recuperation continued. By April 1, 1865, he was judged to be well enough to return to the regiment. He sailed from Annapolis to Wilmington, North Carolina, and made his way overland to Goldsboro, where he reunited with his comrades of the 154th New York. Somehow he found the strength to make the final marches in North Carolina—and a particularly grueling march to Washington when the war ended—before he was mustered out with the 154th on June 11, 1865, near Bladensburg, Maryland.[26]

Bill Hawkins returned home in broken health, and he never fully recovered. Folks could not help but compare his appearance before and after the war. In 1880, E. D. Northrup viewed a photograph taken when Bill enlisted in 1862. Then, Northrup noted, he was a fine looking man in the prime of life. Now Northrup could only comment sadly, "H. shows [the] effects of Andersonville." Tom Aldrich, Bill's fellow Andersonville survivor, delivered a speech about his prison experiences to a group of Cattaraugus County veterans in the postwar years. "The most of you know Hawkins," Tom commented. "Some of you knew him before the war and when he enlisted; look at him anytime since he came out of that *Hell*

Hole and tell me if he is one half the man he would have been if he had never been there, and now he draws from the Government a pension of four dollars per month." Aldrich added bitterly, "Here is another example of the gratitude of a grateful country." Pensions were a crucial issue for veterans. Like Bill, many of them returned from the front with broken bodies, greatly reduced in their capacity to provide for themselves and their families. Would the government recognize their disabilities and lend them a helping hand?[27]

During the four decades he survived the war, Bill dealt repeatedly with the Federal Bureau of Pensions. He applied for an invalid pension in 1879. He claimed to be almost wholly disabled from the effects of diarrhea, dysentery, and dropsy incurred as a prisoner of war, and appointed his old captain, Dan Allen, as attorney to push the claim. As Tom Aldrich mentioned, Bill's initial pension payment was four dollars a month. But as the pension laws were liberalized in passing years, his monthly stipend rose—to six dollars in 1886, twelve dollars in 1887, fourteen dollars in 1890, thirty dollars in 1904. Along the way, Bill's file in the Pension Office at Washington bulged with proofs of disability, surgeon's certificates, and affidavits from doctors and friends, among them Tom Aldrich and other former regimental comrades and prisoners of war. Doctors reported that Bill suffered from chronic diarrhea; rectal disease; rheumatism in his back, hips, and legs; heart trouble; and lung problems, marked by frequent coughing and spitting up blood. His upper teeth were all missing, his lower teeth were loose, and his gums spongy and ulcerated from the effects of scurvy. "I doubt if there is a sound organ in his whole body," a doctor stated in 1887. "He is a physical wreck." Moreover, Bill's mental state seemed impaired. The doctor assessed him as "a wreck in mind as well as body."[28]

His wretched physical condition often shackled Bill in misery. As the thick sheaf of documents in his pension file confirmed, he was unable to perform manual labor, even to get to his barn. He was confined to his house and his bed for months on end. His family life had its ups and downs. A widower when he served in the war, Bill married a woman named Harriet at an unknown date in the postwar years. She bore him a son they named William and left him a widower once again when she died of heart disease in 1891. Bill married for the third time in 1894, taking as his bride a widow, Mary Morgan Smith, who had lost her husband the same year Bill lost Harriet. It was a May-December marriage; Mary was twenty-six, Bill was in his sixties. They had two children, Harold D., born in 1898, and Maria J., born in 1900. By her tenth wedding anniversary, Mary Hawkins felt she had three children to care for. She had to feed and dress and bathe her broken husband just like her two little ones.[29]

Despite what the war had done to him, Bill valued his memories. In the postwar decades, he kept those memories alive by his involvement in veterans' fraternal organizations. He was a charter member of Ellicottville's Grand Army of the Republic (GAR) post on its formation in 1881 and remained a loyal comrade for the rest of his life. He carried his Andersonville cane with pride. And in 1887 he became a charter member and first chaplain of the Cattaraugus County Ex-Union Prisoners of War Association.[30]

Bill Hawkins passed away at his home in the Beaver Meadows section of Ellicottville on September 30, 1906. His obituary noted, "He died of a complication of ailments, contracted while in the army." A host of friends turned out for the funeral on October 3, which was held at the East Otto Methodist Episcopal Church. There Bill had enlisted, his townsfolk had welcomed his return home from prison, and his comrades had presented the Andersonville cane. Now they came to bid him goodbye. Among the crowd of mourners were about forty Civil War veterans, about half of them comrades from the 154th New York. Seven survivors of Company B attended, including Bill's Andersonville friend Tom Aldrich. The church's minister offered an "eloquent and touching" sermon, and Bill's former captain, Dan Allen, added a few remarks. Tom Aldrich and five other members of Bill's old regiment acted as pallbearers and conveyed the remains to the cemetery. Ellicottville's GAR post, assisted by GAR men from other towns, conducted the organization's funeral exercises at the grave.

Bill's obituary contained a lengthy summary of his military career, furnished by an anonymous comrade, which concentrated on his sufferings as a prisoner. It also included an unusual tribute to the deceased's character:

> By the death of Mr. Hawkins the country has lost a patriotic citizen and the community a kind and sympathetic friend. Whenever he heard of anyone in distress, his services were at once offered. There are few families within his own neighborhood which sickness or trouble have visited, which do not hold a warm place in their hearts in remembrance of personal services he had rendered them. His life has been an humble one, unselfish in its devotion to his fellow man. How much more worthy has he filled his humble station by unselfish endeavor than many, who forget the sorrows of fellow beings in their own endeavor for personal fame. How satisfying is such a life.[31]

Having seen "the sorrows of fellow beings" at their unimaginable worst during the war, Bill Hawkins could not turn his back on the more mundane troubles of his friends and neighbors in his years of peace. The war had not wrung him of compassion.

CHAPTER EIGHT

Private Alvin Hitchcock

Company A

Looming over a rhododendron on a back road in the Cattaraugus County town of Randolph, a cast-iron sign with neatly painted green letters identified Sample Hill Cemetery. A row of tall maples lined the Sample Hill Road front; the rest of the graveyard was surrounded by woods and fields. Next to a clump of cedars near the center of the small lot lay the grave I had come to visit.

The low afternoon sun swathed the stone in shade. This small wedge of pebbly concrete with its pale green bronze plaque stood apart from the other graves, isolated on a damp patch of thinning grass under the cedars. The plaque's inscription, and a flag waving above a bronze American Legion medallion, denoted a soldier's grave.

Like Martin Bushnell, this poor fellow had been an uncounted casualty of the war. But his tale was in some ways sadder than Bushnell's woeful saga. Martin had his beloved Fannie Jackson tending him in his duress. This forlorn soldier, thrown into an isolated and esoteric corner of the army medical establishment, had no angel nurses. When Martin was discharged, he returned home to his family's loving welcome. This soldier's family reunion was brief and traumatic.

Some of the sadness surrounding this grave stemmed from its location. The soldier buried here, unlike Martin Bushnell, did not rest among family members. He had been cruelly torn away from them in life, under extraordinary circumstances. It seemed an additional indignity that he was separated from them in death. Alvin Hitchcock of Company A of the 154th Regiment was the only member of his family buried in Sample Hill. All the other Hitchcocks were interred in other Randolph cemeteries.

Alvin's grave has not been neglected by the current generation of Hitchcocks. Thanks to one branch of the family tree, it looks better today than it did several years ago. Visiting Sample Hill Cemetery in the autumn of 1999, James Hitchcock of Randolph, a great-grandson of one of Alvin's brothers, noticed that the roots of a tree were upending Alvin's stone, tilting it at a precarious angle. Jim and his wife, Vicki, wrote to Randolph's town supervisor, requesting the grave site's repair. Within a month, town workers cut down the tree, removed its roots, and reset Alvin's stone on level ground.[1]

According to Vicki Hitchcock, Alvin's family has not forgotten him, and apparently he has not forgotten his family. In the summer of 2002, Vicki visited the nearby Lily Dale Assembly, the largest remaining spiritualist colony in the country. During a session with a medium, Vicki asked if a Civil War soldier named Alvin Hitchcock wished to speak. Yes, the woman responded. Then she began to talk about Alvin's stay in the hospital, about how he was so stricken he had not realized what was happening, and about how the ordeal had been much harder for his family than for him. She spoke of his remains being conveyed on a long journey by train and wagon, accompanied by male relatives, to bring him home from the hospital. She said he had been so grateful not to be left at that dreaded hospital. She gave a minute description of his headstone, and detailed the recent repairs to the grave site. She said Alvin appreciated the flag left by his grave every year on Memorial Day.

Vicki was flabbergasted. Somehow, almost 140 years after Alvin Hitchcock died, this necromancer had channeled his spirit! In her trance, the woman had accurately summoned the pathetic closing chapters of his story. Other than Alvin's name, Vicki had not provided an iota of information to this stranger. "I have to believe she was getting this information from him," Vicki wrote to me. Vicki was certain that she and Alvin had communicated for a brief time in the medium's cottage. "I don't know if you believe in this," Vicki told me, "but thought I would pass on the information anyway."[2]

In March 1864, at the 154th New York's winter camp in Lookout Valley, Tennessee, Alvin Hitchcock's life began to disintegrate. The soldiers were living in log huts roofed with tents and topped with chimneys made of barrels or mud-caulked sticks. The shanties stood in ten parallel rows along cleanly swept company streets trimmed with boughs of evergreens. Close by stood the more substantial quarters of Major General Joseph Hooker, several precisely cut log slab buildings that had been proudly constructed by the 154th Regiment for its favorite general. Surrounding headquarters, the little city of huts housing the rest of the Eleventh Corps sprawled across the flat valley floor, wreathed in a shroud of campfire smoke. Nearby surged the mighty Tennessee River, hemmed in every direction by mountains, with majestic Lookout towering above them all.

The entire landscape radiated the aura of a historic shrine. Four months before, the Union army had won a renowned battle in this rugged terrain, lifting the siege of Chattanooga and decisively defeating their Confederate opponents. Orchard Knob, Lookout Mountain, Missionary Ridge: their names were now indelibly inscribed in the American lexicon. All winter long, the soldiers had relived their victory on the hallowed battlefield. When spring came to this dramatic and celebrated setting, Alvin Hitchcock started to decline mentally and emotionally.

It began when he was sent to the brigade hospital on March 24 with a severe case of pneumonia. Surgeon Henry Van Aernam of the 154th New York made the diagnosis. He noted that Hitchcock exhibited a "slight mental alienation" from the onset of his illness. Six days after the young soldier was admitted to the hospital, his mental health worsened. Hitchcock's aberration, Van Aernam observed, became very prominent. Within the next forty-eight hours the inflamation in Hitchcock's lungs seemed to abate entirely. But this improvement in his physical condition was paradoxically offset by "a very evident increase of the mental disturbance." Alvin Hitchcock's mind was unraveling.[3]

Before his illness, Surgeon Van Aernam recalled, Hitchcock had been "quiet, modest, and rather taciturn." By April Fool's Day, Alvin's personality had been transformed. Shyness had given way to rambunctiousness. Now he was talkative to the extreme, and when he was not jabbering, he was likely to break into song and dance. All of his outbursts were exuberantly cheerful, so he seemed to pose no threat to himself or others. He compliantly obeyed Surgeon Van Aernam's orders. But boisterousness was not his only peculiarity.

Hitchcock harbored a bizarre delusion. "Sometimes he imagines himself and General Hooker in joint command of the army," Surgeon Van Aernam observed. The conceit was firmly fixed in Alvin's mind: the army's destiny rested in the hands of Hooker and Hitchcock. This situation led to an embarrassing moment for Van Aernam one early April day when the surgeon entered Hooker's cabin and found Private Hitchcock there, babbling to the general. The two co-commanders, having a cordial council of war at headquarters, made an odd pair. Hooker was a robust six-footer, florid of face, assured in manner, erect in carriage, fond of wearing thigh-high boots, resplendent in the uniform and insignia of a major general, always appearing, as an officer of the 154th put it, "every inch the general." Hitchcock was three inches shorter and twenty-seven years younger, pale and pinched from his bout with pneumonia, humbly clad in the worn outfit of a private, a nervous tic twitching around his blue eyes. The doctor apologized profusely for his patient's intrusion, but Hooker amiably replied that he liked to listen to Hitchcock. When Van Aernam informed Hitchcock he must return to his regiment and guided him to the door, Alvin turned to "Fighting Joe" with a final order: "General Hooker, next Thursday we will have this army over to Ringgold and will make the Rebs get up and dust as they never dusted before!"[4]

Clearly, Alvin Hitchcock was insane and could no longer function as a soldier.

"I can learn of no hereditary tendency to insanity," Henry Van Aernam wrote when Hitchcock went mad, but that proved to be untrue. Mental illness had long stalked the Hitchcocks. It was another tragedy, like childhood death or fatal accidents, that befell families. Otis and Sarah (Delano) Hitchcock settled in Cattaraugus County about 1823 and raised seven boys and five girls on a farm on the present-day Caswell Road in the township of Randolph. Alvin, the youngest, was born in 1841. Two of his Hitchcock siblings did not survive childhood. One of Alvin's brothers apparently died before Alvin was born; the other was killed when thrown from a horse.

Several members of the Hitchcock clan were struck with madness. One of Alvin's sisters went insane at age twenty-three, but reportedly recovered after a confinement of six months at the New York State Lunatic Asylum in Utica. One of his maternal aunts went insane at a young age, and was dead by the time her nephew's problems developed. A paternal aunt was insane. And Alvin's father Otis was described by the family as "a very excitable and nervous man"—terms that in those times could have signaled a mental imbalance.[5]

Alvin displayed no signs of mental disturbance during his youth. But around 1859, at age eighteen, he contracted typhoid fever and fell into a deep delirium. According to his family, he acted "silly, childish, and playful" for a month and a half after recovering from the physical illness. Then the aberration faded. Over the next three years his health was delicate and he was easily excited, but he continued to work on the farm with his parents and two older brothers (the other siblings had dispersed). When the 154th Regiment was raised, twenty-one-year-old Alvin enlisted at Randolph on August 8, 1862, to serve three years. Surgeon Van Aernam examined the new recruit and certified that he was "free from all bodily defects and mental infirmity which would, in any way, disqualify him from performing the duties of a soldier." On September 24, Alvin was mustered in as a private of Company A of the 154th.[6]

None of Hitchcock's letters have been located, so his reaction to army life remains unknown. Nor were any substantive mentions of him made in the surviving letters of his comrades. Only a bare outline of his service can be gleaned from the muster rolls and other surviving records.

Alvin was present with his company during the regiment's railroad trip to Washington and its early marches in Virginia. Like William Chittenden and many others, he was prostrated with sickness brought on by exposure during the November 1862 march from Fairfax Court House to Thoroughfare Gap and back. Alvin was sent to the Reserve Hospital of the Eleventh Corps at Fairfax on November 21, diagnosed with bronchitis. On December 21 he was admitted to Ward F of Harewood Hospital in Washington, where his complaint was listed as "general debility." After three months of recuperation, he returned to duty on March 25, 1863.

More hardships soon followed. Alvin was captured at Chancellorsville in the disaster of May 2 and spent the next week trudging under guard with the regiment's gaggle of prisoners to Richmond, where they were confined in Libby Prison and on Belle Island. Their stay was fortunately short. On May 15, a squad including Alvin was paroled at City Point on the James River, and shipped by steamer down the James and up Chesapeake Bay to the parole camp at Annapolis, Maryland, where they arrived on May 18. Five days later Alvin was sent to the camp hospital suffering from constipation, but within a week he was shipped via the Potomac River to the convalescent camp at Alexandria, Virginia. There he rejoined his parolee comrades and remained until their exchange was processed that fall.

Finally free to return to their regiment, Hitchcock and about ninety other men traveled west by railroad and rejoined the 154th New York at its camp at Bridgeport, Alabama, on October 3. Alvin and the others took part in the subsequent Chattanooga battle and march to the relief of Knoxville, and settled into winter camp at Lookout Valley. With spring came the April Fool's tragedy.

Alvin had fought in two battles, had been a prisoner of war, and had been hospitalized twice for physical ailments. If he manifested any mental illness during those ordeals, it went unrecorded. Unlike the fever case of his teenage years, Alvin's mind had survived these ailments unimpaired. Then springtime brought his bout of pneumonia, and his descent into madness.[7]

After Hitchcock's impromptu confab with General Hooker, it was obvious to Surgeon Van Aernam that something had to be done with his delusional patient. New army regulations regarding insane soldiers had been adopted in September

1863. They were no longer to be discharged in the field by a surgeon's certificate of disability, as had been the practice. Rather, they were to be sent to the Government Hospital for the Insane at Washington, D.C. There, expert asylum doctors would decide if a discharge for insanity was warranted. Van Aernam was to follow a strict procedure in this process. He was to submit through the proper channels a certificate describing Hitchcock's insanity, whereupon the military department's commanding officer would issue an order providing transportation of the patient to Washington. In the capital, the adjutant general's office reviewed applications for commitments; ultimately they required the approval of Secretary of War Edwin M. Stanton. Discharges from the service at the government asylum also required the authorization of the adjutant general's office.[8]

Officers of the 154th New York carefully followed the rules in Alvin Hitchcock's case. Military procedure's slow wheel was set in motion on April 16, 1864, when Surgeon Van Aernam composed a certificate declaring Hitchcock was "suffering from insanity and has been for sixteen days past," ever since his April Fool's decline. The doctor provided a detailed summary of Alvin's case. "He was well when [he] enlisted," Van Aernam added, "and has always been a very exemplary soldier." Colonel Patrick Henry Jones of the 154th simultaneously addressed a letter to the assistant adjutant general of the Department of the Cumberland, recommending that Hitchcock be sent to the government asylum. Jones also suggested Private Emory Sweetland of Company B as a suitable escort to accompany Hitchcock on the journey to Washington. "Sweetland," the colonel explained, "is one of the nurses in the hospital, and fully acquainted with the temper and humor of the patient." Like Van Aernam, Jones praised Alvin's conduct prior to his illness. "Hitchcock was an excellent and exemplary soldier," he wrote, "and is respectfully recommended to the consideration of the officers to whose charge he is to be entrusted."[9]

Up the chain of command the paperwork climbed. On April 17 Hitchcock was examined by the surgeons-in-chief at the brigade and division levels, and they endorsed his commitment. First Brigade commander Colonel Adolphus Buschbeck granted his consent, followed by Second Division commander Brigadier General Adolph von Steinwehr. Eleven days later, on April 28, General Hooker approved the recommendation to commit his delusional co-commander. The next day, the documentation reached the Chattanooga headquarters of Major General George H. Thomas, commander of the Department of the Cumberland, who immediately responded with Special Field Order Number 120, detailing Private Sweetland to take charge of Private Hitchcock and deliver him to the authorities at the Washington asylum. Sweetland was given fifteen days to complete the duty and return to his regiment; the quartermaster's department was ordered to provide the two soldiers with the necessary transportation. On April 30, General Thomas endorsed the order and forwarded it to Brigadier General Lorenzo Thomas, the army's adjutant general, in Washington.[10]

"The weather is splendid," Emory Sweetland wrote to his wife from Lookout Valley on May 1, 1864, "[with] warm showers occasionally. The trees are draped up in their green suit and the grass is getting quite a start. I have picked some flowers and will send them to you in a magazine." He made no mention of his upcoming assignment; apparently the orders had not yet arrived. Several more lovely Tennessee spring days passed before he and Alvin Hitchcock boarded a train for the long trip to Washington.[11]

As Colonel Jones had correctly assessed, Sweetland—kind, caring, gentle—was an ideal nurse for Alvin. Almost thirty years later, Emory retained vivid memories of their journey together. Hitchcock's condition had improved somewhat; he was quieter than usual. Alvin's behavior during the trip was so unexceptional, in fact, that people encountered along the way had no inkling he was insane.

The order from Washington arrived in Lookout Valley covered with the endorsements of the various generals, to which had been added those of General William T. Sherman, commander of the Military Division of the Mississippi, and Secretary of War Stanton. But delays occurred before Sweetland and his charge could secure transportation on a northbound train. An average of 135 railroad cars were arriving in Chattanooga from Nashville every day, loaded with supplies for Sherman's imminent campaign into the Georgia interior, and the two soldiers had trouble swimming against that mighty tide. They had to wait a day and a half before they caught a train heading north.

They spent their first night in Nashville. The provost guard tried to make them stay in the unfinished Maxwell House hotel, which years later lent its name to the famous brand of coffee. Construction of the immense brick building had begun in 1859, but lapsed when the war started. Since then the unfinished pile had been used as a Confederate barracks and a Union army prison. The place had steadily deteriorated. The previous September some eighty men had been killed or injured when a staircase collapsed. Sweetland considered the Maxwell House a "black hole" and refused to be lodged there. He then discovered the power of the endorsements affixed to his order. When the guard saw Stanton's signature, Sweetland and Hitchcock were permitted to find their own place to stay in Nashville. They spent a comfortable night in the home of a Quaker family.

Another delay occurred in Louisville, where the two were unable to get a train. Stanton's signature once again proved to be an open sesame. Sweetland and Hitchcock soon found themselves aboard the splendid steamship *Queen of the West,* bound up the Ohio River to Cincinnati. There they experienced yet another delay before boarding a train to finish the last leg of their journey to Washington.

A year and a half before, Alvin had marched through the capital in good health. Now he reentered the city with a crippling illness, under a nurse's care. As had happened so often before on their trip, the two encountered an obstacle on arriving in Washington. Once again provost guards attempted to run them into a compound holding soldiers on their way to the front. Emory and Alvin were marched at bayonet point to the pen. From inside floated the taunting catcall, "Fresh fish!" Sweetland demanded to see the commanding officer. A blustering lieutenant appeared and insisted that all returning soldiers must be held in the pen. Sweetland responded that he was traveling on Sherman's and Stanton's orders; if detained, he would report the incident. The lieutenant obstinately demanded to see the order, and once again the secretary of war's endorsement worked its magic. The abashed lieutenant stepped back and allowed the two to go on their way.

At the War Department office of the army's surgeon general, a guard passed them into a large room. A tall, robust, handsome man in a civilian suit was going through papers at a table; Sweetland took him for a clerk. He turned out to be the surgeon general himself, William A. Hammond, a reformer who had greatly improved the army's medical department since his appointment to the post two years earlier. Putting down his papers, Hammond read Sweetland's orders, glanced briefly at Hitchcock, and said, "That is the man standing there." Yes, Sweetland replied. "I suppose everybody on the road has told you he is sane," Hammond remarked. Yes, Sweetland replied. "He is insane enough," Hammond responded, pointing out the nervous twitching around Hitchcock's eyes. "He never will recover fully." Hammond then ordered Sweetland to accompany Hitchcock to the Government Hospital for the Insane, in the Anacostia section of the city.[12]

The final strand of red tape was a letter from army surgeon R. O. Abbott, medical director of the Department of Washington, to Adjutant General Lorenzo Thomas, requesting an order to admit Private Hitchcock to the government asylum. On May 11, 1864, with Thomas's order in hand, Emory Sweetland guided his patient on the final leg of their journey, through southeastern Washington to a hill overlooking the Potomac and Anacostia rivers, past the gates into the asylum's extensive grounds, and through the doors of the red-brick hospital's four-story, crenellated main tower.

Alvin Hitchcock was admitted to the Government Hospital for the Insane as

Case Number 1419, his illness diagnosed as "acute mania," his first name mistakenly listed as "Allen." Ironically, a few days before, a soldier named Joseph Hooker, suffering from "periodic mania," had been admitted as Case Number 1410. He was not the famous general of Alvin's acquaintance, of course, but a private of the 32nd U.S. Colored Troops. (Adding to the irony is the fact that General Joseph Hooker himself, after he was wounded in the right foot at Antietam in 1862, had been treated at the asylum by his old friend Dr. Charles H. Nichols, the hospital's superintendent.)[13]

The Government Hospital for the Insane was one of several asylums established in the prewar years as a result of the urging of Dorothea Lynde Dix, the indefatigable crusader on behalf of the mentally ill and future wartime superintendent of army nurses. In the 1850s, Dix persuaded Congress that Washington had attracted people from all over the country "whose minds are more or less erratic," and who "ramble about poorly clad and suffering from want of food and shelter." The institution founded as a result of her lobbying was the only Federal hospital to treat the mentally ill. Its patients were limited to members of the army and navy and residents of the District of Columbia.

The hospital's site near the confluence of the Potomac and Anacostia was chosen in the belief that "humane treatment in pleasant surroundings could open the road to healing for people with mental illness," a journalist recently wrote. "It was hoped that the careful landscaping and panoramic view of the capital might have a calming, helpful effect on the institution's inmates." Ground was broken in 1852. The building, designed by Thomas U. Walter (architect of the Capitol dome and wings), opened its doors to the first patients in 1855.

The hospital's capacity increased from slightly more than a hundred before the war to almost three hundred at the conflict's end. About 1,230 mentally ill Union soldiers were admitted during the war. Although regulations stipulated that all insane soldiers were to be sent there, the Federal asylum received only a small percentage of mentally troubled soldiers. Many others were committed to local asylums, released to relatives, or discharged from the service by officers who ignored the rule.

Patients entering the Washington hospital were diagnosed according to standard nineteenth-century classifications, unchanged since the days of the ancient Greeks. Those exhibiting disordered thinking were said to be suffering from "dementia." Depression, withdrawal, lethargy, and suicidal tendencies were attributed to "melancholia." Patients who were agitated and anxious—like Alvin Hitchcock—were said to have "mania."

Unfortunately, details of Alvin's treatment at the Government Hospital for the Insane are unknown; some fifty years would pass before the institution began to keep individual case histories. All the record reveals—other than the fact he drew $6.26 worth of clothing during his stay—is that on June 17, 1864, after one month and six days of confinement, Alvin Hitchcock was released as "Recovered." He left Washington with his discharge from the army, given by order of Secretary of War Stanton and dated June 14.[14]

Alvin somehow managed to find his way back to his family in Randolph. They were dismayed to find that, discharge notwithstanding, he was obviously still mad. The formerly quiet son and brother had been transformed into a nonstop chatterbox. At night he was sleepless, at meals he ate very little. He filled the house with talk. He brimmed with speculative schemes, jabbering for hours about buying property, purchasing government currency, getting his hands on gold. He claimed he could transmute brass and iron into gold. Beneath his money fixation, Alvin had not left the war behind. His enemy now was Copperheads, as Northern war opponents were termed. He concocted ruses to deceive devious Copperhead politicians and raise a regiment of Copperheads for service at the front. He would reach those objectives by an act of metamorphosis: commanding the war resisters while slithering among them in the guise of their namesake, a copperhead snake.[15]

Alvin's mania was now entwined with dementia; his mental processes had obviously deteriorated. What was the Hitchcock family to do? One of Alvin's sisters had been cured of mental illness at the state asylum in Utica. Perhaps Alvin could recover there as well.

Less than two weeks after his dismissal from the government hospital in Washington, on June 28, Alvin's family committed him to the New York State Lunatic Asylum. Founded in 1843, it was one of the first large, state-funded mental hospitals in the country. Like the Government Hospital for the Insane, it inhabited an imposing structure. While the Washington hospital resembled a medieval fortress, the Utica asylum presented a stately classical facade. The building looked like a university hall or a statehouse, until one pondered the barred windows and the high wooden fence surrounding its well-kept grounds.

Although Otis Hitchcock was listed as correspondent in the commitment papers, he was not with his son in Utica. Alvin's brother Milo Hitchcock and a neighbor, Charles Woodworth, accompanied him to the hospital.

Inside the asylum, the three men were led from the spacious main hall to a small examination room, where an admitting doctor chatted with Alvin, quizzed his brother about his medical and mental history, and examined the commitment papers. Alvin entered the asylum as a private patient. Payment for his treatment was insured by bonds from his father and brothers Milo and Edwin. Legal control of Alvin now passed from his family to the asylum. After goodbyes from his brother and friend, an attendant led Alvin away to his ward. Wards closest to the central administrative offices and medical staff departments housed the quietest, best behaved patients. Assigned to the farthest halls were less controllable patients—patients like Alvin.[16]

The patients in Alvin's ward lay in the asylum's notorious "Utica cribs"—covered beds in which the occupants were restrained and immobilized. Alvin was placed in one of the cribs, strapped down at his wrists and ankles. The day after his arrival, his arms and legs were found to be badly bruised. "Done before coming here," the examiner noted. This disclaimer might have been self-serving—physical abuse of patients by attendants was not uncommon—but it was possible that Alvin had chafed at his restraints and hurt himself. He had been noisy all night, adding to the bedlam in the chaotic back ward. His laughing, whistling, singing, and talking were constant. "Seems tremendously elated by his delusions," the doctor observed. He continued to shun food. He could not feed himself, and did not care to be fed. Attendants noted that he did not refuse to eat, but he was "so delirious that he does not know enough to take food nor chew it when put in his mouth." Spoon fed, he gulped down and gagged on his meals. His tongue was white, his pupils dilated. He voided excrement unconsciously.[17]

Two days later, on July 1, Alvin's excitement continued. A doctor ordered a warm bath, followed by cold applications to the head. The treatment did not work. Alvin was noisy all night, beating his arms and legs against his crib. On July 2 he was back at the front, still in the war, shouting about driving horses and hollering military orders. Attendants tried a different restraint, tightening a sheet tightly over his chest and fastening it to the sides of his crib. A doctor ordered ice applied to his back. An "anodyne" was administered to sedate him. But his mania continued, day after day. A doctor next noted his condition on July 11. Strapped down in his crib, he was throwing his arms about, twisting and rubbing his hands. His tongue and teeth were covered with a dark coating. His eyes were dull. He managed to swallow some eggnog, beef soup, tea, and milk.

On July 13, 1864, the final entry was made in his case record: *Died. Exhaustion—acute Mania.*[18]

Less than a month after his discharge from Uncle Sam's service, Alvin Hitchcock was gone. Like so many others, he was one of the war's uncounted fatalities: no longer a soldier, but dead nonetheless from soldiering and a family history of severe mental illness.

CHAPTER NINE

Private Barzilla Merrill

Company K

When King David of ancient Israel was overthrown by his son Absalom and fled into the wilderness, he was succored by a Gileadite, Barzillai, whose Hebrew name meant *made of iron*. On Absalom's death, David resumed the throne and invited Barzillai to join him in Jerusalem. Barzillai protested, pleading he was too old to accompany the king to the city. He begged David, "Let thy servant, I pray thee, turn back again, that I may die in mine own city, and be buried by the grave of my father and of my mother." [1]

Barzilla Merrill no doubt was familiar with the story of his biblical namesake. As Merrill marched into Virginia's Wilderness in the spring of 1863, he too hoped to return home to live out his years, to die and be buried beside his family in Cattaraugus County. And he hoped his teenaged son, Alva, who was with him in the army, would also return to enjoy a lengthy life at home.

Alva is another Old Testament name. A descendant of Esau, Alvah was a chief of the Edomites, a people eventually conquered by their frequent foes the Israelites. The name Alvah meant *injustice*. [2]

In the Wilderness, Barzilla and Alva Merrill came to a place called Chancellorsville, named after an obscure crossroads inn. There, during the first three days of May 1863, a terrible battle was fought. "The word [Chancellorsville]," wrote Civil War historian Bruce Catton, "has been a scar on the national memory ever since." Chancellorsville surely scarred the Merrill family's memory for generations, right up to the present day. They have never forgotten the heartbreak that struck their ancestors in 1863.[3]

Late in the afternoon of May 2 of that year, Barzilla and Alva Merrill and the rest of the 154th New York relaxed near an old tavern in a clearing carved from dense woods. Several days of marching through the Wilderness had brought them to the verge of battle. Suspense and apprehension had been high among the men as the movement unfolded and distant fighting erupted. But this day had been one of inactivity, and the evening promised more quiet. The Eleventh Corps appeared to be positioned well to the army's rear. Although rumors had circulated about a Confederate movement past their front, as the afternoon shadows lengthened, the threat seemed to diminish. With sundown approaching, the men chatted as they cooked their suppers, smoked, played cards, and prepared for a peaceful night's sleep.

Suddenly, shockingly, the peace was shattered. Under the red sunset, the western woods exploded with a roar of gunfire and the shrill keen of the rebel yell. Terrified deer and rabbits darted from the trees and zigzagged wildly across the fields. As the regiment hurriedly took up arms and fell into line, Barzilla and Alva watched with astonishment as their fellow Eleventh Corps troops bolted and ran, smashed to flinders by the powerful Confederate onslaught, swarming past the brigade at Dowdall's Tavern in a roiled, panicked mess of men, horse-drawn artillery, and mule-driven wagons. Few of the fugitives could be persuaded to join the brigade as it formed near the tavern, perpendicular to the road in a shallow rifle pit. Some troops rallied on the brigade's right, stretching that flank toward the woods. Anchoring the brigade's left flank was the 154th New York.

As the last Yankee fugitives scampered past the brigade's line and into the woods behind, out of the smoke emerged deep lines of Confederates, filling the clearing from side to side, filing through the forest beyond, their red battle flags and burnished rifles glowing in the twilight. The 154th New York and its brigade, with the small clump of rallied comrades on their right, were all that stood between Jackson's force and the rest of the Union army, a mile or more back through the forest. Barzilla and Alva watched the enemy surge over the rolling countryside toward the rifle pit like an immense gray wave, sweeping all resistance from its path. When orders were shouted to open fire, father and son shot and reloaded and shot and reloaded as fast as they could. The Confederates did the same. The rifle pit offered slight protection; men began to bleed and writhe and scream and moan. Among those hit was Barzilla Merrill, who was slightly wounded in the shoulder.

The Confederates were staggered by the Yankee line's fire, but they could not be stopped. Far to the right, they outflanked and shattered the rallied Union troops. Then they sent the regiments of the 154th's brigade reeling in turn. The 29th New York and 27th Pennsylvania fled to the rear. The right half of the 73rd Pennsylvania joined the rout. But the 73rd's left half, seeing the 154th standing fast, stood by the New Yorkers. The Confederates now closed in on that tiny force, the last Eleventh Corps troops on the field.

Colonel Patrick Henry Jones of the 154th, down with a wound in the hip, gave the order for the regiment to retreat. The men now had to leave the rifle pit and cross an open field to the woods in their rear, all the while exposed to the concentrated Confederate fire. It was no retreat in precise alignment—they ran, every man for himself. During the chaotic withdrawal across that bullet-swept field, the regiment took its heaviest losses. The survivors plunged into the woods and stumbled toward the Union lines, Confederates howling in pursuit, darkness deepening by the second. Left behind in the hands of the enemy were the regiment's killed and badly wounded. Among them was Barzilla Merrill, dead of a gunshot to the head.

Did Alva Merrill see his father fall? Was he by Barzilla's side for a last embrace and hasty parting word? Did he think his father was still alive, running through the woods somewhere to save his skin? Or maybe just wounded back there by the tavern, or nabbed by some younger, faster Reb, and now a prisoner of war? What Alva knew, we will never know.

We do know that he remained ready to fight. During the rout, blundering through the dark woods, some members of the 154th fell into enemy hands. Alva managed to escape, but in the confusion he and some comrades were separated from the regiment. They spent the night lost on the battlefield, listening to a raging fight. The next morning the little squad fell into line with other Union troops. Alva divided some coffee with his company mate, Private Marcellus W. Darling, and the hungry young men anticipated a restorative breakfast. But just as the coffee came to a boil, the Confederates unleashed an attack on the position. In the ensuing battle, Alva was killed by Darling's side.[4]

When the Union army retreated from Chancellorsville, the Confederates buried the dead. All across the battlefield, squads set to the grim work. Near Dowdall's Tavern, Barzilla's corpse was dragged together with those of the 154th New York's other killed and tossed into a common burial pit. More than a mile away, Alva's remains received similar treatment.

The roll of the 154th's Chancellorsville casualties provided by Lieutenant Alanson Crosby was published in the *Cattaraugus Freeman* on May 21. Barzilla Merrill was listed (as "Berzelia") with the killed. Reports of his death also reached his hometown of Dayton, Cattaraugus County, via letters from regimental comrades. Alva was listed as missing; his fate was uncertain. At the family home in the hamlet of Cottage, Mrs. Ruba Merrill addressed a letter to Assistant Surgeon Corydon C. Rugg of the 154th, seeking more information about her husband and son. Rugg came from a neighboring town; of the few regimental medical officers, he was the most likely to know about her loved ones. On May 30, Rugg responded "with the sad and to you painful knowledge of the death of both your husband and son." He could write nothing which would bring her comfort, Rugg regretted; he urged her to look to God as the only source of consolation.

Much of the surgeon's letter concerned the disposition of the dead. Rugg minced no words to the bereaved wife and mother in describing the fate of her loved ones' remains. "We were not allowed the privilege of burying our dead," he reported. Rather, Union corpses "were thrown together in piles and covered up" by the enemy. Regarding Barzilla and Alva specifically, he stated, "Their remains cannot be obtained." He added bluntly, "It would be more difficult to find your son than your husband, and you might as well look for a gold dollar in the sea as to try to find either of them."[5]

When the news reached a neighbor of the Merrills—the mother of Alva's tent mate—she composed a poem to honor the fallen father and son. Mrs. Betsey Howlett opened her verses with lines that reflected the sadness of family and friends at the impossibility of burying the loved ones at home, where their remains could be properly mourned:

> They sleep far away from their cherished home;
> No flowery wreath can we place on their tomb.
> But angels stand sentry around their remains;
> They will safely arise with the sanctified slain.

Oh! could we but kneel on the cold sod there,
And bathe it with tears and breathe one prayer.
T'would be a sad pleasure to treasure the scene,
In future days its memory to glean.[6]

Years later, after the war ended, the Merrills' moldering corpses, together with the rest of the Chancellorsville dead, were disinterred and reburied in the Fredericksburg National Cemetery. There, on Marye's Heights, a few steps from the Fredericksburg Battlefield Visitor Center, row after row of stones march up the steep, terraced incline with military precision. Under those stones rest the remains of 15,243 Civil War soldiers. Of them, only 2,473 lie in identified graves. The others—including Barzilla and Alva Merrill—rest beneath small stones marking the graves of the unknown.[7]

Unable to lay their loved ones to rest, not knowing where their remains were laid, the Merrill family did the next best thing: they erected a cenotaph "In Memoriam" to Barzilla and Alva in the Cottage Cemetery, about a half-mile east of the family homestead. On a splendid summer day in 2002, my friend Phil Palen and I visited the memorial. I parked in the cemetery's U-shaped dirt drive in the shade of a line of sugar maples. Elsewhere tall Norway spruces dappled the grass with shadows. Like the other Cattaraugus County cemeteries I had visited, Cottage's two acres were well tended and peaceful. The road was quiet; the day idyllic. A cornfield backed the grounds. Daisies and buttercups poked through the lawn. An American flag on a red pole fluttered in the cloudless sky. A hand pump waited for visitors to water flowers.

We found the polished granite slab near the lot's left rear corner. It stood next to Ruba's grave in a line of Merrill family stones, flanked by two flags in American Legion holders, one for the father, one for the son. A pot of geraniums was evidence that someone still remembered the long-dead soldiers. Cut into the stone beneath Barzilla's and Alva's names and dates was the terse inscription: "Both Killed at Chancellorsville."

On October 25, 1862, Barzilla Merrill sat on the ground in his tent in Virginia with his bayonet serving as a candlestick and his writing paper on his knee. Dipping pen into ink, he wrote a letter to Ruba. In a tiny and neat hand, squeezing two lines into every one, leaving thin margins on left and right, he filled both sides of a sheet from top to bottom. Then he began another. As he ran out of space on a page, his handwriting shrank until, he joked, it looked like "telegraph marks." But he felt compelled to fill each sheet. "It is rather against my will," he wrote, "to send clean paper." During idle times, he added to his letter day after day until an envelope could barely hold the resulting folded wad. In simple but vivid terms he described his surroundings, he opined on the war and its outlook, he poured out his heart's feelings. Often he sent Ruba a separate sheet—conspicuously marked private—containing hints of tender and playful erotic longing and other deeply personal thoughts. In page after page of reporting and philosophizing, he conveyed his war with plainspoken brilliance.[8]

Only a few weeks before, Barzilla had been an unremarkable farmer in his hometown of Dayton, where all of the significant events in his life had occurred. There he was born on March 29, 1818, the fourth of fourteen children (including two adoptees) of Heman and Amelia Merrill. There he wed Ruba Cole on February 28, 1839. There the children were born: Eber and Achsah, who died in infancy; Nancy, born in 1843; Alva C., born on March 8, 1845; and Irving, born in 1850. There Alva enlisted on July 27, 1862, at age seventeen, either with his parents' permission or by fibbing that he was eighteen. There, about a month later, Barzilla enrolled on August 30 and followed his son into the service.[9]

Now both were privates in Company K of the 154th New York Volunteers, one of eight pairs of fathers and sons in the regiment. (Family ties abounded in the 154th—every tenth man had a brother with him and there were countless other relatives.) But the Merrill father and son no longer lived together. Boys liked to be together, Barzilla explained to Ruba, as did "old steady men." Alva wanted to tent with a young Dayton friend, twenty-six-year old Private Horace H. Howlett. Barzilla chose three middle-aged men as his tent mates. Alva maintained his own regular correspondence with Ruba; his father sent her occasional reports on their son. "He is a good boy and keeps quite steady," Barzilla wrote after less than two months in Virginia, "but I think that if he was now to home, he would not be so anxious to enlist again—though he don't complain." Alva and Horace enjoyed each other's company very well, Barzilla was pleased to report. Both were "first rate boys" who "seem to think as much of each other as two brothers." They minded their own business and kept themselves clean. "I have watched the boys and tried to advise them some," Barzilla observed, "and I think they have a mind to be men." Their tent was nearby and "we borrow and lend and live quite neighborly." Horace was "a man throughout," a steady, prudent, whole-hearted, well-respected young man who had earned Barzilla's respect and love. Alva confessed to his mother, "You better believe that I and Horace takes a lot of comfort together. If one gets any good thing, the other has half. I don't know what I should do without him. I know I should be homesick if he was not here."[10]

In his first letter from Virginia, written at Camp Seward on Arlington Heights, Barzilla voiced a wish he would periodically repeat. "I would like to draw you a picture of how it looks here," he told Ruba, "but I can't." In a simple string of words, however, he precisely sketched the scene: "plenty of men, guns, cannon, music, horses, wagons, and mules and tents," in a desolate, ruined landscape swept by clouds of red dust. The Union's military might awed him. Secessionism seemed to be terminally ill, with only months to live—there were Northern soldiers enough "to bury the creature outright and have his funeral preached." What part Barzilla would play in this outcome was uncertain. "What awaits me in the future I don't know," he admitted, "but I leave all in the hands of God and I expect to go forth and try and do my duty at all times and in all places." He asked Ruba to remember him in her secret devotions.[11]

When the regiment marched to Fairfax Court House, Barzilla found an equally menacing martial array—ten to fifteen regiments were camped nearby, their drums beating almost constantly. "We are in a complete bustle," he wrote. "Things look quite like war around here, and when the men comes out on dress parade their shiny bayonets looks savage." They drilled every day and went through the motions of mock battles. "I always liked realities better than motions," he stated, "but in this case I presume that the motions would be the most pleasant to the eye." A real battle seemed unlikely: no rebels were reported in the vicinity. "If there was, I think they would fare slim," Barzilla declared. "Our team about here is pretty strong." He thought there were enough soldiers in the field to go where they pleased—if they were managed properly.

Barzilla's new world was unlike any he had known before. Since he left New York State, he had not seen the inside of a house, or sat in a chair, or laid in a bed. He had not spotted a cow or a sheep in Virginia's denuded fields, but he had seen rifle pits and earthworks and trees scarred by bullets. No longer his own man, he belonged to Uncle Sam. His equipage was stamped "U.S." All of the many horses and mules in view were branded with the same letters; they were painted on the fleets of wagons. "Some days I feel a little lonesome and think of home and the folks to Dayton," he admitted, "but I pass it off as soon as possible and enjoy myself as best I can." His health was excellent—"I feel keen as a brier," he wrote, apparently his highest standard. But he was troubled by the high price of tobacco, a dollar a pound. He did not know how he could get along without it, but figured he would "have to stand up to the rack, hay or no hay."

Barzilla wondered if he could do without something else. "My lodging is not first rate," he confided to Ruba. "You know that I like a good bed and a good bed fellow of the right stripe, but I can't have either of these." He daydreamed about calling at home and eating supper with her, in no hurry to leave before morning to return to Virginia. He wavered on how best to address this delicate topic. "I think of things I can't write," he confessed one day; another day he admitted, "I feel some like writing a kind of roguish letter." [12]

He found the solution in private notes. Sometimes he would write letters the neighbors could read, he informed Ruba, and sometimes that would not do. She had to read through the letters herself first and see. If he wrote anything that she did not want to read, she could scrap it. "But I write the truth, and they say the truth will stand anyhow," he declared—and it would not cost much for her to drop a note in the stove after reading it. And so he told her that he needed something that did not grow in Virginia, it only grew in Dayton and provided immediate relief and good flavor. He told her that he thought of her in their bedroom, that he wanted to try his "old nest and old bed fellow" one night and lay his hand over her waist. He told her that Assistant Surgeon Rugg advised that he take a warm hunk of boiled fat pork to bed with him, and added slyly, "I suppose he meant to have me put it to my feet." [13]

The war cast a shadow over his reveries. Once again he wished he could draw a landscape for Ruba. Instead he resorted to words to picture the Fairfax countryside: hilly woodlands dotted with white tents in all directions, heavy canvas-covered baggage wagons pulled by two to four spans of horses or mules clogging the roads on either side of the regiment's camp, the unharnessed teams standing all night "in the broad stable of all outdoors." Writing one evening after cleaning and greasing his boots and shoes, alone in his tent in the glow of a makeshift fireplace, he declared himself "as comfortable as a biscuit." "I am thin in flesh," he reported, but as tough and hearty as a pig. He had not had a hard word with anyone in the regiment. He had been well treated by his comrades. "I have got above living in old snowy Cattaraugus," he teased. "Now my home is in the sunny South." But sometimes he thought his tent was pitched in Sodom; immoral behavior among the soldiers was widespread. "After I get laid down nights I have a chance for reflection," he noted, "and I try in weakness to call on the name of the Lord."

"I have an occasional thought come over me about my little home to Dayton and folks there," he conceded, "but I dry up and expect to reside a spell longer in old Virginia." He assured Ruba, "You know I would like to see you and the children and all the rest of the folks, but there seems to be something to be done here yet—if we ever get about it." But the thing moved slowly; his gun had not yet been loaded. His determination nonetheless remained strong. "I am here to try and do my duty as a soldier for my country and the old flag," he declared.

When he was through he should be glad to come home, but not until then. He asked Ruba to cheer up and enjoy herself as best she could until he returned. "I expect to come sometime if providence permits." [14]

Here was the crux of Barzilla's war—the constant internal battle between his sense of duty and his desire to return home. His morale hinged on the outcome of this clash. "Pa is as cheerful as any of them," Alva reported when the regiment marched to Thoroughfare Gap. "I shall be very glad to have the time come when I can go home," Barzilla wrote from the gap, "but I have done what I thought was my duty coming here, and now my business is here and I expect to stand up like a man and do my duty and if necessary fight for the old flag." He related the regiment's march and its uneventful stay at the gap with his usual thoroughness and color. When the maneuver produced nothing except a lengthened sick list and petered out in a return to Fairfax, Barzilla's spirits drooped. "We have the mumps some here in the army and some have the dumps," he told Ruba. "I try and enjoy myself as well as I can and keep as contented as possible. Some days I get the blues a little and get to thinking about home and wife." He hoped that matters would shape up so he could return home by spring, that the good Lord would take the work in hand and bring about an honorable and speedy close to the war. When orders arrived for another march, he admitted he did not know when or where they would go, but he knew where he wanted to go—"I would like to go home if all was right here." He emphasized that although he was not homesick, he hoped the end of the war would be hastened, but he would wait patiently for the Lord to interpose on behalf of their cause.

"The thing ain't right as it now is," he declared. "The men [are] here and the women there and you know that don't work very well either way." He voiced much concern about their correspondence, requesting Ruba to write frequently and punctually, thanking her for sending stamps and envelopes, regretting that some of his mail had apparently been lost, suggesting that they number their letters to keep better track of them. He sadly reported that he was unable to keep all of her letters, so after reading them over he destroyed them—"I hated to do so." He enclosed notes to Nancy and Irving (his "Chub" or "Chubby"). He offered Ruba advice about home and farm matters, but added, "I don't know as I will want to advise you much. I think that you are getting along first rate."

He and Alva both recovered from hard colds brought on by raw, chilly weather. He felt a little lazy and weak from a lack of exercise, and his dark eyes were bothered by the constant clouds of campfire smoke. His black hair and beard were getting long; he combed them every day "pretty slick," but wished Ruba could give him a haircut and fix him up a little. One night, after his tent mates retired, he laundered his clothes and gave himself a thorough bath. "I wished you [were here] to wash my shoulders and back," he told his wife, "but I got along." [15]

When the regiment marched from Fairfax to the vicinity of Falmouth, averaging eight miles per day, often in ankle-deep mud, Barzilla stood it fairly well. He had recovered his health and added some flesh—he carried 136 pounds on his five-foot, six-inch frame—but stiff knees had made him a little clumsy. "I feel that I am growing old some," he confided to Ruba, "but I guess that I stand it about as well as the generality of the men." He had become toughened to camp life and found he did not mind it as much as he thought he might. He had yet to be excused from duty and had answered to his name at every roll call.

"I have had some peculiar feelings about this war," he admitted. Sometimes his faith was strong that God would stop "this man-slaughter business." The recent disastrous defeat at Fredericksburg was particularly deadly; "It was a wholesale slaughter on our side," one that had cast a pall of depression over the army. Many of the soldiers were discouraged and disaffected. In camp, Barzilla tried to keep as quiet about current affairs as possible, but he revealed his doubts to Ruba. Sometimes he thought that the nation was so wicked it would perish. The war effort was managed altogether differently than he expected, and had he understood its imperfect workings he would have stayed home—"But I came in good faith and I shall trust the consequences." He had a great many anxieties, both in Virginia and at home. Ruba had been sick and he wished he could be with her. "I begin to think that I have been away from home a long time," he wrote, but there was little prospect of returning soon. He had been dreaming about fresh-looking, red-cheeked Ruba recently, and he hoped to again enjoy the privileges of his home circle. [16]

Alva wrote to his mother the same day. "It seems hard to have Pa deprived of the comforts of life as he is," he observed. "If he was only at home I could stay and feel a great deal better about things than I do now." He liked to have his father with him, he reassured his mother, but he felt that Barzilla's place was at home and it would be better if he was there to see to things. [17]

The next day Barzilla confessed, "I rather had the blues yesterday." He had slept it off and felt rather keen. He was somewhat uncomfortable at times, he explained, but "it works off" and he was all right again. It was Christmas Eve, 1862, the night to hang up stockings. He wished he was home to put something into her stocking, to sleep once again in his old nest with his old bed fellow. He thought that he would lay close to her. [18]

On the pleasant first morning of 1863, while Alva and Horace were away on a New Year's Day visit, Barzilla sat in their tent and wrote all day, hurriedly filling page after page, not bothering to read them over. He cautioned Ruba not to let anyone else read the letter—"Some curious notions comes into my head when I write." He had long contemplated informing her of his opinions of the war. She might call him a secessionist sympathizer, but that is not true. He loved his country and its government and he felt like weeping over the nation's deplorable condition. He lacked words to describe his feelings, but felt safe to say one thing: "Unless God by his almighty power interposes, we are lost, lost as a nation."

He had never been more disappointed than he was with how the war was being conducted. The common soldiers were blameless; they volunteered intending to crush the rebellion and save the Union and had done everything asked of them. The blame for the failure fell on the country's "leading men," including the top generals, who did not think of the welfare of their country or the well-being of their soldiers, but instead coveted their large salaries and harbored jealousies of one another. "They all seem to want to be the largest toad in the puddle," Barzilla observed; when one of them made a move, another tried to take his head off. This selfishness and pettiness came at the expense of a great many lives. As a result, the soldiers were discouraged, disheartened, disappointed. The Union forces were diminishing as the men, badly exposed to winter weather in their poor tents, sickened and died in great numbers. Government horse and mule teams were poor and jaded. Good campaigning weather had been wasted in inactivity. Many men had been killed in battle.

For his part, Barzilla tried to take things cooly, but he occasionally felt uneasy and his thoughts drifted to home. For the past week he had had a hard cold, a cough and sore lungs, but the sickness was loosening and he felt better. Camp smoke still bothered his eyes. His thoughts turned to the destruction he had witnessed in Virginia. It was disturbing to see Northern folks come to Virginia and wantonly destroy property. He did not know whether it was right or wrong, but he did think that he and Ruba would not like to see their property treated that way. The South instigated the war, but its small farmers were suffering while the leading men who fomented the conflict prospered. He wished the war could be settled. It would have been materially better for both sides to have it cease, to stop killing folks and let the soldiers return to their homes and families. "But we as a nation are guilty," he felt, "and we need chastening."

He confided to Ruba his own undivided feelings. He was blessed by the Lord and intended to conduct himself so as to receive God's approving smiles. When he laid down at night he asked the Lord's blessings for himself and his family.

Sometimes he saw evidence that his prayers were answered. "Sometimes I enjoy my mind first rate and I feel clear," he noted; "at other times not so well." One thing was sure: he had no disposition to join in the wickedness—card playing, swearing, "all kinds of obscene talk"—that surrounded him every day. He had not had a word of trouble with anyone in the army.

Hardly a day passed without a soldier's funeral. As he wrote, muffled drums announced a nearby funeral procession. For the first time, he commented on the possibility of his own death. "I feel anxious that the Lord will spare my life to come home again and live and die with my family," he wrote, uncannily echoing his biblical namesake. He tried to reconcile himself and bend to the will of God. "I feel rather solemn today," he told Ruba. "I want you to pray for me and I know that you do. I hope the time will soon come round when we shall meet."

He and the rest of the regiment agreed that they wanted the war to end so they could go home. "But we have got on the harness," he declared, "and we are going to keep it on until we see the thing through, and no whining." With that expression of determination, bedtime arrived, so he closed his letter to bunk down. Some of the men kidded him, saying he was going to his tent to lie down in despair. But he had got a lot off his chest today, and on the whole he felt "a little keen." [19]

In the ensuing weeks Barzilla stood picket on the banks of the Rapphannock River, in sight of plenty of Confederate soldiers on the opposite shore. Some of his comrades had conversed with the Rebs and found them to be as dispirited as their Yankee counterparts. If not for the "big toads," Barzilla guessed, Northern and Southern soldiers would not quarrel or fight much. He told Ruba he had learned two things in the army: a man could endure a great deal of fatigue, and he could get along without many of the comforts of home. A cup of coffee with a little sugar and four or five hardtack made up a meal; a pint cup and a spoon served as his dishes; pine or cedar boughs covered with dried grass and topped with a blanket formed his bed. But he had no complaints. They had built comfortable huts for winter quarters. Chimneys had lessened the smoke. He took an occasional bath in warm water—scrubbing "clean enough to sleep with my wife"—and donned fresh clothes. He shaved his upper lip but cultivated a heavy crop of jaw whiskers. He had recovered from another cold and his health was good. Still, a somber thought nagged. "Some of us will live through it and go home, and some will fall and sleep in Virginia without doubt." He hoped to be favored with the privilege of returning home, he stated, "But I want to see this trouble cleared up and removed first, if I can." [20]

After the humiliating Mud March in January 1863, when torrential rains mired the army's upriver movement in a viscous bog and the immobile men were taunted by the enemy, Union morale plunged to new depths. "I see by a little examination that the men in the army are getting uneasy and discontented," Barzilla noted after slogging back to camp, "and I am inclined to think that it would not take a great many more [such] moves to cause a break in our army." Many of the men cursed army commander General Ambrose E. Burnside. Sometimes it seemed to Barzilla that the army would do nothing to accomplish its purpose. If so, he asserted, it would be the fault of the leaders, not the soldiers, who served in good faith. Taken all together, he wrote, "Things look rather dark now."

When several inches of snow whitened the camp, he once again wished he could draw Ruba a picture. Instead he described four regimental encampments surrounding forty or fifty heavy covered wagons, with dozens of mules hitched to wagons or stumps, standing with their front and rear hooves together, shivering in the wet and cold. One morning as he rummaged in his knapsack he came across a photograph of Ruba and was flooded by thoughts of home. He wanted to see one handsome, good-looking Cattaraugus County woman, "about like yourself," he informed Ruba; attractive women were scarce in Virginia. Some soldiers said they would give a quarter to see a good-looking woman, but Barzilla did not think a mere look would satisfy them. "I judge from my own feelings," he admitted; he wanted to kiss one too, that would do him. But he bore his infirmities as best he could, he promised his wife. He had not even had a "grist ground by hand" yet, so she could see he was all right and might go off "half touched." "I made up my mind when I left home," he assured Ruba, "that I would come home [as] pure and clean as I was when I left."

He continued to keep his person and clothes clean, his hair and beard neatly combed. Some soldiers were filthy—one looked "worse than an Indian"—and some were infested with lice. He still had not had any trouble with other men. A number of his comrades called him Uncle Merrill. He still expected to return home. He would feel like a bird released from a cage to be his own man again, not under the control of the "big bugs."

"Well, I guess I have written about trash enough for this time," he closed a letter. He noted that other men received small notes inside longer letters from their wives. Barzilla liked to receive "choice news" from Ruba by this method and encouraged her to send some. Alva wanted to read her letters, but sometimes his father found "little sections I think he had better not read" and refused to let the boy see them. Writing to his mother the same day, Alva complained, "When Pa gets a letter from you, he has to read it three or four times before he will let me

read it, so I have concluded not to ask him to let me read any more of his letters."
The private note was the solution to this dilemma.[21]

Several days later the regiment moved to the vicinity of Stafford Court House
and erected a new winter camp. A week after settling in, Barzilla composed a
lengthy private note to Ruba while in a randy mood. He asked her how she liked
sleeping alone that winter. He supposed she was content not to have someone
disturb her and keep her awake—or perhaps she "would like to be woke up
and crowded a little tightly." He wanted to do just that thing for her; he was
keen as a brier and clean enough to get between sheets with her. "I sojourn in a
strange land," he observed, "a land of all men and no women." But some high-
ranking officers had their wives in camp. The other night he was guarding brigade
headquarters and he heard a "strange noise" coming from the tent. That was the
advantage the big men have, he thought. So the world went, "all towards twenty-
one." He would make up for lost time when he returned home.

A visitor to camp from home had remarked that he did not think much about
women. A soldier had replied that if he had been in Virginia for five months
eating nothing but hardtack, he would think about them. The soldiers said that
calico would look good to them, but Barzilla thought they meant something
other than calico—he could think of other things he would like to see besides
calico. Sometimes he felt like he just must go home, but he knew he could not
under the circumstances, so he bore his infirmities as best he could. He guessed
he would live through it and see his wife again. Sometimes he thought he was a
fool to join the army; other times he thought it was his duty to be in Virginia;
yet again he was disgusted with what he observed of the war effort. "So I have
my trials about it," he confessed. When he looked back the time seemed short,
but looking ahead, time stretched to a great length. He hoped providence would
arrange for his speedy return home, to its front bedroom, warm kitchen, and beloved inhabitants. He would keep up good courage and hope for the best. In the
meantime, if Ruba wanted to send him any thoughts that had a bearing in this
direction, "a little of this stripe," he asked for it in a scrap by itself.[22]

He thought he had some news "from the fine end" when he found three small
strips of paper tucked into her next letter, but he was disappointed. "If you can't
give me nicer little letters then you did in your last," he scolded, "I would not
give much for them." They were "pretty much a fudge after all." But his dis-
content dissolved quickly. "I wish you could see me now," he bragged in a long
letter composed over two days. "I think you would see something worth looking
at." His cheeks, arms, and legs were round and plump, his hair was cut and his
whiskers trimmed—on the whole he looked about as good as new. He would

have liked to measure legs with Ruba; he thought his would be largest. He had talked with his captain about getting a furlough, but he wondered if a ten-day leave was worth the twenty-five- to thirty-dollar transportation expense (his to pay) and six-day travel time, which added up to a costly four days at home. He also had talked with his tent mates about sending for their wives to make a visit to Virginia. "We find one difficulty to get along with," he noted, "and that is we han't sleeping rooms enough in our house to lodge three couple."

Snow had been falling since the previous night when he resumed his letter. His shanty was snug with its warm fireplace and, he teased, no scolding wife. It was hard for him to believe five months had passed since they parted. He often thought of the last time they spent together. He repeated his oft-voiced desire to return home, his hope that providence would order it, his realization that he would have to wait. The regiment had been plagued by sickness, he noted; Company K had been reduced from more than eighty men to fifty-six or so. "But I have been wonderfully favored on all or nearly all sides since I came here," he observed, "for which I feel thankful." He had not had a bad time to stand picket or do guard duty. He had never been healthier or tougher or heavier; he could haul around luggage like a horse. Never would he have thought he could stand what he had endured. Sometimes he got tired, but as long as his bed was dry, a good rest revived him. To date he had slept on beds of oak leaves, pine and cedar boughs, corn stalks, hay, straw, and the open ground. He stood it all like a horse. The Lord had been with him and blessed him and given him strength many times, for which he was thankful.

He closed by wishing he could send Ruba a kiss in the letter; instead he sent his love and bid her goodbye for the present. But then he continued with a little private letter. Sometimes, he stated, he felt as keen as possible when he wrote. On other occasions he almost felt it would be a relief to drop a tear over his writing. He probably thought as much about his family as any man should and he felt anxious to see home soon. "I often feel that I wish that I had been a better man and a better Christian," he solemnly admitted, "and had taken things more pa- tient." Reviewing his life, he found many things he wished were not so, "but the past is gone forever; it can't be recalled." With divine help he intended to live as a Christian man. Today he looked beyond the "musty trash of earth" to behold a heavenly mansion prepared for him. It was Sunday, and he wished he could at- tend the old home church. He was glad that God ruled in heaven. Sometimes, when he witnessed the wickedness practiced in the world, he thought God would be justified to sink the nation. The army was a wicked place that sometimes made him heartsick. "Ruba," he declared, "my mind is as clear as a bell to day." But he wished he could talk with her; he could not fit all of his thoughts onto a bit of paper.[23]

Days passed in plodding monotony—"All is quiet on the Potomac," Barzilla reported—but a flood of words continued to gush from his pen. He defined the army as a hydra-headed monster and a piece of the devil's invention. Following a twenty-four-hour picket tour with no sleep, he sarcastically declared that he was in good trim to write, with quick and discerning thoughts coursing in a clear head. Ruba would hardly recognize him. His weight was up to 140 pounds, his face was plumping up, his joints were getting limber, his hands were becoming smooth. With a little of her hair dye to brush into his hair and whiskers, he thought he could do anything as well as he did twenty-four years earlier—"and I think I could do some things better."[24]

It was not right, he felt, for him to have nothing to do while Ruba had so much to contend with at home. He wished he could be there to help her with her chores, but nothing could be done about it—she would have to do the best she could alone. He was getting tired of having nothing to do. He had his ups and downs. Some days he got the blues, thought he was a fool for enlisting, felt tried and perplexed; but he knew that would not do and tried to avoid that train of feeling. Other days he felt lively and buoyant, his mind clear and sound. He thought he was in the right position to pass through the current scenes. He had had some "sunny spots" and "happy seasons"—as good as he ever experienced—since he came to Virginia, but he had also endured some trials as sore as any he had passed through in his life.

Sometimes Barzilla thought that God had turned a deaf ear to people's prayers. Why, he wondered, did God permit things to continue as they were? On the other side of the leaf, he felt that the wickedness practiced in the nation's high places deserved punishment. Why were noble men suffered to fall, or weather the storms of life in camp, all for the wickedness of others? While voicing these questions, he did not want Ruba to think he was embracing skeptical views with regard to duty. He was only saying he could not solve the questions. Perhaps she could help him on these points. He stressed that he still held on to God's promise. In addition, "I am learning lessons here that will be of use to me after I get home." He tried to glean knowledge when and where he could. The army was "a good place to study human nature." He found "some men that are men in mind and body, and a great many that are only men in body." A well-developed mind looked better to him than ever before. Some superior officers had small minds and large bodies, according to their own conceit. Selfishness—one of man's meanest traits—was widespread.

Barzilla felt that the nation's troubles would be overruled for the people's good; the clouds would disperse and God would show a smiling face. He hoped that the nation would be cleansed and left to stand on the broad basis of a government unimpaired by wickedness. Again he wondered why the innocent suffered with the guilty in the war. The war's instigators were the leading men, who get big pay. The common soldiers, who had enlisted with good motives, had been deceived to a great extent. He wished he could speak with Ruba because he could not convey all of his observations in writing—they would be too lengthy. "When I get home," he promised, "we will talk."[25]

During this period, Alva worried about his parents. He did not think Barzilla would be able to stand the coming warm weather and hoped he would be discharged. If his father returned home to attend to things there, Alva could stay at the front and feel a great deal better. The situation saddened the boy. It agonized him to know that his mother was without someone to care for her. "I have not been homesick yet," Alva asserted, "but Pa wants to get home on furlough the worst kind [of way], and I hope he will have a chance before long." He added, "I hope that we shall all come home before long."[26]

But Alva's assessment of Barzilla was off target. As winter waned, both father and son thrived. Barzilla considered himself as "tough as a pig," with a "constitution like a horse," his body "clean as a penny" to boot, with "no lice, no sores." Alva was a half-inch taller and outweighed his father; Barzilla described him as a great, stout fellow, curly haired and heavy-boned, whom he guessed he could not "handle" anymore. "I think that there is considerable Cole about [him] by some means," Barzilla teased Ruba about their fair-skinned, hazel-eyed boy. "I hardly know how it happened. Can you tell me anything about it?"

One of Barzilla's tent mates had received a box of goodies from home and the men were living on the top shelf, savoring light wheat bread and strained honey. "We han't but one thing to hinder us from having things as we want it just now," Barzilla told Ruba, asking her to guess what it was in her next letter. Then he turned to a more sober subject, the progress of the war—a topic that heated him up sometimes, despite his efforts to remain cool. He wished the nation could be rid of its trouble so the soldiers could return home to their families, but if his health permitted he intended to stay and "help pick the bone." He refused to "grunt around a while" and leave the regiment to return home with a discharge. It would not do justice to Dayton, nor to the 154th New York. "I came with the regiment," he declared, "and I want to go with the regiment." He loved his country as well as ever. He remembered that some men professed a "warm attachment" for their country before they enlisted, but on reaching the front quickly managed to wangle a discharge and get home. "My spunk is good yet," he contended. "It makes me disgusted to see men sing another tune so quick."

In his opinion he had not done a thing to be ashamed of since joining the army and he intended to continue conducting himself in a manner that would allow him to hold his head up when he returned home. As usual he had social feelings and wanted to have a "pretty lively visit" with folks in Dayton. "I have had the blues shit on [me] right hard some days," he confessed. But he broke the fit with a large dose of thoughts of home, "and the harder the fit the larger the dose, and it works very well." He tried to keep his best foot forward and his countenance cheerful.

After the evening roll call, Barzilla continued his letter in Alva and Horace's tent. The young men were out on duty. He sat alone on the edge of their bed near a cozy little fire with a board from a hardtack box across his knee for a desk. For more than five months, he calculated, he had lived "a kind of widower life." And while he could stand this solitude, he thought of Ruba often. "I would not grudge a V," he told her, "if you could spend the night with me tonight." The bed was just right for two to sleep ("or rather lay") on; he wanted to put his arm around her and give her a good hug and a sweet kiss. He remembered the first kiss he ever put on her cheek. He recalled many pleasant seasons the two had shared; he also reflected on times that he wished had not occurred. "My affection for you is probably as strong as it ought to be," he assured Ruba, "for I have had a trial of this [separation] during the past five or six months." A flood of recollections swept over him, from the time twenty-six years before when he and Ruba stood at the end of the rain trough at the back door of her father's house and had a talk, to an apparently unforgettable occasion when she sat by the front window. He recalled how she looked when her name was still Cole, with her hair cut short beneath a black ribbon headband and a white cape around her neck. Not only that, "I can remember how other things look that you have got, and on the whole *all* is right." These musings were interrupted by the officer of the day, who ordered the candle extinguished, so Barzilla continued to write by firelight. Finally, tired and sleepy, he closed by saying he did not hear from her as often as he wished. He looked for a little letter from her—"get it up nice," he pleaded—and sent his love to the children.[27]

Three days later, snow fell over the quiet camp. Barzilla reported a better feeling had emerged in the army, with less fault-finding. He discussed the military situation but admitted that speculating about what might happen was futile. Distant cannon fire had been heard recently, but his brigade had yet to be called on. The army appeared to be reduced in numbers and some regiments were soon due to be discharged.

Old Virginia, he informed Ruba, resembled the Seneca Indian reservations back home in western New York. Fences were burned, buildings razed, the few families left had little to eat. Slaves were a curiosity to Barzilla; he found most of them were half-breeds and some "nearly white." In a tidy slave cabin with a large, old-fashioned fireplace, he met four mulatto adults and about a half-dozen youngsters. One of the women was nearly white and good looking; if she had been in Dayton and nicely dressed, Barzilla thought, she could have passed quite well for white. Some of the masters' houses were in good shape. Others were crumbling, their plantation grounds overgrown with scrub.

In camp, Uncle Sam had opened a nearby bakery. Massive amounts of dough were mixed in huge vats and baked in smoke-belching ovens; each soldier received a fresh loaf every day. A bristling battery of fifteen cannon was planted on a hill above the regiment's camp. "They look savage," Barzilla thought. Some men's wives were visiting the front. It did Barzilla good to see a nice Yankee woman in camp. He wondered if Ruba should visit. He had tried a widower's life for six months now and was beginning to feel uneasy about it. "What is to be done?" he asked plaintively. "I feel as though something should be done some way for me soon." He asked Ruba to advise him what to do.[28]

Writing after a three-day picket tour and little sleep, Barzilla felt rather thick-headed. Around 3:00 that morning there was a slight scare when a gun was fired and the picket guard was called to arms. It was a false alarm. "This makes the third or fourth time that I have been called immediately to my gun," Barzilla reported, "and no bones broke yet."

In line after line he offered advice about the farm and war news and rumors. He suggested that Ruba buy herself a good black silk dress. There was not as much time to write nowadays as before, he noted; he had been busy doing laundry, attending to his regimental duties, standing guard around camp, keeping his musket in order. He again urged Ruba to fill an occasional leaf "with matters that we would not talk about in company." She might think he was improper or impolite, but he wrote what he felt.[29]

Several days later he composed another long letter. After relating the latest war news and speculation, he stated he would like to be where he could do the most good, that he came South not for profit or promotion, he came to take a gun and bayonet. Now he had them; he had learned to use them, and "they are a very good carnal weapon." He expected to stand by and help pick the bone of contention. He had no fuss other than with the leaders, who might not be of the right stripe, but he left them to "the disposer of wants."

Horace Howlett had accidentally cut his foot badly with an ax the other day, Barzilla reported. He had been sent away to a hospital. Barzilla did not say whether Alva had a new tent mate or not. Instead he returned to thoughts about the war. A summer campaign seemed likely; Barzilla hoped it would bring the conflict to an honorable close. He had no particular anxiety to stay in Virginia once that end was reached.

He described the interior of his hut to Ruba. The walls were not ornamented with engravings, he noted, but rather with guns, bayonets, cartridge boxes, haversacks, and canteens. Most of the time, he assured her, his mind was well composed; sometimes he felt a little uneasy, but he dispensed with those worries as soon as he could. He despised the eternal complaining and faultfinding he heard on all sides. Yes, most of the time his head was as clear as a bell, but his eyesight was failing, especially by candlelight or at twilight. He had some shortness of breath, which he attributed to lack of exercise.

He reserved the last page "for a little fun." A "strange phenomena" had been seen in camp this morning. A woman rode by on horseback and her white underskirts showed, which "waked up the boys considerable I assure you." He wanted to see his nice little handsome, delicate wife quite badly, he assured Ruba, and that was not all he wanted—but he had to learn the art of self-denial, "which by the way is a very good lesson to learn." He guessed he would stand it a while longer, but he could not stop writing about it. "I would like to take a lodging under the left wing of my hen," he wrote. "I may get hard up by and by unless I should just see my frau." He called this last page "a kind of masonic letter," that is, secret.

The date was March 29, 1863, his forty-fifth birthday. Barzilla supposed that if he was out of the army now he would be clear of the draft. But he had enlisted for a long scrape, three years. That was not as long, however, as the scrape he and Ruba were in, "for the length of life" via the matrimonial vow. Again he reflected over the past quarter-century or so—years that included a good many sunny spots and the occasional thunderstorm. It did not do any harm to review the past, he felt. He had serious thoughts, although Ruba may have doubted it from what he wrote. But his wild oats were not all sown yet, and probably would not be for some time. "I like a little fun," he wrote. "Deliver me from gloom and a long face."

But gloom darkened his meditation. "Sometimes I have a thought that it is possible that I shall never see home again," he wrote, "but I leave this all with the disposer of wants." Barzilla did not know if it was wrong to give room to a thought of that kind. He did not worry about it; he expected to come home and spend his declining years with his wife. He asked Ruba to pray that he would return. "I am as likely to fall here as others have been," he acknowledged; disease had taken many. Barzilla thought he was acquainted with the human system enough not to abuse his health unnecessarily. On that note, he asked her to send him a half-pound of good, fine-cut tobacco. The army did not furnish tobacco, but he thought he had better not stop using it.[30]

April brought signs that the army might move, but Barzilla thought that the weather and roads had to improve before a campaign could commence. The troops were in good health and spirits, he believed, and if they had good leaders they would succeed. "I think that light begins to dawn," he wrote. He hoped the war would end soon.

Reflecting on their relationship, Barzilla wrote, "Ruba, I have not laid up anything that has happened, and I hope you won't." He was sorry that they ever had an unkind word; there was no need of any such thing. But the past was gone and could not be recalled. It might be so ordered that they should never meet again on earth, but he expected to meet her on the other shore. Should providence favor, he expected to come home. He felt no depression of spirits and he thought the war would come out right. He looked for this and expected it and felt as though it was his duty to help achieve the victory.

In her last letter she had stated that if he was home, they would have a good sleep. He offered a correction: "I don't think that we would have slept at all. We would want to visit, etc." He left one nice little article at home that he wanted, but unless Ruba came and brought it to him he could not have it. But that was not convenient for her, he assumed, so he would have to do without. He supposed self-denial was quite a lesson to learn. He again requested "some delicate news" in separate notes that he would not have to share with Alva. He presumed that a man and wife had a right to talk or write a little on nice points if they chose. Living like a widower for the past six months, it was a matter of course that he thought a little about the finer sex. He had got along better than he expected on this point, but he had an occasional thought in that direction. "I hardly know how it happens," he claimed.

He and Ruba never appreciated the privileges they enjoyed, it seemed to Barzilla. He recalled times when he was at home and the children were at school. He would come in the house and get some water and a little lunch and have a nice time with her. It pleased him to think of these things now. He wondered if she was too old to have such fine feelings, or if she had an occasional flit in that direction. According to his mother, he had not been weaned yet. He was about the same old coon. He apologized for the abuse Ruba received from him the night she sat by the front window.[31]

He enclosed notes to the children. In response to a letter from Nancy, he encouraged her to learn to write rapidly and spell correctly. As a sort of game, he intentionally misspelled many words, so that his daughter "may have the privalage of critassing thisere lines . . . and correkt me in your next lettor to me. I have bin riting to ma and fell some tiord and it may be I shal spel bad." "Look clost," he urged her.[32]

A week later, Barzilla worried that Ruba's mind was taxed with concerns about home matters. He too had experienced six months of toil and anxiety, but he had also enjoyed some happy seasons. A friend had taken him safely and shielded him from harm all the way thus far; he felt like praising the Lord for his wonderful goodness to him. On review, he saw God had a watchful eye over him: he had had no accidents, had not been sick, had a good appetite and slept well—in all, had been wonderfully favored. He placed his trust in providence and thought he would be taken safely through the strife and again enjoy the privileges of his quiet home. He thought much of home and the loved ones he had left behind, but duty called him to be in Virginia. As soon as he could see that his duty was to go home, he would feel thankful.

He had aged. There were some gray hairs on his neatly combed head. He thought Ruba would not like the look of his face, the lines around his mouth; but as long as she could not see him, it was all right.[33]

The next day, April 10, 1863, Barzilla finally had an important event to relate. The Eleventh Corps, to which the 154th New York belonged, had just been reviewed by President Abraham Lincoln. Barzilla typically wished he could draw a picture of the scene for Ruba. Instead, he suggested she might find a woodcut of the review in *Frank Leslie's Illustrated Newspaper*—he had noticed an artist sketching on a distant hilltop. But as usual, he did a fine job picturing the scene in words. There was President Lincoln, hat in hand, on a dark bay horse at the head of a gang of horsemen. Lincoln's familiar portrait did not do him justice, Barzilla thought; he was an intellectual looking man with a well-shaped forehead, although he looked care-worn and pallid. Army commander Joseph Hooker and the Eleventh Corps commander, one-armed Oliver Otis Howard, led a flock of their fellow generals and other big men. Four or five women tagged along, attired in long, black riding dresses and black hats. Masses of soldiers occupied a large plot of ground. The men made a fine appearance; they were well clothed and in good condition, and when they wheeled in double columns at half distance to pass in review before the president and generals while brass bands played stirring tunes, the scene was sublime. Ruba probably would not understand what "double columns at half distance" meant; he did not have room to explain.

As he captured the spectacle with his pen, Barzilla was distracted by constant noise—talk, laughter, drumbeats. "Some times I get tired of it," he conceded, "and feel as though I would like a few days of quiet life." He occasionally felt confused when he tried to write, but on the whole he got along very well. Alva, sick with a hard cold, had stayed in camp and missed the review. The cold was working loose; Barzilla thought their boy would get along in a day or two. There were a great many exposures to bad weather in soldiering, but Barzilla stood it like a horse. Swarthy by nature, he was suntanned darker than Ruba had ever seen him. He accounted for this by noting he had been "turned inside out for the past six months"—he had not seen the inside of a house, nor spoke to a woman, nor sat in a chair. He doubted that he could lay on a soft bed.[34]

A letter from her arrived and he responded immediately. He was writing to her every day now, and because he squeezed two lines into every one, his letters got in more than hers did—although he admitted his content was "probably nonsense." He offered much advice about home and farm matters, but concluded by suggesting, "You will have to calculate to get along as best you can." Irving was still too young to be of much help. Ruba should not work outside too much, in her husband's opinion, because she was not tough enough to stand it. Barzilla still hoped to get a furlough, but he was highly uncertain of the prospects.

The uncertainty of military life bothered him. Orders were received only to be countermanded; orders to march any day were just as likely to result in a month's delay. There was never a hint as to what was to come. This insecurity gave him a great many anxieties. He speculated—correctly, as it turned out—that another attempt would be made that spring to cross the Rappahannock. The roads were drying up and the weather was milder. In the meantime, he had found amusement playing baseball and was pleased to find his athletic skills had not diminished.

He decided to write a separate sheet to respond to some remarks Ruba made in her letter. Some people of his acquaintance, he mused, seemed to have a great many unnecessary troubles and anxieties to contend with, and they seemed to want others to be miserable with them. He thought it was a pity for people to get into such a state. People should watch their heart's emotions; they should have the right kind of shoots spring up and weed out the noxious plants. It was a great lesson to be acquainted with one's own heart. There were a great many comforts and much merriment to be enjoyed in life. Sometimes it required some effort, but a choice had to be made. Some chose foolishly, others wisely.

He signed off, "From your little man."[35]

The next afternoon, Sunday, April 12, 1863, Barzilla filled the last sheet of his letter. He was in a contemplative mood and he wrote passages unlike any he had written before. He offered Ruba a meditation on grace, God's enabling help to humankind. His words had a biblical tone and cadence, but they were not quotes from prophets or saints—they were simply the words of a philosophical farmer-turned-soldier, deep in a reverie.

He told Ruba he guessed he would "drop a thought or two" on the word grace—a commonly used, short word, but one big with meaning. He found we need grace in the sunshine to keep ourselves humble, and grace in a thunderstorm to remove the dark, looming cloud. We need grace in health to teach us to prize the privilege, and grace in sickness to teach us patience, and how to prize health. We need grace to do every duty. We need grace to carry a joyous cup with a steady hand, and to drink the bitter cup with an unmurmuring spirit. We need grace to have prosperity and adversity sanctified, and grace sufficient enough to say at all times, the will of God be done.

Barzilla sometimes tried to examine himself to see if he had grace enough to meet all emergencies. "Some times I think I have," he stated; "at other times I fear that I lack." He wanted to struggle to achieve a graceful existence, to have daily evidence that he had enough of God's grace to prepare him for any and every emergency he might be called to endure. He declared, "I can feel the fire burn." He never was in a place where he needed a larger share of God's grace than in the army. Thus far he had found God's grace sufficient.

Nearing the bottom of the page, he closed his letter with a few lines:

> I want to place myself and all I have, family and cares, into the kind care of a just God, hoping that all will be ordered right, and also hoping that things will be so arranged that we as a family may have the privilege of reuniting under the paternal roof. I look for this time to come, and I expect it; and further, sometimes I feel that I have an evidence of it. One thing I can say—thy will, O God, be done.
>
> Barzilla Merrill to Wife[36]

They were the last lines Ruba Merrill ever received from her husband. The next morning Barzilla and Alva and the rest of the regiment left camp and marched away on the road that led to the Wilderness. Barzilla, made of iron for the Union cause, was about to be thrust into the inferno at Chancellorsville.

CHAPTER TEN

Private Clark E. "Salty" Oyer

Company G

Sometimes during his long and vibrant life, momentous experiences came to Clark E. Oyer in pairs. Twice he sailed the seas. He was twice wounded, twice captured, twice imprisoned, and twice busted from noncommissioned officer to private in the Civil War. He married twice in the postwar years, and was twice divorced. He had two children.

Oyer was a chronic roamer and adventurer. In the postwar decades he led a nomadic life, regularly moving from place to place and state to state. When asked in 1906 to list his residences since the war, he confessed, "I can't make any positive statement." Around 1918, slowed at last by old age and infirmities stemming from his army days, he alighted in California at the home of his only son and spent his final years rambling under the sunny skies of Los Angeles. A stroke killed the peripatetic old veteran on April 29, 1923, at the age of eighty-six years, nine months, and twenty-five days.[1]

Jesse Oyer buried his father in one of Los Angeles's oldest extant cemeteries, Rosedale, on West Washington Boulevard. A typical nineteenth-century urban memorial park, incorporated in 1884, it drew visitors not only to attend the graves of loved ones, but also to admire its beautifully landscaped grounds. Today a pilgrim to Rosedale heads west from downtown Los Angeles about two miles on the Santa Monica Freeway and exits at Normandie Avenue. The cemetery is a few blocks north. Over the years the surrounding neighborhood has deteriorated, but Rosedale remains a pretty and peaceful oasis, sixty-five acres of ornamental trees, shrubs, flowers, and monuments. This being Los Angeles, the cemetery is home to the remains of several show business celebrities, among them the actress Hattie McDaniel, best known for her Oscar-winning role as Mammy in the classic Civil War film *Gone With the Wind*.[2]

In Rosedale, Clark Oyer rejoined the Boys in Blue. In a special section of the cemetery, surrounded by trees, marked by a tall flagpole, and guarded by an immense cannon, hundreds of veterans of the Grand Army of the Republic rest in neat rank-and-file rows. Each granite headstone is carved with a shield enclosing the veteran's name, rank, company, and regiment. The cannon is aimed directly over the row containing Clark Oyer's stone. Around him lie men who served in regiments from Pennsylvania, New Hampshire, Michigan, and Missouri, before following the setting sun to the California coast.

Beneath the rustling palms, each silent stone guards a soldier's story. Few could have been as rollicking as Clark Oyer's.

His comrades of the 154th New York called him Salty in recognition of his prewar career as a sailor. He was listed as such in Company G's descriptive book; his hometown clerk classified him as a seaman. But his nautical nickname and several tattoos—a star on his left hand, his initials on his left arm, a spread eagle and flag on his right forearm—are the only other evidence of his life at sea. Nothing is known of his ships or his voyages or his ports of call.[3]

It is unknown how long he had been ashore when he enlisted at age twenty-six on August 18, 1862, in his hometown of Ellicottville, Cattaraugus County. His father, Peter D. Oyer, apparently took a dim view of Clark's enrollment. During the recruiting drive that led to the formation of the 154th Regiment, the elder Oyer declared that fools aplenty were volunteering. He added that the fools were not dead yet, but their chances were good. "Keep clear of them," was old man Oyer's advice. Salty ignored it. "You perhaps think I am a strange fellow for enlisting," he wrote to an uncle about a month later, "but that is all right." He voiced only one reason for joining up: "I could not stay out there."[4]

"Out there" perhaps referred to Peter Oyer's remote, hilly farm near the Ellicottville hamlet of Plato—a place Clark had fled at least once before, when he went to sea. Clark was the only child of Peter and Mary (Clark) Oyer, born on the sixtieth anniversary of Independence Day—July 4, 1836—in the nearby town of Franklinville. About eight years later, his mother died. Two years after that Peter married again and moved to Plato. Rachel Vedder Oyer bore him five sons before she died giving birth to twins in 1860; the babies also perished. Peter would marry yet again, and father two more children. But when Clark left for the war, the Oyer farm was an all-male preserve of his father and five young stepbrothers.[5]

As a soldier, Salty Oyer was always on the lookout for a little fun, an escapade, extra food, and any advantage of any sort that would ease his life in the army. But he seemed prone to mishaps, and as often as not, his ambitions were thwarted. A typical example occurred during the march from Fairfax Court House to Falmouth, Virginia, in December 1862, when Salty and two comrades fell behind the regiment to do some unauthorized foraging. During their brief two months of service in Virginia they had become quite proficient at plundering food—a skill noted by their division commander, Brigadier General Adolph von Steinwehr, who declared that if he had three regiments with foragers as good as those of the 154th New York, he could steal Richmond.

Salty and his friends came across a spot the Confederates had used as a slaughterhouse. The blood-soaked ground was dotted with rotting beef heads and offal. Some fat hogs, snorting and slobbering, rooted in the refuse. After several missed potshots, Salty and his pals killed and skinned a fine specimen. Lugging the carcass, they hustled to overtake the regiment. But they were stopped by two mounted Union soldiers, a major and his orderly. Both were German-Americans, a predominant ethnic component of the Eleventh Army Corps, to which the 154th New York belonged. In a thick accent, the officer denounced the three privates as loafers and rascals and demanded to know why they were straggling. "Getting rations," they replied, stating the obvious. "You have plenty," the major replied; "crackers, sugar, coffee, meat, all such things." That pronouncement made, the hog was slung onto the orderly's horse and the two Germans rode away to prepare a feast, leaving Salty and his comrades in empty-handed disgust.[6]

The next time Salty was the victim of a thief, he extracted some revenge. Again the perpetrator was a German-American. One night in May 1864, near Resaca, Georgia, as Salty slept with his haversack's strap under his head, he was awakened by a tugging at his neck. He found a soldier standing over him, who explained in a German accent that he was looking for his regiment. Salty gave the wanderer directions and went back to sleep. The next morning he discovered his full haversack was gone and an empty one left in its place. While his comrades cooked breakfast and jibed him about his loss, Salty fumed. But the boys—as he surely knew—were with him. After breakfast several of them accompanied Salty to the German's regimental camp, where Salty confronted the thief. Words were exchanged. Someone yanked off Salty's hat and a 154th boy jerked it back. Salty aimed a kick at the thief. But before the confrontation escalated into a brawl, cooler heads prevailed and a settlement was reached. Much of Salty's provisions and his tin cup were returned to him, and the German got a kick in the pants from his captain.

A month later, by a quirk of happenstance, Salty witnessed a cruel fate befall his antagonist. During a fight near Kennesaw Mountain, Salty was acting as a file-closer—keeping the men in line—when he spotted the haversack thief sneaking behind the 154th's line. Salty ordered him back to his regiment. As the fellow turned to go, a bullet smashed through his mouth.

Sometimes circumstances seemed to conspire to foil Salty's whims. One night during the three-day battle of Chattanooga in November 1863, he saw a distant stream glittering white in the moonlight. Thirsty, he crept up to it with his empty canteen—only to discover it was a mirage, nothing but a road's pale dust. A month later, on a bitterly cold evening, he and his company comrade and good friend Private Esley Groat, both lacking overcoats, ducked into an abandoned Chattanooga house to spend the night. Groping their way around stacks of wooden boxes in the darkened rooms, they were delighted to find fireplaces. As they prepared to kindle a blaze, providence sent a guard to stop them. The place was an ammunition storehouse.

A month after Salty nearly blew himself up in Chattanooga, the regiment was assigned to cut timber to corduroy a road through the Tennessee woods. Salty felled a tree; as it toppled earthward, it snapped a military telegraph wire. Worried about interrupting important army communications, he decided to splice the wire's two frayed ends. But when they touched he received an electrical shock— "a steady stream of dispatches," he joked—and he dropped the wires and left the repair job to the authorized linemen.

Even fraternizing with the enemy backfired on Salty. When entrenched Union and Confederate troops confronted each other near Atlanta in August 1864, informal truces led to occasional trading between the foes. Yankee coffee for Reb tobacco was the usual exchange. The trick was to keep on the sly from officers, who were under orders to prevent fraternization. During a quiet period, Salty decided to try his luck and clambered over the breastworks. When within hailing distance of the enemy line he let out a call. In response a lieutenant rose from the Confederate trench and shouted, "Stop right there and go right back!" Without a word, Salty pivoted and returned to the Union line, never looking back, his spine tingling in dread of flying bullets.

Sometimes he had better luck. When the regiment briefly camped at Germantown, Virginia, in December 1862, Salty and Esley Groat pulled off a theft and flimflam to perfection. One evening a ration of whiskey was delivered to the company officers, to be issued to the men the next morning. Company G's full wooden pail was entrusted to First Lieutenant Commodore Perry Vedder, an ambitious self-promoter who Salty and his pals had derisively nicknamed "Yawpy Boy." For safekeeping, Vedder put the bucket atop a hardtack box inside his tent. Late that night, while Yawpy Boy slept, Salty and Es snuck into his tent and stole the pail. They filled the canteens of conspirators in their own company and Company B—whose tents backed up to Company G's—and put the empty pail back in Vedder's tent. Then they hid the bootleg canteens.

The next morning, when Company G turned out for its morning nip, Vedder discovered the theft. The lieutenant and his first sergeant, Salmon W. Beardsley, searched the company quarters. Entering Oyer and Groat's tent, Beardsley asked for their canteens. "Hanging up there," Es gestured. Beardsley shook the canteens and found them empty. Elsewhere, the search did not turn up a drop of the missing whiskey. Yawpy Boy, bewildered, ordered another bucket of whiskey from the commissary, which he dutifully doled out to the company. Salty and Es and their partners in crime got mellowly drunk on the newly issued ration, augmented by the many canteens of stolen whiskey they had hidden under brush and blankets. On top of that, they made some cash selling whiskey to officers who had gotten wind of their surplus.

It was the type of shenanigan that especially pleased Salty, Es Groat, and their good friend Private Bradford Rowland, who together took some pride in being the company cutups. They loved to play pranks—ambushing friends with squirt guns, smoking them out of their winter huts by blocking chimneys with flat stones, sneaking grains of gunpowder into a dupe's pipeful of tobacco, pegging a comrade to the ground while he slept, sandwiching another sleeping soldier between two logs, covering him with brush, and startling him awake with a shout. Officers were often targets of the trio's chicanery. During a time of short rations around Chattanooga, they stole a bushel of corn from a lieutenant's tent (meant for that dignitary's horse), took it to a mill where Es and Brad ground it fine, and relished hoecakes while the other men gnawed hardtack.

Any officer, it seemed, was fair game for their pranks, but bullying officers were favorite targets. As the regiment approached Chattanooga in October 1863, Salty and some other men were ordered to dismantle a roadside fence to make way for some cavalry. As they labored, a young, self-important German staff officer rode up waving his revolver and ordered them to "stir along." Salty gave the lieutenant a "lauf-pass"—whatever that was—and marked the man in memory for retribution. The opportunity came seven months later, at the Battle of Resaca. During the night of May 15, 1864, the 154th New York was ordered to construct a road into a captured Confederate hilltop redoubt set between the lines, so the artillery pieces therein could be hauled away. Part of the regiment wielded picks and shovels while the rest lugged rails up the hill. Suddenly the Confederates opened fire, sending the workmen scrambling to the rear. Trotting down the hill, Salty spied his old antagonist swinging his sword at the fugitives and sneering, "Dese tam dogs won't stand!" Salty barreled into the German and sent him tumbling down the hill.

Salty, Es, and Brad were among the bad boys of Company G, card playing, gambling, drinking, smoking, swearing, thieving hooligans who contrasted sharply—and clashed frequently—with their more Christian brethren. They held mock prayer meetings, snidely misquoted Scripture, clipped the U.S. Christian Commission insignia off of stationery and sewing kits donated to the soldiers, and refused to accept the Commission's pocket testaments. Es Groat gathered one batch of unwanted Bibles and stuffed them in an unsuspecting comrade's knapsack. On the ensuing march, the victim couldn't figure out why his load seemed so heavy. While a prayer meeting was in progress inside the chaplain's wall tent at a Virginia winter camp, the scoffers dropped some cartridges down the chimney. The resulting explosions burned holes in the tent and scattered the worshippers like "scared chickens."

A rare squabble among the three rogues ended ludicrously. It happened during the famine at Chattanooga. Salty was frying bacon in a long-handled skillet in the fireplace of their winter hut while Es and Brad lounged in their bunks. Suffering from a toothache, Salty was in a grumpy mood. So when the two observers repeatedly urged him to flip the bacon before it burned, he quickly lost his patience. "Say two words," he growled, "and in the fire it goes." Brad inanely replied, "Two words." True to his word, Salty tossed the bacon into the fire.

It was an uncharacteristic sacrifice. Food was always on their minds; they were constantly on the lookout for whatever eatables they could beg, borrow, or steal. At the very beginning of their service, while the regiment was forming at Camp Brown in Jamestown, they ran the guard, climbed a tree near the cookhouse, and broke through the roof to plunder the place. By the end of the war they had pilfered cattle, hogs, sheep, turkeys, chickens, geese, fruit, sorghum, and other delectables across substantial portions of Virginia, Maryland, Tennessee, Georgia, and the Carolinas.

Near Goose Creek, Virginia, where they camped for a week in June 1863, Salty and his pals discovered a land of milk and honey. The area's rich farms offered a plentiful harvest of mutton and eggs and ducks and cherries. Camp was pitched near the plank home of an elderly woman, who kept a constant wary eye on the

Yankees after they stole some of her butter. The thieves coveted some beehives in her yard, but the crone's vigilance kept them at bay. Night fell, the hours dragged on toward midnight, and still the old lady sat watchful guard over her hives. Finally Salty and his friends could resist temptation no longer. They made a rush, yanked an open-bottomed hive onto a blanket, and darted off into the darkness. Having anticipated such a foray, the woman let out a long, loud blast on a horn. The racket roused the 154th's commander, Colonel Patrick H. Jones. He ran up to the house, heard her complaint, and promised that the thieves would be apprehended and punished. But the next morning, when Jones's coffee was accompanied by a plate of dripping honeycomb, talk of punishment ceased.

During the occupation of Atlanta, Salty—then a sergeant—commanded a squad of men on the picket line. He began his duty conscientiously. "I always made it a point to go outside of the line," he related, "and explore a little and satisfy myself what was ahead of us." During his reconnaissance he came upon a two-acre squash patch. "As we were on half rations," he noted, "I just considered that something worth looking after." He picked a couple of squash and returned to the picket post. His charges were eager to raid the field. Salty was worried about the severe punishment he would suffer if caught allowing his men to leave their post. But hunger trumped prudence, and he directed the boys toward the squash. Meanwhile, he reported, "I kept a sharp lookout all around." Suddenly trouble appeared over the top of a nearby hill in the form of the division officer of the day, coming to inspect the picket line. Rushing from the thicket where the men had stacked their muskets, Salty bustled up to the unfamiliar officer with an officious salute and a barrage of blather. Somehow he convinced the gullible fellow not to examine his part of the line. "I did not get into any trouble," he reported with relief, "and the boys got squashes galore."

Incorrigibly resistant to discipline, Salty, Es, and Brad incurred several drumhead courts-martial and punishments. Infractions twice derailed Salty's career as a noncommissioned officer. At the organization of the regiment he was mustered in as a sergeant, but within a few weeks after reaching Virginia he had been reduced to the ranks for an unknown offense. By April 1863 he had earned promotion to corporal. "Salty," Es told him, feigning distaste at living with a figure of authority, "I guess we will choose new tent mates." But the comrades stuck together. That November 1, Salty regained his sergeant's chevrons. A year later, however, he fell again, to rise no more. Marching near Atlanta on October 25, 1864, he repeatedly dropped out of line to squat by the roadside with diarrhea. With each stop, he found it harder to catch up with the company. Then he grabbed the wrong haversack by mistake, and in returning to exchange it for his own, he fell far behind the column. He finally caught a ride with his friend Brad, who was driving a wagon loaded with corn. When Salty arrived late in camp, the company commander charged him as absent without leave. A regimental court-martial was convened in Major Lewis D. Warner's tent. Salty admitted to being away from the company during the march, and Warner recommended he plead guilty. Once more, Salty was a private; he would remain a private for the rest of his service.

It was probably for the best. The few times Salty got to exercise authority as a noncommissioned officer, the results were laughable. At winter camp in Lookout Valley, Tennessee, in March 1864, the temporary absence of First Sergeant Richard J. McCadden put Salty in charge of Company G's daily one-hour drill. It was his first experience at the task, and he failed miserably. As the men went through the familiar evolutions, their hapless sergeant struggled to remember the proper commands. It was "like calling cotillion" to him. He finally gave up, marched the men back to the company street, and dismissed them. The captain ran up to the sergeant and demanded to know what was going on. Salty explained that he could perform the drill to perfection, but he could not direct others through the movements. His career as a drillmaster ended.

At the end of that month the regiment was ordered to make a reconnaissance to Trenton, Georgia. Salty was still Company G's ranking sergeant. Seized by some sudden sartorial impulse, he bought a box of paper collars from the regimental sutler and distributed them to the men. During a quick inspection as they lined up to march, Salty noticed that some of the boys had their collars on upside down, others were wearing them inside out. Then, as they stepped off, it began to rain. The wet collars wilted. That day Company G's line of march could be traced by discarded paper collars. Salty had failed as a drillmaster; now he failed as a haberdasher.

For all of his foolishness as a noncommissioned officer, Salty made a generally obedient private. For all the many times he lagged behind the column, whether stricken with the runs or chasing after chickens, he would be found in camp at night. For all the trouble he caused with his mischief, he did his duty. At the Falmouth, Virginia, winter camp in early 1863 he was excused from duty a few times owing to a lame back, but generally he was present to pitch in and do his load of work. Unlike many others—"bummers," Salty called them—who slunk to hospitals seeking discharges, or maneuvered themselves to safe noncombatant posts behind the lines, or simply slipped away as deserters, Salty stuck with the regiment, even after it began to fight battle after bloody battle.

An incident that occurred during the Atlanta campaign crystallized for Salty the difference between bummers and true soldiers. The regiment happened across a skulkers' hideaway, where they found a human skull mounted on a pole above a placard reading, "Thus we serve all rebels that fall into our hands." Salty and his comrades were shocked—they had developed too much respect for the enemy to treat them with such puerile contempt. The ghastly trophy, Salty reported, "created much indignation among the soldierly portion of the regiment," who tore it down.

By that time, Salty was a veteran of many battles. His first was Chancellorsville. As an ex-sailor he was, appropriately, the first to step forward on the evening of April 28, 1863, when volunteers were sought to scull boats across the Rappahannock River at Kelly's Ford, Virginia, and secure the opposite shore. As the men paddled across the moonlit stream, Confederate pickets unleashed a hasty volley that splashed harmlessly into the water. By the time Salty's boat touched the southern shore, the enemy had fled. That night he made a bed of some loose cotton. In the morning, he awoke covered with cotton, looking like he had been tarred and feathered.

Four evenings later, Salty and his friends lounged near Dowdall's Tavern in a clearing in the tangled forest called the Wilderness. They had torn down a house and used its timbers to top a shallow rifle pit they had scraped out of the ground. Veteran troops told them they were fools—a shell would send the lumber flying and kill them all. But Salty was unconcerned. Sunset was approaching; all was quiet and he looked forward to a peaceful night. Then the forest exploded with the shocking fury of Stonewall Jackson's famous flank attack. Down the road to the west, cannon roared, musketry rattled, and the rebel yell howled. The regiment had time to take position at the far left of a Union line in the shallow rifle pit that stretched across the road near the tavern. The men watched in shock as panicked Union troops ran past their line, refusing to be rallied. Then came an intimidating sight: masses of Confederate regiments were rolling across the clearing toward them. Fire erupted from both sides, and a cloud of smoke shrouded the battlefield. The Confederates were momentarily staggered, but their overwhelming numbers were not to be stopped. As they neared the rifle pit, the 154th New York fled, scattering into the woods to the rear and leaving behind many killed, wounded, and captured.

Their hearts pounding, the Yankees plunged through the darkening forest. Much of the regiment dispersed, but Captain Matthew B. Cheney somehow managed to keep Company G together during the retreat. Emerging from the trees into a clearing, the company reformed to confront the enemy. A staff officer rode up and shouted, "Hold them back, boys! Don't let them get through!" Then he went silent. The men glanced back and saw him scrambling away from his mount. The horse had been shot and lay on the ground, flailing its legs in agony. As the officer fumbled for his revolver to put the beast out of its misery, Sergeant Alexander Bird shouted to him, "Goddamn you, you have got something to do yourself now!"

Twice during the evening's chaos, Salty was hit by bullets. A spent ball struck his pants pocket, in which he had a plug of tobacco recently sent from home by his father. The ball hit the wad, cut it in two, and dropped harmlessly down his pant-leg into his boot. The second shot was more harmful—it pierced his boot and opened a bloody wound in a toe. As the company fell back again, Salty received permission from Captain Cheney to go to the rear. Alex Bird hurriedly washed the blood from Salty's foot and bandaged the wound. Then Salty hobbled to the Chancellor house, headquarters of the Army of the Potomac's commander, Major General Joseph Hooker. There he rested until enemy artillery fire began to knock bricks from the house. Salty limped to a safer spot.

Three days later Dick McCadden wrote, "Clark Oyer . . . is slightly wounded but will be able for duty in a few days." That day Salty was admitted to the Eleventh Corps hospital at Brooks Station. Medical records listed his wound as a "vulnur sclopeticum [of the] toe, slight." His convalescence was, as McCadden had predicted, of short duration.[7]

In other combats, Salty had better luck. At the battle of Chattanooga in November 1863 the regiment was minimally engaged, skirmishing with the enemy across a rugged terrain of woods, ravines, and a deep railroad cut. At one point Company G came under fire in a cornfield. As bullets whistled through the stalks, the men hugged the ground. Private Jeremiah O'Hern called to his friend Salty. There was no reply. O'Hern called again; still no response. "Salty, are you there?" O'Hern screamed, and Salty finally looked up. His face was slathered in mud.

In the first battle of the Atlanta campaign, at Dug Gap on Rocky Face Ridge, Georgia, on May 8, 1864, Salty was assigned to the regiment's skirmish line. The scattered row of soldiers toiled up the wooded mountain's steep slope in advance of the main line of battle. As they neared the crest, they hid behind trees from a hail of enemy bullets. A soldier to Salty's right was hit and begged piteously to be carried to the rear. He was from another regiment, but nevertheless aroused Salty's sympathies. Salty shouted the request to Dick McCadden. The first sergeant replied that Salty would be foolish to attempt a rescue—he would surely be shot if he did. But Salty and a comrade of the wounded skirmisher gathered him in their arms and carried him partway down the mountainside. There Salty slumped to the ground, panting with exhaustion. Within five minutes, the wounded man died.

The main line began its assault of the mountaintop palisades. A company comrade, firing up the slope from behind a nearby rock, asked Salty if he was going to join the attack. It depended, Salty replied, on how the charge progressed; if the attackers meant business, he would go with them. And so when the regiment stormed up the ridge right up to the shadow of its rocky brow, he went with them. Below the mass of jumbled boulders at the crest, Salty ducked behind a tree. A short distance in front of him he spotted a company comrade, Private William Wilson, sheltered by another tree. A core of the regiment rushed with the colors to the crest. They were met by a blaze of gunfire. Many fell killed or wounded; survivors leaped from the palisades to safety. The national flag fell to the rocks, its bearer killed. Several men were shot in succession trying to save the banner. A corporal finally retrieved it. The attackers fell back down the mountainside, hurried by bullets and huge boulders sent crashing down the slope by the enemy.

Salty shouted to Billy Wilson to dart from tree to tree and join him in the retreat. But as Billy scampered back, an officer of another regiment—"a young kid," according to Salty—yelled to Salty to shoot Wilson for running. Furious, Salty stepped from behind his tree and berated the whippersnapper. Billy had gone farther up the mountain than he or any of his men had, Salty snarled, and he turned and trotted away.

Down the ridge Salty and Billy scrambled, zigzagging through the trees, jumping fallen limbs and low rocks. Finally out of danger, they halted for a brief rest and a drink of water. But both of their canteens were empty. Salty proposed that they go to a nearby creek to fill their canteens. On the way, they ran into trouble: a provost guard, who had been ordered to halt all stragglers. Salty emphatically suggested that the man walk to the end of his beat and not look back. The fellow took the hint and Salty and Billy reached the creek with no further hindrance.

Darkness had fallen by the time the two drank to each other's health. Then they were startled by female voices. Two women were calling for their cows. Salty crawled into a dense thicket and shouted at the dim figures—they were approaching a Yankee picket line and should go away. He would take care of their cows. Then he and Billy spread their blankets and slept until dawn. When they returned to the regiment that morning, the boys were delighted to see them. Dick McCadden was just about to report them missing in action; almost a quarter of the regiment had been killed, wounded, or captured on the ridge. Salty and Billy, McCadden declared, had fired the company's last shots of the battle.

About a month later, during the fighting on June 15, 1864, at Gilgal Church, Georgia, Salty was wounded for the second time. Weakened with diarrhea, he was excused by the regimental assistant surgeon from carrying a gun. While the regiment deployed as skirmishers and began driving the enemy through the pine woods, Salty led an officer's horse to the rear. But then he volunteered to do his part by carrying ammunition to the men. He scrabbled through the pines to the front and was standing by an officer behind a cottonwood tree when a bullet slammed into his foot, somersaulting him to the ground. A gash along his shoe's counter was ringed with lead. On removing the shoe he found a shallow cut in his heel, but no other damage. Once again Salty had been struck by a relatively harmless gunshot. Knowing it could have been worse, he patted the tree and said, "I like to have these things between me and the balls."

Salty first became a prisoner of war at the Battle of Gettysburg. After a wet morning's march from Maryland on July 1, 1863, the 154th New York got its first look at Gettysburg from the heights of Cemetery Hill. As fighting raged beyond the town, the weary soldiers took a short breather. They wolfed a cold lunch and filled their canteens. Company G uprooted and moved a picket fence. The men were ordered to prick powder into the percussion cap nipples on their muskets. Finally orders arrived to hurry to the front.

Salty never forgot the "pitiable sight" that confronted him during the double-quick march down from the hill through the streets of Gettysburg. Wounded Union soldiers were crawling on their hands and knees into the shelter of alleys. Some were clinging to wounded horses, the poor beasts barely able to drag them along. Panicked civilians carrying packed satchels were fleeing town. Women were crying and wailing that their homes would be burned. Brave young girls were ladling water to the passing soldiers. As they hustled through the tumult, Salty turned and asked a sergeant where they were going. He joked, "Down into town to do provost duty."

In the outskirts of town the regiment filed to the right through a carriage gateway into a brickyard. The 154th New York took position in front of the brick kilns, behind a post-and-rail fence set on a raised bank, with the 134th New York on its right and the 27th Pennsylvania stretching up the leftward slope, toward the brickyard owner's house. Almost immediately the enemy appeared in front, his long lines stretching to the horizon on both flanks, and firing erupted from both sides. Overlapping the right of the Yankee line and decimating it with enfilading volleys, the Confederates sent the 134th New York and the right-most companies of the 154th reeling. Salty saw Union men "dropping . . . like sheep." Company G was second in line at the regiment's left and held its ground a bit longer than the beleaguered right flank. Salty managed to fire seven shots at the advancing horde before he heard an order to retreat.

Returning the way he had come, he darted past a kiln to the brickyard's gate, only to find the street swarming with Confederates. The 27th Pennsylvania had been driven from its position, leaving the 154th New York virtually surrounded by the enemy. Salty ran to hide in the house's cellar. Scrambling down the steps, he found the place crowded with Union soldiers. They had entered a perfect trap. Confederates poured down the stairs, disarmed the Yankees with ease, and herded them outside. To his chagrin, Salty found himself a prisoner of war.

Emerging into the smoky sunlight, Salty discovered that much of his regiment had been captured. Brad Rowland, who had surrendered to a musket-wielding Reb at the brickyard fence, was a fellow prisoner. Five bullets had pierced Rowland's uniform during the fight, but he was unhurt. Salty and Brad, "fast friends and chums," determined to stick together during the coming ordeal. They made a resourceful pair. Brad—like Bill Hawkins of Company B—turned out to be a shrewd trader with a knack for procuring supplies. As for his partner, "Salty's sailor life," Brad declared, "had accustomed him to take care of himself, and his care and judgment were fine." Salty and Brad relied on each other to survive their imprisonment. As Brad put it, "Each believed that the preservation of his life [was] due to the other."

During the march through Maryland and Virginia on their way to Richmond, Brad bartered diligently and kept himself and Salty well provisioned. To satisfy Salty's craving for tobacco, Brad always ended a swap by saying, "Well, throw in some tobacco and we'll make it a bargain!" When Brad showed Salty the day's loot, Salty joyfully praised his pal's prowess, but always ended by asking, "Well, Brad, did you get any tobacco?" Brad was usually able to reply, "Yes, Salty, and here it is!"

Incidents of the march lodged in their memories. Several days after starting, the prisoners crossed a bridge submerged under two feet of rushing water in a swollen stream. A Reb cavalryman clubbed the men to keep them skating across the slippery planks. As he urged his horse up the embankment on the opposite shore, it shied and bucked, throwing him into the stream. The delighted Yankees catcalled, "Grab a root!" "Swim!"

The bullying cavalryman was the exception to the rule. "The Reb guards," Brad recalled, "used the prisoners first rate and with indulgence." On one occasion the captives jumped an orchard fence to pick apples, carefree and laughing. A guard mildly told them, "Now Yanks, you mustn't, it's agin orders." When the prisoners persisted, he flailed at one of them with the flat of his bayonet. It broke, doing the Yankee no harm, and the embarrassed Reb departed, never to return to that portion of the line. Another kindly guard once watched a sutler sell tobacco to the prisoners from his wagon. If the Yanks reached too close to him, he slashed at them with a Bowie knife. The guard, disgusted with the sutler's meanness, cocked his musket and told him not to hack at the prisoners any more or he would blow his brains out.

The Yankees had a miserable time crossing the Potomac River. They had to wade through hip-deep water in a pouring rain to a ferry boat. On the Virginia shore they were corralled in a field of tall clover and spent the night wet to the skin as a heavy fog settled over them. Marching through the Shenandoah Valley, they were taunted by civilians. "You want to go to Richmond, don't you?" the Virginians would shout. "I guess you'll get there now!" "Have you heard from Vicksburg?" Salty and Brad countered, reminding their tormentors of the recent surrender of the Confederates' Mississippi stronghold.

It was during the march through the valley that Salty was first plagued by attacks of diarrhea. Despite the extras Brad obtained to supplement their meager rations, Salty's body rebelled. More and more often he had to drop out of the line and squat by the roadside to relieve himself.

On reaching Richmond, the prisoners were confined on Belle Island. As the summer days plodded by, Salty and Brad sank into suffering. Their clothes rotted to rags, their bodies shriveled with hunger and festered with lice-bites and filth. Brad later vowed that he owed his life to a regimen insisted on by his friend. Salty patted a low ridge of sand to form a pillow, and enjoined Brad to "lie down much, and not waste strength and hasten digestion of food by constant walking about and fretting, as most prisoners did." So while the other inmates milled miserably about the fetid camp, Salty and Brad reclined inert on the sand. Salty's passive routine, Brad swore, was the key in "how to live and preserve [our] strength and health." But while Brad's health remained stable, Salty's diarrhea became chronic.

The two successfully resisted a malady that haunted many of the prisoners: depression. They grew concerned about their company comrade, Private Truman D. Blowers, who became "utterly discouraged—weak, sick, and crying." Salty and Brad nursed him as best they could. They shared their meager supply of flour, spooning it into his mouth, giving him a drink of water, and telling him to swallow it slowly. Despite their solicitous care, Blowers's demoralization deepened.

One day, watching guards haul "the usual number of starved corpses" out of the prison compound, Blowers told Salty and Brad that in a few days he too would be carried out in the same manner. Blowers was right, Brad realized. "In his then condition of body and mind the statement was all too true." But what could Brad and Salty do? They knew that "falling in with the idea, and pouring disheartening sympathy, and offers to receive his dying requests and messages, and sending such to his friends," was what *not* to do. Instead, Brad and Salty "wisely adopted the course of raillery to provoke him to rouse his spirits." They subjected Blowers to a mock examination. They felt his forehead and told him he had a bad case of the sweats, which "was a sure sign he would die in a day or two." They dubbed him "Sweat Brow" and taunted him until Blowers lost his temper. Still they nagged him. "The reaction that followed," Brad claimed, "was so beneficial that it saved his life." Newly energized, Blowers survived his imprisonment, to be mustered out with Company G at the end of the war and live until 1920 — thanks to Salty and Brad.

Salty and Brad had no intention of being carried lifeless out of Belle Island. Within weeks after entering the prison, they joined a plot to escape the place by buying their way out. Dick McCadden masterminded the scheme. Leaving Salty recumbent on the sand, Dick and Brad circulated among their comrades and collected about five hundred dollars in greenbacks. They then approached a guard and requested an interview with Lieutenant Virginius Bossieux, the camp commander. Permission was granted. A detail was carting away corpses from the vicinity of headquarters when Brad and Dick were ushered into Bossieux's office. The ragged, filthy Yanks laid the greenbacks on the lieutenant's desk. Beside the cash they put a list of the names and numbers of the contributing prisoners.

Negotiations proceeded politely. Dick and Brad informed Bossieux that they wished to be aboard the first truce boat that arrived. They asked him to forward the list to headquarters in Richmond and request parole for those enumerated. They were simply prisoners of war like thousands of others, they told Bossieux, but if he could do anything for them, they wished he would. They "did not want to *buy* him," they stressed, "but would make him a little present." The deal was quickly clinched. The lieutenant raked the cash into his desk drawer without counting it, told the prisoners he was much obliged, and gave them some instructions.

The next afternoon a detail of sick prisoners was culled to be paroled at City Point, down the James River, as part of a standard quota. At the same time, orders were issued that certain well ones, to be named later, would make up rest of the quota. The bribery conspirators glowed with satisfaction. But that evening an officer read through the list without naming the Company G boys. Their hearts sank. Had Bossieux betrayed them? Bill Hawkins ribbed Salty, telling him he would have to raise more money. But then the officer reread the order, and six additional names were called: Richard McCadden, Truman Blowers, George W. Bailey, Othnial Green, Bradford Rowland, and Clark Oyer.

"Goodnight, Bill!" Salty cried to Hawkins as he leaped to his feet. Brad was so weak from starvation that he could barely move, but when his name was called he thought he could jump over a table. Two of the party were unable to go. Bailey stayed behind to care for Green, his brother-in-law, who was too sick to leave. (Ten months later, the two would die five days apart at Andersonville.) As the four others prepared to depart Belle Island, regimental comrades—including Hawkins—were forlorn. They pressed the quartet with messages for their families and friends and said sad goodbyes. "Boys," Brad callously told them, "you will have to raise another five hundred dollars."

Salty and Brad received their paroles at City Point on August 2 and boarded a ship bound for Annapolis, Maryland. The weak and emaciated prisoners, scarcely able to crawl on Belle Island, "were filled with new life," Brad observed, "and walked aboard with firm step and alacrity." As the men stepped from the gangplank onto the ship, each was handed a pork sandwich made with thick slabs of bread. A chilly sea breeze swept the deck, so Salty and Brad huddled for warmth near the boilers. As Brad gobbled two large bites of his sandwich, Salty took a dainty bite from his own. Then, to Brad's surprise, Salty declared, "I suppose the fishes are hungry," and flung the remainder of his sandwich into the river. He urged Brad to do the same. "Not much!" Brad replied. "You don't catch me throwing away my victuals that way!" He tore a third mouthful. As he chewed, Salty warned him to follow his example and get the food out of his sight at once, if he wished to stay alive. Brad, by now a firm believer in Salty's fitness theories, tossed his sandwich overboard. Years later, Brad still believed that "the sound judgment and care over [me] that Salty exercised, saved [my] life." For, Brad swore, seven prisoners who yielded to ravening hunger and devoured their sandwiches in a rush died from the effects thereof during the voyage.

At the Annapolis parole camp, Salty and Brad and another Company G man, Private George W. Hess, with their eyes open as usual for the main chance, somehow managed to finagle permits to absent themselves on a regular basis. Initially they used their free time to hunt chickens and turkeys. But then they ran across a doctor, a native of New York State, who owned a large farm outside of town. He was desperate for workers, so he hired the three parolees to husk corn for seventy-five cents per day. They enjoyed meals superior to those at camp, and spent comfortable nights bedded down in a shed. But they felt their pay was inadequate, so they slacked off. By day, while two of them slept, the third would husk corn and throw the ears onto a huge pile. Whenever the farmer approached the barn, the man on duty would rouse his companions, "and then all three husked lustily, as Cattaraugus farmer boys know how to do." After a few weeks Salty tired of the job. He quit and returned to camp. When Brad and George went back to Annapolis a weekend or two later, they were surprised to find Salty and their other comrades gone. The parolees had been exchanged and shipped by steamboat to Alexandria, Virginia. From there they were shipped by rail to the regiment, now in Alabama.

Salty spent a few days at the College Green barracks in Alexandria before he was transferred to the parole camp. There he happily reunited with Colonel Jones and Yawpy Boy Vedder (now a captain) and members of Company G who had been captured at Chancellorsville. As he had in Annapolis, Salty managed to spend a lot of time foraging outside the camp, hitching rides on wagons and trains to get back and forth. He also was pleased to discover a comrade working in the cookhouse, who provided him with plenty of grub.

By October 1863 Salty had rejoined the regiment and reunited with his friends Brad Rowland and Es Groat. He was still suffering from diarrhea; it continued to plague him in the coming camps and campaigns in Tennessee and Georgia. "I have had the Tennessee quickstep so long that I am pretty weak," Salty wrote to an uncle in December. "If I only had a box of those pills that we used to get, I think they would straighten me up again. But we don't get any medicine here that is [of] any account at all." The regimental medical staff—Surgeon Henry Van Aernam, Assistant Surgeons Dwight W. Day and Corydon C. Rugg, and Hospital Steward Charles Harry Matteson—took their turns dosing Salty with the standard remedies—opium, calomel, camphor, or turpentine—to no avail. Often they excused him from duty, or let him march without his knapsack or musket, or permitted him to ride in a wagon. Sometimes Salty could not reach the sinks in time and fouled his pants. Es and Brad would launder for him. Salty never completely got over it; he would have the trots for the rest of his life.[8]

Sherman's March to the Sea offered the men a comestible cornucopia, all free for the foraging. Trekking across central Georgia's breadbasket, Salty reveled in pancakes, butter, roast pork, corn, sweet potatoes, wild honey, and the largest turkeys he had ever seen. "Two thrown over the back of a mule made a load!" he marveled. He had the perverse pleasure of watching Yawpy Boy Vedder chomp on a piece of honeycomb and get stung on the tongue by a bee, rendering him temporarily mute. Salty delighted in the destructive aspects of the march, happily thrusting rails through the trestlework of the Ogeechee River railroad bridge, for instance, readying it for the torch. But on December 3, 1864, Salty had a somber moment. He and Es Groat explored a deserted log stockade at Millen, which had recently held thousands of Union prisoners. The ground inside the pen was studded with hollowed-out humps of dirt, formed by the wretches for shelter. The place haunted Salty with dark memories of Belle Island. He lectured Es on the horrors of prison life and vowed that he would run through shot and shell before he would ever be captured again.

A week later, Sherman besieged Savannah. The luxurious bounty his men had enjoyed in Georgia's heartland now dwindled to monotonous rations of rice, all that was to be gleaned from the coastal countryside. Salty was dissatisfied with this meager fare. On December 12, he huddled with Corporal William P. Haight and Private Delos Peck of Company E in the regiment's entrenchments by the Savannah River and stared across the water at Hutchinson Island. Some decent foraging could be done over there, the three decided. So they commandeered a boat and assembled a crew of five black men—John Brooks (division commander General John White Geary's cook), the servant of a captain of the 33rd New Jersey, and three newly liberated slaves. As the eight men poled across the river, they discovered they had mistimed their voyage. The tide was ebbing. Approaching the levee surrounding the island, their boat grounded in mud. As they bemoaned their misfortune, about twenty Rebs suddenly rose from behind the embankment and leveled their muskets at the hapless seamen. One drawled, "Come in out of the wet."[9]

It was only nine days since Salty had sworn to Es Groat that he would never again be captured. Now he was a prisoner of war for the second time. On shore, a Confederate lieutenant berated the Yankees for "tearing Georgia all to pieces," and accused them of coming to the island to scout a location for a battery. When the officer threatened to shoot the eight men, a small Reb at his side pointed his cocked musket at Salty and volunteered, "Yes, Lieutenant, I'll shoot him." Salty and his comrades had heard of foragers being executed by their captors, but these threats were idle. The lieutenant turned out to be "a nice young fellow." Another Reb, searching Salty, found a two-dollar bill in his pocket. "Now you better leave that," Salty said. "I shall want it to buy tobacco with when I get over in the city." You cannot buy any tobacco there, the Reb responded. "Oh yes I can," Salty insisted. The kindhearted soldier quietly crumpled the bill into a small wad and, when none of his companions were looking, dropped it into Salty's hand.

That night, Salty and the other prisoners were ferried in a small boat across the river to Savannah. There they were confined in the stone carriage house of a wealthy property owner. Fumbling around in the darkness, Salty found two blankets, identified by white cotton tags as the property of a Reb officer. Bill Haight had an overcoat to keep him warm; Salty and Delos Peck were coatless. So Oyer and Peck commandeered the blankets and tore off the tags. Salty's blanket would come to be a talisman to him.

After a couple of hours the prisoners were rousted, interrogated by a Confederate provost marshal, and marched up Bull Street to Oglethorpe Barracks. Built to house Federal troops in the 1830s, the building had more recently been the headquarters of Savannah's police force. As a prison, Salty thought, the place was absolutely "tony." But he enjoyed the comfortable quarters for only a few days.

Staring out a diamond-shaped window in the front door one afternoon, Salty saw a familiar figure approach across the old parade ground. It was the lieutenant who had captured them on Hutchinson Island. Salty and Peck quickly opened a trap door and tossed their purloined blankets into the cellar. The Yankees greeted their captor with delight and plied him with questions about doings at the front. After hemming and hawing a bit, the youthful officer said he had a disagreeable question to ask his new-found friends. Some blankets had been stolen from the carriage house; did the prisoners know where they were? "Oh, no," came the reply. "Oh, no—have not seen them." The lieutenant thoroughly but fruitlessly searched the room and left. He was barely out of sight when a corps of black drummers beat the call for guard mounting on the square. A guard opened the door and ordered the prisoners to gather their traps and prepare to move. After some worried deliberation, Salty and Peck decided to retrieve their stolen blankets. "Might as well be shot as to freeze to death," Salty reasoned. Blankets in hand, they marched from the barracks to Savannah's city jail.

Their new home was a distinct step down from Oglethorpe Barracks. Salty, Haight, and Peck were tossed into a cramped cell. Its stone floor was so small that they had to contort their bodies to sleep. It also was within sight and hearing of the whipping post, at which blacks were often lashed. Rations consisted of bull's head soup. Salty's bowl always seemed to have a beef's eye in it. To leave a mark, he wrote his name repeatedly on the cell walls. When the 154th New York eventually occupied Savannah, Captain Vedder was posted at the jail as a provost marshal and spotted Salty's signatures among the graffiti.[10]

After several days in the dank jail, Salty and the others were evacuated under cover of darkness. The Confederates were abandoning Savannah, but they were not leaving their prisoners behind. The captive Yankees crossed the river on a pontoon bridge—planked-over scows, Salty observed, covered deep with rice and straw to muffle the thumping of the marchers. On the South Carolina shore the prisoners were herded aboard railroad cars. They rode until the track ran within shelling range of Union gunboats prowling the Broad River. Then they detrained and walked the rest of the way to Pocotaligo, where the Coosawhatchie and Salkehatchie rivers merged to form the Broad.

At Pocotaligo, Salty huddled with dozens of other Yankees under the watchful eye of an elderly captain and his young guards. Two carbines were pointed at the prisoners; as they stood with their hands aloft, a guard relieved them of their valuables. Salty lost his only cash, the two-dollar bill the kindly Reb had let him keep at his capture. The robbery complete, the guards herded the Yankees aboard a train. They rode to Charleston, where they were locked in the three-story, octagonal city jail. Salty was housed in a large upstairs room with a fireplace. When a prisoner in an adjacent tower wanted to smoke his pipe, Salty leaned out a window with a firebrand and, ignoring the drop, stretched far enough to offer the man a light.

A few days later the prisoners were herded aboard another train and rode to their ultimate destination: a stockade at Florence, South Carolina. Hurriedly established in September 1864 when Andersonville was threatened by Sherman's campaign in Georgia, the Florence prison soon confined many of the Andersonville prisoners in a strikingly similar environment. About a mile and a half east of the hamlet of Florence—a railroad stop set in a vast pine forest—the log stockade enclosed twenty-three and a half acres of sandy land pocked with holes dug by the prisoners for shelter. A stream bisected the camp, bordered by a swampy marsh. Within two months after it opened, more than fifteen thousand wretched prisoners were crowded into the Florence stockade. By the time Salty arrived, the population had dropped by about four thousand. Perhaps a quarter of them had been exchanged, badly sick. The rest had died. At the edge of the woods north of the main gate, trenches were filled with thousands of corpses.[11]

The new batch of Yankees was greeted by the prison's commandant, Lieutenant Colonel John F. Iverson. After asking the arrivals how they had fared in Charleston, the colonel admitted that his hotel was not much of an institution, but he would do as well for them as he could. Salty pegged Iverson as a gentleman who kept his word. But Iverson's good intentions went for naught—Florence was as bad a hell hole as Andersonville.

Prowling the stockade, Salty came across several regimental comrades, filthy, skeletal survivors of Andersonville. Among them were Thomas R. Aldrich of Company B, Robert J. Woodard of Company C, and Private Thomas D. Spiking Jr. of Company F, who shared a brush shanty. They invited Oyer, Haight, and Peck to join their mess.

For a while the sextet fared relatively well, thanks to a scam pulled off by Tom Spiking. It was triggered when a civilian from Cheraw, South Carolina, visited Florence and was granted permission to mingle with the prisoners. He was looking specifically for New Yorkers, and soon came across Salty's gang. The man related that his son was held at the camp for Confederate prisoners in Elmira, New York, and he hoped to arrange for the boy to receive some relief. The quick-witted Spiking claimed he had an uncle who was a merchant in Elmira. If a letter could be smuggled to this uncle, he would furnish the South Carolinian's son with comforts—provided, of course, that the South Carolinian reciprocate to the New York boys in Florence. A deal was struck. Spiking composed a letter to his imaginary uncle and handed it over. The grateful civilian gave the New York squad a hundred dollars in Confederate bills and departed the stockade. A day or two later a basket of provisions and vegetables was delivered to Spiking from his new friend.

But this fortunate arrangement came to an end when Spiking and Bill Haight received paroles of honor to help construct crude sheds in a corner of the stockade to serve as a hospital. Prisoners were paroled to work both inside and outside the stockade. With upraised hands, they took an oath: "You do solemnly swear that you will not attempt to escape, that you will not associate with niggers, trade with citizens, smuggle anything into the stockade—so help you God, you Yankee louse-picking sons of bitches!" Salty was jealous of Spiking and Haight and yearned for a work parole to get him out of the fetid stockade. His jealousy must have deepened when he learned that the two had broken their oath and escaped.

One day, while he was admiring his shoes (which were in fine shape by prison standards), inspiration struck. Surely such a well-shod prisoner would be paroled to work outside the stockade hauling firewood from the swamps. But Salty's interview for the post went badly. "How long have you been in here?" a Confederate officer asked. "Three months," Salty lied. "You are one of Hooker's men, ain't you?" inquired the officer, glancing at the Twentieth Army Corps' star badge on Salty's cap. "Yes," Salty confessed. "I thought so," the officer replied. "You've been tearing Georgia all to pieces. You get back in there." Salty trudged back across the dead line into the stockade's stinking squalor.

As at Belle Island, Andersonville, and other prisons, a black market flourished among the Florence prisoners. Speculators cornered the market on sweet potatoes. Others fashioned buckets of cedar staves and peddled water for a button, or a chew of tobacco, or a spoonful of cornmeal. A strong voice would bellow, "Who wants a pail of water?" "I do," a faint voice would reply. "Where are you?" "Here I am." A button would be cut off the sufferer's jacket and the deal completed.

Salty noted a more gruesome trade. "One rule of the prison," he observed, "was that if a man died in your tent and you carried him out in the morning, you could carry in a stick of wood the size of the body. This created heavy speculation and competition, and watches had to be kept sharp to keep other prisoners from stealing the body, and getting the prize. It often occurred."

With the departure of Haight and Spiking, Salty's mess was reduced to Tom Aldrich, Bob Woodard, and Delos Peck, all of them torpid with fever. "I then had the brain fever," Peck later wrote, "and was unconscious for several days." Tom Aldrich noted, "*Salty* was the only one able to stand up." As Salty related, "I used to draw the rations for us all [and] then hire a burly Tennessean to split the wood, paying him out of our supplies. I would build the fires, sift some corn meal, use the hulls for a sort of coffee after browning them, [and] make some mush, also a corn dodger. Then I would have some warm water ready and awaken the boys, assist them to a sort of bath, and if they could partake they done so of our poor, poor fare." Tom Aldrich, like Brad Rowland before him, credited Salty's care with the preservation of his life. "I was near death's door at Florence," Aldrich wrote after the war, "as was three or four of my tent mates, and if it had not been for Clark Oyer or Salty, as we call him . . . I think I should have occupied a place in the National Cemetery there now." [12]

One day Salty stumbled on John Brooks and another of the blacks who had been captured on Hutchinson Island; they had been incarcerated as Union soldiers rather than sold into slavery. They were "filthy, sick, and rotting," Salty observed. Salty shared the offhanded racism of his time and always referred to black people as "niggers." But he tendered care to the two black men with the same concern he showed for his white messmates. He forced them to "get up and take care of themselves," believing "neglect to care for cleanness—filth—had much to do with disease." Salty was pleased to see his prescription worked and the health of the two improved. His kindness to them would be repaid.

Bit by bit, the prisoners sold off or bartered away their possessions. Bill Haight sold a thirty-dollar silver watch to a guard for three hundred Confederate. Tom Aldrich traded photographs of his girlfriends for bread. But the men clung to certain items. Salty prized a silver ring and the blanket he had stolen in Savannah. Delos Peck cherished a gold ring that never left his finger. One morning, as Salty watched Aldrich and Woodard stir awake, Peck remained flat on his back with his blanket pulled over his face. "Not a sign of life or a move of any kind could I see," Salty noted. Perverse as it seemed, the death of his friend could mean life to Salty and his mates. As per prison practice, Peck's corpse would bring the mess a large chunk of firewood. And that gold ring—"I would be able to sell that ring," Salty realized, "and perhaps buy a little rusty bacon, and that would give a little different taste to our miserable fare." Salty crawled to Peck and pulled down the blanket. The supposed corpse grinned at Salty and said, "I ain't dead yet!" "The fact was," the surprised Salty admitted, "he was better, and that source of revenue was cut off."

As the days dragged by in the stockade, events outside hastened the ending of the war. When Sherman's army penetrated South Carolina and approached the Florence area, Confederate officials rushed to ship the prisoners elsewhere. And so Salty's second imprisonment was—like his first—of short duration. After about two months in the stockade, late in February 1865, he was one of a group of prisoners sent to Wilmington, North Carolina.

Too weak to walk, Salty crawled on his hands and knees to the flatcars strung out along the railroad at the Florence depot. He thought he was afflicted with "brain fever"—he actually had pneumonia—and the trip was an unremembered blur. Much of the time he was unconscious. He lay helpless on the flatcar or on the ground at station stops, but nobody stole his precious blanket. Sometimes he awoke to find a bottle of water left by a kindly soul. At Wilmington, Salty sold his silver ring for three Confederate dollars and tried without success to buy a biscuit. Then, as rain fell, the ragtag prisoners were loaded back onto the cars for a trip inland to Goldsboro. Confederate guards ordered two husky Yankees to help Salty aboard the train. When the duo tried to abandon him, Salty cried, "Johnny, they are leaving me!" A sympathetic guard ordered, "Yanks, you take him along—you don't leave him," and Salty swelled with gratitude.

The train pulled into Goldsboro and the prisoners were unloaded to form in files on an abandoned picnic ground and draw rations of cornmeal. Salty ate and fell asleep. When he awoke, there was not a prisoner or guard in sight. He had been left behind, no doubt mistaken for dead in his slumber.

He had nothing to eat and no shelter, other than his threadbare blanket. Then a bit of luck clattered up in the shape of an old black man piloting a mule-driven wagon. He helped Salty aboard and carried him about a mile to a fairground. The place had become a campground for freedmen, as liberated slaves were called. Salty crawled into a cross-shaped building, gathered an armful of straw on the floor, wrapped himself in his blanket, and collapsed into sleep. For several days he lived among the freedmen at the fairground, depending on their kindness for relief.

An old black woman peddled raw turnips in the camp. When she met Salty, her stock was already depleted. Disappointed, he told her he wanted something made from wheat flour. The next day she brought him some white bread and a bottle of milk, and Salty dined like royalty. Some Samaritan white citizens sent him some "dainties," and his strength grew. But he was plagued by lice. In distress, he heeded the advice of the turnip peddler. She handed him a clean white rag and said, "Honey, put it around your neck, and when it gets full you just shake it." It helped a bit, and he was more comfortable.

While the Negroes and even some of the local whites treated him well, Salty suffered some mean treatment from a strapping Yankee cavalryman—probably an escaped prisoner—who meandered onto the fairgrounds. He had a pie, but did not offer to share any with Salty. When Salty tried to snatch a piece, the man callously kicked him away. Salty crawled back to his straw pile in tears.

The Confederacy was collapsing when Reb soldiers rounded up Salty and sent him from the Goldsboro fairgrounds to North East Ferry, where a burned railroad bridge spanned the Neuse River. There he was paroled on March 4, 1865. He boarded a small stern-wheeler under a flag of truce and was shipped back to Wilmington. The ship's Texas cabin was crowded with black soldiers; like Salty, they were former prisoners of war. They sang Union songs as the craft steamed down river toward the ocean. The shores were lined with ex-slaves hefting bundles, hoping to get away, begging to be taken aboard.

By the time Salty's ship docked at Wilmington the city had fallen to the Yankees. Once again, Salty was back under the old flag. But even surrounded by boys in blue, he felt alone—he had not seen any of his regimental comrades since he left Florence. He was housed in a decrepit rebel plank barracks, but each rough room had a welcome brick fireplace. There he became chums with a Norwegian sailor. This tar had been captured forty miles offshore on a scuttled U.S. ship, and later wounded by buckshot in the nose and both hands while attempting to escape from a train. Despite his bandaged, useless hands, the Norwegian helped Salty gather wood for heating and cooking by kicking boards off of fences; Salty would carry the kindling back to the barracks.

As usual, Salty hunted around Wilmington for extra food. Once he used a bucket to fish some submerged onions from the water near a dock. A New York soldier gave him some onions plundered from a warehouse, and Salty and his Norwegian friend enjoyed meals of roasted onions. An officer presented Salty with a new pair of pants, a welcome present, Salty noted, since his old pair was "deficient."

One day while the Norwegian was off running an errand, Salty hobbled down to the wharf and discovered a boat loading paroled prisoners bound for Annapolis. When an officer asked if he wanted to go, Salty did not hesitate to say yes—he did not even bother to return for his roasted onion and potato. In the milling crowd on the dock, Salty was delighted to find John Brooks and his companion. Now the kindness Salty had shown the two Negroes at Florence was repaid. One of them gave him a three-cent stamp, which he traded for an apple. Next Salty acquired an overcoat, which freed him to leave his ragged, filthy, beloved blanket behind.

Heavy gales delayed the boat's departure, so the parolees were put back ashore and ordered to spend the night in a warehouse. Salty and his two companions instead sought more comfortable shelter in a black man's house, where a fireplace kept them warm. During the night, one of his friends discovered Salty's toes were swollen and painful, perhaps the result of frostbite. The next afternoon, when the wind died down, John Brooks hefted Salty onto his back, carried him aboard the boat, and deposited him in the hold near the boilers. The heat soon drove Salty on deck, where he perched on the windlass.

As the vessel rocked on the ocean swells, a number of Union soldiers from eastern Tennessee, just mustered out of the army and seasick on their first voyage, crowded the rails to retch. One of them noticed Salty sitting with aplomb, observing their misery, and asked his advice. "Breathe with the heave of the ship," Salty instructed the landlubber: take a deep breath on a long heave; release it when the ship dipped into a trough. The fellow followed Salty's suggestion and within a half-hour was well. Then his companions followed his example and, Salty was pleased to note, "all got well and chipper." They rewarded their hero by swaddling him in their blankets and sharing their rations all the way to Annapolis.

When the ship docked in Maryland on March 14, Salty hobbled down the plank clutching two canes and passed a gauntlet of guards from the garrison, who treated him to drinks of whiskey before a surgeon put a stop to it. As Salty was lowered onto a stretcher, he bid his black comrades a heartfelt goodbye and told them he would write letters of recommendation on their behalf. But after they parted, he never saw or heard from them again. He never forgot them, however.

At the Navy Yard Hospital in Annapolis Salty was diagnosed with chronic diarrhea and scabies, a contagious skin disease caused by mites and marked by itching. He was given a bath and new clothing, a pair of drawers and a long white nightshirt. A few days later a woman volunteer from the U.S. Sanitary Commission—the large civilian agency devoted to Union soldiers' relief—asked Salty if there was anything he wanted. A pair of slippers, he replied, and a pocket handkerchief. When the slippers arrived he found they had purple linings. Several days later a surgeon was examining Salty's feet and asked him how long his toes had been purple. "Ever since I got my new slippers," Salty said, but he was kidding. His feet hurt so badly he could not stand the pain of being shod, and he had not worn the slippers.

A pair of Roman Catholic priests came by the hospital one day to minister to the patients. At Salty's bedside they asked if he was a church member. "No." "What, not any church?" "No." "Can we bless you?" Yes, Salty guessed it would not hurt him any. A few days later some Protestant clerics went through the same routine. After a while, all of the clergymen realized they were dealing with a hopeless case and left Salty alone. For his part, Salty was perfectly content to be a "retired Christian."

Reminiscing about the war decades later, Salty glossed over the last months of his service—his stay in the Navy Yard Hospital at Annapolis, broken up by a lengthy (and overstayed) furlough home, his transfer to hospitals in Baltimore and Wilmington, Delaware, and his final discharge, on July 6, 1865, at Elmira, New York. No doubt the retired Christian was acutely bored by hospital life and often tempted by diversion; his cravings were probably frustrated more often than not. But he was sadly broken down by his wartime afflictions and he needed the long recuperation. According to Oyer family tradition, Salty was so debilitated on his return home that his family spoon-fed him soup until he got better.[13]

He never entirely recovered. That autumn he found he was unable to do farm work. He wore plasters on his lame back; he could not load hay bales onto a wagon; his labor was constantly interrupted by diarrhea attacks. But farm life was not for Salty anyway, so he returned to the sea. For about nine months in 1866 he served as a signal quartermaster aboard the U.S. Revenue Cutter *Commodore Perry*. The Revenue Cutter Service, a precursor of the U.S. Coast Guard, enforced tariff and trade laws, prevented smuggling, protected the collection of Federal revenue, and aided mariners in distress. The *Commodore Perry* had been constructed by Buffalo shipbuilders and launched in 1864. During Salty's tour of duty, the cutter served on the Great Lakes out of Erie, Pennsylvania.[14]

Salty's second round as a sailor was his last. Back ashore, he finally found light work that agreed with him, as a cook in lumber camps. The job also satisfied his wanderlust. His migrations took him (in no particular order) to Stillwater and Perham, Minnesota; Alpena and Thunder Bay River, Michigan; Imboden and Ravenden Springs, Arkansas; Diamond Springs and Eureka, California; and Mead, Trent, Chattaroy, Hillyard, Spokane Falls, and Orting, Washington, with occasional returns to Cattaraugus County.[15]

He supplemented his income with an invalid pension for his Civil War service. By 1920 a board of doctors found him to be suffering from diarrhea, rheumatism, heart disease, and senility, but nevertheless declared, "His general condition is very good." He was tough; he was a survivor.[16]

Oyer never could settle down, and his rambling no doubt adversely affected his family life. He married a woman named Sarah Davis in Alpena, Michigan, in 1871. They had two children; Mattie was born in 1873 and Jesse followed in 1879. Salty and Sarah were divorced in St. Cloud, Minnesota, in 1886. For two decades he enjoyed a carefree bachelor life. Then, in 1909, at age seventy-three, he married a widow named Ellen Burd in Coeur d'Alene, Idaho. They were living in Orting, Washington, when Salty's son, Jesse, joined them to spend a winter. Ellen later bitterly recalled that Jesse "got his father to go with him to California for he wanted his money"—by 1920, Salty's Civil War pension came to seventy-two dollars a month. Having decided to join Jesse in the sunshine, Salty asked Ellen for a divorce. "I told his lawyer he could have it," she wrote, adding balefully, "but he seen many a sorry day." [17]

He loved to reminisce about his Civil War service and touch base with his old regimental comrades. He was proud of the record the 154th New York had posted in the war. "You know we all think our dear old Regiment *The Regiment*," he wrote, "for there was regiments and regiments, but ours like Auld Lang Syne [was] the grandest of them all." When circumstances permitted, he joined a local Grand Army of the Republic post; his name is listed on a GAR monument in Evergreen Cemetery in Mead, Washington. Occasionally he had the pleasure of reuniting with his regimental comrades back in Cattaraugus County. And one memorable day he joined fifteen of them—including his old friend Brad Rowland—in Gettysburg. The veterans trooped out to the site of the old brickyard, where a twenty-foot monument marked the center of the 154th's line of battle on July 1, 1863. Bedecked in ribbons and badges, the men gathered around the granite obelisk for a group photograph, gazing northward across the quiet fields over which the Confederates had charged some thirty years before. Salty leaned against the sloping base of the shaft and let memories wash over him as the exposure was made. It is, fittingly, his only known portrait. [18]

CHAPTER ELEVEN

Private Francis "Blind" Patterson

Company G

Some eighty thousand people are buried on eighty rolling acres in Woodlawn Cemetery—more than twice the living population of Elmira, New York. On a flat in Section M, Lot 183, stands the headstone of a Civil War veteran whose tale forms a notorious chapter of Elmira history. In his day, Blind Patterson (as he was universally known) was a celebrity for all the wrong reasons. His fame exploded beyond Elmira to the nation as a whole in the summer of 1887, when he found himself at the center of a series of extraordinary events. A few months later, he tumbled back into obscurity. A decade passed before he garnered his last headlines in death and sank into the realm of the forgotten.

Signs pointed the way to Woodlawn's true celebrities: Elmira native Hal Roach, the Hollywood director and producer of movie and television fare who lived to be a centenarian, and Ernie Davis, the "Elmira Express," the all-around athlete and first black Heisman Trophy winner, who died of leukemia at age twenty-three. Woodlawn's brightest star is Mark Twain. His wife was Elmira's Olivia Langdon; the Sam Clemens family spent summers on the city's outskirts at Olivia's sister's home, Quarry Farm. Twain consequently was in town when Blind Patterson captured the nation's consciousness. One might think that Twain would be attracted to the story—it sounded like one of his own.

I sensed Blind Patterson's presence during my time in Elmira, conjuring him meandering the streets and alleys, as he had more than a century before. I stayed at a bed and breakfast in the historic Near Westside neighborhood, just blocks from Patterson's last home. Walking the old slate sidewalks, I twice came across "Blind Crossing" signs. One morning, during the course of pleasant breakfast talk with fellow guests at the B&B—Bill and Karen from Baltimore—I summarized Blind Patterson's story. Our conversation meandered elsewhere. Then Karen stunned me by saying she has retinitis pigmentosa. She is slowly, irreversibly going blind.

Frank Patterson, Blind Patterson's great-great-grandson and namesake, naturally feels an affinity for his handicapped ancestor. Frank is afflicted with multiple sclerosis. He is still able to get around, but he tires easily and falls occasionally when his legs numb up. On disability since 1992, he keeps busy teaching and caring for the disabled. I met Frank at his house in Horseheads, north of Elmira, on a mid-November day. He knew of his ancestor's Civil War service and blindness, but was unaware of the celebrity and its circumstances. I had cautioned Frank in telephone conversations that the tale was of the black-sheep-of-the-family, skeleton-in-the-closet kind. I wondered how he would react when he heard all the sad, sordid details.

We sat at his kitchen table as I spun out the story. A cheerful, friendly, open man, Frank listened to me intently and peppered me with questions. Amazed at the sensational tale, he said repeatedly, "It sounds like a movie." He spoke movingly and wisely about trials and tribulations that shatter people's hopes and crush their spirits and break up their families. He was deeply touched by the tragedies that had overwhelmed Blind Patterson and his family: war, affliction, poverty, desperation. The tale should be told, he said; to my gratitude, he offered me his full support in its telling.

We drove to Woodlawn Cemetery. Fallen leaves were gathered in piles on Elmira's curbs and scattered in drifts across the cemetery grounds. Frank had not visited his ancestor's grave in about ten years, but he quickly found it. Inscribed across the top of the stone was the word *Husband*. To the left, tilting backward after a century of shift, a smaller, darker stone identified the wife. Both markers were inscribed with dates of birth and death; his listed his Civil War company and regiment. Ordinary in every way, the two graves camouflaged a scandalous tale that had made their occupants the talk of the town.

Francis Patterson was born on March 1, 1837, in Greene, Chenango County, New York. His parents, Reuben and Electa, took him at a young age to the seat of adjacent Broome County, Binghamton. There the boy apparently went unschooled, never learning to read or write. In his early teens, Frank spent about a year in his father's Chemung County hometown, Elmira. He then returned to Binghamton, where he boated on a canal in the summer and worked for various employers in the winter. During one canal packet trip at age sixteen or so, Frank was struck in the head by a bottle under unknown but readily imagined circumstances. The wound left a scar above his right eye.[1]

A justice of the peace married Frank Patterson and Helen M. Greek in Elmira on April 18, 1856. Frank was nineteen, a year and a half younger than his bride. In the spring of 1857 the Pattersons moved west to Cattaraugus County and settled in Olean to raise a family. Frank worked as a teamster and in 1860 resumed canal boating during the warmer months, making trips from Olean to Albany the following two summers. A Federal census taker counted four Pattersons in June 1860: Frank, Helen, three-year-old Abram, and one-year-old Electa Ann. Another child, Helen, would arrive in a year or two. Living with the family was an eighteen-year-old laborer, Frederick Greek, probably Helen's brother. Another Greek, a girl named Ida, soon joined the family as an adopted daughter. Frank owned a very modest $150 in real estate; his personal estate had no value. Olean residents considered him a "hard character" and a "dissipated man." "Pretty rough kind of a fellow," thought William Canning, a native Scotsman who worked with Patterson for a few weeks in the summer of 1862, loading lumber in an Olean sawmill. Canning, worthy to note, heard Frank often complain of weak eyes.[2]

After another Monday at the mill, on the night of August 4, 1862, Frank Patterson and William Canning volunteered in Olean. Both were mustered in on September 24 as privates of Company G, 154th New York. "When I entered the army," Frank later said, "I was a strong, robust, healthy man." The descriptive book listed him as five feet, eight inches tall, with a dark complexion, dark hair, and black eyes. (Regimental comrades would remember Frank's dark eyes as peculiarly piercing.) Two weeks after the muster-in, on October 6, while the regiment was at Camp Seward on Arlington Heights, Virginia, Frank was assigned to duty as a teamster in the regimental quartermaster's department. His war would be fought from the back of the near pole mule of a six-mule team, hauling a wagonload of regimental stores.[3]

Each of Frank's few surviving letters is in the hand of a different scribe. In dictating his missives to Helen, Frank offered only a bit of war news. Instead, he concentrated on his family and their well-being. Frank Patterson might have been a rough-and-tumble type, but he consistently expressed himself as a loving and conscientious husband and father.

Composing a letter during the Thoroughfare Gap expedition in November 1862, Frank used a popular opening line: "My dear but absent wife, it is with much pleasure that I take this opportunity to let you know that I am well and hoping that these few lines will find you the same." He had been sick in the hospital for two weeks, but he was "getting tough again" and fully expected to recover his health. He had been driving his mules for the past week. He believed (incorrectly) he would receive an extra seven dollars a month for his teamster duty and promised to let Helen know for sure when he received his first pay. His thoughts were with her and the children. He wondered where they were living, and offered some words of advice for his son: "Tell Abe he must be a good boy and mind his Ma and take good care of the children."

"My dear," Frank dictated, "I don't think we will be in any fight this winter, but I don't know. But I think the war will be settled before long, and my dear I hope it will be, for I want to come home and see you and the children. My dear, I want you to write often for I want to hear from you every week, if not oftener. And my dear, write every week whether I write or not and I will write as often as I can." [4]

On the regiment's return to Fairfax Court House, Frank received two welcome letters from Helen. He responded as soon as he had a few spare minutes and a willing amanuensis. His health continued to improve; he was still driving his team. The departure from Thoroughfare Gap he described as a "skedaddle," made on the double-quick on a rainy night. Frank's war news was cursory, however, compared to his lengthy expressions of concern for his family and its welfare. "Write and tell me whose house you live in and how you get along," he asked Helen. "I don't know when we will get our pay, but as soon as I get it I will send it to you. I wish I could see you and the children. I think we will all be home in the spring. I hope so." He again admonished young Abe to mind his mother and help her all he could. "You must write to me often," he begged Helen, "for you don't know how much good it does me to hear from home." He promised to send her his photograph. "We are right in the woods, so you see I have no chance [now] to get my likeness. But when I get a chance, I will have it taken." He closed by sending a kiss to her and the children, a sign of affection that became routine in his letters. [5]

On January 31, 1863, Frank dictated a letter to Helen from the regiment's camp on the Rappahannock River near Falmouth. "We have a pretty hard time now," he noted. "The mud is so deep that we can hardly get around." He did not offer an account of the recent dispiriting Mud March, having more pressing concerns on his mind. "Helen, you say that you do not get any letters from me," he stated. "I write as often as I can. We have been on the tramp all of the time. You think I do not think anything of you, but that is not so. There is not a day that I do not think of you and the children, and I hope sometime to be at home with you." He had finally received his pay. Keeping four dollars for himself, he enclosed the balance—twenty dollars—in a check made out to Helen. Disgruntled by the late payment, the regiment's first after four months of service, he threatened to desert if need be to support his family. "If I cannot get my pay so that I can support my family here," he vowed, "I shall go where I can." But Frank also urged Helen, "You must keep up good courage and do as well as you can." He added a postscript, pointing out that Helen's name was misspelled on the check and she would have to endorse it similarly.[6]

Helen picked up Frank's letter one morning at the Olean post office. She broke the seal, extracted the epistle, and tossed the envelope on the sidewalk. Strolling along, she reached the part of the letter that mentioned the check. She had discarded it with the envelope! A search failed to turn it up. An Olean newspaper ran an account of Helen's misfortune under the headline, "Serious Loss." "She is a worthy woman," the item stated, "quite poor and has a family of children to support, and the loss of course is quite serious for her. We trust if anyone is lucky enough to find the money they will return it at once." Whether Helen recovered her money is uncertain.[7]

Snow blanketed Camp John Manley near Stafford Court House on a cold and stormy day in March 1863. "I would like to be at home with you today," Frank told Helen. "What a pleasant time we would have. But that cannot be at present, but I hope the time is not far distant when we shall be together again. But when it will be, God only knows. But one thing is sure—this war cannot always last." In the meantime, he promised to send forty dollars in extra pay as soon as he received it. "That will help me a good deal," he declared. He reported his health was good.[8]

He was still well when he wrote from Camp John Manley on April 12. Rumor had it the paymaster would visit the regiment the next day. Frank thought he could send money again soon. But there was a complicating factor—the regiment would march up the Rappahannock the next morning. "Where we will go from there I cannot tell," he said, "unless we cross the river."[9]

None of Frank's letters are known to survive to describe what happened next. Two weeks after his April 12 letter, the regiment crossed the river as Frank had surmised, and days later he experienced his first battle. The wagon train was in the rear at Chancellorsville, but still came under artillery fire; a man was killed and a span of mules was torn to pieces. Several weeks later, during the march to Gettysburg, Frank had his most noteworthy venture as a teamster. It grew from a plot hatched by several of the regiment's officers. They were behind in their financial accounts for company clothing and equipment, and personally liable for the balance. The incriminating ledger books were put into a bag, and Frank Patterson was appointed to "lose" it. On June 14, 1863, as the wagons crossed Bull Run, Frank dutifully dumped the bag of books into the creek. It was for this illegal exploit that he was best remembered by veterans of the regiment, until he became famous as Blind Patterson.[10]

Years later, Frank told the rest of his story repeatedly. Details of place and time varied from telling to telling, but the gist remained consistent. At some point during the spring or summer of 1863, he was injured in the chest when thrown from his mule during a collision with another wagon on a hill. After the accident he spent several days in the regimental hospital. That summer his eyes began to trouble him, at first stinging and itching, then turning sore, red, and inflamed. He attributed the problem to exposure to campfire smoke, aggravated by a cold. One of the regiment's assistant surgeons prescribed a small bottle of eyewash, which proved ineffective.[11]

After the Battle of Gettysburg—where the wagon train was kept safe well to the rear—and the return to Virginia, the 154th was assigned to duty at Alexandria, forming details to guard conscripts on their journey by rail to the front. Frank turned in his wagon and mules and rejoined his company. In late September he was sent from Alexandria with a southbound trainload of conscripts. On returning, he found the regiment had departed, bound by rail to the west, part of a relief force sent from the Army of the Potomac to support the beleaguered Army of the Cumberland in Tennessee. Frank and other stranded soldiers were herded aboard a train and rode off in pursuit. During the journey he pondered a letter he had received from home. Helen and one of the children were sick; they were not expected to live.[12]

One of the regimental comrades left behind with Frank was Private Wellman P. Nichols of Company C. Noticing Patterson's red eyes, Nichols surmised Frank had been on a drunk. The two struck up a conversation. They talked for hours as the train rattled through the Maryland countryside. Finally, they reached an agreement: together, they would desert. One of Frank's fellow teamsters, Private Zeno Besecker of Company I, overheard the planning and tried to dissuade the two, to no avail. Besecker also noticed Frank's inflamed eyes, but did not think much about it. Patterson was, after all, "a dissipated man when he could get anything to drink."[13]

The connivers' opportunity came when the train approached Benwood, West Virginia, on the Ohio River just south of Wheeling, on October 3, 1863. Here the soldiers were to detrain, cross the river on a pontoon bridge to Bellaire, Ohio, and board another westbound train. As the locomotive slowed for the Benwood stop in late afternoon, Patterson and Nichols jumped from their boxcar. They apparently stopped in a saloon for a meal, then headed north. Frank later claimed they were left by the train, but it is clear the two planned to desert; they would each come to charge the other with concocting the scheme. The first night they slept in a haystack. For the next several days, they tramped northward. After trading their uniforms for civilian dress, they had no problems boarding in houses. When they reached Oil City, Pennsylvania, they parted.[14]

Here a gap appears in Frank's story. Later he claimed that he continued on to Olean, walking and hitchhiking rides in wagons, led (in one version) by a boy traveling in the same direction. But evidence points to Frank's arrival in Olean about four months after he parted with Nichols in Oil City. Where was he in the meantime? "Probably," an investigator surmised years later, "on the Genesee Valley Canal and doubtless under an assumed name." Frank denied the charge, but admitted that his memory was very poor.[15]

Frank remembered there was snow on the ground when he arrived in Olean, apparently on or about February 3, 1864. A black family friend, Sarah Johnson, was visiting the Patterson home because one of the children was sick. She never forgot Frank's entrance—he crawled through a side window. "Good heavens, Frank," Helen exclaimed. "Where did you come from?" As Frank warmed by the stove, Sarah noticed his black eyes gleaming in the lamplight. When she saw him several days later, however, he was wearing a bandage over his eyes.[16]

In the twelve days immediately after Frank's return to Olean, Dr. Charles Hurlbut made nine house calls to the Patterson residence, running up a $9.25 bill. Meanwhile, accusations flew in the Patterson family. Frank's mother, brother, and sister all came to blame Helen for causing his eye problems by infecting him with venereal disease. Frank's mother even accused Helen of running a brothel while he was in the army, polluting him with the "bad disorder" when he was home on furlough. This gossip spun from family friends like Sarah Johnson to Olean at large. Later, rumors swirled that Dr. Hurlbut botched an operation on Frank's eyes and burned them out with caustic. Frank himself remembered the doctor applying tea leaves to his eyes.[17]

Frank denied ever having a venereal disease. He consistently maintained that his eye troubles developed during his service, and that by the time he arrived at Olean he was blind. Helen thought Frank's problem stemmed from a cold caught "while beating his way home after deserting." To a friend, she vented annoyance at having to care for her blinded husband.[18]

A couple of days after Frank climbed back into her life, Helen reported him to the local recruiting officer, who came by the Patterson house, examined Frank, and arranged to have him admitted to a hospital in Dunkirk, in neighboring Chautuauqa County. During his time there, Frank later claimed, "I became crazy and was out of my head." Apparently he was in Dunkirk for a week or two at most before returning home. Back in Olean, he wore a green eye shade and carried a bucksaw, sawing wood to earn money.[19]

In the meantime, Private Patterson had been officially reported as a deserter; he was now liable to be arrested. Company G's muster roll noted that he owed the government $22.85 for the loss of his Enfield rifled musket and a full set of equipment. A certain O. S. Hardy apprehended Frank in Olean on March 2, 1864. Hardy then accompanied Frank back to Dunkirk and turned him over to the district provost marshal, Captain George W. Palmer, who paid Hardy thirty dollars for Frank's arrest and took charge of the blind prisoner. On March 21, Palmer escorted Patterson to the Dunkirk depot and aboard an eastbound train. That night, the captain turned Frank over to the guardhouse jailors at Barracks Number Three of the sprawling state military depot in Elmira. A day or two later, Frank was admitted to William Street Hospital.[20]

Frank said he was "blind as a post" when he reached Elmira. One doctor told him his case was hopeless. Another accused him of blinding himself by contaminating his eyes. The best the physicians could do was to recommend that Frank continue using eyewash to alleviate soreness. Years later, a nurse recalled the pathetic sight of Frank being led around the hospital with his eyes bandaged, totally blind.[21]

Luckily for Frank, his sister, Olive E. Hooker, was renting a house in Elmira. When Olive learned on March 23 that Frank was in town, she went to the hospital and received a pass for him to stay at her home. Every day she escorted him to the hospital to report.[22]

Frank related this good news to Helen on March 24, in a letter perhaps dictated to Olive. He had more welcome tidings: the doctors had recommended his discharge from the army. And upon his discharge, he was amazed to relate, he was to receive his bounty (a stipend promised him on enlistment) and back pay—despite his desertion! Here was a nest-egg on which to build a new life, Frank figured, and Elmira seemed to be the place to build it. "Helen," he declared, "if you will move here, you can get a good living. There is a society here that gives to all soldiers' wives." Olive benefitted from that charity, Frank noted, "and you can [do] the same." And despite his blindness, Frank would do what he could to support his wife and children. He promised Helen that he would have a house ready for her if she came to Elmira, and that he would pay to ship their household goods from Olean. If she needed money to make the journey, he urged her to let him know. He also advised her to ignore any old debts, "for they can't take anything you have got." "Now Helen," Frank pleaded, "if you will only come here we will be all right, for then we can take comfort together, and I will be to home with my family, and I can get a plenty of provisions and a load of wood." He closed with some tender and ironic words: "Tell all the children that Pa wants to see them all. Kiss the children for me, and a kiss for you."[23]

On April 9, 1864, William Street Hospital's chief surgeon, W. S. Thompson, signed duplicate copies of a "Certificate of Disability for Discharge" for Francis Patterson. He judged Frank to be totally blind in both eyes, "the result of disease contracted since enlistment." He also noted that Frank had been dropped from the rolls of his company as a deserter. Four days later Frank's discharge was granted by Department of the East headquarters in New York City, with a stipulation: "Pay to be suspended until satisfactory explanation be furnished of his absence." When the paperwork arrived back in Elmira on April 16, Frank was discharged from the army. He left the service without a cent of the bounty and pay he had anticipated.[24]

By the time Helen and the children joined Frank in Elmira, the place's promise had vanished. She found him a mile and a half out of town, on the Water Cure Hill farm of Thomas Bennett. Frank was living in a small house on the property and working for his landlord in lieu of rent. Bennett and his neighbors thought Frank must have had some degree of sight in his sore, inflamed eyes. After all, he worked with the men, cutting brush and clearing land, and he walked back and forth to town by himself. Patterson's blindness was not a problem for Bennett; his behavior was. Frank raised too much hell for his landlord's taste. He drank a lot of liquor on Water Cure Hill and threw wild parties for a hard crowd, including strumpets from Elmira's female House of Corrections.

When Helen walked into this squalor, she was furious. She and Frank quarreled constantly. She left him speechless when she ranted that he had brought "the bad disorder" back from the army—the same charge Frank's relatives had hurled at her. Whenever Helen started up about that, Frank clammed up. Bennett quickly grew tired of the Pattersons and their problems and evicted them.[25]

They moved into the city. Elmira's overseer of the poor, Howard M. Badger, made two official payments to Frank during the summer of 1864. Badger also privately hired the blind man to do whatever odd jobs he could handle. Frank proved to be particularly adept at sawing wood; he used a special stick to measure his cuts. That fall, walking together through Badger's cornfield, Helen picked the ears and handed them to Frank to husk. Perhaps the Pattersons supplemented their wages with aid from a local soldiers' relief society, as Frank had suggested when he asked Helen to join him in Elmira.[26]

Pain and headaches continued to plague Frank. He sought relief from Dr. Thomas S. Updegraff of the Elmira Surgical Institute, considered to be "an oculist of great skill." Updegraff told Frank that his eyesight could not be restored, but that medicine could relieve his pain. He also advised his patient to stay away from women and whiskey, attributing Frank's difficulties to venereal disease. Two Elmirans later stated that they witnessed Updegraff operate on Patterson's eyes, but no mention of an operation by either the doctor or Frank has been found. Updegraff recalled seeing Patterson only two or three times.[27]

There was nothing doctors could do for Frank. Blind and poor, he was left to his own skills and the mercy of the world to support his family. He worked for a while in an Elmira brickyard. Autumns he husked corn. He found his steadiest work sawing wood. A boardinghouse tenant named Herman Joerg watched his landlady arrange a deal with Frank: a bundle of old clothes for some wood-saw-ing. The astonished Joerg watched Frank "go to the pile of wood, take off a stick, put it on the saw-back, and saw it"—just like a sighted man. Joerg was even more astounded when the blind man pointed to a distant barrel and asked its contents. Cider, Frank was told. Patterson was all set to tap the barrel before he learned the cider was sweet. Frank, strictly a hard cider man, sneered, "I would not give a damn for sweet cider."[28]

Helen went to work, too. Some six years after he marveled at Frank's wood-sawing abilities, Herman Joerg was a student in an Elmira law firm. Helen Patterson cleaned the office. One day Frank stormed into the place, demanding her wages. Helen protested, complaining to the lawyers that her husband had beaten her. Her eyes were black; she bared bruised arms. Frank, belligerent as ever, claimed the discolorations were smudges of coal dust.[29]

Blind Patterson became a familiar sight on the streets of Elmira. He soon found that begging yielded a better living than his bucksaw. In 1867 some benevolent soul bought Frank a hand-organ to aid his panhandling. The day he received the present, Frank got drunk and smashed it to pieces. At first, Abram Patterson led his father around town. When the young man married, Frank trained a shepherd dog to be his guide. Elmirans marveled at the animal's abilities. "The success of the dog," an observer noted, "ever since has been the wonder of the people." The animal led Frank to his favorite haunts and guided him home when he was drunk. Frank managed to stay out of serious trouble with the law, but he was regularly tossed into jail on intoxication or vagrancy charges. Elmira's overseer of the poor did what he could for him. Now and then he was admitted to the local veterans' home, but he could not be made to stay and always returned to his dog and the streets. Winters were especially hard for Frank; he often was arrested and sent to the Chemung County Poorhouse. "Everyone in Elmira knew Blind Patterson," a reporter later stated, "and though few liked him, he excited much pity."[30]

Things would have been so different, if only Frank had been able to get a pension for his army service.

A Federal act of 1862 had provided for pensions to be paid to the widows, orphans, and dependent relatives of soldiers who had died, and to wounded, injured, and disabled Union veterans. A totally disabled private was to receive eight dollars per month, a rate that increased as the years passed when higher amounts were granted for severe disabilities. No pension, however, was to be granted for an injury not originating during a veteran's service, while in the line of duty. This stipulation would be the stumbling block in Blind Patterson's path to a pension.[31]

When Frank first got out of the army, during his summer on Water Cure Hill, he told Tom Bennett that his eyes had gone bad in the service, but that he had not applied for a pension because he had no discharge. Within two years, he changed his mind. On May 30, 1866, in front of two witnesses who swore that "his habits are steady and good," Francis Patterson marked his X on a pension application in Elmira. The form itself was provided by Washington, D.C., pension agents Gardner and Burgess, whose names were printed on the document as the duly appointed attorneys to press Frank's claim. The veteran stated that his eyesight was harmed by campfire smoke and aggravated by a cold, that he went blind by New Year's Day 1864, and that he was hospitalized in Dunkirk and Elmira—the same story he would repeat numerous times thereafter.[32]

Into the ponderous maw of the Pension Bureau's machinery went Frank's petition, filed in Washington on June 12 as Invalid Application Number 109,848. A routine inquiry brought a copy of Frank's record from the adjutant general's office. That fall an affidavit from Olean arrived in Washington. William Lennon, a former private in Company I of the 154th New York, swore he saw Frank often while in the service and remembered well his sore eyes. The Pension Bureau sent special examiners—detectives in all but name—to Olean to investigate the case. They determined that Lennon was a worthless drunkard and an illiterate to boot; it appeared that his affidavit had been signed by the justice of the peace in front of whom it had supposedly been sworn. When Lennon subsequently disappeared, his affidavit was judged to be a forgery.[33]

This type of shenanigan was familiar to the experienced special examiners. They knew that veterans would sometimes fib about their cases, and get old comrades to tell white lies on their behalf. The examiners fought this collusion by interviewing as many principals as could be located, judging the validity of their testimony by their moral reputation. This method was detrimental, of course, to a claimant like Blind Patterson. To one special examiner, Frank's reputation was so bad that "any statement made by him would be unworthy of consideration unless corroborated by credible persons." His claim was riddled with "evident falsehoods." Frank hurt his own case when he told Elmirans various fanciful stories about how he lost his eyesight. In depositions to pension agents, however, the essence of his story remained consistent. No matter; as a social pariah, Blind Patterson's veracity was worthless. Now this liar had attempted to bolster his claim with apparently false testimony.[34]

A few months after the Lennon affidavit entered Frank's file, a score of Elmirans, among them members of the Ladies Relief Association and former superintendents of the Soldiers Home, sent a petition to the commissioner of pensions on Frank's behalf. They described him as an "industrious and worthy man" with a wife and four children to support, "now hopelessly blind and entirely destitute," unable to work and constantly attended by one of his children, presumably Abram. "We would respectfully suggest that he is very needy," read the petition, "and seems to be worthy of a pension." The Elmirans requested an investigation of the case and the granting of a pension.[35]

Their words went unheeded; Frank's pension application was rejected. William Lennon's testimony had been discredited and Frank's agents had not provided additional evidence. Neither Frank in Elmira nor his agents in Washington could come up with the addresses of any other of his regimental comrades, most of whom were back in Cattaraugus County. From 1866 to 1881, Blind Patterson did nothing to further his claim but repeat his story in sporadic depositions and change one ineffective Washington pension agent for another. Then a confluence of people and events swept Frank to a pension—and to notoriety.[36]

During the decades following the war, tens of millions of dollars were paid annually to hundreds of thousands of Union veterans and their loved ones. Thousands of employees processed, investigated, and adjudicated cases at the Pension Bureau's massive Washington headquarters, issuing certificates, mailing checks, conducting an immense correspondence, and filing staggering numbers of records. About a quarter of a million pensioners were largely satisfied with the bureau's service. But many veterans, like Blind Patterson, were frustrated in their efforts to receive a pension. The claims of some had been denied, the applications of others were tied up in red tape. Others, like Frank, were unable to prove that their disabilities originated during their service.

Coming to the rescue of these pensionless veterans were the pension agents, quasi-attorneys who handled for a fee the business of claimants with the bureau. Frank wasted his money paying Washington agents who did not accomplish anything for him. They squandered a ripe opportunity to gain a sympathetic ear from 1869 to 1871, when the former surgeon of the 154th New York, Henry Van Aernam, served as commissioner of pensions during President Grant's first term. Dissatisfied with his Washington agents, Frank hired an Elmira attorney, who proved to be equally ineffective. After fifteen years of failure, Blind Patterson had just about given up on receiving a pension when his hopes were revived—in his hometown of Elmira, no less—by Dr. Robert N. Mills.[37]

Mills later said he met Patterson during the war, when Frank was confined in the hospital in Elmira before his discharge. Frank remembered a later encounter, apparently around 1880, in the streets of Elmira. "How are you getting along?" the doctor asked the blind beggar. "I'm getting along the best I can," Frank replied. Mills commented, "I suppose you are getting a good big pension." On hearing Frank's story, the doctor offered to help.[38]

On the surface, Robert Mills appeared to be entirely respectable. A native of Greene County, Virginia, he married an Elmira woman who was teaching school in Mills's hometown around the time the war broke out. Rumor had it that Mills served as an assistant surgeon in the rebel army. In 1864, the couple moved to Elmira. A square-faced man with carefully trimmed gray muttonchops and neatly brushed dark hair, the doctor carried his tall, stout, powerful-looking frame with military bearing. He was a dapper dresser, a husband and father, a property owner. He had an intellectual look about him. Beneath his presentable facade, however, lurked a villain so heinous that one man declared of him, "Language would fail to describe his character, as black as it is." Mills was considered by upright Elmirans to be a drunkard, a perjurer, a congenital liar, a scoundrel holding no social, moral, or medical standing in the community. Every election day, he sold his vote for five dollars. He boasted of committing adultery with various women. Elmira's medical community shunned him. He was reputed to be a specialist in treating venereal diseases and an abortionist, or a "a reducer of the census," as someone euphemistically put it.[39]

This not-so-good doctor lubricated Frank with alcohol and smooth-talked him into an understanding. Dr. Mills and his good friend Captain John Laidlaw would act as Frank's agents and get him a pension. Laidlaw, a veteran of the 161st New York Volunteers, was a well-respected family man and alderman who worked in a shoe factory. The two had experience in these matters, having helped ex-soldiers get pensions in deals that, unbeknownst to Frank, were crooked. Now Mills and Laidlaw looked to reap a substantial windfall from Blind Patterson's plight. In 1879, Congress had passed the Arrears Act, stipulating that veterans and their loved ones who applied for a pension before July 1, 1880—as Frank Patterson had—and whose claims were approved, were to be paid from the date of the soldier's death or discharge rather than the date the claim was approved. Such pensioners consequently would receive large sums in retroactive payments. If Blind Patterson's case, then lingering in the rejected file, was reopened on the discovery of new evidence and was approved, he would receive a whopping sum to cover all the years since his discharge. Mills and Laidlaw could deliver this to him, they promised—for a consideration. The two sharpers must have been delighted with the blind beggar's response. All he wanted out of the deal, Frank insisted, was a twenty-five hundred-dollar house, the seventy-two-dollars-per-month pension, and a horse and cart with which to gather bones. Mills and Laidlaw could have the rest of the settlement.[40]

Frank Patterson grew to consider Robert Mills his best friend—indeed, his only friend. The doctor regularly gave the blind beggar money, food, and medical attention. When others kicked Frank out, the doctor took him in. Patterson relied on Mills. Helen trusted him, too. "We will stick with him," the couple vowed, "if we die in the gutter."[41]

Mills and Laidlaw got on Frank's case with an urgent efficiency quite unlike the slothful ineffectiveness he was used to from his Washington agents. Somehow they connected with a veteran of the 154th New York living in Elmira, Wilkes J. Miller, former private of Company A. Miller knew Blind Patterson from Elmira's streets; he had not known Frank during the war. But when Mills and Laidlaw got him drunk and promised him a hundred dollars and the best suit in Elmira, Miller was quite willing to sit for a deposition and swear—as coached by the duo—that he knew Frank Patterson well in the service and witnessed Frank's eyes become sore and inflamed during the summer of 1863.[42]

Armed with the Miller deposition, Mills and Laidlaw took Blind Patterson to Washington in September 1881. They lodged at an Eleventh Street boardinghouse, promising the landlady liberal compensation for their room and board—once Frank's pension came through. A fellow boarder was Colonel Amos T. Bissell, journalist and editor of the *Grand Army Journal*, with Pension Bureau connections reaching all the way up to Commissioner William W. Dudley. A. T. Kinney, a Pension Bureau special examiner who was rumored to be distantly related to Laidlaw, was another boarder. Bissell had been involved with Mills and Laidlaw in a shady pension case, and he had met with the two in Washington about the Patterson case months before. Mills and Laidlaw told Bissell there was money in it for him if he could convince his friend Commissioner Dudley to pass Patterson's claim. As for Kinney, he would take testimony and provide a favorable report for a one thousand-dollar payment. Mills had Kinney over a barrel, Bissell observed, having performed an abortion on a young lady at the special examiner's request. Bissell also noted that Mills, Laidlaw, and Patterson were largely drunk during the few weeks they stayed in Washington.[43]

"Now we have the case right," John Laidlaw exclaimed when Kinney's cooperation was assured, but the conspirators' ill-laid plans came to naught. Bissell accompanied the Elmirans on several visits to Commissioner Dudley's office. On another occasion he hand-delivered Frank's discharge to the commissioner. Dudley called for Patterson's file and promised to give the case his special attention. In the end, however, he informed the Elmirans that additional evidence was needed to drop the desertion charge against Frank. Mills and Laidlaw were angry with Bissell over the result, but Laidlaw nonetheless slipped the journalist ten dollars for his trouble. Kinney had no better luck than Bissell. Preparing to take Frank's deposition, the special examiner routinely mentioned that a false statement was punishable by arrest and jail. Frank became so frightened that Mills and Laidlaw were hard pressed to calm him down and keep him in Washington. On one occasion they tracked him to the depot, where they found him ticket in hand, ready to return to Elmira.[44]

Kinney eventually traced Wellman Nichols to Pennsylvania and deposed him regarding his desertion with Frank. Then Kinney submitted the evidence he had gathered together with a recommendation to admit Patterson to the pension rolls. But Nichols later recanted his testimony and charged Kinney with bullying him, warping and garbling his statements, and putting words in his mouth. The bureau, rightfully dissatisfied with the special examiner's work, assigned a new man, Theodore Smith, to the case. Commissioner Dudley himself ordered a thorough reexamination of the Patterson claim, centering on whether Frank's eyes were diseased when he deserted.[45]

Special Examiner Smith began his work in Elmira, where he took testimony from Blind Patterson and Wilkes Miller, both of whom stuck to their stories. Smith then traveled west and interviewed veterans of the 154th New York in Cattaraugus County. To a man they recalled Frank Patterson as a rowdy, quarrelsome drunk, but they did not remember his having bad eyes. Back in Elmira, Smith forwarded affidavits and a report to Commissioner Dudley, together with a recommendation that Frank's claim again be rejected.[46]

A few months later a Pension Bureau official sent a memo to the chief of the special examiner division. "The weight of evidence appears to be against this case," he wrote. Commissioner Dudley wanted additional evidence obtained to determine when Patterson's eye problems began. "This case is important," the bureaucrat wrote, "in that it is a case of total blindness, and an adverse decision would bear hard upon the claimant—and it should not be adversely decided until all means of information have been exhausted. Neither should it be allowed, until it is *clearly* shown to be meritorious." [47]

On May 3, 1882, Frank Patterson's pension claim was rejected in Washington. "The claimant is unable to prove origin of disease in line of duty," the document noted. Evidence strongly suggested Frank's eyesight had gone bad after he deserted. When the news arrived in Elmira, Mills and Laidlaw went back to their plotting, and Blind Patterson continued to beg. [48]

Five years passed. The Patterson marriage fell apart. Helen ran out of patience with Frank and left him around 1883. Adding insult to injury, she moved in with Fred "Dutch" Frank, a rag peddler who lived in a tenement at the foot of Spanish Hill, just over the Pennsylvania state line from the New York State town of Waverly. Blind Patterson reportedly responded by moving in with a certain Mrs. Buckley. Meanwhile, significant changes were made at the Pension Bureau in Washington. Commissioner Dudley was replaced in 1884; the next year Dudley's successor was followed by John C. Black of Illinois, a brevet brigadier general during the war who had been awarded the Medal of Honor. This was considered an auspicious change by claimants and their agents. Dudley, it was said, "immediately after a soldier filed his claim, had that soldier covered with detectives and branded on the back as a thief unless his claim had been disposed of." To the more lenient Black, "a soldier's claim [was] an honorable debt due him from the government." [49]

In the spring of 1886, Dr. Mills told an Elmira druggist he soon expected "a good big pile." "When the money comes," Mills added, "you and I will go to New York and have a *grand* time." That fall, an Elmira blacksmith who had known Blind Patterson for twenty years happened on the beggar in the street. "Frank," the man said, gesturing to Patterson's dog, "you have still got your old guardian leading you around." "Yes," Frank replied, "but we have got a scheme on hand, and if it works all right I will be on the top shelf, and lay aside the old dog." [50]

Mills and Laidlaw had learned from their earlier failure; they now sought the assistance of a lawyer. After listening to the two go on about poor old Blind Patterson, Andrew B. Galatian of Elmira agreed to take the case and get the charge of desertion against Patterson removed. The lawyer proved to be a cooperative sort. He let Mills and Laidlaw lounge in his office for hours on end, talking about the case. He opened a dark back room in his office to the doctor and the captain for a meeting with Wilkes Miller. Plied once again with booze and offered a bribe ten times larger than before—a thousand dollars—Miller again swore that he knew Frank Patterson intimately in the army and that Patterson had suffered from sore eyes before he deserted.

Miller made his affidavit on January 4, 1887. Less than two weeks later, Galatian personally filed the affidavit at the adjutant general's office in Washington. Three days after that, on January 20, an assistant adjutant general wrote to Francis Patterson (in care of Galatian) to notify him that the charge of desertion had been dropped; Frank's record would now show he was sick before his discharge. When Mills and Laidlaw met Galatian at the Elmira depot and heard the news, they "danced for joy." Anticipating a quick payment, Frank notified Elmira's postmaster, "Please do not let anybody excepting John Laidlaw have any of my mail." But no mail arrived. A week later, back in his usual routine, Blind Patterson was sent to the Chemung County Jail on an intoxication charge; he would be confined for about three weeks. Galatian, Mills, and Laidlaw visited him there. With Mills and Laidlaw acting as witnesses in Frank's cell, Patterson officially appointed Galatian his attorney. The jailor heard Mills and Laidlaw assure Frank that he would soon be released, that he would soon have plenty of money, that all he had to do was ask and his wants would be gratified. For his part, Frank grumbled that Mills and Laidlaw were "damned scoundrels" who were out to cheat him of his pension.[51]

Frank was still in jail when Mills and Laidlaw returned to Galatian's back room with several bottles of liquor and a new witness, Edward Porter of Olean. Porter had served as quartermaster and captain in the 154th New York and suffered a long imprisonment after his capture at Gettysburg. He had not known Frank Patterson, but he was moved by the story of this needy old regimental comrade and wanted to do what he could to help. Porter's willingness to help Blind Patterson was strictly altruistic; he had no interest in accepting a bribe for his perjury. Porter wondered if he would recognize Patterson. Although quite willing to drink his hosts' booze, he turned down their offer to introduce him to a local "nymph." Drunk, the former captain swore that he often saw Frank Patterson in the service and that Frank complained of sore eyes and worried about losing his eyesight prior to the Battle of Gettysburg.[52]

A week later, Mills and Laidlaw had a drunken Wilkes Miller make another affidavit in Galatian's office. Galatian then traveled again to Washington, where on

March 15 he filed the new affidavits in person at the Pension Bureau. On March 21 the adjutant general's office notified Commissioner Black that the Patterson desertion charge had been dropped.[53]

The commissioner responded by declaring the Patterson case special and assigning a couple of special examiners to investigate it. A letter was sent to the Olean postmaster asking for Edward Porter's community standing and reputation for truthfulness; the official, misreading the name, replied that Edward *Parker* stood well in Olean. A special examiner tracked Ed Porter to the Soldiers Home in Bath, New York; the ex-captain stuck staunchly to his story and added a few gratuitous details. In Elmira, Wilkes Miller faithfully repeated his story, quoting Frank as saying before Gettysburg, "Wilkes, what am I going to do? If I don't get help I'm going blind altogether."[54]

Blind Patterson's cronies had outfoxed the mighty Pension Bureau. Based on the seemingly ironclad testimony of Wilkes Miller and Ed Porter, there was nothing to do but approve the Patterson claim. Various legal and medical reviewers signed off on the case, ten dollars were deducted as Andrew Galatian's fee, and Application 109,848 was approved on May 14, 1887. Two days later, pension certificate number 359,849 was issued in Francis Patterson's name, enrolling him in the bureau's Syracuse Agency. Clerks calculated the payment. From eight dollars per month commencing the day after his discharge in 1864, the rate had risen incrementally to seventy-two dollars per month. Frank's retroactive payment totaled a whopping $13,337.99—a sum equal to more than a quarter of a million dollars today. It was the largest Civil War pension payment ever made. A voucher was issued to Frank for the money and mailed with his certificate to Elmira on June 1.[55]

Three days later, Blind Patterson picked up the voucher at the Elmira post office and immediately took it to Attorney Galatian's office, where it was properly executed and returned to the post office to be mailed to the pension agent at Syracuse, Major T. L. Poole. That same day the Elmira city attorney, Hosea H. Rockwell, heard about Frank's windfall. Rockwell also heard rumors that Dr. Mills claimed to be Blind Patterson's guardian. Rockwell knew Frank had no guardian, and he suspected that Mills and Laidlaw were about to fleece Frank, who, after all, was "a drunkard and entirely incompetent to use money." Seeking to prevent the duo from robbing the blind beggar, Rockwell met with Elmira's overseer of the poor, Edward Marvin, and Chemung County judge Seymour Dexter. Affidavits were obtained from local physicians attesting to Frank's habitual lunacy and drunkenness, and Marvin and Rockwell petitioned the court to appoint a guardian for the blind veteran. Rockwell also dashed off a letter to Pension Agent Poole in Syracuse, summarizing the actions he had taken and requesting that Poole not pay the voucher until a guardian had been named.[56]

Poole responded three days later, promising Rockwell he would delay Patterson's payment. "The amount granted Mr. Patterson is undoubtedly the largest pension ever paid in the United States," Poole observed; the agent considered it "very important that great care should be taken to see that he [Patterson] and those entitled to share in the same are protected."[57]

Mills and Laidlaw somehow got wind of Rockwell's guardianship effort and realized they had to act fast. The two grifters visited Elmira lawyer Charles H. Knipp and had him draw up a power of attorney for Mills to receive and dispense Frank's money. Then they mulled over the guardianship threat. On June 9, Knipp, Mills, and Patterson took a train to Syracuse and confronted Poole, demanding Frank's payment. Poole replied that he had information that made it advisable to withhold payment for the present. Knipp then played his money card. He telegraphed his law partner, E. B. Youmans, who happened to be the chief clerk of the U.S. Treasury in Washington. Knipp explained how Rockwell had stopped the payment of an allowed pension claim to a "mentally perfect" man, and suggested that his partner could sway pension officials to persuade Poole to make the payment. Youmans immediately made a call at the Pension Bureau. Commissioner Black was out of the office, so Youmans met with the acting commissioner, William E. McLean. Youmans laid out the case; he told McLean that he had seen Blind Patterson and his dog on Elmira's streets for years; Frank was a habitual drinker but not insane. McLean called up the file, looked it over, requested some legal advice, and finally wired Poole in Syracuse and ordered him to make the payment. That evening, Poole reluctantly made several drafts totaling $13,302.00 and gave them to Frank, who turned them over to Mills.[58]

Within days after returning to Elmira, Frank had signed most of his money over to the doctor. Mills in response threatened to "carve Patterson up" if he spilled the beans. But Blind Patterson had what he wanted—a seventy two dollars-per-month pension, some spare cash (he gave his daughter Electa Ann Moore thirty dollars), and a house. On Charles Knipp's advice, Frank purchased a $3,050 mortgage on the Fishler House hotel in Wellsburg, south of Elmira near the Pennsylvania line. One of Blind Patterson's dreams had come true—he now owned his own home. The deal was consummated on June 14.[59]

Helen Patterson, meanwhile, hearing of Frank's good fortune, had quickly returned to her newly rich husband, who welcomed her back with delight. At the urging of Dr. Mills, the reunited couple had left Elmira. They appeared on foot at the Halfway House on the Horseheads Road around June 11 and asked for a room. They stayed two nights, kept to their locked room, had their meals sent up, and saw only two visitors. A deputy sheriff frightened Frank by serving notice of the Elmira guardianship proceedings. Dr. Mills spent a half-hour with the Pattersons and on leaving urged the innkeeper to stay mum about his guests. On June 14, Frank and Helen returned to Elmira to buy the Fishler House. They also stopped by a church and were married for the second time—without an intervening divorce. This measure, probably suggested by Dr. Mills, was taken to provide the Pattersons with a marriage record; no documentation of their 1856 nuptials survived. Dr. Mills and the Pattersons' daughter, Electa Ann Moore, witnessed the ceremony. Now Frank had a bride to carry over the threshold of his new house.[60]

Elsewhere in Elmira on that eventful June 14, clouds were gathering to cast a shadow over this sunny scene. An aggrieved Wilkes Miller sat down with a Pension Bureau special examiner and admitted twice accepting bribes, in 1881 and 1887, to provide false affidavits in the Patterson pension case. After the money came in, Miller had been snubbed by Mills. Wilkes had seen the doctor emerge from a bank stuffing a large roll of bills into his pocket. Miller approached Mills and asked if he was going to hold up his end of their agreement. Mills laughed in Miller's face. With a dismissive wave of his hand he sneered, "We don't owe you anything," and walked away. Now, Miller got his revenge on Mills by blowing the whistle on the fraud.[61]

Hearing of Miller's confession, lawyer Andrew Galatian quickly moved to protect himself, composing a letter to the acting pension commissioner to report the fraud, claiming he was astounded to learn of Miller's disclosure, and expressing his sincere regret to have been connected with the case. "I sympathized with the blind man believing his claim to be just," Galatian declared, "but now when it is too late I find that it is a fraud, and that I have been the victim of misplaced confidence." For their part, pension officials thought that Galatian knew more than he let on, but they could never come up with enough evidence to implicate the lawyer as a willing accomplice.[62]

Dr. Mills and Blind Patterson had an appointment with Charles Knipp that June 14 to discuss a strategy for Frank's guardianship hearing. They never showed up.[63]

At four o'clock that afternoon, Mills paid an Elmira liveryman an exorbitant ten dollars to rent a pair of horses and a carriage to go to Troy, Pennsylvania. At first the doctor said he needed a driver, but then he changed his mind. That evening John Laidlaw came by the stable for the rig and team. The captain clattered off and picked up the Pattersons. The trio drove south, across the state line into Pennsylvania. Frank and Helen were on the lam.[64]

That night Laidlaw and the Pattersons reached Troy, Pennsylvania, after a twenty-five mile ride. They checked into the Troy House. Laidlaw was firmly in charge of the party, the hotelkeeper observed. He admitted he was getting Blind Patterson out of Elmira to escape the authorities, and refused to allow Frank and Helen to be registered. All three guests had obviously been drinking. After a meal, they took an omnibus to the Troy railroad depot, expecting Mills to join them by train from Elmira. But the doctor was drunk; he fell asleep, missed the stop, and woke up in Williamsport. He immediately telegraphed the Pattersons, asking them to join him the next day. When Laidlaw checked out of the Troy House on the morning of June 15, he tried to obliterate his signature from the hotel register. Then he and the Pattersons got in their buggy and drove to Williamsport.[65]

In the meantime, Mills and Laidlaw had become wanted men. Elmira City Attorney Rockwell issued warrants for their arrest for conspiracy to defraud Blind Patterson. A telegram to the Washington, D.C., police requested them to arrest and hold Mills, who was believed headed in that direction.[66]

The doctor, unaware of these developments, arranged accommodations for the Pattersons at the Sherman House in Williamsport. When they arrived, John Laidlaw parted with his fellow conspirators; he would rendezvous with Mills later. Mills made frequent visits to the Pattersons' room, where Frank and Helen were drinking. The landlord finally tired of the trio and threw them out. During his brief stay in Williamsport, Mills cashed the remaining pension checks. The local bank did not have $6,950.00 in currency on hand, so the tellers paid him in gold. He swept the heavy pile of five , ten , and twenty-dollar coins into a satchel. Down the street he bought two smaller bags to hold the loot, one for him and one for the Pattersons. He stopped at a jeweler's and bought a fifty-dollar gold watch and chain, blathering with the shopkeeper about investing in local real estate. He gave an innkeeper a ten-dollar tip and suggested he buy his wife a new bonnet. Then he escorted Frank and Helen to the depot and put them on an afternoon westbound train to Lock Haven. He would catch a later train, heading elsewhere. The gang was temporarily breaking up.[67]

Frank and Helen registered at the Central Hotel in Lock Haven just before supper on June 16. Over the next several days, Helen spent fifteen or twenty dollars on clothes, but the Pattersons' largest expenditure was for liquor, which they drank in their room. Frank deposited twenty-three hundred dollars in the Lock

Haven State Bank, all but two hundred of it in gold coin. The Pattersons had only one visitor during their stay in Lock Haven: David M. Pratt of Elmira, cashier at the Second National Bank, who on June 17 had been appointed by Judge Dexter as Blind Patterson's guardian. When Frank refused to return to Elmira with Pratt, the guardian ordered the Lock Haven bank to freeze the Patterson funds. With that setback, Frank and Helen left Lock Haven on June 21 on an eastbound morning train.[68]

Meanwhile, the Pension Bureau increased the pressure on the Blind Patterson pension case. In Washington, Commissioner Black on June 18 urged swift and vigorous action to push the investigation and prosecute the fraud's perpetrators. That same day, the chief of the special examiner division ordered his man in Elmira, Charles H. McCarthy, to carefully and thoroughly investigate the case. If fraud was found, steps were to be taken to seize the ill-gotten money. McCarthy worked conscientiously. At one point during the investigation he spent forty-five days combing more than a hundred villages in an unsuccessful search for a single witness. On June 21 the supervising examiner of the Hudson District, Thomas J. Shannon, was ordered to proceed to Elmira and take charge of the probe. As soon as Shannon arrived, he got to work. He and McCarthy interviewed an uncooperative Andrew Galatian. The special examiners strongly suspected the lawyer was in on the plot, but they could not piece together enough evidence to charge him. Wilkes Miller had already confessed to being bribed—the big break in the case—but he stubbornly stuck to his story about Patterson's bad eyes until Shannon and McCarthy broke him down after a sixteen-hour interrogation. Ed Porter proved to be equally obstinate. The special examiners grilled him in Olean from 4 P.M. on June 23 until after midnight, when he finally, reluctantly confessed that his affidavits, made while he was drunk, were false.[69]

While Shannon and McCarthy tightened the noose in New York State, Dr. Robert Mills's flight ended in his native Virginia. There he had fled to the isolated home of his sister, Pattie M. Mills, in Stanardsville, the Greene County seat, a hamlet in the shadow of the Blue Ridge. For days, Mills recklessly spent loot and bragged about his "cords of money." He bought sister Pattie a six hundred-dollar plot of land, paying in gold coin. He repaid old loans, granting exorbitant interest. He delighted in paying highly inflated prices for a cow (one hundred dollars) and a saddle (twenty dollars). He cheerfully gave five dollars to an "Old Auntie" of long acquaintance. He gave cash to relatives who stuffed it in envelopes and sent it via registered mail to other relatives in Missouri and Texas. He lied about fat fees from a flourishing surgical practice in Elmira. He told a hotelkeeper he had five hundred dollars in gold in his pocket and could show him thousands more. He told several people that the most gold he had ever carried at once was thirteen thousand dollars worth—it weighed so much, he often had to stop and rest.[70]

It all came crashing down for the doctor at 6:30 A.M. on June 23, when he sauntered out of Pattie's house into the waiting arms of a special examiner and a county sheriff. Inside, the authorities found John Laidlaw asleep on a sofa. Dr. Mills's wife, Julia, also was present. She at first denied that any pension loot was hidden in the house, but soon produced a bag containing more than four thousand dollars in gold coin. Mills and Laidlaw were arrested. Julia Mills accompanied her husband to Washington, where a search of her person revealed $635 in bills in her bosom. All of the money, Dr. and Mrs. Mills admitted, was part of the Patterson plunder. Some $5,725 was turned over to the Pension Bureau's assistant chief clerk that day, and diligent investigative and legal follow-up work in the Stanardsville area recovered more of the loot. On June 24, Elmira's chief of police and a Washington detective escorted Mills and Laidlaw aboard an Elmira-bound train.[71]

Frank and Helen, in the meantime, rode back to New York State, arriving at the Waverly depot on the evening of June 22. They immediately recrossed the state line to Dutch Frank's Pennsylvania tenement, Helen's former haunt. Dutch was not home, so the Pattersons broke in and holed up. "Pat and his wife while here kept quite shady," an observer reported, "and took care not to linger very long on the New York side of the line." A seventeen-year-old son of Dr. Mills joined the Pattersons on the afternoon of June 23; that night the boy bought tickets for Washington, D.C., and the three boarded a southbound train. Helen hauled along a trunk full of goods from Dutch Frank's place. "Blind Patterson," a wag noted, "is in as hard luck now as he was when a pauper, for detectives are on his trail, a blood-thirsty paramour of his wife is after his heart, and everybody else is after his money."

After a night in the capital's Cutler House, the trio journeyed on to Stanardsville, where they expected to meet Dr. Mills and were shocked to learn that their friend had been arrested. They continued their flight southeastward to Gordonsville, a railroad town. But before they could board a train, they were nabbed on June 28 by a U.S. marshal and the same special examiner who had arrested Mills and Laidlaw. The officials hustled Frank and Helen and young Mills aboard a northbound train, and the old veteran bounced over the same landscape he had traversed twenty-four years before, when he had escorted recruits to the front after Gettysburg, just before the fateful railroad journey west and his desertion. But Frank's thoughts were on Helen, not the war. "The old man showed much jealousy of his wife," his escorts noticed, "and insisted that she retire with him to the smoking car, away from the wiles of a suspected admirer." At Alexandria, Frank and young Mills waived further hearing and consented to be taken to Elmira. In Washington, Frank, Helen, and the Mills boy were searched. Helen was carrying the loot—a $2,300 certificate of deposit on the Lock Haven bank and $62.53 in cash.[72]

On June 29, the Pension Bureau officially suspended payment of Blind Patterson's pension. He had given away most of his huge settlement, squandered a bit of it, and relinquished the rest to the authorities. In all, pension officials recovered more than eleven thousand dollars in New York, Pennsylvania, and Virginia. Robert Mills and John Laidlaw were in jail in Binghamton, awaiting a hearing. That day they were joined by Ed Porter, recently arrested in Olean. Wilkes Miller was free in Elmira; he would be the government's star witness against the cabal. Frank Patterson was aboard yet another train, heading to New York State to join his co-conspirators in jail.[73]

By this time, the press was having a field day with the Blind Patterson story. The *Elmira Daily Advertiser* broke the news of "The Largest Pension Yet" on June 11; the next day, the *New York Times* related "A Blind Beggar's Fortune." Newspapers followed up with stories about Frank's purchase of the Fishler House mortgage, his lunacy hearing, and his rebuffing of David Pratt. Coverage exploded when Wilkes Miller's confession revealed the fraud. The *Elmira Tidings* broke the story on Sunday, June 19. Monday's papers broadcast it to the nation. Subsequent reporting chronicled the flight and arrest of the fugitives and their return to New York State.[74]

Mills and Laidlaw were garrulous to reporters. The captain stoutly maintained his innocence to a Washington correspondent en route to the Binghamton jail. "Why should I fear anything?" he asked. "I didn't run away from Elmira." He knew nothing about a fraud. Mills was nervous and excited; his fingers trembled as he spoke. Like Laidlaw he was adamant about his innocence, categorizing the whole affair as a "spite action" by Hosea Rockwell. When they reached the Elmira jail, Mills and Laidlaw bought a box of cigars and puffed away during an interview. "I am just as calm as when I was facing rebel bullets in the war," Laidlaw boasted. "And you can add to that," said Mills, "that I am just as calm as when I was facing Union bullets in the war."[75]

Newspapers followed every step of the story. On the morning of June 28, Mills and Laidlaw were arrested at the Elmira jail by Federal officials, charged with perjury, handcuffed together, and escorted to Binghamton. Within days they were joined by their accomplices, Ed Porter and Blind Patterson. Bail for each of the four was set at five thousand dollars. Only Mills could meet it. Elmira's mayor, John B. Stanchfield, traveled to Binghamton to post the bond. Mills immediately returned to Elmira and denounced the newspapers—to a reporter, of course—for prejudging him. The doctor then turned his attention to supervising the construction of an addition to his house. Laidlaw could have raised bail, but refused it. There would be no bail for poor Porter and Patterson.[76]

Blind Patterson broke his silence to a reporter and an artist from an Elmira paper. While the artist struggled to capture his squirming subject's likeness, the reporter scribbled down Frank's thoughts. He had had a hard life. Now that his money was gone, he had no friends. He asked often after Helen and spoke highly of his "old woman." He worried that Dutch Frank had won her back again. "Me and her has had a hard life," Frank said, "and now that I ain't got any money I'll be worse. I'd a had my money if they'd a left me alone. . . . I wanted to take it and buy me a little home and have an easy time." Frank closed the interview with another inquiry about Helen.[77]

It took four legal proceedings to decide the case. Each generated a wave of publicity. A preliminary hearing was held before a Federal commissioner at Binghamton on July 6. After Wilkes Miller, Ed Porter, Andrew Galatian, and other witnesses testified, the commissioner held Patterson, Mills, Laidlaw, and Porter for trial at the next term of the Federal court in Buffalo, and upped their bail to seven thousand dollars each. "'Blind' Patterson looked fat and hearty," a reporter noted, "and seemed unconcerned about the result."[78]

Over the next few days the prisoners were transferred to the Buffalo jail. Helen made headlines when she returned to Dutch Frank's tenement in Waverly. She told a reporter that she was only picking up some things and intended to rejoin her husband. Helen followed the story closely in the papers and did not hesitate to write to editors to complain of inaccuracies in their coverage.[79]

A grand jury indicted Mills, Laidlaw, and Patterson in Buffalo's Federal court on the morning of September 24 for transmitting false affidavits to the commissioner of pensions. The prisoners pleaded not guilty. The judge raised their bail to ten thousand dollars each. On the motion of John Stanchfield, counsel for Mills and Laidlaw, the cases were held over to the November term of the Federal court at Auburn, New York. A reporter described Blind Patterson as having "the helpless, patient look on his face peculiar to the sightless. He has a big, round head, with thick iron-gray hair that once was black. His face is smooth-shaven, with the exception of a small round patch of hair on his chin. He held a stout stick in his hands and showed as little interest as if he were deaf as well as blind."[80]

More than seventy-five witnesses gathered on November 17 for the Auburn trial. When the defendants entered the courtroom, many Elmira friends shook their hands. After two days of testimony—"Patterson proved himself to be a first-class witness in his own behalf," an onlooker noted—the case went to the jury at 12:50 P.M. on November 19. At 2:15 the next morning, the jurors returned to the courtroom. "A half dozen flickering gas jets cast a yellowish, sickly light about the judge's bench and over the twelve sleepy jurymen as they filed into their seats," a reporter wrote. They were hopelessly deadlocked; the judge discharged them and carried the case over to the spring term of the court in Utica. Bail for both Mills and Laidlaw was reduced to seven thousand dollars; Blind Patterson's bail dropped to five hundred dollars. "The prisoners appeared to be much disappointed at the outcome of the trial," observed a reporter, "and returned to jail three very sorrowful men."[81]

Olive Hooker convinced an Elmira alderman to post her brother's bail, and she accompanied Frank home in mid-December. A newspaperman noted, "The faithful dog that has been eyes for the old man so long was glad to see his master and again become his escort." Frank's townsmen largely believed that he deserved his pension and that he would be acquitted in the next trial. Laidlaw also had Elmirans' sympathy; he too was bailed out and returned home. Dr. Mills also was bailed out, only to be immediately rearrested and charged in another case of pension fraud.[82]

The U.S. District Court convened in Utica on March 20, 1888, in an uncomfortably crowded courtroom. An estimated 150 Elmirans were in town as witnesses, attorneys, and officers. After some preliminary maneuvering, the trial got under way on the morning of March 22. Wilkes Miller, Ed Porter, and Andrew Galatian led off two days of testimony from a string of witnesses, all of it raptly reported in the newspapers. "What Patterson said in his own behalf," a reporter wrote, "was given, in spite of the efforts of counsel to confuse him, in a way that amused as well as convinced the jurors and spectators." With tears in his eyes and a quavering voice, Frank said "it had cut him to his heart to have his wife abused" in the press. Pension supervising examiner Tom Shannon thought that Frank was poorly clad intentionally, to look "pinched with poverty." "Patterson," Shannon mused, "although uneducated, is shrewd." Dr. Mills caused a sensation on the first day of testimony when he fell from his seat in a fit and had to be carried from the courtroom. The district attorney took an hour and a half to sum up his case, pointing out that the government had spent more than twice the amount of Patterson's pension windfall in trying the case. After a few hours of deliberation, the jury returned to the courtroom at 8 P.M. on March 26 with a verdict of not guilty for all three defendants. The large crowd burst into boisterous applause. Mills, Laidlaw, and Patterson individually thanked each juror. Their legal troubles finally behind them, Blind Patterson and Laidlaw went home to Elmira. Mills was held in the other pension fraud case; when it came to trial a few days later, the doctor was taken from the courtroom "pale and seemingly bewildered." Spectators thought he had gone mad.[83]

Francis Patterson was dropped from the pension roll on November 7, 1887. On March 3, 1888, his record as a deserter was restored by the adjutant general's office. About a month later, a special examiner suggested that legal proceedings be instituted to reclaim money in the hands of Patterson's guardian, David Pratt, including the $3,050 mortgage on the Fishler House and $2,300 in cash. With that money in legal limbo, Blind Patterson applied again for a pension. "I have not a dollar in the world to support myself or my family," he stated. "I am now utterly destitute, old, infirm, and unable to obtain the necessaries of life. Since the close of the war I have been and am now an object of charity, buffeted from door to door, and dependent upon the kindness of strangers to keep me from starvation's door." A group of influential Elmirans urged that the disputed monies be restored to Pratt, a reliable and competent guardian who would not misuse the funds. Meanwhile, the Blind Patterson case was summarized in the annual report of the commissioner of pensions as proof that "the Pension Bureau is not always responsible for the failure of justice."[84]

"Where are Blind Patterson's friends?" asked an Elmira newspaper in August 1888. "A few months ago they were hovering about him thicker than flies about the bunghole of a molasses barrel." Now Frank and Helen were in court, pleading guilty to charges of disturbing the peace and intoxication. For days they had been on a rip-roaring drunk in a hovel on an Elmira alley; neighbors had repeatedly complained about their vile language, noise, and filth. "The stench arising from the place," a reporter wrote, "drove two policemen out of it quicker than if they had been struck by bullets." Frank was "dirty beyond description, unshaved and unkempt, and the odor which filled the room from his presence would have made a bone factory smell like attar of roses." Helen "presented a worse sight and dirtier appearance than her husband." She asked Frank how she should plead. "Tell the truth, baby," Frank replied. "Truth is truth the world over." Frank "loves his baby," the reporter noted. The Pattersons were sentenced to sixty days in jail.[85]

The attorney general eventually recommended to the commissioner of pensions that Blind Patterson was entitled to the frozen funds. Commissioner Black therefore granted permission to Pratt to distribute the sums held by him, and $4,807.53 seized from Julia Mills and Helen Patterson was also turned over to the guardian. Frank and Helen were able to purchase a house at 724 West First Street in Elmira; whether Frank ever got his wished-for cart and horse to gather bones is unknown. Several times he applied to be readmitted to the pension roll, but each time he was rejected. Once he was turned down because of his "vicious habits."[86]

Frank Patterson was paralyzed after a brief illness and died at his home at 6:45 P.M. on April 30, 1897. Headlines in all the Elmira newspapers trumpeted the passing of "A Famous Elmira Character." "Probably no one man or character about town," one paper observed, "was known by more people than he." The funeral was held at the Patterson home on May 2. A minister officiated. A reporter noted, "A large number of the old soldier friends of the deceased were present and many beautiful floral offerings were received." After Frank was buried at Woodlawn, Helen published a card of thanks in the newspapers: "To all my neighbors and friends who assisted me by kindly words, actions, beautiful flowers and other evidences of sympathy in my bereavement, the loss of my husband, I extend my sincere thanks." It was an entirely proper ending to a highly irregular life.[87]

Helen applied for a widow's pension after Frank's death, but she had no better luck than her husband had. She was rejected because the War Department considered Frank's discharge to be dishonorable. She received another blow when Frank's estate was settled and a judge ordered the sale of the West First Street house, forcing to her move several times during her last years. In 1902 she fell on a sidewalk and was severely hurt; she received an eight hundred dollar settlement from the city, which helped ease her situation. Helen died on September 4, 1904, and was laid to rest in Woodlawn beside Frank.[88]

Toward the end of her life, Helen Patterson wrote annually to the commissioner of pensions, requesting the return of Frank's discharge. She never received it; the discharge remained in her husband's pension file in Washington. The documents in a typical Civil War pension file fit into a single folder, two or three at most. Blind Patterson's file, the largest Civil War invalid case file ever, consists of fourteen folders bulging with the correspondence, depositions, notes, newspaper clippings, bank deposit slips, telegrams, subpoenas, and witness lists that chart his remarkable story.[89]

CHAPTER TWELVE

Private Oscar F. Wilber

Company G

The weather turned hot and humid for my last Cattaraugus County cemetery visit. Five Mile Cemetery was set in a flat surrounded by wooded hills on Church Road in the town of Allegany. The grounds were bordered on their back and sides by cornfields. Across the road, a row of small houses faced the graveyard. A wrought-iron fence opened to the usual dirt drive. Only a half-dozen cedars were scattered about the cemetery, so most of the stones baked in the sun. It was just the sort of muggy July day, I thought, on which Oscar F. Wilber had died in a hospital in our nation's capital 141 years before. To the left of my parking spot, in the very first row of markers, I spotted the flag flying over Wilber's grave.

The inscribed granite wedge appeared to be a replacement stone. Beside it, three older stones of family members were sunk in the grass, their inscriptions illegible. To their left was a taller monument to the Wilber family, with inscriptions for Oscar's parents on the front and for him and a brother and sister on the right side. Oscar's stated that he died at the age of twenty-five years, four months, and eleven days.

As I sat writing some notes in the shade of a tree opposite Oscar's grave, a new friend joined me. Thomas T. Krampf of nearby Hinsdale is a collateral descendant of Colonel Patrick Henry Jones of the 154th New York, which is how we came to correspond. Two nights before, Tom and I had met for the first time when he hosted a talk I gave at the library in nearby Olean. Today we met to continue our conversation. As the noontime sun scorched the cemetery, we discussed the Civil War, the Wilber family, and Oscar's sad demise. And we talked about writing—Tom is a poet, the author of several published volumes of verse. Then we took some photographs of Oscar's stone, said our goodbyes, got in our cars, and drove away.

It was a while before I was struck by the coincidence of meeting a poet at the grave of Oscar Wilber. For it was Oscar's encounter with America's greatest poet that drew me to his story in the first place.

Walt Whitman was not yet a colossus of American literature when he met Oscar Wilber in 1863. His reputation as a poet rested on a slender volume of verses, *Leaves of Grass,* then in its third edition. The book had brought its author considerable notoriety—many considered it obscene—but little in the way of royalties. Before the war began, Whitman had spent his time avoiding his dysfunctional Brooklyn family, palling around with horse-car drivers in Manhattan, and drinking with fellow bohemians at Pfaff's saloon on Broadway. He had lost his job as an editor of a Brooklyn newspaper and was not writing much. He was depressed. Only his naturally buoyant personality kept him from sinking into chronic despondency.

The war reinvigorated him. When his soldier brother was wounded in battle in Virginia, Walt journeyed to the front to look after him. In Washington's sprawling military hospitals, he found a new calling. In wards teeming with sick and shattered soldiers, he wandered row after row of beds dispensing comfort to the sufferers. A part-time government job left him plenty of time to distribute treats and trinkets to the patients, to write letters for them, to listen to their stories, to hold their hands, to temper their trials with tenderness. He recorded certain of his hospital encounters in bloodstained notebooks. So he met and wrote about Oscar Wilber.[1]

Whitman estimated that he visited between eighty thousand and a hundred thousand hospitalized soldiers during the war. The stories of some of those soldiers eventually made their way from the private pages of his notebooks into the public realm of print. This first occurred when Walt reworked certain notebook sketches into lengthy articles for the *New York Times.* Among the profiles in a December 1864 piece was "Death of a New-York Soldier," Walt's account of his meeting with Oscar Wilber. Titled "A New York Soldier," the same sketch appeared a decade later in a collection of Whitman's wartime writings in the *Weekly Graphic,* another New York newspaper. The following year, 1875, Whitman privately published his book, *Memoranda During the War,* which included sketches of some fifty soldiers. Among them was "A New York Soldier." Since its appearance in those early sources, Walt's story of Oscar has been reprinted numerous times in collections of Whitman's writings.[2]

Walt Whitman certainly put a snippet of Oscar Wilber's real war into the books; countless readers have pondered the account of "A New York Soldier." But the rest of Oscar's story remained untold. Whitman's readers never learned, for example, that Walt was not the only good Samaritan who tended Oscar during his last days—nor was the poet alone in chronicling this particular mortality tale. Likewise, the fact that another famous Civil War personage met and cared for Oscar remained concealed. And Oscar's own voice—only faintly echoed in Whitman's piece—was not stilled at his demise. It lived on, in the letters he had sent home to his family, lovingly tucked away and preserved through the generations.

During the Civil War, Wilber family farms stood across from Five Mile Cemetery in Allegany and were scattered along the road running north through the Five Mile Run valley into the town of Humphrey. Seven sons of Freeman Wilber, a Rhode Island native and Revolutionary War veteran, had moved en masse from Onondaga County, New York, to the Five Mile tract in 1830. One of the brothers was Alanson Wilber, who purchased and worked a small Humphrey farm. Alanson's wife was Sally D. Richmond. Their third child and first son, Oscar Franklin Wilber, was born March 20, 1838. Five siblings followed Oscar. Alanson died in 1852, leaving his widow to raise the eight children. By 1860, Sally was dependent on Oscar for the family's support. The Wilber household then included Sally's mother, Oscar's invalid older sister, Rosina, a younger sister, and three younger brothers. The farm was now in Oscar's name. Oscar worked it and also hired out to his uncle, Nathan Wilber, on a neighboring farm, turning over his wages to Sally.[3]

Five Wilber cousins left the Five Mile Run valley to enlist. Twenty-four-year-old Oscar was the third to go. It must have been a difficult decision for him to leave his mother and siblings. He volunteered only after his Uncle Nathan promised to handle his financial affairs and look after Sally in his absence. Oscar enlisted in the neighboring town of Hinsdale on August 11, 1862. On September 24, he was mustered in as a private in Company G of the 154th New York. Three of his Wilber cousins—Milo (age eighteen), and brothers Darius (age twenty) and Lyman (age eighteen)—also served in Company G. The fourth cousin, Charles (age twenty-four), was a private in Company I.

Seventeen of Oscar's wartime letters survive, eleven of them to his Uncle Na-

than, the others to his mother. Reflecting the weight of his family responsibili-
ties, they are filled with sometimes labyrinthine references to money matters and
questions and suggestions regarding the farm. In addition to the business minutia, they relate Oscar's particular experience of the war, and his reactions to it.[4]

His first letter to Nathan sketched the highlights of the trip to the front:
the stop in Elmira to receive their arms and accouterments; the slow ride from
Baltimore to Washington over heavily guarded track; Old Abe's nice house in
the capital; the rolling countryside surrounding Washington, cropless, desolate,
scarred by entrenchments; tents and soldiers as thick as flies around Camp Seward
on Arlington Heights; a fort containing a cannon large enough for a man to crawl
into. Just a week after leaving western New York he had seen more than he had
ever imagined, but none of the sights could compare with home: "I like Cattaraugus the best," he asserted.[5]

Nine days later Oscar informed his uncle of the move to Fairfax Court House
and the regiment's assignment to Major General Franz Sigel's corps. "I guess
we shall have to fight," Oscar opined, because Sigel was a fighter: "You know he
has been boxing with the rebels for some time." Captain Matthew B. Cheney
thought that Company G "shall have to fight right along." All Oscar had to say
about the prospect was he wanted no one at home to trouble about him. But
he requested their prayers. "I wish I was a good Christian," he wrote, in one of
the few religious references of his correspondence. "I try to live like one, but
you know that there is everything to lead a man astray." He would do the best
he could as a soldier, Oscar promised. He expected the war to end by spring. He
added the typical soldier's refrain: please write. His uncle had more time to write
than he did; he was often busy with drill or standing guard or other duties. "Nathan, write all the news," Oscar pleaded. "Write me a good long letter."[6]

By the time of Oscar's next letter, the regiment had marched to Thoroughfare
Gap. The men had seen their first battlefield, having traversed the site of the two
combats at Bull Run. "Now I will tell you a little about war," Oscar informed
his uncle, launching into a graphic description of the horrors he had witnessed: a
leg, severed below the knee, still standing in its boot; a rain-washed face protruding from the soil; a desiccated, shriveled forearm, shot off at the elbow; a head
severed from its body; countless corpses of men barely covered by a few inches of
dirt; decaying horses littering the ground. "Uncle Nathan Wilber," wrote Oscar,
"you don't know how bad it looked."

Turning from the gruesome sights of the battlefield, Oscar related some better
news. The men had enjoyed a fine beef dinner, having confiscated several cattle
from local rebels. "Our boys went at them like wolves," he reported; the beeves

were immediately shot, quickly dressed, and soon were broiling over campfires. One of the beasts was a young bull that tried unsuccessfully to escape. The men bragged that they had whipped him at Bull Run. In following days the soldiers proved as proficient in plundering and butchering hogs, sheep, and chickens.[7]

Like many of his regimental comrades, Oscar took sick during the expedition to Thoroughfare Gap. He was one of several men who came down with the mumps. Some were so ill they were sent to the hospital, but Oscar resisted going and thought he was better off for it. By the time the 154th returned to Fairfax, he was feeling "quite smart," recovering his strength, and "getting pretty stout." But he stressed to his uncle that the home folk had no idea of the hardships of soldier life. Some days all they got to eat was one hardtack and a little piece of beef. (During the worst of his illness he could not eat hardtack and bought luxuries like cheese, butter, and pies from sutlers at inflated prices. Consequently he was broke.) After spending all day outdoors, the soldiers lay at night in mud and water two or three inches deep, wrapped in a single blanket beneath thin cloth tents, through which the rain ran unimpeded. If they could have his barn to sleep in, Oscar informed Nathan, the soldiers would think that they were well provided for. "We have to fare harder than your cattle does," he declared. "Uncle Nathan," Oscar admonished, "if you are drafted, you better hire a man to come in your place if it costs you all you are worth to hire him; for what is a man's property worth when he is dead?" But Oscar thought he would live to return home. He asked his uncle to pray for him, "and I will pray for myself."[8]

A few days later Oscar wrote to both his uncle and mother. He had received a "kind letter" from Sally the previous night. "Oh," he exclaimed, "how glad I was to hear from you, Mother. I began to think that you had all forgotten me." He continued to recover from the mumps, he reported, feeling well enough but still a bit weak. Cousins Charles, Milo, and Darius all had been sick. Times were dull, he noted; there was no war news to convey. Initial expectations of fighting had diminished. Oscar told Sally that he did not expect to be in battle for a good while, and it may be that the regiment would never have to fight. "I hope not, anyhow," he admitted. "For my part, I don't want to fight." He reiterated his opinion—and that of most of the soldiers—that the war would be settled by spring and he would return home.[9]

The regiment had made a muddy march to the vicinity of Fredericksburg by the time of Oscar's next surviving letters. Finally he confronted the rebels; the enemy was in plain sight across the Rappahannock River. Company G was detached from the regiment to support a nearby battery. Talk among the troops centered on the recent bloody defeat at Fredericksburg, in which Major General

Ambrose E. Burnside had repeatedly ordered his army to make hopeless attacks up a slope against well-entrenched Confederates. Veterans dubbed the battle "General Burnside's slaughter yard."

When orders to march arrived in the middle of the night in mid-January 1863, the regiment expected to see action. The men quickly cooked some meat, rolled up their blankets, and started off as quietly as they could, having been ordered to make no noise. After covering a couple of miles they loaded their muskets and fixed bayonets before continuing, apprehensive about an attack by enemy cavalry. It never came. Reaching their upriver destination, they put their muskets aside for axes, shovels, and picks, and worked building roads and a bridge. The labor appeared to be in preparation for a strike at the enemy. "Well, Mother," Oscar wrote, "if we have got to fight with them we might as well be about it, for I have got sick of it." He was homesick. "Mother, did you think that I had forgotten you?" he asked. "If you did think so, you thought wrong, for there ain't ten minutes in a day but what I think of some of you. Oh, how I would like to step in our house and see you all." [10]

On completing its assigned road work, the regiment was ordered to accompany the pontoon train to the river as Burnside's grand offensive began. Oscar described the ensuing Mud March as "the worst time that I ever see." Rain began falling and continued throughout the night and into the next day. The soldiers, the teams hauling the pontoons, the artillery—all bogged down in knee-deep mud. Soaked to the skin, Oscar estimated his saturated knapsack weighed sixty pounds. "I am a-going to stop writing right here about that march," he declared with disgust, "for I don't like to write about it." [11]

By the time of his next letter, army life had settled back into routine dullness. The big news was that the regiment had received its first pay. Uncle Sam had broken his agreement by only paying the soldiers a portion of what they had coming, Oscar declared, but he would not find fault with him, "for I know that old Uncle Sam has got his hands full. [It is] more than he can do to pay off the soldier." Uncle Sam was getting poor, Oscar thought, but he was "a long-winded old fellow, slow and sure." The soldiers would eventually get their withheld pay. Oscar drew $21.20; he sent a fourteen-dollar check to his uncle together with specific instructions on endorsing and cashing it to pay the family's land tax. He wanted Sally to have six dollars to buy herself a new dress or anything she had a mind to obtain. [12]

Early in February the regiment moved a short distance to the vicinity of Stafford Court House and constructed a new winter camp on a pleasant site with good sources of water and plenty of timber to use for building materials and fuel. After the brief flurry of activity, the soldiers languished in boredom once again. "Nathan, I wish that I was to your house today, where I could clasp my hands with you and your family," Oscar confided to his uncle. "Oh, what a happy day that would be to me." In a photographer's small tent, dark and crowded with other customers, he had two tintypes taken at a dollar apiece. He was not pleased with the results; nevertheless he told his mother to take the picture of him wearing a cap and his sister Rosina to have the one of him with a hat. In a note to Rosina he stated that he thought he would live to see her again—"For we hain't got only two years and a half to stay; that ain't but a little while. It soon will pass away and I can come home." He added, "Rosina, you see that I ain't discouraged yet."[13]

In mid-March, Oscar reported more dull times. Drilling and standing picket were the soldiers' only duties. "Mother, I don't think that there will be much more fighting in Virginia," Oscar guessed. "Nothing more than some skirmishing." He kept good courage and expected the war to end by fall. He asked his mother not to trouble about him; his health was good and he carried 180 pounds on his five-foot, ten-inch frame. "I don't trouble about myself," he declared. "All the trouble I have is about you and the rest of the family." He thanked his brother closest in age, sixteen-year-old Wallace, for notes he and two younger brothers had sent him. "I had rather have a letter from them and you," Oscar informed Wallace, "than to have one from old Abe Lincoln."[14]

On April 28, 1863, Oscar finally had some significant news to send to his mother. The regiment had marched up the Rappahannock River to Kelly's Ford, leaving its knapsacks behind in the Stafford camp. Three days after arriving at the ford, Oscar was detailed to return to camp with the wagon train. Two weeks later his squad was ordered to rejoin the regiment, bringing along the knapsacks. Oscar and his companions went through the baggage, removing overcoats and dress coats and turning them over to the quartermaster, leaving each soldier with spare clothing consisting of two shirts, two pairs of socks, a pair of shoes, and a woolen blanket. Then they loaded the knapsacks and eight days' worth of rations aboard wagons and made the two-day journey to the ford.

"Mother, I think that we shall have to fight pretty soon," Oscar accurately predicted. "I think that our men will attack the rebels in two or three days." He finished writing with thoughts of home. "Now Mother, I shall have to close my letter, and I want you to write as soon as you get this. Tell all the family that I would like to see them. . . . Mother, write soon and write all of the news. Direct your letters as before. Goodbye. Write soon."[15]

Four days after Oscar wrote his letter, the 154th New York underwent its baptism of fire at Chancellorsville. When the regiment was driven from the rifle pit near

Dowdall's Tavern by Stonewall Jackson's mighty attack on the evening of May 2, 1863, most of the soldiers scattered in flight. But Captain Matthew Cheney managed to keep Company G together. Cheney even halted the company as it fell back through the woods and called the roll to make sure all of his men were present. Other members of the 154th attached themselves to Cheney's intact command. Oscar and his comrades spent a harrowing night on an improvised picket line, under fire a good part of the time. At five o'clock on the morning of May 3, Cheney reported to Brigadier General George Sears Greene, commander of a brigade in the Twelfth Corps, who directed the 154th men into a section of rifle pit alongside his troops.[16]

Later that morning, the battle exploded along Greene's line. This combat proved to be even fiercer than the one Cheney's men had fought the previous evening. In fact, the fighting on May 3 cost the Union and Confederate armies 21,357 casualties, making it the second bloodiest day (after Antietam, September 17, 1862) in American history. Among the thousands of men stricken in this horrific bloodbath was Oscar Wilber.[17]

Greene's troops were at a disadvantage in the fight. "The position was a bad one for our men, as the Rebs were out of reach of our muskets," a member of the 154th New York wrote; "but their shells made considerable havoc among our men there, as they could do nothing [to defend themselves] and were badly exposed." During the artillery barrage, a shell exploded amid Company G and a fragment tore into Oscar's right hip. The force of the blow broke his femur in two. Appalled company comrades saw the shattered white bone protruding from Oscar's mangled flesh. Oscar called piteously for Captain Cheney, who was posted behind the rifle pit. Cheney hurried down into the trench to examine Oscar. But there was little the captain or Oscar's comrades could do for him in the heat of battle—and when Greene's line was driven in retreat, Company G had to leave Private Wilber behind.[18]

What happened to Oscar thereafter was told by those who encountered and cared for him in his plight. The first of these Samaritans was a Confederate soldier.

Philip J. Friedrich was a veteran of many battlefields, having served since the war's opening. Ten days after Fort Sumter surrendered, he enlisted at Holmesville, Mississippi, in the Quitman Guards, which was designated Company E of the 16th Mississippi Infantry. After serving under Stonewall Jackson in the Shenandoah Valley, the regiment joined the Army of Northern Virginia and fought in the Seven Days battles and at Second Bull Run, Antietam, and Fredericksburg. But Friedrich was not a soldier in the ranks. He was a musician, a member of his regiment's brass band. On the battlefield, he and his fellow musicians were detailed to act as stretcher-bearers, gathering the wounded and carrying them to field hospitals in the rear.[19]

While scouring the Chancellorsville battlefield for his regiment's wounded in the wake of the fighting, Philip Friedrich came across Oscar. "Although an enemy," Friedrich wrote, "I could not refuse attending to his wounds, as far as I was able." A day had passed since Oscar fell. He asked the friendly Mississippian to write to Sally, to tell her that he wished she and Rosina would have his land as long as they lived. This Friedrich considered Oscar's dying request, for, he wrote, "The wound I should judge is a mortal one." The Mississippian seized the opportunity to send his note "by some of the prisoners who will soon return north and by this means convey the sad intelligence." He added, "I do so knowing that the facts of the matter communicated is better than to live in suspense as regards the fate of your son."[20]

Suffering greatly, Oscar remained on the battlefield in the hands of the enemy for ten days. During that time, his gaping wound was never dressed. Finally he was retrieved under a flag of truce, together with many other Union wounded, about two weeks after the battle. An ambulance conveyed him back across the Rappahannock to the hospital of the Second Division, Eleventh Corps, near Brooks Station, not far from the 154th New York's camp.

Cousin Milo Wilber visited him there on May 22 and immediately wrote to Sally. Her son did not think he would survive, Milo reported. "Oscar wanted me to tell you that he was willing to die," Milo wrote. "He thought he was prepared to die, and I think he was. He says you must not trouble yourself about him." Milo relayed Oscar's wishes as to the distribution of his property. He wanted his mother and sister to have the farm and be supported upon it as long as they lived. Steers, cows, and money were to be divided among relatives, and debts paid. "If Oscar lives, he will make it all right himself," Milo related, "and if he don't, he wants it to go as I have wrote." Oscar was settling his affairs, little knowing that months of agony stretched before him.[21]

A letter from Sally to her son arrived in camp on the night of May 28, and Milo immediately delivered it to his cousin. He found Oscar on the gain, he reported the next day. "I have considerable hopes of him yet," Milo informed his aunt. "He has good care and I think he will get along yet." Once again, Oscar told his mother not to trouble herself about him.[22]

The regimental armorer, Private William Charles of Company F, had a long talk with Oscar on June 7. "He is becoming *very weak*," noted Charles in a letter to his wife. In his decline, Oscar was turning to religion for solace. He had rarely mentioned spiritual matters in his letters and did not appear to be a particularly devout soul. But on death's door, he became fervid with faith.

In the devout Charles, Oscar found Christian sympathy. Oscar told his visitor that he could not live but for a few days. Asking Charles to pray for him, he declared, "I do not wish to die without having Jesus Christ my friend." Charles replied that he would pray for Oscar and Oscar must do the same for him. Oscar agreed, and added, "Oh, what a happy time that would be, if we could only meet in heaven." As Charles departed, he promised to return the next day and read some Bible verses to Oscar. "Now religion and the Bible are his only *comforts*," Charles observed. "Oh, how sorry he feels that he neglected religion so long."[23]

Five days later, Oscar called on a regimental comrade and family friend, Private Danford L. Hall of Company I, to be his amanuensis. Hall, too, had been wounded at Chancellorsville, shot in the left thigh, his hipbone broken—a wound similar to Oscar's but much less dangerous. Writing to Sally Wilber, Hall reported that Oscar's leg was badly swollen, but his appetite was good and his countenance looked first rate. "He says you need not trouble about him," Hall wrote, "for he is willing the Lord will have his way; for he says he is perfectly reconciled." Perhaps responding to a suggestion of Sally's, Hall wrote, "He says you need not think of coming down to see him, for it would not do any good." Oscar wanted to see all of his family, Hall related, and if he lived, he would—but if he did not live, he wanted them all to meet him in heaven. Then Hall reiterated Oscar's requests regarding the future of the farm and the dispersal of his money. Oscar sent his respects to family and friends and asked anyone holding anything against him for forgiveness, as he forgave them. At the close of the letter, Oscar signed his name.[24]

Two days after Hall wrote for him, on June 14, Oscar was conveyed from the Second Division hospital about seven miles to Aquia Landing, at the confluence of Aquia Creek and the broad Potomac River. There he and other severely wounded soldiers were put aboard a ship bound for Washington, where the men were to be admitted to various hospitals. The vessel docked at the capital's Sixth Street wharf the next day. The shot-riven men were unloaded onto the pier to await assignment and transportation. Oscar laid on the wharf overnight before he was moved. A few torches cast a flickering light over him and his fellow sufferers.

As many as a thousand wounded were arriving daily at the Sixth Street wharf in the aftermath of Chancellorsville. Soldiers covered the pier and nearby ground, lying on blankets and old quilts, exposed to the weather, bloody rags bound around their wounds. Attendants were few, primarily the harassed ambulance men, who arrived in clusters and backed their rigs up one after another to take up their sad loads. The drivers had forsaken their usual light ambulances for heavy wagons drawn by four-horse teams. The most extreme cases were carried off on stretchers. Few civilians lingered at the wharf. Wounded soldiers had become so common, people had grown callous to their plight. The few onlookers were struck by the soldiers' stoicism. Whatever their condition, they rested patiently until their turn to be moved. No matter how badly wounded, they made little fuss; occasionally a soldier would scream in pain as he was lifted into an ambulance.[25]

Before night fell on June 15, Oscar noticed a lean, muscular, bearded man surveying the woeful scene at the wharf with a ferret-eyed intensity. Oscar caught the stranger's eye and motioned to him to approach. Future historians would describe Lafayette Curry Baker as a sinister, feared, execrated, venal, arrogant, unscrupulous scoundrel. Baker's twentieth-century biographer would term him dangerous, wicked, and merciless. But in meeting with Oscar, this villain showed a compassionate side.[26]

Beyond being natives of western New York and serving the Union cause, Oscar Wilber and thirty-six-year-old Lafayette Baker had nothing in common. As a teenager, Baker had moved with his family from Genesee County, New York, to Michigan. On reaching adulthood, he returned to the eastern states and married a Philadelphia girl. In 1852 he sailed to California, where he was active as a Vigilante in San Francisco. He returned east in 1861. During the long voyage, Baker studied a book about Francois Vidocq, a famous French detective, and found his inspiration. He would be a detective. Baker's ship landed in New York City shortly before the firing on Fort Sumter. With war a reality, Baker hurried to Washington and offered his services to General Winfield Scott, commander-in-chief of the Union armies.

General Scott sent Baker to Richmond to spy on the enemy government. Although captured by Confederate authorities and interrogated by Jefferson Davis himself, Baker managed to escape and return to Washington. The success of his mission won him the trust of Secretary of State William H. Seward. Baker did cloak-and-dagger work for Seward until 1862, when internal security came under the aegis of the War Department. There Baker found another trusting patron in Secretary of War Edwin M. Stanton. Baker became a special provost marshal for the War Department and chief of a secret police force, the National Detective Bureau. He now controlled the government's espionage and security apparatus, and Allan Pinkerton—who had heretofore handled those reins—returned to his private detective agency in Chicago. On May 5, 1863, while Oscar Wilber was lying wounded on the Chancellorsville battlefield, Baker was appointed colonel of the 1st District of Columbia Cavalry (often called "Baker's Raiders"), a regiment devoted to suppressing Confederate insurgency in the Washington area.

Wearing his various hats, Baker directed his agents in a ruthless war against traitors, spies, and saboteurs, earning the hatred and fear of war opponents. Unionists were also alienated by his arrogant and unscrupulous methods of secret investigations and arbitrary imprisonments. Baker converted Washington's Old Capitol Prison into an American Bastille and during the course of the war filled its filthy cells with thousands of citizens: political prisoners, Southern secessionists, quinine smugglers, speculators, Copperheads, crooked contractors, counterfeiters, bounty jumpers, gamblers, insubordinate officers, and common criminals—male and female, guilty and innocent alike. In the prison's Room 19, Baker and a subordinate interrogated prisoners. By the end of its first year of operation as a prison, approximately five hundred inmates had died in the Old Capitol. Baker's two-story brick headquarters at 217 Pennsylvania Avenue, swarming with stool pigeons, scoundrels, and thieves, has been described as "the nation's most feared address."[27]

Oscar had no idea that the stranger by his side was one of the most feared and reviled men in the country. To young Wilber, this gentleman was a sympathetic soul who was willing to help him. Oscar introduced himself and described how he had been wounded. He gave Baker Sally's address and $4.50 in cash to send to her. He also asked Baker to relay some news to her. Baker wrote to Sally the next day, addressing her as "Dear Friend" and sending her news of her son, "a fine, noble looking young man."

> He told me he thought he could not live but a few days. He is wounded very bad in the meaty part of his thigh. It was where it could not be taken off or either could it be set, and now he is reduced quite low and I should not think it strange if he dropped off in a few days. I became very much interested in him and told him I would do all in my power to assist him. He is very much resigned to his hard fate and says he is willing to die, and that his constant prayer has been ever since he was wounded that he might be prepared to die when the time comes. He is now in one of the hospitals in this city, and I shall look him up before it will be time to receive a letter from you. They could not tell me what hospital he would be left in when I left him. Now if you have anything to communicate I will do it with pleasure, or if you should want to come here to see him, you come to me and I will go with you to see him. You direct to C. Baker, 217 Penn Avenue, Washington, and I will see that he receives your letters, if he is living. The money enclosed is the same he gave me. From a friend.[28]

Friend Baker thinly disguised his identity by signing himself "C. Baker." Whether he followed up on his promise to visit Oscar in the hospital is unknown;

he certainly would not have had a problem tracking the wounded soldier down. Nor is it known if Sally communicated with Baker. Apparently she was unable to act on his suggestion to visit Oscar in Washington.[29]

Oscar was admitted to Armory Square Hospital on June 16. Its eleven wooden pavilions—each 150 by 25 feet—were set in a row beside the sludgy canal at the foot of Seventh Street (on the site of today's National Air and Space Museum). The central building housed a reception room, post office, dispensary, linen room, officers' quarters, and offices for the chief surgeons. One end of each fifty-bed ward contained a bathroom, water closet, and the ward master's room. Oscar was assigned to Bed 47 in Ward K. The hospital's chief surgeon, D. Willard Bliss, diagnosed Oscar's injury as a "Compound comminuted fracture of [the] femur." "When brought to this hospital he was very much prostrated," Bliss observed. He added, "No previous history could be obtained from him."[30]

Oscar encountered a whole new cadre of caregivers at Armory Square. The hospital's employees included physicians, stewards, medical cadets, nurses, clerks, cooks, launderers, gardeners, grave diggers, janitors, guards, and a chaplain. And the wards received a steady stream of visitors from outside—delegates from local, state, and national soldiers' relief agencies; members of fraternal groups or religious congregations; private individuals; and relatives who traveled to Washington to look after their loved ones. Several of these Samaritans befriended Oscar and communicated with Sally Wilber on his behalf.[31]

On June 29, Oscar dictated a letter to his mother to one of his new friends, Edwin S. Shaw. He was about the same as when he last wrote, Oscar reported. His wound was slow to heal, but he was lucky that it did not give him pain much of the time. His appetite remained good and he rested well nights. He wanted to see his family very much but could not. He supposed they wanted to see him as well but likewise could not, so instead he asked for their prayers. Again his thoughts turned to Jesus. "I thank God, dear Mother, that I can lay here and think of his goodness to me," he stated. "I can lay here and think of the sufferings of the Savior [and] how he died for me and rose again to show me that I too, [although] a man, are of heaven; and I shall dwell with him."

Oscar then turned to more earthly matters. "Dear Mother," he said as Shaw's pen scratched away, "I want the boys to be good boys and mind their mother. If they love their brother that lays here sick and wounded and perhaps never will see them again, they will love and respect her." He sent his love to certain relatives and told them that if he was not permitted to meet them again on earth, "I trust I shall in heaven." He asked if Uncle Nathan had received a check for fifty-four dollars sent in a previous letter. He requested that she send her letters to him at the hospital in care of a certain George H. Willson.[32]

As the hot summer days and weeks passed, Oscar's condition worsened. His stomach became very irritable, Surgeon Bliss noted, and he was constantly nauseous. So a visitor named A. J. Pratt found him on the night of July 20. The following day Pratt took a sheet of Treasury Department stationery (perhaps he was an employee) and wrote to Sally. Oscar wanted his mother to know "that he has not much hope of recovery, but that he feels entirely reconciled to depart and be with Christ, which is far better he believes and feels than to remain longer here. When his 'Father' calls him, he is (he says) entirely willing and prepared to go to the home of many mansions." Oscar had given a friend twenty-five dollars to send to Sally a few days before; Pratt now asked if she had received it. "Write to him at once, as he is very anxious to hear from you," Pratt requested. He closed on an ominous note: "He will have every attention, but I . . . cannot hold out much hopes of his recovery. He is growing weaker daily." [33]

Oscar's hospital was Walt Whitman's favorite haunt. "I devote myself much to Armory Square Hospital," the poet informed his mother, "because it contains by far the worst cases, most repulsive wounds, has the most suffering and most need of consolation—I go every day without fail, and often at night—sometimes stay very late—no one interferes with me, guards, doctors, nurses, nor any one—I am let to take my own course." Whitman and Chief Surgeon Bliss admired each other. Walt described the doctor as "one of the best surgeons in the army." Testifying in the postwar years in support of a pension for the poet, Bliss declared, "No one person who assisted in the hospitals during the war accomplished so much good to the soldier and for the government as Mr. Whitman." Under the circumstances, it seemed inevitable that Whitman would be drawn to Ward K's Bed 47. [34]

On the afternoon of July 22, Whitman spent a long time with Oscar. That night Walt jotted details of the encounter in his hospital notebook. Oscar had asked Whitman to read a chapter in the New Testament. The poet agreed, and asked what he should read. "Make your own choice," Oscar replied. Whitman opened a Bible to the close of one of the Gospels and read the chapter on the last hours and crucifixion of Christ. Oscar asked Walt to read the following chapter, relating the resurrection. The passages pleased Oscar very much. With tears in his eyes, he asked the visitor if he enjoyed religion. "Probably not, my dear, in the way you mean," Whitman replied. Oscar responded that religion was his main reliance. Smiling sweetly, he said he did not fear death. "Why Oscar, don't you think you will get well?" Whitman asked. "I may," Oscar replied, "but it is not probable." He then told Walt about his condition: "His wound was very bad, it discharges much   he had also, for quite a long time diarrhea, altogether prostrating him." Whitman closed his sketch with some comments about the dying soldier. "He behaved very manly, calm, and sweet," the poet wrote, "spoke slow and low, had large, fine eyes, very eloquent / mother Mrs. Sally D. Wilber, Allegany P.O., Cattaraugus Co. N.Y." [35]

When Whitman revised his notebook entry on Oscar for newspaper publication, he added a few details. He said that he had several such interviews with Oscar. He described Oscar as a poor, wasted young man. He said that he read the Gospel chapters very slowly, "for Oscar was feeble." He expanded on his response to Oscar's question of whether he enjoyed religion: "Perhaps not, my dear, in the way you mean, and yet, maybe, it is the same thing." He confessed that he held little hope for Oscar's survival: "I felt that he was even then the same as dying." He condensed his assessment of Oscar's behavior, and added an intimate detail: "He behaved very manly and affectionate. The kiss I gave him as I was about leaving, he returned fourfold." [36]

It seems likely that Walt Whitman wrote to Sally Wilber about her son. Unfortunately, no letters he sent to her are known to survive.

Edwin Shaw returned to Oscar's bedside on July 23 and wrote for him to Sally. Her son was "quite low," Shaw reported, "and the chances are against him for getting well." Shaw continued, "He does not seem to suffer much from pain, yet I can see that he is failing daily." But Shaw noted that Oscar was resigned to his fate: "He wishes me to say to you that he is willing to die, and says he is prepared for the moment that will relieve him from the care and evil influences that human nature is subject to while in this life."

Shaw had written to Mrs. Wilber earlier concerning her son, but as yet had not received an answer. Now he enclosed twenty-five dollars, "the amount he has on hand"—apparently the same sum mentioned by A. J. Pratt three days before. Shaw informed Sally, "He wants to hear from you very much, as he thinks he will not live but a short time." He closed by inviting her to write to Oscar in his care. Then he added a postscript—Oscar had just received Sally's letters. [37]

A. J. Pratt visited Oscar on the evening of July 28 and wrote to Sally the next day. Oscar had received a letter from her dated July 24, and felt very grateful for it. "He is not able to sit up and write himself," Pratt reported, "or he would be glad to do it." Pratt then transmitted Oscar's message to his family:

He desires me to say that he is daily growing weaker and feels that his earthly career is drawing to a close, but that his mind is calm and in perfect peace, being stayed on the Lord Jesus Christ, who he feels is near to support and comfort him as he passes through the dark valley. His wound, he desires me to say, is running very much and he is unable to keep anything on his stomach. He says Mr. Shaw, the gentleman he gave the $25 to send to you, has forwarded it and no doubt 'ere this you have received it. The reason he has not sent it before was that he had told him to keep it for a while. He sends his kind love and blessing to you, whom he calls his dear Christian Mother, and also to all the children, Rosina and Wallace and the boys, and to Grandma. He knows altho' about to be taken from you and never more to see you on this side [of] the grave, that the good Lord our Heavenly Father will watch over and protect the dear ones at home. He asks you all to seek Christ and endeavor daily to become more like him, that he is ready to go and feels it will be better for him.

Pratt added a postscript to his letter the following day: "July 30th Saw Oscar last evening; he had not eaten anything during the day and is rapidly fading."[38]

At four o'clock in the afternoon of July 31, 1863, Oscar Wilber died from exhaustion. Whether A. J. Pratt, Edwin Shaw, Walt Whitman, or any other Samaritan friend was by Oscar's side when he expired is unknown. Nor do we know who wrote to Sally Wilber to inform her of her son's passing. Any letters she received regarding Oscar's death have long since been lost to history.[39]

Oscar's lifeless body was not allowed to rest in peace. Surgeon Bliss, intrigued by Oscar's wound, performed an autopsy. Slicing through the flesh of Oscar's hip and leg, he exposed the shattered femur, wrenched it out of its hip socket, and sawed off its lower end. The specimen was cleaned, packed together with documentation, and delivered to the surgeon general's office. Oscar's broken hipbone has remained in Washington ever since. Today it is part of the collection at the National Museum of Health and Medicine's Armed Forces Institute of Pathology.[40]

Sally Wilber had her son's dismembered remains shipped home to Cattaraugus County, to rest beneath his stone in peaceful Five Mile Cemetery.

Acknowledgments

Research, often performed with the aid of helpful people, serves as a pleasant counterbalance to the solitary art of writing. Many kind folk shared materials that found their way into these tales. For help in general, I turned as always to Lorna Spencer, curator of the Cattaraugus County Memorial and Historical Museum in Little Valley, New York—sadly, for the last time, as Lorna has retired and the museum has moved. Phil Palen, my longtime history-loving friend from Collins, New York, put me up, accompanied me to some of the Cattaraugus County cemeteries on a perfect summer day, and shared some of Martin Bushnell's letters. The Department of Manuscripts and University Archives of the Cornell University Libraries in Ithaca, New York, made available the E. D. Northrup papers, which contain a valuable trove of postwar material.

I am lucky to have homes away from home on my research trips. On my annual trips to western New York I had the pleasure of staying with my aunt, Floris Dunkelman Sarver, in Getzville. My old friend Christopher L. Ford and his wife, Michelle, and son, Wesley, welcomed me into their Fairfax, Virginia, home during my research at the National Archives. In Gettysburg, Paul Kallina and Carolyn Quadarella made me comfortable in their perfectly located home, just a few doors down from Coster Avenue and the monument to the 154th New York. And I had a hospitable way station at the Macungie, Pennsylvania, home of my cousin Paul Sarver and his wife, Kay.

Maureen Koehl, Town of Lewisboro Historian, South Salem, New York, shared Joel Bouton's letters. Brenda Beasley Kepley of the Old Military and Civil Records branch at the National Archives in Washington, D.C., and William A. Owensby Jr., director of the Nashville National Cemetery in Tennessee, both provided pieces of the Milton Bush puzzle. Martin Bushnell's letters, diary, and portrait were shared by his grandnephew, the late Frank M. Bushnell of Napoli, New York. Miller and Jeannette Nichols, Kansas City, Missouri, presented me with a copy of their published version of Fannie Jackson's diary. Richard E. Chittenden of Ventura, California, offered help on the family of his great-grandparents, William and Mary Chittenden. My cousin John Sarver, of East Lansing, Michigan, stood in for me in visiting and photographing the Chittendens' grave. James A. Crosby of Kirkland, Illinois, has been a longtime champion of his relative, Alanson Crosby, and an enjoyable correspondent.

John C. Griswold's great-granddaughters, sisters Ruth Griswold of Gerry, New York, and Margaret Griswold Green of Allegany, New York, shared family letters and photographs. The bulk of Griswold's letters were provided by the Fenton Historical Society of Jamestown, New York. James and Vicki Hitchcock of Randolph, New York, shared valuable material on Alvin Hitchcock. Doris Williams of Orange City, Florida, shared the letters of her great-grandfather Barzilla Merrill and his son Alva. Doris's daughter, Louise Koenig of Olean, New York, provided Assistant Surgeon Corydon C. Rugg's letter. Dr. James S. Brust of San Pedro, California, kindly visited and photographed Salty Oyer's grave in my stead.

Frank Patterson of Horseheads, New York, provided the photograph of his great-great-grandfather, Francis Patterson, and the moral support I needed to tell the Patterson tale. Stuart McConnell of Pitzer College in Claremont, California, kindly suggested some worthwhile sources on pension fraud. The staff of the Steele Memorial Library in Elmira offered help during my newspaper searches. George and Beverly Geisel of Hamburg, New York, shared the letters of Beverly's collateral relative, Oscar Wilber. Martin G. Murray of the Washington Friends of Whitman in Washington, D.C., provided a copy of his Whitman article and identified Lafayette Baker in Oscar's story.

My sincere thanks to all, and to any I have inadvertently omitted.

Family plays an important role in most of the tales collected here. I am pleased to dedicate this book to my sister, Amy, and her family, and to send my love to my wife, Annette, and son, Karl.

Notes

Introduction

1. Mary Jane Chittenden to William F. Chittenden, October 12, 1862.

CHAPTER ONE
CORPORAL JOEL M. BOUTON, COMPANY C

1. Lloyd Lewis, *Sherman: Fighting Prophet* (New York: Harcourt, Brace and Company, 1932), 635.

2. Maureen Koehl, "Joel M. Bouton, one of brave fallen on bloody Gettysburg," *Lewisboro [New York] Ledger,* June 28, 2001, 15–16A. Maureen Koehl, Town of Lewisboro Historian, kindly provided copies of Bouton's letters to Hoyt.

3. Joel M. Bouton to Stephen M. Hoyt, September 12, 1860.

4. Bouton to Hoyt, October 8, 1860.

5. Bouton to Hoyt, November 17, 1860.

6. Bouton to Hoyt, December 25, 1860.

7. Bouton to Hoyt, February 1, 1861.

8. Bouton to Hoyt, March 11, 1861.

9. Bouton to Hoyt, April 8, 1861.

10. Franklin Ellis, ed., *History of Cattaraugus County, New York* (Philadelphia: L. H. Everts, 1879), 99; Bouton to Hoyt, April 29, 1861; descriptive book, Company C, 154th New York, National Archives, Washington, D.C.

11. Bouton to Hoyt, June 3, 1861.

12. Bouton to Hoyt, July 13, 1861.

13. Bouton to Hoyt, August 17, 1861.

14. Bouton to Hoyt, November 10, 1861; flyer for the Olean Academy, November 1861.

15. Bouton to Hoyt, January 7, 1862; Bouton to Hoyt, March 11, 1862.

16. Bouton to Hoyt, March 11, 1862.

17. Bouton to Hoyt, May 22, 1862; William Adams, ed., *Historical Gazetteer and Biographical Memorial of Cattaraugus County, N.Y.* (Syracuse: Lyman, Horton and Co., 1893), 93.

18. Bouton to Hoyt, September 2, 1862.

19. Descriptive book, Company C, 154th New York; Bouton to Hoyt, October 26, 1862.

20. Bouton to Hoyt, December 7, 1862.

21. Bouton to Hoyt, January 7, 1863.

22. Bouton to Hoyt, February 11, 1863.

23. Bouton to Hoyt, March 3, 1863; Bouton to Hoyt, March 29, 1863.

24. Bouton to Hoyt, March 29, 1863; Stephen Welch diary, March 17, 1863; Amos Humiston to Philinda Humiston, December 2, 1862.

25. Bouton to Hoyt, May 18, 1863; Lewis D. Warner diary, May 13, 1863; Thaddeus L. Reynolds to his family, May 20, 1863.

26. Bouton to Hoyt, June 6, 1863.

27. Lewis D. Warner diary, June 15, 1863.

28. Register of deaths, descriptive book, Company C, 154th New York; E. D. Northrup, notes of an interview with Henry Van Aernam, October 17, 1893, Edwin Dwight Northrup Papers, #4190, Department of Manuscripts and University Archives, Cornell University Libraries, Ithaca, New York.

29. "Letter from Maj. Warner—The 154th," undated clipping, quoting letter of Lewis D. Warner, July 10, 1863; "Letter from Maj. L. D. Warner," undated clipping, quoting letter of Warner, August 19, 1863, both courtesy of the New York State Military Museum and Veterans Research Center, Saratoga Springs, N.Y.; "The 154th New York," *Cattaraugus Freeman,* July 23, 1863, quoting letter of James W. Phelps, July 19, 1863.

CHAPTER TWO
PRIVATE MILTON H. BUSH, COMPANY K

1. Nashville National Cemetery brochures, courtesy of William A. Owensby Jr., Director; "Report of Interment," Milton H. Bush, Nashville National Cemetery. Today the railroad bisects the cemetery, which has grown to 65.5 acres and more than 33,600 interments.

2. Descriptive book, Company K, 154th New York, National Archives, Washington, D.C.; Bush genealogical information courtesy of Elaine Waiters.

3. Mark H. Dunkelman, *Camp James M. Brown: Jamestown's Civil War Rendezvous* (Jamestown, N.Y.: Fenton Historical Society, 1996), passim.

4. Col. Patrick H. Jones to Brig. Gen. William D. Whipple, April 2, 1864, in 154th New York Regimental Letter Book, courtesy of Ellicottville Historical Society, Ellicottville, N.Y. (hereafter cited as Jones to Whipple); Gustavus J. Ackley, Conewango, Records of Soldiers by Towns, Cattaraugus County Memorial and Historical Museum, Little Valley, N.Y.; descriptive book, Company K, 154th New York.

5. Jones to Whipple; muster-in roll, Company K, 154th New York, September 25, 1862, National Archives. Ackley is first borne on Company K's October 31, 1862, muster roll. The same roll lists Bush with the remark, "Mustered out of service Sept 27th 1862." Ackley is listed in Company K's descriptive book; Bush's entry is apparently a later insertion, and lists him as absent without leave.

6. Henry Cunningham to a friend, October 11, 1862, courtesy of Cattaraugus County Memorial and Historical Museum, Little Valley, N.Y.; register of men discharged, descriptive book, Company K, 154th New York; William Adams, ed., *Historical Gazetteer and Biographical Memorial of Cattaraugus County, N.Y.* (Syracuse: Lyman, Horton and Co., 1893), 149.

7. George W. Newcomb to Ellen Newcomb, February 28, 1863, courtesy of Alexander G. Lynn.

8. George W. Newcomb to Ellen Newcomb, March 6, 1863, courtesy of Lewis Leigh Collection, Book 36, #90, U.S. Army Military History Institute, Carlisle Barracks, Pa.

9. Jones to Whipple.

10. Marcellus W. Darling to his family, April 5, 1864.

11. Jones to Whipple.

12. David S. Jones to Edward Jones, March 27, 1864; muster roll, Company K, 154th New York, June 30, 1864, National Archives; Bush medical records, National Archives.

13. Bush medical records, National Archives; Frank R. Freemon, *Gangrene and Glory: Medical Care during the American Civil War* (Madison, N.J.: Fairleigh Dickinson Univ. Press, 1998), 169–70.

14. Register of deaths, descriptive book, Company K, 154th New York.

15. Special Order Number 282, Extract 63, War Department, August 26, 1864, in 154th New York Regimental Letter Book.

CHAPTER THREE
CORPORAL MARTIN D. BUSHNELL, COMPANY H

1. Fannie Jackson, manuscript of undated address to "Young People, Citizens & Soldiers," courtesy of Frank M. Bushnell (hereafter cited as Jackson address), 6–9; Joan F. Curran and Rudena K. Mallory, eds., *On Both Sides of the Line, by Fannie (Oslin) Jackson, 1835–1925: Her Early Years in Georgia and Civil War Service as a Union Army Nurse* (Kansas City, Mo.: Miller and Jeanette Nichols, 1989), 42–47.

2. Jackson address, 2–3; Curran and Mallory, *On Both Sides of the Line,* 1–41.

3. Jackson address, 4–6; Curran and Mallory, *On Both Sides of the Line,* 29–41.

4. William G. Le Duc, *Recollections of a Civil War Quartermaster* (St. Paul, Minn.: North Central Publishing Company, 1963), 124–25; Jackson address, 10–11; Curran and

Mallory, *On Both Sides of the Line,* 50–56, 104–6; William G. Le Duc to whom it may concern, May 15, 1864, and recommendations of Thomas Audas and William F. Cady, May 20, 1864, in Fannie Jackson pension records, National Archives, Washington, D.C.

5. Jackson address, 10–11; Curran and Mallory, *On Both Sides of the Line,* 49–59.

6. Clara (Waite) Burroughs, "Genealogy of the Family of Amasa Bushnell, Pioneer, Napoli, Cattaraugus Co., N.Y.," typescript, 1959.

7. Bushnell military records, National Archives; Bushnell to his parents, July 1, 1863, courtesy of Frank M. Bushnell.

8. Bushnell to Frank Congdon, November 6, 1863, courtesy of Phil Palen.

9. Bushnell to Frank Congdon January 25, 1864, courtesy of Phil Palen.

10. Bushnell to his parents, March 12, 1864, courtesy of Frank M. Bushnell; Bushnell to Frank Congdon, March 12, 1864, courtesy of Phil Palen.

11. Bushnell to his parents, June 3, 1864, courtesy of Frank M. Bushnell.

12. Martin D. Bushnell diary, June 24, 1864, courtesy of Frank M. Bushnell; Emory Sweetland to Mary Sweetland, June 25, 1864; Bushnell military records, National Archives; E. D. Northrup, notes of an undated interview with Stephen Welch; Stephen Welch to E. D. Northrup, November 9, 1895, both in Edwin Dwight Northrup Papers, #4190, Department of Manuscripts and University Archives, Cornell University Libraries, Ithaca, N.Y.; *The Medical and Surgical History of the War of the Rebellion* (Washington, D.C.: Government Printing Office, 1877) part 2, vol. 2, p. 481; Frank R. Freemon, *Gangrene and Glory: Medical Care during the American Civil War* (Madison, N.J.: Fairleigh Dickinson Univ. Press, 1998), 48–49, 109.

13. Bushnell diary, June 25 and 26, 1864; Sweetland to Mary Sweetland, June 25, 1864.

14. Bushnell diary, June 27–30, 1864.

15. M. C. Woodworth to whom it may concern, November 2, 1889, Fannie Jackson pension records; Curran and Mallory, *On Both Sides of the Line,* 62–62, 65.

16. Curran and Mallory, *On Both Sides of the Line,* 68–69; Jackson address, 12–13. The paisley robe is in the collections of the Cattaraugus County Memorial and Historical Museum, Little Valley, N.Y. A card accompanying it reads, "Robe worn by Martin Bushnell . . . when in hospital in Ga."

17. Curran and Mallory, *On Both Sides of the Line,* 70; Bushnell diary, July 7–8, 1864.

18. Jackson address, 13; Bushnell diary, July 10–13, 1864; Curran and Mallory, *On Both Sides of the Line,* 70–71.

19. Bushnell diary, July 14–24, 1864; Curran and Mallory, *On Both Sides of the Line,* 72.

20. Curran and Mallory, *On Both Sides of the Line,* 72–75.

21. Bushnell diary, August 2–10, 1864; Curran and Mallory, *On Both Sides of the Line,* 75.

22. Bushnell diary, August 16–17, 23, 1864; Curran and Mallory, *On Both Sides of the Line,* 76–78, 92, 131.

23. Bushnell diary, August 24–30, 1864; Curran and Mallory, *On Both Sides of the Line,* 79.

24. Curran and Mallory, *On Both Sides of the Line,* 86–89; Bushnell diary, September 8–23, 1864.

25. Curran and Mallory, *On Both Sides of the Line,* 93–101, 106; Bushnell diary, Septem-

ber 24–25, 1864; Jackson address, 17–20; Le Duc, *Recollections of a Civil War Quarter-master,* 130.

26. Bushnell diary, October 1, 1864; Curran and Mallory, *On Both Sides of the Line,* 101–2.

27. Bushnell diary, October 2–November 13, 1864; Curran and Mallory, *On Both Sides of the Line,* 112; Fannie Jackson to Martin D. Bushnell, March 1, 1865; George C. "Guy" Waterman to Martin D. Bushnell, October 30, 1864, courtesy of Frank M. Bushnell.

28. Bushnell diary, November 14–December 31, 1864; Bushnell to his family, April 28, 1865, courtesy of Frank M. Bushnell.

29. Alfred Jay Bollet, M.D., *Civil War Medicine: Challenges and Triumphs* (Tucson, Ariz.: Galen Press, 2002), 159, 228; Bushnell's "Certificate of Disability for Discharge," August 12, 1865; "Declaration for Invalid Pension," August 24, 1865; affidavit of George C. Waterman, August 29, 1865, all in Bushnell pension records, National Archives; Frederick Phisterer, *New York in the War of the Rebellion, 1861 to 1865* (Albany, N.Y.: Weed, Parsons and Company, 1890), 160; Curran and Mallory, *On Both Sides of the Line,* 131; Clara (Waite) Burroughs, "Genealogy of the Family of Amasa Bushnell."

30. Jackson address, 20–22; Curran and Mallory, *On Both Sides of the Line,* 107–18.

31. Curran and Mallory, *On Both Sides of the Line,* 119–28, 131; Le Duc, *Recollections of a Civil War Quartermaster,* 130; Jackson pension records.

32. Curran and Mallory, *On Both Sides of the Line,* 129–30; Clara (Waite) Burroughs, "Genealogy of the Family of Amasa Bushnell."

CHAPTER FOUR

PRIVATE WILLIAM F. CHITTENDEN, COMPANY D

1. William F. Chittenden (hereafter cited as WFC) to Mary Jane Chittenden (hereafter cited as MJC), August 31, 1862. The Chittenden correspondence is in the collection of the author.

2. Biographical sketch of Clyde C. Chittenden in John H. Wheeler, *History of Wexford County, Michigan* ([Logansport, Ind.]: B. F. Bowen, 1903), 325; biographical sketch of Hiram M. Chittenden in *The National Cyclopaedia of American Biography,* 63 vols. (New York: James T. White and Company, 1927), 17:404; genealogical notes on the Wheeler family, courtesy of Richard E. Chittenden; 1860 U.S. Census, Town of Yorkshire, Cattaraugus County, N.Y.; "Pioneer Dies," obituary of WFC in *State Journal,* Lansing, Michigan, June 4, 1923, 1; documents in WFC pension file, National Archives, Washington, D.C.

3. Muster-in roll, Company D, 154th New York, September 24, 1862, National Archives.

4. WFC to MJC, September 6, 1862.

5. WFC to MJC, September 9, 1862.

6. WFC to MJC, September 19, 1862; WFC to MJC, October 2–3, 1862.

7. WFC to MJC, October 5 and 7, 1862; WFC to MJC, October 9, 1862.

8. WFC to MJC, October 10–13, 1862.

9. WFC to MJC, October 20, 1862.

10. MJC to WFC, undated letter fragment circa October 1862. MJC occasionally referred to herself as "Jennie," and WFC sometimes addressed her as such. For simplicity's sake, I refer to her as Mary throughout.

11. MJC to WFC, October 6 and 9, 1862.

12. MJC to WFC, October 12, 1862.

13. MJC to WFC, October 28–30, 1862.

14. MJC to WFC, October 31, 1862.

15. WFC to MJC, November 2–4, 1862.

16. WFC to MJC, November 7, 1862.

17. WFC to MJC, November 12, 1862.

18. WFC to MJC, November 13, 1862; WFC to MJC, November 16, 1862.

19. MJC to WFC, circa November 1862.

20. MJC to WFC, November 12–13, 1862.

21. MJC to WFC, November 20, 1862.

22. WFC to MJC, December 1–2, 1862; WFC to MJC, December 3–4, 1862; WFC to MJC, December 7–8, 1862.

23. WFC to MJC, December 1–2, 1862; WFC to MJC, November 22–25, 1862.

24. WFC to MJC, November 22–25, 1862; WFC to MJC, November 27–28, 1862.

25. WFC to MJC, December 1–2, 1862; WFC to MJC, December 3–4, 1862.

26. MJC to WFC, December 7–8, 1862.

27. MJC to WFC, December 9, 1862.

28. MJC to WFC, December 14–15, 1862; Hiram M. Chittenden to WFC, undated.

29. WFC to MJC, December 19, 1862.

30. WFC to MJC, December 20, 1862.

31. WFC to MJC, undated fragment, circa December 1862.

32. MJC to WFC, undated fragment, circa December 1862.

33. MJC to WFC, December 28, 1862.

34. MJC to WFC, January 1–2, 1863.

35. WFC to MJC, May 27, 1863; WFC to MJC, April 7, 1863; WFC to MJC, undated fragment, circa April 1863.

36. WFC to MJC, April 24, 1863; WFC to MJC, May 13, 1863; WFC to MJC, May 16, 1863.

37. WFC to MJC, May 16, 1863; WFC to MJC, May 17, 1863.

38. WFC to MJC, May 20, 1863; WFC to MJC, May 24, 1863; WFC to MJC, May 27, 1863; WFC to MJC, May 28–29, 1863.

39. WFC to MJC, May 30, 1863.

40. MJC to WFC, April 23, 1863; MJC, poem dated April 9, 1863.

41. MJC to WFC, April 23, 1863; MJC to WFC, April 30, 1863.

42. MJC to WFC, May 22, 1863.

43. Certificate of Disability for Discharge, June 3, 1863, WFC pension file, National Archives.

44. Documents in WFC pension file, National Archives; Wheeler, *History of Wexford County,* 325; "Pioneer Dies," *State Journal,* June 4, 1923, 1.

45. Wheeler, *History of Wexford County,* 325–27.

46. *The National Cyclopaedia of American Biography,* 17:404–5; Allen Johnson and Dumas Malone, eds., *Dictionary of American Biography,* 22 vols. (New York: Charles Scribner's Sons, 1930), 2:77–78; Henry Van Aernam to Lieut. E. L. Phillips, December 21, 1891, courtesy of J. Richardson Lippert II. For more on Hiram M. Chittenden, see Gordon B. Dodds, *Hiram Martin Chittenden: His Public Career* (Lexington: Univ. Press of Kentucky, 1973), and Bruce Le Roy, ed., *H. M. Chittenden, A Western Epic: Being a Selection from His Unpublished Journals, Diaries and Reports* (Tacoma: Washington State Historical Society, 1961).

CHAPTER FIVE

CAPTAIN ALANSON CROSBY, COMPANY D

1. Franklin Ellis, *History of Cattaraugus County, New York* (Philadelphia: L. H. Everts, 1879), 318; "Record of Death and Interment," Alanson Crosby military records, National Archives, Washington, D.C.; E. D. Northrup, notes of an undated interview with Addison G. Rice, Edwin Dwight Northrup Papers, #4190, Department of Manuscripts and University Archives, Cornell University Libraries, Ithaca, N.Y. (hereafter cited as EDN Papers).

2. "Death of Capt. Alanson Crosby," *Cattaraugus Union,* July 21, 1864; "Capt. Crosby," *Cattaraugus Freeman,* July 21, 1864; William Adams, ed., *Historical Gazetteer and Biographical Memorial of Cattaraugus County, N.Y.* (Syracuse: Lyman, Horton and Co., 1893), 635–36, 643; Marlynn McNallie Olson, *A Guide to Burial Sites, Cemeteries and Random Stones in Cattaraugus County, New York* (Randolph, N.Y.: Published by the author, 1996), 123–25; Ellis, *History of Cattaraugus County,* 318; Lorna Spencer, Curator, Cattaraugus County Memorial and Historical Museum, Little Valley, N.Y., to author, March 25, 2002.

3. "Interesting Narrative of the Escape of two Officers of the 154th Regt. N.Y.S. Vols. from the hands of the Rebels," *Jamestown [New York] Journal,* March 18, 1864, quoting Alanson Crosby to Samuel G. Love, February 28, 1864 (hereafter cited as Interesting Narrative).

4. Adams, ed., *Historical Gazetteer and Biographical Memorial of Cattaraugus County,* 363–64, 651–52. In newspaper articles cited below, Crosby's first name is sometimes spelled Allanson, but in this authorized biographical sketch, in pension documents signed by his mother, and in other sources it is spelled Alanson. He signed his letters using only his first initial.

5. "A Tribute to the Memory of the Late Capt. Allanson Crosby," *Cattaraugus Freeman,* August 11, 1864, quoting letter of anonymous correspondent of August 4, 1864.

6. "We notice that our friend and former townsman, A. Crosby, Esq.," *Cattaraugus Freeman,* July 24, 1862; muster-in roll, Company A, 154th New York, September 24, 1862, National Archives; Adams, ed., *Historical Gazetteer and Biographical Memorial of Catta-*

raugus County, 494; "First Company from Cattaraugus!" *Cattaraugus Freeman,* August 14, 1862; "Camp 'James M. Brown,'" *Cattaraugus Freeman,* August 21, 1862.

7. "First Company from Cattaraugus!" *Cattaraugus Freeman,* August 14, 1862; "Camp 'James M. Brown,'" *Cattaraugus Freeman,* August 21, 1862; "From Camp 'James M. Brown,'" *Cattaraugus Freeman,* September 4, 1862.

8. "From the 154th Regiment," *Cattaraugus Freeman,* November 6, 1862, quoting Crosby's letter of October 23, 1862.

9. "From the 154th Regiment," *Cattaraugus Freeman,* December 18, 1862, quoting Crosby's letter of December 8, 1862; "From our Cattaraugus Regiment," *Cattaraugus Union,* November 28, 1862.

10. "From the 154th Regiment," *Cattaraugus Freeman,* March 19, 1863, quoting Crosby's letter of March 9, 1863.

11. "Losses in the 154th Regiment," *Cattaraugus Freeman,* May 21, 1863, quoting Crosby's letter of May 13, 1863.

12. Interesting Narrative; "Letter from Lieut. Allanson Crosby," *Cattaraugus Freeman,* July 30, 1863, quoting letter to Manley Crosby, July 17, 1863.

13. "We are informed that Lieutenant A. Crosby . . . ," *Cattaraugus Freeman,* August 6, 1863.

14. Special Order Number 134, Headquarters Eleventh Corps, July 22, 1863, in regimental records of the 154th New York, National Archives; Lewis D. Warner diary, July 24, 1863; Charles W. McKay, "Three Years or During the War, With the Crescent and Star," *The National Tribune Scrap Book* (n.p., n.d.), 136; "Detailed," *Cattaraugus Union,* July 31, 1863; "In Town," *Cattaraugus Freeman,* September 16, 1863; "Adjutant Crosby," *Cattaraugus Freeman,* January 1, 1864; "Gone to the Front," *Cattaraugus Freeman,* April 21, 1864.

15. Lewis D. Warner diary, April 28, 1864; Henry Van Aernam to Amy Melissa Van Aernam, April 28, 1864; William A. Farlee to E. D. Northrup, January 28, 1879, EDN Papers.

16. E. D. Northrup, notes of interview with Samuel Hogg, January 6, 1896, EDN Papers.

17. E. D. Northrup, notes of interview with Emory Sweetland, February 18, 1891, EDN Papers.

18. "Letter from Col. P. H. Jones," *Cattaraugus Freeman,* July 7, 1864, quoting letter of June 24, 1864; Stephen R. Green to Ann Eliza Jane Green, June 20, 1864, courtesy of Phil Palen.

19. "Letter From Capt. C. P. Vedder," *Cattaraugus Freeman,* August 18, 1864, quoting letter to Manley Crosby of July 24, 1864.

20. Horace Smith diary, June 30, 1864; "Record of Death and Interment," Alanson Crosby military records, National Archives, Washington, D.C.

21. Lewis D. Warner diary, July 15, 1864; "Letter from Major L. D. Warner," unidentified newspaper clipping, quoting letter to A. E. Fay, July 28, 1864, courtesy of Cattaraugus County Memorial and Historical Museum, Little Valley, N.Y. Warner wrote for publication on a regular basis to Fay, co-publisher of the *Olean [New York] Times.*

22. Horace Smith diary, August 4, 1864; Adams, ed., *Historical Gazetteer and Bio-*

graphical Memorial of Cattaraugus County, 364; "Letter From Capt. C. P. Vedder," *Cattaraugus Freeman,* August 18, 1864, quoting letter to Manley Crosby of July 24, 1864.

23. "Death of Captain Allanson Crosby!" *Cattaraugus Freeman,* July 14, 1864; "Death of Capt. Crosby—Meeting of the Bar," *Cattaraugus Freeman,* July 21, 1864.

24. Roy P. Basler, ed., *The Collected Works of Abraham Lincoln,* 8 vols. (New Brunswick, N.J.: Rutgers Univ. Press, 1953), 7:431–32.

25. "A Tribute to the Memory of the Late Capt. Allanson Crosby," *Cattaraugus Freeman,* August 11, 1864, quoting letter of anonymous correspondent of August 4, 1864.

CHAPTER SIX

CAPTAIN JOHN C. GRISWOLD, COMPANY F

1. Susan Griswold (hereafter cited as SG) to John C. Griswold (hereafter cited as JCG), May 7, 1863.

2. Ibid.; "Death of Lieut. John C. Griswold," *Fredonia [New York] Censor,* May 13, 1863.

3. SG to JCG, June 3, 1863.

4. Susan Griswold obituary, *Fredonia [New York] Censor,* April 6, 1864; Margaret Griswold Green to author, October 1, 2002.

5. "A Noble Pioneer. The Late Capt. John C. Griswold," *Fredonia [New York] Censor,* August 3, 1892; "John C. Griswold," in *The Centennial History of Chautauqua County,* 2 vols. (Jamestown: Chautauqua History Company, 1904), 2:271; "Memorial of Capt. John C. Griswold, Adopted by the Board of Supervisors of Chautauqua County, N.Y., Nov. 17, 1892," author's collection; Margaret Griswold Green to author, October 1, 2002.

6. Muster-in roll, Company F, 154th New York, September 25, 1862, National Archives, Washington, D.C.

7. JCG to SG, October 1, 1862, courtesy of the Fenton Historical Society, Jamestown, N.Y. (as are all of JCG's letters except where noted); JCG to Cassius Griswold, October 3, 1862.

8. JCG to SG, October 11, 1862; JCG to SG, October 18–19, 1862; JCG to SG, October 21, 1862.

9. JCG to SG, October 26, 1862; Henry A. Munger letter, no salutation, October 19, 1862.

10. JCG to SG, October 21, 1862; JCG to Cassius Griswold, November 26, 1862.

11. JCG to SG, October 26, 1862; JCG to SG, November 1, 1862.

12. JCG to SG, November 8, 1862; JCG to SG, November 16, 18, 20, 1862; "Tribute to a Deceased Soldier," *Fredonia [New York] Advertiser,* January 16, 1863; "Tribute to a Deceased Soldier," *Fredonia [New York] Censor,* January 21, 1863.

13. JCG to SG, November 16, 18, 20, 1862; JCG to Cassius Griswold, November 26, 1862.

14. JCG to SG, November 27, 1862.

15. JCG to Cassius Griswold, December 26–28, 1862.

16. Ibid.; JCG to SG, March 16, 1863.

17. JCG to SG, February 4, 6, 7, 1863; JCG to SG, January 17–18, 1863.

18. JCG to SG, February 22, 1863.

19. Ibid.

20. JCG to SG, March 9, 13, 1863.

21. JCG to SG, March 22, 1863; JCG to SG, April 5, 1863.

22. JCG to SG, April 12, 1863.

23. JCG to SG, April 19, 26, 1863; William Charles to Ann Charles, April 23, 1863.

24. SG to JCG, May 5, 1863.

25. Dana P. Horton to SG, May 11, 1863; Homer A. Ames to SG, May 12, 1863, both courtesy of the Fenton Historical Society.

26. SG to JCG, June 3, 1863; Henry C. Loomis to SG, May 14, 1863, author's collection; Dana P. Horton to SG, May 15, 1863, courtesy of the Fenton Historical Society; Thomas Donnelly to SG, May 21, 1863, author's collection.

27. JCG to SG, May 22, 1863.

28. Dana P. Horton to SG, May 23, 1863, author's collection.

29. Homer A. Ames to SG, May 24, 1863, author's collection; Dana P. Horton to SG, June 2, 1863, author's collection.

30. JCG to SG, May 30, 1863.

31. SG to JCG, June 3, 1863.

32. JCG to SG, June 8, 1863.

33. SG to JCG, June 12, 1863.

34. JCG to SG, June 23, 1863.

35. JCG to SG, August 6, 1863; JCG to SG, September 22, 1863.

36. JCG to SG, October 2, 1863; JCG to SG, October 12, 1863; JCG to SG, October 20, 1863.

37. JCG to SG, November 1, 1863.

38. JCG to SG, November 10, 1863; JCG to SG, November 18, 1863; JCG to SG, November 25, 1863; JCG to SG, December 2, 1863.

39. Susan Griswold obituary, *Fredonia [New York] Censor,* April 6, 1864; JCG to SG, December 2, 1863.

40. JCG to Lieut. Col. Dan B. Allen, December 11, 1863, author's collection.

41. Susan Griswold obituary, *Fredonia [New York] Censor,* April 6, 1864.

42. Special Field Order Number 335, Headquarters Department of the Cumberland, December 14, 1863, National Archives; Col. Patrick H. Jones to JCG, January 13, 1864, courtesy of Fenton Historical Society; muster roll, Company F, 154th New York, February 29, 1864, National Archives; Special Field Order Number 59, Headquarters Department of the Cumberland, February 28, 1864, National Archives; Milon J. Griswold to SG and Cassius Griswold, March 2, 1864, author's collection.

43. JCG to SG, February 15, 1864.

44. JCG to SG, February 20, 1864.

45. JCG to Cassius Griswold, March 14, 1864.

46. Ibid.; Susan Griswold obituary, *Fredonia [New York] Censor,* April 6, 1864.

47. JCG to Cassius Griswold, March 22 and 26, 1864; JCG to his niece, March 30, 1864, courtesy of Vince Martonis, Historian, Town of Hanover, New York.

48. "We are pained to learn . . . ," *Fredonia [New York] Censor,* May 11, 1864; Homer A. Ames to Cassius Griswold, May 1, 1864, author's collection; Special Field Order Number 119, Headquarters Department of the Cumberland, April 28, 1864, National Archives.

49. "John C. Griswold" and "Cassius M. Griswold," in *The Centennial History of Chautauqua County,* 2:271.

50. "A Noble Pioneer. The Late Capt. John C. Griswold," *Fredonia [New York] Censor,* August 3, 1892.

51. "Memorial of Capt. John C. Griswold, Adopted by the Board of Supervisors of Chautauqua County, N.Y., Nov. 17, 1892."

52. Ibid.; William D. Harper, "The Enlistment and in Camp at Jamestown and the Several Camps While in the Service of the United States."

CHAPTER SEVEN

PRIVATE WILLIAM HAWKINS, COMPANY B

1. "East Otto," *Cattaraugus Republican,* September 9, 1882; "In Memoriam," *Ellicottville [New York] Post,* October 10, 1906 (William Hawkins obituary); E. D. Northrup diaries, March 5, 1881, and September 2, 1882, Edwin Dwight Northrup Papers, #4190, Department of Manuscripts and University Archives, Cornell University Libraries, Ithaca, N.Y. (hereafter cited as EDN Papers); William Adams, ed., *Historical Gazetteer and Biographical Memorial of Cattaraugus County, N.Y.* (Syracuse: Lyman, Horton and Co., 1893), 551; William Marvel, *Andersonville: The Last Depot* (Chapel Hill: Univ. of North Carolina Press, 1994), ix.

2. Descriptive book, Company B, 154th New York, National Archives, Washington, D.C.; Town Clerk, East Otto, N.Y., William Hawkins listing in Register of Soldiers, New York State Archives, Albany, N.Y.; William Hawkins listing under East Otto, Records of Soldiers by Towns, Cattaraugus County Memorial and Historical Museum, Little Valley, N.Y.; 1860 U.S. Census, East Otto, Cattaraugus County, N.Y.; "General Affidavit," John Hawkins, July 8, 1907, in William Hawkins pension file, National Archives. In 1860 Hawkins was a laborer on Orson H. Malley's farm.

3. Muster-in roll, Company B, 154th New York, September 24, 1862, National Archives; William Hawkins interview notes, probably made August 7 and 8, 1880, EDN Papers.

4. Except where noted, the rest of Hawkins's story comes from the William Hawkins interview notes, EDN Papers.

5. Lonnie R. Speer, *Portals to Hell: Military Prisons of the Civil War* (Mechanicsburg, Pa.: Stackpole Books, 1997), 104–5.

6. Horace Smith diary, July 18, 20, 22, and 23, 1863. Smith, another Gettysburg captive, was a sergeant in Company D of the 154th New York.

7. Speer, *Portals to Hell*, 92, 119–22.

8. "Proof of Disability" by Simeon V. Pool, October 17, 1881, Hawkins pension file.

9. Buel Bishop died in Richmond on February 1, 1864; Alansing Wyant was reported to have died in Richmond at an unknown date.

10. Clark E. Oyer interview notes, undated; Bradford Rowland interview notes, February 7, 1891; Bradford Rowland, Clark E. Oyer, and Esley Groat interview notes, undated, all in EDN Papers.

11. Speer, *Portals to Hell*, 205.

12. The identity of the two men who died during the railroad trip is uncertain.

13. Marvel, *Andersonville*, 68.

14. Ibid., 17, 21, 38, 45, 53, 54–55, 71, 101, 111, 180.

15. Thomas R. Aldrich, "The Experience of Thomas R. Aldrich Late of Co. B 154th New York Volls. while a prisoner of war from May 8, 1864 until February 22nd, 1865," Patricia Wilcox Collection, Fairport, N.Y. (hereafter cited as Aldrich account).

16. Ibid.

17. Franklin Goodrich is buried in Grave 3042 of the Andersonville National Cemetery.

18. Hawkins did not mention Herburt by name; he is identified in Marvel, *Andersonville*, 11, 65–67.

19. This prisoner apparently was either New Yorker Francis Devendorf, shot on July 13, 1864, or Pennsylvanian William Unversagt, killed on July 27, 1864. Marvel, *Andersonville*, 145, 157, 172, 287 n. 58.

20. On other prisoners' resentment of the Regulators, see Marvel, *Andersonville*, 144.

21. Aldrich account.

22. Ibid.; Marvel, *Andersonville*, 67–68, 86, 169; "In Memoriam," *Ellicottville [New York] Post*, October 10, 1906. Orso Greeley survived his imprisonment; Charles Allen died of dropsy at Savannah on October 7, 1864.

23. Othnial Green is buried in Grave 5202 and George Bailey in Grave 5697 of the Andersonville National Cemetery.

24. Speer, *Portals to Hell*, 277–79.

25. Hawkins identified the commandant as Captain Bowes; the correct identification is in Speer, *Portals to Hell*, 278.

26. "Physician's Affidavit" of Elijah Dresser, November 22, 1879; "General Affidavit" of M. W. Butterfield, January 21, 1888, both in Hawkins pension file. The East Otto church meeting is mentioned in "In Memoriam," *Ellicottville [New York] Post*, October 10, 1906.

27. Aldrich account.

28. Hawkins pension file, passim; quote is from "Physician's Affidavit" of E. L. Fish, M.D., September 3, 1887.

29. Hawkins pension file, passim

30. "In Memoriam," *Ellicottville [New York] Post*, October 10, 1906; Cattaraugus County Ex-Union Prisoners of War Association Charter, January 22, 1887, courtesy of the

Franklinville (N.Y.) American Legion Post; "County Ex-Prisoners of War Association," *Ellicottville [New York] Post*, March 23, 1887.

31. "In Memoriam," *Ellicottville [New York] Post*, October 10, 1906.

CHAPTER EIGHT

PRIVATE ALVIN HITCHCOCK, COMPANY A

1. James Hitchcock to Dale Senn, Supervisor, Town of Randolph, October 11 and November 12, 1999, courtesy of Jim and Vicki Hitchcock, Randolph, N.Y.

2. Jim and Vicki Hitchcock to author, July 25, 2002.

3. Henry Van Aernam, Surgeon's Certificate of the Insanity of Alvin Hitchcock, April 16, 1864, Alvin Hitchcock military records, National Archives, Washington, D.C. (hereafter cited as Van Aernam, surgeon's certificate).

4. Ibid.; E. D. Northrup, notes of an interview with Henry Van Aernam, undated, Edwin Dwight Northrup Papers, #4190, Department of Manuscripts and University Archives, Cornell University Libraries (hereafter cited as EDN Papers); Walter H. Hebert, *Fighting Joe Hooker* (Indianapolis: Bobbs-Merrill, 1944), 154; Lewis D. Warner diary, November 2, 1863; Alvin Hitchcock entry, Company A descriptive book, National Archives.

5. Van Aernam, surgeon's certificate; Mrs. Edward Hitchcock Sr., comp., *The Genealogy of the Hitchcock Family* (Amherst, Mass.: Carpenter and Morehouse, 1894), 319–20; New York State Census, Town of Randolph, June 25, 1855; U.S. Census, Town of Randolph, Cattaraugus County, N.Y., July 30, 1860; D. G. Beers, J. H. Goodhue, and E. F. Sanford, *Atlas of Cattaraugus County, New York* (New York: D. G. Beers and Co., 1869); New York State Archives, Albany, New York State Office of Mental Health, Utica State Hospital Patient Case Records (Alvin Hitchcock), vol. 20, pp. 380–81 (hereafter cited as Hitchcock case record).

6. Hitchcock case record; U.S. Census, Town of Randolph, Cattaraugus County, N.Y., July 30, 1860; muster-in roll, Company A, 154th New York, September 24, 1862, National Archives.

7. Alvin Hitchcock military, prisoner of war, and medical records, National Archives; Colby M. Bryant diary, May 2–24, 1863; Stephen Welch diary, May 2–24, 1863.

8. Eric T. Dean Jr., *Shook Over Hell: Post-Traumatic Stress, Vietnam, and the Civil War* (Cambridge, Mass.: Harvard Univ. Press, 1997), 118–19, 279–80.

9. Van Aernam, surgeon's certificate; Col. Patrick H. Jones to Brig. Gen. William D. Whipple, April 16, 1864, Alvin Hitchcock military records, National Archives.

10. Endorsements on reverse of Jones to Whipple; Special Field Order Number 120, Head-Quarters Department of the Cumberland, April 29, 1864, Alvin Hitchcock military records, National Archives.

11. Emory Sweetland to Mary Sweetland, May 1, 1864.

12. E. D. Northrup, notes of an interview with Emory Sweetland, February 28, 1891, EDN Papers; Albert Castel, *Decision in the West: The Atlanta Campaign of 1864* (Lawrence: Univ. Press of Kansas, 1992), 93; James A. Hoobler, *Cities under the Gun: Images*

of Occupied Nashville and Chattanooga (Nashville: Rutledge Hill Press, 1986), 101. At the time of the meeting, Hammond was on trial in a court-martial. Ira M. Rutkow, *Bleeding Blue and Gray: Civil War Surgery and the Evolution of American Medicine* (New York: Random House, 2005), 291–95.

13. R. O. Abbott to Brig. Gen. Lorenzo Thomas, May 12, 1864, Alvin Hitchcock military records, National Archives; entry for Alvin Hitchcock, "Register of Cases, Government Hospital for the Insane," National Archives; Hebert, *Fighting Joe Hooker,* 146.

14. Lawrence L. Knutson, "D.C. Hospital Now Endangered Place," Associated Press report, June 10, 2002; John T. Hubbell and James W. Geary, *Biographical Dictionary of the Union: Northern Leaders of the Civil War* (Westport, Conn.: Greenwood Press, 1995), 142; Dean, *Shook Over Hell,* 116–17, 121–23; Ellen Dwyer, *Homes for the Mad: Life Inside Two Nineteenth-Century Asylums* (New Brunswick: Rutgers Univ. Press, 1987), 5; C. H. Nichols, Superintendent, Government Hospital for the Insane, clothing voucher, May 23, 1864, Alvin Hitchcock military records, National Archives; entry for Alvin Hitchcock, "Register of Cases, Government Hospital for the Insane," National Archives. Congress changed the name of the hospital to St. Elizabeth's in 1916, and in 1987 the Federal government transferred the institution's operations to the District of Columbia. Poet Ezra Pound was its most famous inmate, confined there from 1946 to 1958 after he was found mentally incompetent to answer charges of treason during World War II. Today St. Elizabeth's houses about six hundred patients, including John W. Hinckley Jr., would-be assassin of President Ronald Reagan. As detailed in Knutson's article, in June 2002 "the National Trust for Historic Preservation placed St. Elizabeth's on its annual list of 11 most endangered historic places, calling its more than 100 rapidly deteriorating buildings irreplaceable architectural marvels."

15. Hitchcock case record.

16. Ibid.; Dwyer, *Homes for the Mad,* 8–9, 13–14, 117–18.

17. Hitchcock case record; Dwyer, *Homes for the Mad,* 14, 21–22.

18. Hitchcock case record.

CHAPTER NINE

PRIVATE BARZILLA MERRILL, COMPANY K

1. II Samuel 17:27–29, 19:31–39, KJV.

2. Genesis 36:40, KJV.

3. Bruce Catton, *Never Call Retreat* (Garden City, N.Y.: Doubleday, 1965), 144.

4. Corydon C. Rugg to Ruba Cole Merrill (hereafter cited as RCM), May 30, 1863; Marcellus Warner Darling, *Events and Comments of My Life* (n.p., n.d.), unpaginated.

5. George W. Newcomb to Ellen Newcomb, May 15, 1863, author's collection; Rugg to RCM, May 30, 1863.

6. Betsey Phelps Howlett, manuscript poem, "Composed and written by Mrs Betsey Howlett, on the death of Barzillai and Alva Merrill, who died at the battle of Chanslorville in May, 1863."

7. Brochure, "Fredericksburg National Cemetery."

8. Barzilla Merrill (hereafter cited as BM) to RCM, October 25, 1862; BM to RCM, October 20, 1862.

9. Mary Thrasher, *Merrill Genealogy: Descendants of Barzilla Merrill, 1764–1850* (Cooperstown, N.Y.: Crist, Scott and Parshall, 1907), 15–16, 23–24.

10. BM to RCM, November 11, 1862; BM to RCM, March 7, 1863; BM to RCM, November 24, 1862; BM to RCM, December 7, 1862; BM to RCM, January 1, 1863; BM to RCM, January 7 and 9, 1863; BM to RCM, March 8, 1863; BM to RCM, October 5, 1862; Alva C. Merrill (hereafter cited as ACM) to RCM, November 23, 1862.

11. BM to RCM, October 5, 1862; BM to RCM, October 11, 1862.

12. BM to RCM, October 14, 1862; BM to RCM, October 18, 1862; BM to RCM, October 19, 1862.

13. BM to RCM, October 20, 1862.

14. BM to RCM, October 25, 1862; BM to RCM, October 28, 1862; BM to RCM, October 31, 1862.

15. ACM to RCM, November 8, 1862; BM to RCM, November 4, 1862; BM to RCM, November 7, 1862; BM to RCM, November 11, 1862; BM to RCM, November 15, 1862; BM to RCM, November 16, 1862; BM to RCM, November 24, 1862; BM to RCM, November 30, 1862; BM to RCM, December 4, 1862; BM to RCM, December 7, 1862; BM to Irving Merrill, February 15, 1863.

16. BM to RCM, December 19, 1862; BM to RCM, December 20, 1862; BM to RCM, December 23, 1862.

17. ACM to RCM, December 23, 1862.

18. BM to RCM, December 24, 1862.

19. BM to RCM, January 1, 1863.

20. BM to RCM, January 7 and 9, 1863; BM to RCM, January 11, 1863; BM to RCM, January 13, 1863.

21. BM to RCM, January 25, 1863; BM to RCM, January 29, 1863; BM to RCM, February 2, 1863; ACM to RCM, February 2, 1863.

22. BM to RCM, February 12, 1863.

23. BM to RCM, February 21 and 22, 1863.

24. BM to RCM, February 25, 1863; BM to RCM, March 2, 1863; BM to RCM, March 7, 1863.

25. BM to RCM, March 7, 1863; BM to RCM, March 8, 1863.

26. ACM to RCM, March 1863.

27. BM to RCM, March 17, 1863.

28. BM to RCM, March 20, 1863.

29. BM to RCM, March 24, 1863.

30. BM to RCM, March 29, 1863.

31. BM to RCM, April 2, 1863.

32. BM to Nancy Merrill, April 2, 1863.

33. BM to RCM, April 9, 1863.

34. BM to RCM, April 10, 1863.

35. BM to RCM, April 11, 1863.
36. BM to RCM, April 12, 1863.

CHAPTER TEN
PRIVATE CLARK E. "SALTY" OYER, COMPANY G

1. Clark E. Oyer (hereafter cited as CEO), "Declaration for Invalid Pension," May 11, 1906, CEO pension file, National Archives, Washington, D.C.; "Standard Certificate of Death" for CEO, Registrar-Recorder/County Clerk, County of Los Angeles, Los Angeles, Calif.

2. Msgr. Francis J. Weber, *Rosedale Cemetery, Mortuary and Crematory* (Los Angeles: Rosedale Cemetery, n.d.); Dr. James S. Brust to author, August 2, 4, and 6, 2003.

3. CEO, "Declaration for Invalid Pension," May 11, 1906; Town Clerk, Ellicottville, N.Y., Register of Soldiers, New York State Archives, Albany; "Surgeon's Certificate," July 11, 1906, CEO pension file, National Archives.

4. Peter D. Oyer to unknown recipient, August 24, 1862; CEO to Jacob Oyer, September 22, 1862, both courtesy of Phyllis Oyer, Rochester, N.Y.

5. Phyllis Smith Oyer, *Oyer and Allied Families: Their History and Genealogy* (Interlaken, N.Y.: Heart of the Lakes Publishing, 1988), 113–14.

6. Unless otherwise noted, the account of CEO's Civil War service is drawn from notes of Edwin D. Northrup's interviews with CEO on August 30–31, 1886, June 23, 1893, August 25, 1893, and unknown dates; with Bradford Rowland on February 7, 1891, and March 3, 1893; with CEO and Bradford Rowland on August 29, 1886, June 28, 1893, August 21, 1893, and unknown dates; and with CEO, Bradford Rowland, and Esley Groat on unknown dates, all in the Edwin Dwight Northrup Papers, #4190, Department of Manuscripts and University Archives, Cornell University Libraries, Ithaca, N.Y. (hereafter cited as EDN Papers).

7. Richard J. McCadden to his mother, May 5, 1863, author's collection; CEO's medical record, War Department, Surgeon General's Office, January 31, 1884, CEO pension file.

8. CEO to Jacob Oyer, December 15, 1863, quoted in Oyer, *Oyer and Allied Families,* 166–67; Affidavits of Bradford Rowland, August 9, 1886; Esley Groat, August 9, 1886; Alexander Bird, August 9, 1886; Charles Harry Matteson, August 10, 1886; Dwight W. Day, undated; Corydon C. Rugg, September 20, 1887; "Certificate of Medical Examination," November 17, 1920, all in CEO pension file.

9. William Alan Blair, ed., *A Politician Goes to War: The Civil War Letters of John White Geary* (University Park, Pa.: Pennsylvania State Univ. Press, 1995), 218.

10. On Oglethorpe Barracks and Savannah's jail, see Walter J. Fraser Jr., *Savannah in the Old South* (Athens: Univ. of Georgia Press, 2003), 223, 242, 304, 306.

11. Lonnie R. Speer, *Portals to Hell: Military Prisons of the Civil War* (Mechanicsburg, Pa.: Stackpole Books, 1997), 273–77.

12. Delos Peck, State of New York Bureau of Military Record prisoner of war question-

naire; Thomas R. Aldrich, "The Experience of Thomas R. Aldrich Late of Co. B 154th New York Volls. while a prisoner of war from May 8, 1864 until February 22nd, 1865."

13. Record of CEO's service, War Department, Adjutant General's Office, January 27, 1883; CEO's medical records, Surgeon General's Office, January 31, 1884, both in CEO pension file; Oyer, *Oyer and Allied Families,* 165.

14. Paul H. Silverstone, *Warships of the Civil War Navies* (Annapolis, Md.: Naval Institute Press, 1989), 189; telephone conversation with Robert Browning of the U.S. Coast Guard Historian's Office, Washington, D.C., March 10, 2004.

15. Affidavits of Octavius P. Vedder, August 31, 1886; CEO, September 4, 1886; Robert M. Curtiss, September 3, 1887; Michael Gillespie, September 27, 1887; Bureau of Pensions questionnaires filled out by CEO, May 2, 1898, July 5, 1898; CEO, "Declaration for Invalid Pension," May 11, 1906; CEO, "Declaration for Pension," March 18, 1907, all in CEO pension file.

16. "Certificate of Medical Examination," November 17, 1920, CEO pension file.

17. Bureau of Pensions questionnaire filled out by CEO, March 10, 1915; Ellen McCulloch to E. W. Morgan, Acting Commissioner, October 28, 1930, CEO pension file.

18. CEO to E. D. Northrup, February 26, 1894, EDN Papers; undated photograph, author's collection.

CHAPTER ELEVEN

PRIVATE FRANCIS "BLIND" PATTERSON, COMPANY G

1. Francis Patterson depositions, October 14, 1881, November 15, 1881, June 30, 1887; "Transcript of Record of Death" for Francis Patterson, May 5, 1898, both in the Francis Patterson pension file, National Archives, Washington, D.C.

2. "Declaration for Widow's Pension," Helen M. Patterson, May 13, 1897; Helen Patterson affidavit, April 13, 1898; Francis Patterson depositions, November 5, 1879, September 28, 1881, November 15, 1881; Theodore Smith to Commissioner of Pensions, November 30, 1881; Petition of Edward Marvin, Elmira Overseer of the Poor, June 4, 1887, all in Patterson pension file; 1860 U.S. Census, Olean, Cattaraugus County, N.Y.; "'Blind' Patterson," *Elmira [New York] Daily Gazette and Free Press,* May 1, 1897, 1.

3. Wellman P. Nichols deposition, June 30, 1887; William Canning deposition, December 20, 1887; William Canning witness summary; Francis Patterson deposition, July 1888; Descriptive List of Deserters from 154th Regiment; Jesse K. Green deposition, November 18, 1881, all in Patterson pension file; descriptive book and muster-in roll, Company G, 154th New York, National Archives; *Biographical Review: The Leading Citizens of Livingston and Wyoming Counties, New York* (Boston: Biographical Review Publishing Company, 1895), 160–61; John D. Billings, *Hardtack and Coffee: The Unwritten Story of Army Life* (Williamstown, Mass.: Corner House Publishers, 1993), 282.

4. Francis Patterson to Helen Patterson, November 11, 1862, Patterson pension file.

5. Francis Patterson to Helen Patterson, November 1862, Patterson pension file.

6. Francis Patterson to Helen Patterson, January 31, 1863, Patterson pension file.

7. "Serious Loss," unidentified newspaper clipping, Newspaper Clipping Collection, New York State Military Museum and Veterans Research Center, Saratoga Springs, N.Y.

8. Francis Patterson to Helen Patterson, March 21, 1863, Patterson pension file.

9. Francis Patterson to Helen Patterson, April 12, 1863, Patterson pension file.

10. Charles Harry Matteson interview notes, October 6, 1893; Clark E. Oyer interview notes, undated, both in EDN Papers.

11. Francis Patterson depositions and affidavits of November 5, 1879, September 28, 1881, October 14, 1881, November 15, 1881, June 30, 1887, July 1888; Francis Patterson Invalid Army Pension Application, May 30, 1866, all in Patterson pension file.

12. Francis Patterson depositions of July 31, 1879, and November 15, 1881, Patterson pension file.

13. Wellman P. Nichols affidavit, November 29, 1881; Zeno Besecker deposition, November 22, 1881, both in Patterson pension file.

14. Francis Patterson depositions and affidavits of July 31, 1879, September 28, 1881, November 15, 1881, and June 30, 1887; Zeno Besecker deposition, November 22, 1881; Wellman P. Nichols depositions of November 29, 1881, and June 30, 1887; Wellman P. Nichols witness summary, all in Patterson pension file; John E. Clark Jr., *Railroads in the Civil War: The Impact of Management on Victory and Defeat* (Baton Rouge: Louisiana State Univ. Press, 2001), 150; regimental returns, 154th New York, October 1863, National Archives.

15. Francis Patterson depositions and affidavits of July 31, 1879, September 28, 1881, November 15, 1881, November 19, 1881, and June 30, 1887; Charles H. McCarthy to John C. Black, July 31, 1887, all in Patterson pension file.

16. Francis Patterson deposition, November 19, 1881; Charles H. McCarthy to John C. Black, July 31, 1887; Sarah Johnson witness summary, all in Patterson pension file.

17. Charles H. McCarthy to T. J. Shannon, July 17, 1887; Charles H. McCarthy to John C. Black, July 31, 1887; A. B. Galatian to Gen. J. J. Bartlett, June 14, 1887; Witness Summaries of H. W. Chamberlain, Dr. Charles Hurlbut, Sarah Johnson, Obadiah Patterson, Sarah E. Patterson, and Bennett T. Zimmer, all in Patterson pension file.

18. Francis Patterson depositions and affidavits of July 31, 1879, September 28, 1881, October 14, 1881, November 15, 1881, November 30, 1881, and June 30, 1887; Francis Patterson Invalid Army Pension Application, May 30, 1866; A. S. Coleman to W. W. Dudley, April 2, 1882; Mary McMahon witness summary, all in Patterson pension file.

19. Francis Patterson depositions and affidavits of January 10, 1871, July 31, 1879, November 15, 1881, and June 30, 1887; George D. Sidman to John C. Black, December 16, 1887, all in Patterson pension file.

20. Muster roll, Company G, 154th New York, October 31, 1863, National Archives; Descriptive List of Deserters; "History of the Fraud: With the Names and Relation to It of the Various Actors Therein," unsigned, undated manuscript (hereafter cited as History of the Fraud), 2; Francis Patterson deposition, January 10, 1871; transcript from Records, Surgeon General's Office, September 23, 1871; "Case of Francis or Frank Patterson," unsigned, undated manuscript, all in Patterson pension file.

21. Francis Patterson depositions of November 5, 1879, and September 28, 1881;

James W. Williams witness summary; James Williams deposition, June 23, 1888, all in Patterson pension file.

22. Olive E. Hooker deposition, June 23, 1888; Robert Shay deposition, June 23, 1888, both in Patterson pension file.

23. Francis Patterson to Helen Patterson, March 24, 1864, Patterson pension file.

24. Francis Patterson's Certificate of Disability for Discharge (two copies), April 16, 1864, Patterson pension file.

25. Witness Summaries of Thomas Bennett, Moses B. Hills, and Phillip E. Mungar, Patterson pension file.

26. Howard M. Badger deposition, June 25, 1888, Patterson pension file.

27. Francis Patterson deposition, November 5, 1879; Charles H. McCarthy to John C. Black, July 31, 1887; Charles A. Chapin deposition, November 4, 1887; Witness Summaries of Charles A. Chapin, Seymmur Dexter, Moses B. Hills, and R. H. Ransom, all in Patterson pension file.

28. George W. Jackson and Herman Joerg Witness Summaries, Patterson pension file.

29. Herman Joerg witness summary, Patterson pension file.

30. Francis Patterson depositions of November 5, 1879, and July 1888; Hiram Straight deposition, October 20, 1881; H. H. Rockwell to T. L. Poole, June 4, 1887; James Armstrong deposition, September 19, 1887; George D. Sidman to Thomas J. Shannon, December 18, 1887; "A Blind Veteran's Sudden Wealth," unidentified newspaper clipping, all in Patterson pension file; "Famous Pension Fraud," *Buffalo Daily Courier,* June 1, 1893, clipping in EDN Papers; "'Blind' Patterson," *Elmira [New York] Daily Gazette and Free Press,* May 1, 1897, 7.

31. Stuart McConnell, *Glorious Contentment: The Grand Army of the Republic, 1865–1900* (Chapel Hill: Univ. of North Carolina Press, 1992), 143; Gustavus A. Weber, *The Bureau of Pensions: Its History, Activities and Organization* (Baltimore, Md.: Johns Hopkins Press, 1923), 4–5; William H. Glasson, *Federal Military Pensions in the United States* (New York: Oxford Univ. Press, 1918), 125–29.

32. Thomas Bennett witness summary; Francis Patterson, Invalid Army Pension Application, May 30, 1866, both in Patterson pension file.

33. History of the Fraud, 4; William Lennon affidavit, October 3, 1866; Theodore Smith to Commissioner of Pensions, November 30, 1881; Charles C. McCarthy to John C. Black, July 25, 1887, and July 31, 1887, all in Patterson pension file.

34. Theodore Smith to Commissioner of Pensions, November 30, 1881, Patterson pension file.

35. Petition of Elmirans to Commissioner of Pensions, February 15, 1867, Patterson pension file.

36. Francis Patterson depositions, January 10, 1871, June 11, 1879, July 31, 1879, November 5, 1879, and September 7, 1880; Agreement between Francis Patterson and George Burgess, August 8, 1870; Articles of Agreement between Francis Patterson and S. R. Bond, August 2, 1871; Power of Attorney of Francis Patterson, appointing S. R. Bond to replace Gardner and Burgess, June 11, 1879, all in Patterson pension file.

37. Francis Patterson to W. W. Dudley, October 3, 1881, Patterson pension file; McConnell, *Glorious Contentment,* 144–45.

38. Note, June 20, 1879; Francis Patterson deposition, June 30, 1887, both in Patterson pension file.

39. "On Mills," document by anonymous writer; A. B. Galatian to J. J. Bartlett, June 14, 1887; Typescript Overview of Case by unknown writer, circa July 6, 1887 (hereafter cited as Typescript Overview), all in Patterson pension file; "Uncle Sam Around," *Elmira [New York] Telegram,* June 3, 1887, 5; "Dr. Mills at Liberty," *Elmira [New York] Daily Advertiser,* June 30, 1887, 5; "Mills, Laidlaw & Co.," *Elmira [New York] Telegram,* September 25, 1887, 1.

40. Hiram R. Enoch to John C. Black, June 29, 1887; George H. Patchin witness summary, both in Patterson pension file; "Old soldiers in this vicinity who know Capt. John Laidlaw," *Elmira [New York] Telegram,* July 24, 1887, 5; McConnell, *Glorious Contentment,* 146–47; Weber, *The Bureau of Pensions,* 15–16; Glasson, *Federal Military Pensions in the United States,* 163–65, 173, 182.

41. Charles H. Knipp and George H. Patchin Witness Summaries, Patterson pension file; "Patterson at Waverly," *Elmira [New York] Telegram,* June 26, 1887, 8.

42. Wilkes J. Miller depositions of September 5, 1881, November 15, 1881, and June 27, 1887, Patterson pension file.

43. Anna M. Baden and Amos T. Bissell Witness Summaries; Amos T. Bissell deposition, December 7, 1887; Hiram R. Enoch to John C. Black, June 29, 1887; Francis Patterson deposition, June 30, 1887; John Delany to A. T. Bissell, circa September 27, 1888; case summary, all in Patterson pension file.

44. Amos T. Bissell witness summary; Amos T. Bissell deposition, December 7, 1887; Francis Patterson to W. W. Dudley, October 3, 1881; History of the Fraud, 6–7, all in Patterson pension file.

45. History of the Fraud, 6–7; William W. Dudley, Letter of Instructions, November 12, 1881; Wellman P. Nichols depositions of November 29, 1881, and June 30, 1887, all in Patterson pension file.

46. Francis Patterson deposition, November 15, 1881; Wilkes J. Miller deposition, November 15, 1881; Jesse K. Green deposition, November 18, 1881; Chauncey Pipher deposition, November 22, 1881; Charles M. Mallery deposition, November 22, 1881; Emery Osterstuck deposition, November 23, 1881; Henry Martin deposition, November 29, 1881; Theodore Smith to Commissioner of Pensions, November 30, 1881, all in Patterson pension file.

47. Illegible signatory to Chief, Special Examiner Division, January 16, 1882, Patterson pension file.

48. Original Invalid Pension rejection, May 3, 1882, Patterson pension file.

49. A. B. Galatian witness summary; John Delany to A. T. Bissell, circa September 27, 1888, both in Patterson pension file; "Patterson at Waverly," *Elmira [New York] Telegram,* June 26, 1887, 8; U.S. Department of the Interior, *Reports of the Department of the Interior for the Fiscal Year Ended June 30, 1914* (Washington, D.C.: Government Printing Office,

1915), 1:224; Roger D. Hunt and Jack R. Brown, *Brevet Brigadier Generals in Blue* (Gaithersburg, Md.: Olde Soldier Books, 1990), 56.

50. James Armstrong deposition, September 19, 1887; John Bartholomew witness summary, both in Patterson pension file.

51. Wilkes J. Miller affidavit, January 4, 1887; Charles H. McCarthy to John C. Black, July 25, 1887; Assistant Adjutant General to Francis Patterson, January 20, 1887; Francis Patterson to E. F. Babcock, February 5, 1887; Francis Patterson, Power of Attorney, February 15, 1887; History of the Fraud, 8–10; Isaac Garabrant and A. B. Galatian Witness Summaries, all in Patterson pension file; "What Mr. Galatian Says," *Elmira [New York] Telegram,* June 26, 1887, 8.

52. Note attached to Adjutant General's Office report on Patterson case, March 2, 1887; Edward Porter affidavit, March 1, 1887; Edward Porter witness summary; Charles H. McCarthy to John C. Black, July 25, 1887, all in Patterson pension file.

53. History of the Fraud, 10–11, Patterson pension file.

54. John C. Black to Olean Postmaster, March 26, 1887; note by C. S. Stowell, March 28, 1887; John C. Black to Sir, April 6, 1887; John C. Black to Sir, April 6, 1887; Edward Porter deposition, April 12, 1887; Wilkes J. Miller deposition, May 2, 1887, all in Patterson pension file.

55. Original Invalid Claim approval, May 14, 1887; undated slip with payment calculations, circa June 4, 1887; History of the Fraud, 12, all in Patterson pension file.

56. Charles H. McCarthy to John C. Black, July 25, 1887; H. H. Rockwell to T. L. Poole, June 4, 1887; Petition of Edward Marvin, Elmira Overseer of the Poor, June 4, 1887, all in Patterson pension file.

57. T. L. Poole to H. H. Rockwell, June 7, 1887, Patterson pension file.

58. Charles H. Knipp and T. L. Poole Witness Summaries; Charles H. McCarthy to John C. Black, July 25, 1887; History of the Fraud, 13–15, all in Patterson pension file.

59. Francis Patterson deposition, June 30, 1887; T. J. Shannon to John C. Black, July 4, 1887; Charles H. McCarthy to John C. Black, July 31, 1887; Charles H. Knipp witness summary, all in Patterson pension file.

60. Harry Carpenter and Jeremiah Smalley Witness Summaries, Helen M. Patterson affidavit, April 13, 1898; David Keppel affidavit, April 18, 1898, all in Patterson pension file.

61. Wilkes J. Miller affidavits of June 14, 1887, June 27, 1887; History of the Fraud, 20, both in Patterson pension file.

62. A. B. Galatian to J. J. Bartlett, June 14, 1887, Patterson pension file.

63. Charles H. Knipp witness summary, Patterson pension file.

64. Frederick M. Jones witness summary, Patterson pension file.

65. Charles H. McCarthy to John C. Black, July 25, 1887; Louise A. Dewitt deposition, October 31, 1887; George H. Dewitt and Louise A. Dewitt Witness Summaries, all in Patterson pension file.

66. Charles H. McCarthy to John C. Black, July 25, 1887; History of the Fraud, 18, both in Patterson pension file.

67. J. E. Kast, Charles C. Mussina, George H. Patchin, and William H. Sloan Witness Summaries, Patterson pension file.

68. David M. Pratt, George F. Ronian, and W. A. Simpson Witness Summaries; Chemung County Court Order, June 17, 1887, all in Patterson pension file.

69. Chief, Special Examiner Division, to Charles H. McCarthy, June 18, 1887; William E. McLean to T. J. Shannon, June 21, 1887; Charles H. McCarthy to John C. Black, June 21, 1887; Andrew B. Galatian deposition, June 30, 1887; Charles H. McCarthy to John C. Black, July 25, 1887; T. J. Shannon to William M. Dye, June 25, 1887; Wilkes J. Miller deposition, June 27, 1887; Edward Porter deposition, June 28, 1887; History of the Fraud, 39–40; Typescript Overview, all in Patterson pension file.

70. Charles H. McCarthy to John C. Black, July 25, 1887; John C. Black to T. J. Shannon, October 28, 1887; G. E. Blakey, Zeb K. Page, and E. W. Sims Witness Summaries; Typescript Overview, all in Patterson pension file; "How Mills Spent Money in Virginia," *Elmira [New York] Telegram,* July 10, 1887, 8.

71. History of the Fraud, 21–24; Joseph Carter witness summary, both in Patterson pension file.

72. History of the Fraud, 24–26; Typescript Overview, both in Patterson pension file; "Patterson at Waverly," *Elmira [New York] Telegram,* June 26, 1887, 8; "Blind Patterson, the Elmira pensioner," *Elmira [New York] Daily Advertiser,* June 29, 1887, 5; "Dr. Mills at Liberty," *Elmira [New York] Daily Advertiser,* June 30, 1887, 5.

73. John C. Black to T. J. Shannon, November 2, 1887; Hiram R. Enoch to John C. Black, June 29, 1887; Charles H. McCarthy to John C. Black, July 25, 1887; Francis Patterson deposition, June 30, 1887, all in Patterson pension file.

74. "The Largest Pension Yet," *Elmira [New York] Daily Advertiser,* June 11, 1887, 2; "A Blind Beggar's Fortune," *New York Times,* June 12, 1887, 3; "'Blind' Patterson's Money," *Elmira [New York] Daily Advertiser,* June 15, 1887, 5; "Appears to be an Empty Honor," *Elmira [New York] Daily Advertiser,* June 17, 1887, 2; "Will he Capture Them?" *Elmira [New York] Daily Advertiser,* June 18, 1887, 5; "Frank Patterson's Pension," *New York Times,* June 19, 1887, 1; "Blind Patterson's Pension," *Elmira [New York] Daily Advertiser,* June 20, 1887, 5; "Blind Patterson's Pension," *New York Times,* June 20, 1887, 1; "More About 'Blind' Patterson," *Elmira [New York] Daily Advertiser,* June 21, 1887, 2; "Mills and Laidlaw," *Elmira [New York] Daily Advertiser,* June 24, 1887, 5; "Patterson's Friends," *Elmira [New York] Daily Advertiser,* June 25, 1887, 1; "Patterson's Two Friends," June 27, 1887, 5; "Blind Patterson Arrested," *Elmira [New York] Daily Advertiser,* June 29, 1887, 2; "'Blind Patterson' Arrested," *New York Times,* June 29, 1887, 5.

75. "Dr. Mills Interviewed," *Elmira [New York] Telegram,* June 26, 1887; "Patterson's Two Friends," *Elmira [New York] Daily Advertiser,* June 27, 1887, 5.

76. "Mills and Laidlaw," *Elmira [New York] Daily Advertiser,* June 29, 1887, 5; "Dr. Mills at Liberty," *Elmira [New York] Daily Advertiser,* June 30, 1887, 5; "Patterson In the Parlor City," *Elmira [New York] Daily Advertiser,* July 2, 1887; "Uncle Sam Around," *Elmira [New York] Telegram,* July 3, 1887, 5.

77. "Uncle Sam Around," *Elmira [New York] Telegram,* July 3, 1887, 5.

78. "Pat's Big Pension," *Elmira [New York] Daily Advertiser,* July 4, 1887, 5; "Four Conspicuous People," *Elmira [New York] Daily Advertiser,* July 6, 1887, 2; "The examination of Dr. Mills and Captain Laidlaw," *Elmira [New York] Daily Advertiser,* July 7, 1887, 5; "Blind Patterson's Pension," *New York Times,* July 7, 1887, 5; "Fast In the Toils," *Elmira [New York] Telegram,* July 10, 1887, 7.

79. "Laidlaw Goes to Buffalo," *Elmira [New York] Daily Advertiser,* July 8, 1887, 5; "Taken to Buffalo," *Elmira [New York] Telegram,* July 10, 1887, 8; "The Doctor at Buffalo," *Elmira [New York] Daily Advertiser,* July 11, 1887, 5; "Is He There to Stay?" *Elmira [New York] Daily Advertiser,* July 15, 1887, 5; "Mrs. Frank Patterson," *Elmira [New York] Telegram,* July 10, 1887, 8; "Mrs. Patterson Heard From," *Elmira [New York] Telegram,* June 26, 1887, 8.

80. Thomas J. Shannon to John C. Black, September 25, 1887, Patterson pension file; "The Trials Postponed," *Elmira [New York] Daily Advertiser,* September 24, 1887, 5; "Mills, Laidlaw & Co.," *Elmira [New York] Telegram,* September 25, 1887, 1.

81. Thomas J. Shannon to John C. Black, November 20, 1887, Patterson pension file; "Going to Auburn," *Elmira [New York] Daily Advertiser,* November 16, 1887, 5; "Elmirans in Auburn," November 17, 1887, 5; "The Alleged Fraud," *Elmira [New York] Daily Advertiser,* November 18, 1887, 5; "Could Not Agree," *Elmira [New York] Telegram,* November 20, 1887, 1; "Jury Disagrees," *Elmira [New York] Telegram,* November 20, 1887, 1; "About the Mills-Laidlaw Verdict," *Elmira [New York] Telegram,* November 20, 1887, 5; "From a Legal Standpoint," *Elmira [New York] Telegram,* November 20, 1887, 8; "Mills, Laidlaw, Patterson," *Elmira [New York] Daily Advertiser,* November 21, 1887, 5.

82. Thomas J. Shannon to John C. Black, December 14, 1887, Patterson pension file; "Patterson Home Again," *Elmira [New York] Daily Advertiser,* December 15, 1887, 5; "From Frying Pan to Fire," *Elmira [New York] Daily Advertiser,* December 17, 1887, 5; "Mills and Laidlaw Get Bail," *Elmira [New York] Telegram,* December 18, 1887, 1.

83. Thomas J. Shannon to John C. Black, December 18, 1887; Thomas J. Shannon to John C. Black, March 30, 1887, both in Patterson pension file; "Elmirans in Utica," *Elmira [New York] Daily Advertiser,* March 21, 1888, 5; "No Separate Trials," *Elmira [New York] Daily Advertiser,* March 22, 1888, 8; "The Pension Fraud," *Elmira [New York] Daily Advertiser,* March 23, 1888, 5; "Many Witnesses," *Elmira [New York] Daily Advertiser,* March 24, 1888, 5; "The Pension Case," *Elmira [New York] Daily Advertiser,* March 26, 1888, 5; "What the Jury Say," *Elmira [New York] Daily Advertiser,* March 27, 1888, 5; "Blind Patterson Acquitted," *New York Times,* March 27, 1888, 1; "Dr. Mills's Mind," *Elmira [New York] Daily Advertiser,* March 30, 1888, 5.

84. "To Be Dropped" form, November 7, 1887; A. Ward to John C. Black, March 3, 1888; Hiram R. Enoch to John C. Black, April 19, 1888; Francis Patterson deposition, July 1888; Walter Lloyd Smith et al. deposition, July 20, 1888, all in Patterson pension file; U.S. House, *Report of the Secretary of the Interior,* 50th Cong., 2d sess., 1888, Ex. Doc. 1, part 5, vol. 3, serial 2638, 111–12.

85. "A Dirty Pair," *Elmira [New York] Daily Gazette and Free Press,* August 29, 1888, clipping in Patterson pension file.

86. A. H. Garland to Secretary of the Interior, December 10, 1888; Acting Secretary of the Interior to Commissioner of Pensions, December 17, 1888; Bureau of Pensions report, December 29, 1888; John C. Black to Second National Bank and David M. Pratt, January 2, 1889; Rebellion Service Invalid application, August 6, 1891; Declaration for Invalid Pension, August 10, 1892; Declaration for Invalid Pension, August 9, 1893; Francis Patterson deposition, August 9, 1893, all in Patterson pension file.

87. "Transcript of Record of Death," Patterson pension file; "'Blind' Patterson," *Elmira [New York] Daily Gazette and Free Press,* May 1, 1897, 7; "Francis Patterson Dead," *Elmira [New York] Daily Advertiser,* May 1, 1897, 6; "'Blind' Patterson," *Elmira [New York] Telegram,* May 2, 1897, 3; "Francis Patterson Buried," *Elmira [New York] Daily Advertiser,* May 3, 1897, 6; "Card of Thanks," *Elmira [New York] Telegram,* May 9, 1897, 8.

88. Declaration for Widow's Pension, May 13, 1897; Order of Chemung County Supreme Court, February 12, 1898; Helen M. Patterson affidavit, April 13, 1898; Widow's Pension record, May 31, 1898; Commissioner of Pensions to Helen M. Patterson, June 4, 1898, all in Patterson pension file; "Helen M. Patterson," *Elmira [New York] Daily Advertiser,* September 5, 1904, 2; "Helen M. Patterson," *Elmira [New York] Daily Gazette and Free Press,* September 6, 1904, 5.

89. Helen M. Patterson to Commissioner of Pensions, December 21, 1900, January 15, 1901, and May 14, 1902; note on Bureau of Pensions form, July 7, 1914, all in Patterson pension file.

CHAPTER TWELVE

PRIVATE OSCAR F. WILBER, COMPANY G

1. Roy Morris Jr., *The Better Angel: Walt Whitman in the Civil War* (New York: Oxford Univ. Press, 2000), passim; Daniel Mark Epstein, *Lincoln and Whitman: Parallel Lives in Civil War Washington* (New York: Ballantine Books, 2004), passim.

2. Walt Whitman, "Visits Among Army Hospitals At Washington, on the Field and here in New-York," *New York Times,* December 11, 1864; Walt Whitman, "'Tis But Ten Years Since," *[New York] Weekly Graphic,* February 28, 1874; Walt Whitman, *Memoranda During the War* (Camden, N.J.: Published by the author, 1875), 21. Two of the many modern examples are Walter Lowenfels, ed., *Walt Whitman's Civil War* (New York: Alfred A. Knopf, 1961), 101–2; and Walt Whitman, *Complete Poetry and Collected Prose,* ed. Justin Kaplan (New York: Library of America, 1982), 730–31.

3. William Adams, ed., *Historical Gazetteer and Biographical Memorial of Cattaraugus County, N.Y.* (Syracuse: Lyman, Horton and Co., 1893), 744–45; Town Clerk, Humphrey, N.Y., Register of the Town's Soldiers and Sailors, 1865, New York State Archives, Albany; Affidavit of Sally D. Wilber, February 11, 1882, in Wilber pension file, National Archives, Washington, D.C.; Affidavit of Nathan Wilber, February 18, 1882, Wilber pension file.

4. The letters of Oscar F. Wilber (hereafter cited as OFW) to Nathan Wilber (hereafter cited as NW) are courtesy of George and Beverly Geisel; his letters to Sally D. Wilber (hereafter cited as SDW) are from the Wilber pension file.

5. OFW to NW, October 5, 1862.

6. OFW to NW, October 14, 1862.

7. OFW to NW, November 6, 1862.

8. OFW to NW, November 21, 1862; OFW to Rachel Wilber, November 22, 1862, courtesy of George and Beverly Geisel.

9. OFW to NW, November 27, 1862; OFW to SDW, November 27, 1862.

10. OFW to NW, December 23, 1862; OFW to SDW, January 16, 1863.

11. OFW to NW, January 27, 1863.

12. OFW to NW, February 2, 1863; OFW to SDW, February 8, 1863.

13. OFW to SDW, February 8, 1863; OFW to NW, February 21, 1863; OFW to SDW and Rosina Wilber, February 27, 1863.

14. OFW to SDW, March 16, 1863.

15. OFW to SDW, April 28, 1863.

16. Matthew B. Cheney to Rodney R. Crowley, September 3, 1893, Edwin Dwight Northrup Papers, #4190, Department of Manuscripts and University Archives, Cornell University Libraries, Ithaca, N.Y. (hereafter cited as EDN Papers); Matthew B. Cheney to E. D. Northrup, October 8, 1893, EDN Papers.

17. Stephen Sears, *Chancellorsville* (Boston: Houghton Mifflin, 1996), 389.

18. George A. Taylor to Eleanor Taylor, May 20, 1863; Bradford Rowland and Clark E. Oyer interview notes, August 19, 1886; Clark E. Oyer and Esley Groat interview notes, undated; Matthew B. Cheney to E. D. Northrup, April 18, 1894, all in EDN Papers.

19. Philip J. Friedrich military records, courtesy of the Mississippi Department of Archives and History, Jackson, Mississippi.

20. P. J. Friedrich to SDW, May 4, 1863, Wilber pension file.

21. Milo L. Wilber to SDW, May 22, 1863, Wilber pension file.

22. Milo L. Wilber to SDW, May 29, 1863, Wilber pension file.

23. William Charles to Ann Charles, June 7, 1863.

24. Danford L. Hall to SDW, June 12, 1863, Wilber pension file; Danford L. Hall, "Application for Invalid Pension," January 23, 1869, Hall pension file, National Archives.

25. Lowenfels, *Walt Whitman's Civil War*, 65–66.

26. C. Baker (Lafayette C. Baker) to SDW, June 16, 1863, Wilber pension file; Margaret Leech, *Reveille in Washington, 1860–1865* (New York: Harper and Brothers, 1941), 148; John T. Hubbell and James W. Geary, eds., *Biographical Dictionary of the Union: Northern Leaders of the Civil War* (Westport, Conn.: Greenwood Press, 1995), 22–23; Jacob Mogelever, *Death to Traitors: The Story of General Lafayette C. Baker, Lincoln's Forgotten Secret Service Chief* (Garden City, N.Y.: Doubleday, 1960), 18.

27. Mogelever, *Death to Traitors,* 109 (quote) and passim; Hubbell and Geary, *Biographical Dictionary of the Union,* 22–23.

28. Lafayette C. Baker to SDW, June 16, 1863, Wilber pension file.

29. "A Comparison of L. C. Baker Signatures," *North & South* 7, no. 1 (January 2004): 20.

30. Epstein, *Lincoln and Whitman,* 131–32; Oscar F. Wilber records accompanying

Specimen Number 1534, courtesy of National Museum of Health and Medicine, Armed Forces Institute of Pathology, Washington, D.C.

31. Martin G. Murray, "Traveling with the Wounded: Walt Whitman and Washington's Civil War Hospitals," *Washington History: Magazine of the Historical Society of Washington, D.C.* 8, no. 2 (fall–winter 1996–1997): 62–63, 66.

32. OFW (written by Edwin S. Shaw) to SDW, June 29, 1863.

33. Wilber records, National Museum of Health and Medicine; A. J. Pratt to SDW, July 21, 1863, Wilber pension file.

34. Murray, "Traveling with the Wounded," 67, 69–70.

35. Walt Whitman, *Notebooks and Unpublished Prose Manuscripts,* ed. Edward F. Grier, 6 vols. (New York: New York Univ. Press, 1984), 2:654–55.

36. Walt Whitman, "Visits Among Army Hospitals At Washington, on the Field and here in New-York," *New York Times,* December 11, 1864.

37. Edwin S. Shaw to SDW, July 23, 1863, Wilber pension file.

38. A. J. Pratt to SDW, July 29 and 30, 1863, Wilber pension file.

39. Wilber records, National Museum of Health and Medicine.

40. Ibid.

Bibliography

MANUSCRIPT SOURCES

Private Collections

Thomas R. Aldrich Memoir. "The Experience of Thomas R. Aldrich Late of Co. B 154th New York Volls. while a prisoner of war from May 8, 1864 until February 22nd, 1865." Patricia Wilcox Collection, Fairport, N.Y.

Homer A. Ames Letters. Author's Collection.

Joel M. Bouton Letters. Maureen Koehl Collection, South Salem, N.Y.

Colby M. Bryant Diary. Bruce H. Bryant Collection, Salamanca, N.Y.

Clara (Waite) Burroughs Typescript. "Genealogy of the Family of Amasa Bushnell, Pioneer, Napoli, Cattaraugus Co., N.Y." 1959. Author's Collection.

Bush Family Genealogical Notes. Elaine Waiters Collection, Arroyo Grande, Calif.

Martin D. Bushnell Letters. Phil Palen Collection, Gowanda, N.Y.

Martin D. Bushnell Letters and Diary. Frank M. Bushnell Collection, Napoli, N.Y.

Cattaraugus County Ex-Union Prisoners of War Association Charter. American Legion Post Collection, Franklinville, N.Y.

William Charles Letters. Jack Finch Collection, Freedom, N.Y.

Mary Jane Chittenden Letters. Author's Collection.

William F. Chittenden Letters. Author's Collection.

Thomas Donnelly Letter. Author's Collection.

Flyer for the Olean Academy, November 1861. Maureen Koehl Collection, South Salem, N.Y.

Genealogical Notes on the Wheeler Family. Richard E. Chittenden Collection, Ventura, Calif.

Stephen R. Green Letters. Phil Palen Collection, Gowanda, N.Y.

John C. Griswold Letter. Author's Collection.

John G. Griswold Letter. Vince Martonis Collection, Hanover, N.Y.

Milon J. Griswold Letters. Author's Collection.

Susan Griswold Letters. Author's Collection.

William D. Harper Memoir. "The Enlistment and in Camp at Jamestown and the Several Camps While in the Service of the United States." Raymond Harper Collection, Dunkirk, N.Y.

James Hitchcock Letters. James and Vicki Hitchcock Collection, Randolph, N.Y.

Dana P. Horton Letters. Author's Collection.

Betsey Phelps Howlett Poem. "Composed and written by Mrs Betsey Howlett, on the death of Barzillai and Alva Merrill, who died at the battle of Chanslorville in May, 1863." William H. Petersen Collection, East Randolph, N.Y.

Amos Humiston Letters. Allan L. Cox Collection, Medford, Mass.

Fannie Jackson Undated Address. "Young People, Citizens & Soldiers." Frank M. Bushnell Collection, Napoli, N.Y.

David S. Jones Letters. Clara Jones Collection, Salamanca, N.Y.

Henry C. Loomis Letter. Author's Collection.

Richard J. McCadden Letters. Author's Collection.

"Memorial of Capt. John C. Griswold, Adopted by the Board of Supervisors of Chautauqua County, N.Y., Nov. 17, 1892." Author's Collection.

Alva C. Merrill Letters. Doris Williams Collection, Orange City, Fla.

Barzilla Merrill Letters. Doris Williams Collection, Orange City, Fla.

Henry A. Munger Letters. Author's Collection.

George W. Newcomb Letters. Alexander G. Lynn Collection, Chicago, Ill.

George W. Newcomb Letters. Author's Collection.

Clark E. Oyer Letters. Phyllis Oyer Collection, Rochester, N.Y.

Peter D. Oyer Letter. Phyllis Oyer Collection, Rochester, N.Y.

Delos Peck, State of New York Bureau of Military Record Prisoner of War Questionnaire. Author's Collection.

Corydon C. Rugg Letter. Louise Koenig Collection, Olean, N.Y.

Emory Sweetland Letters. Lyle Sweetland Collection, South Dayton, N.Y.

Henry Van Aernam Letters. J. Richardson Lippert II Collection, Franklinville, N.Y.

Lewis D. Warner Diary (1863). John Lewis Spencer Collection, Canandaigua, N.Y.

Lewis D. Warner Diary (1864–1865). Charles H. Warner III Collection, Santa Rosa, Calif.

George C. Waterman Letter. Frank M. Bushnell Collection, Napoli, N.Y.

Stephen Welch Diary. Carolyn Stoltz Collection, Tonawanda, N.Y.

Oscar F. Wilber Letters. Beverly Geisel Collection, Hamburg, N.Y.

Repositories

Cattaraugus County Memorial and Historical Museum, Little Valley, N.Y.

Henry Cunningham Letter
Newspaper Clippings
New York State Census, 1855, Cattaraugus County, N.Y.
Records of Soldiers by Towns
U.S. Census, 1860, Cattaraugus County, N.Y.

Chautauqua County Historical Society, Westfield, N.Y.

George A. Taylor Letters

Cornell University, Ithaca, N.Y.

Edwin Dwight Northrup Papers, #4190, Department of Manuscripts and University
Archives, Cornell University Libraries

Ellicottville Historical Society, Ellicottville, N.Y.

154th New York Regimental Letter Book

Fenton Historical Society, Jamestown, N.Y.

Homer A. Ames Letters
John C. Griswold Letters
Dana P. Horton Letters
Patrick H. Jones Letter

Fredericksburg National Cemetery, Fredericksburg, Va.

Brochure

Kennesaw Mountain National Battlefield Park, Kennesaw, Ga.

Fannie Jackson Letters in Martin D. Bushnell Papers

Mazomanie Historical Society, Mazomanie, Wisc.

Horace Smith Diary

Mississippi Department of Archives and History, Jackson, Miss.

Philip J. Friedrich Military Records

Nashville National Cemetery, Nashville, Tenn.

Brochures
Report of Interment, Milton H. Bush

National Archives, Washington, D.C.

Thomas Audas Recommendation, Fannie Jackson Pension File
[Lafayette] C. Baker Letter, Oscar F. Wilber Pension File
Milton H. Bush Medical Records
Martin D. Bushnell Military Records
Martin D. Bushnell Pension File
William F. Cady Recommendation, Fannie Jackson Pension File
William F. Chittenden Pension File
Alanson Crosby Military Records
Descriptive Books, 154th New York
P. J. Friedrich Letter, Oscar F. Wilber Pension File
Danford L. Hall Letter, Oscar F. Wilber Pension File
Danford L. Hall Pension File
William Hawkins Pension File
Alvin Hitchcock Medical Records
Alvin Hitchcock Military Records
Alvin Hitchcock Prisoner of War Records
Fannie Jackson Pension File
William G. Le Duc Letter, Fannie Jackson Pension File
Muster Rolls, 154th New York
Clark E. Oyer Pension File
Francis Patterson Letters, Francis Patterson Pension File
Francis Patterson Pension File
A. J. Pratt Letters, Oscar F. Wilber Pension File
Regimental Records, 154th New York
Regimental Returns, 154th New York
Register of Cases, Government Hospital for the Insane
Thaddeus L. Reynolds Letters, Reynolds Pension File
Edwin S. Shaw Letters, Oscar F. Wilber Pension File
Milo L. Wilber Letters, Oscar F. Wilber Pension File
Oscar F. Wilber Letters, Oscar F. Wilber Pension File
Oscar F. Wilber Pension File
M. C. Woodworth Letter, Fannie Jackson Pension File

National Museum of Health and Medicine, Armed Forces Institute of Pathology, Washington, D.C.

Oscar F. Wilber Records Accompanying Specimen Number 1534

New York State Archives, Albany, N.Y.

New York State Office of Mental Health, Utica State Hospital Patient Case Records
Town Clerks' Registers of Soldiers and Sailors

New York State Military Museum and Veterans Research Center,
Saratoga Springs, N.Y.

Newspaper Clippings Regarding the 154th New York

Registrar-Recorder/County Clerk, County of Los Angeles, Los Angeles, Calif.

Clark E. Oyer Death Certificate

U.S. Army Military History Institute, Carlisle Barracks, Pa.

George W. Newcomb Letter (March 6, 1863), Lewis Leigh Collection, Book 36, #90
Henry Van Aernam Letters

University of Iowa Library, Iowa City, Iowa

Marcellus W. Darling Letters

PUBLISHED SOURCES

Newspapers

Cattaraugus Freeman, Ellicottville, N.Y.
Cattaraugus Union, Ellicottville, N.Y.
Cattaraugus Republican, Salamanca, N.Y.
Ellicottville [New York] Post
Elmira [New York] Daily Advertiser
Elmira [New York] Daily Gazette and Free Press
Elmira [New York] Telegram
Fredonia [New York] Advertiser
Fredonia [New York] Censor
Jamestown [New York] Journal
Lewisboro [New York] Ledger
New York Times
State Journal, Lansing, Mich.
Weekly Graphic, New York, N.Y.

Books and Articles

"A Comparison of L. C. Baker Signatures." *North & South* 7, no. 1 (January 2004): 20.
Adams, William, ed. *Historical Gazetteer and Biographical Memorial of Cattaraugus County, N.Y.* Syracuse: Lyman, Horton and Co., 1893.
Basler, Roy P., ed. *The Collected Works of Abraham Lincoln.* 8 vols. New Brunswick, N.J.: Rutgers Univ. Press, 1953.
Beers, D. G., J. H. Goodhue, and E. F. Sanford. *Atlas of Cattaraugus County, New York.* New York: D. G. Beers and Co., 1869.

Billings, John D. *Hardtack and Coffee: The Unwritten Story of Army Life*. Williamstown, Mass.: Corner House Publishers, 1993.

Biographical Review: The Leading Citizens of Livingston and Wyoming Counties, New York. Boston: Biographical Review Publishing Company, 1895.

Blair, William Alan, ed. *A Politician Goes to War: The Civil War Letters of John White Geary*. University Park, Pa.: Pennsylvania State Univ. Press, 1995.

Bollet, Alfred Jay, M.D. *Civil War Medicine: Challenges and Triumphs*. Tucson, Ariz.: Galen Press, 2002.

Castel, Albert. *Decision in the West: The Atlanta Campaign of 1864*. Lawrence: Univ. Press of Kansas, 1992.

Catton, Bruce. *Never Call Retreat*. Garden City, N.Y.: Doubleday, 1965.

The Centennial History of Chautauqua County. 2 vols. Jamestown: Chautauqua History Company, 1904.

Clark, John E., Jr. *Railroads in the Civil War: The Impact of Management on Victory and Defeat*. Baton Rouge: Louisiana State Univ. Press, 2001.

Curran, Joan F., and Rudena K. Mallory, eds. *On Both Sides of the Line, by Fannie (Oslin) Jackson, 1835–1925: Her Early Years in Georgia and Civil War Service as a Union Army Nurse*. Kansas City, Mo.: Miller and Jeanette Nichols, 1989.

Darling, Marcellus Warner. *Events and Comments of My Life*. N.p., n.d.

Dean, Eric T., Jr. *Shook Over Hell: Post-Traumatic Stress, Vietnam, and the Civil War*. Cambridge, Mass.: Harvard Univ. Press, 1997.

Dodds, Gordon B. *Hiram Martin Chittenden: His Public Career*. Lexington: Univ. Press of Kentucky, 1973.

Dunkelman, Mark H. *Camp James M. Brown: Jamestown's Civil War Rendezvous*. Jamestown, N.Y.: Fenton Historical Society, 1996.

Dwyer, Ellen. *Homes for the Mad: Life Inside Two Nineteenth-Century Asylums*. New Brunswick, N.J.: Rutgers Univ. Press, 1987.

Ellis, Franklin, ed. *History of Cattaraugus County, New York*. Philadelphia: L. H. Everts, 1879.

Epstein, Daniel Mark. *Lincoln and Whitman: Parallel Lives in Civil War Washington*. New York: Ballantine Books, 2004.

Fraser, Walter J., Jr. *Savannah in the Old South*. Athens: Univ. of Georgia Press, 2003.

Freemon, Frank R. *Gangrene and Glory: Medical Care during the American Civil War*. Madison, N.J.: Fairleigh Dickinson Univ. Press, 1998.

Glasson, William H. *Federal Military Pensions in the United States*. New York: Oxford Univ. Press, 1918.

Hebert, Walter H. *Fighting Joe Hooker*. Indianapolis: Bobbs-Merrill, 1944.

Hitchcock, Mrs. Edward, Sr., comp. *The Genealogy of the Hitchcock Family*. Amherst, Mass.: Carpenter and Morehouse, 1894.

Hoobler, James A. *Cities under the Gun: Images of Occupied Nashville and Chatta-nooga.* Nashville: Rutledge Hill Press, 1986.

Hubbell, John T., and James W. Geary. *Biographical Dictionary of the Union: North-ern Leaders of the Civil War.* Westport, Conn.: Greenwood Press, 1995.

Hunt, Roger D., and Jack R. Brown. *Brevet Brigadier Generals in Blue.* Gaithersburg, Md.: Olde Soldier Books, 1990.

Johnson, Allen, and Dumas Malone, eds. *Dictionary of American Biography.* 22 vols. New York: Charles Scribner's Sons, 1930.

Knutson, Lawrence L. "D.C. Hospital Now Endangered Place." Associated Press news story, June 10, 2002.

Le Duc, William G. *Recollections of a Civil War Quartermaster.* St. Paul, Minn.: North Central Publishing Company, 1963.

Leech, Margaret. *Reveille in Washington, 1860–1865.* New York: Harper and Broth-ers, 1941.

Le Roy, Bruce, ed. *H. M. Chittenden, A Western Epic: Being a Selection from His Unpublished Journals, Diaries and Reports.* Tacoma: Washington State Historical Society, 1961.

Lewis, Lloyd. *Sherman: Fighting Prophet.* New York: Harcourt, Brace and Company, 1932.

Lowenfels, Walter, ed. *Walt Whitman's Civil War.* New York: Alfred A. Knopf, 1961.

Marvel, William. *Andersonville: The Last Depot.* Chapel Hill: Univ. of North Carolina Press, 1994.

McConnell, Stuart. *Glorious Contentment: The Grand Army of the Republic, 1865–1900.* Chapel Hill: Univ. of North Carolina Press, 1992.

McKay, Charles W. "Three Years or During the War, With the Crescent and Star." *The National Tribune Scrap Book.* N.p., n.d.

The Medical and Surgical History of the War of the Rebellion. Washington, D.C.: Gov-ernment Printing Office, 1877.

Mogelever, Jacob. *Death to Traitors: The Story of General Lafayette C. Baker, Lincoln's Forgotten Secret Service Chief.* Garden City, N.Y.: Doubleday, 1960.

Morris, Roy, Jr. *The Better Angel: Walt Whitman in the Civil War.* New York: Oxford Univ. Press, 2000.

Murray, Martin G. "Traveling with the Wounded: Walt Whitman and Washington's Civil War Hospitals." *Washington History: Magazine of the Historical Society of Washington, D.C.* 8, no. 2 (fall–winter 1996–1997): 58–73.

The National Cyclopaedia of American Biography. 63 vols. New York: James T. White and Company, 1927.

Olson, Marlynn McNallie. *A Guide to Burial Sites, Cemeteries and Random Stones in Cattaraugus County, New York.* Randolph, N.Y.: Published by the author, 1996.

Oyer, Phyllis Smith. *Oyer and Allied Families: Their History and Genealogy.* Interlaken, N.Y.: Heart of the Lakes Publishing, 1988.

Phisterer, Frederick. *New York in the War of the Rebellion, 1861 to 1865.* Albany, N.Y.: Weed, Parsons and Company, 1890.

Rutkow, Ira M. *Bleeding Blue and Gray: Civil War Surgery and the Evolution of American Medicine.* New York: Random House, 2005.

Sears, Stephen. *Chancellorsville.* Boston: Houghton Mifflin, 1996.

Silverstone, Paul H. *Warships of the Civil War Navies.* Annapolis, Md.: Naval Institute Press, 1989.

Speer, Lonnie R. *Portals to Hell: Military Prisons of the Civil War.* Mechanicsburg, Pa.: Stackpole Books, 1997.

Thrasher, Mary. *Merrill Genealogy: Descendants of Barzilla Merrill, 1764–1850.* Cooperstown, N.Y.: Crist, Scott and Parshall, 1907.

U.S. Department of the Interior. *Reports of the Department of the Interior for the Fiscal Year Ended June 30, 1914.* Washington, D.C.: Government Printing Office, 1915.

U.S. House. *Report of the Secretary of the Interior.* 50th Cong., 2d Sess., 1888. Ex. Doc 1, part 5, vol. 3, serial 2638.

Weber, Gustavus A. *The Bureau of Pensions: Its History, Activities and Organization.* Baltimore, Md.: Johns Hopkins Press, 1923.

Weber, Msgr. Francis J. *Rosedale Cemetery, Mortuary and Crematory.* Los Angeles: Rosedale Cemetery, n.d.

Wheeler, John H. *History of Wexford County, Michigan.* [Logansport, Ind.]: B. F. Bowen, 1903.

Whitman, Walt. *Complete Poetry and Collected Prose.* Edited by Justin Kaplan. New York: Library of America, 1982.

———. *Memoranda During the War.* Camden, N.J.: Published by the author, 1875.

———. *Notebooks and Unpublished Prose Manuscripts.* Edited by Edward F. Grier. 6 vols. New York: New York Univ. Press, 1984.

Illustration Credits

Milton H. Bush (chapter 2, page 20): Courtesy of the William H. Petersen Collection at the U.S. Army Military History Institute, Carlisle Barracks, Pennsylvania.

Martin D. Bushnell (chapter 3, page 28): Courtesy of the Frank M. Bushnell Collection at the U.S. Army Military History Institute, Carlisle Barracks, Pennsylvania.

William F. and Mary Jane Chittenden with their daughter Ida (chapter 4, page 47): Courtesy of Richard E. Chittenden.

Alanson Crosby (chapter 5, page 68): Courtesy of the William C. Welch Collection at the U.S. Army Military History Institute, Carlisle Barracks, Pennsylvania.

John C. Griswold (chapter 6, page 92): Courtesy of the Ruth Griswold Collection at the U.S. Army Military History Institute, Carlisle Barracks, Pennsylvania.

William Hawkins (chapter 7, page 112): Author's collection.

Barzilla and Ruba Merrill (chapter 9, page 146): Courtesy of the Gerald Merrill Collection at the U.S. Army Military History Institute, Carlisle Barracks, Pennsylvania.

Alva C. Merrill (chapter 9, page 148): Courtesy of the Gerald Merrill Collection at the U.S. Army Military History Institute, Carlisle Barracks, Pennsylvania.

Clark E. "Salty" Oyer (chapter 10, page 170): Author's collection.

Francis "Blind" Patterson (chapter 11, page 197): Courtesy of the Frank Patterson Collection at the U.S. Army Military History Institute, Carlisle Barracks, Pennsylvania.

Index